W9-BTD-006

WITHDRAWAL

The New Sabin

Entries 13514-15803

The New Sabin;

Books Described by Joseph Sabin and His

Successors, Now Described Again on the

Basis of Examination of Originals,

and Fully Indexed by Title, Subject,

Joint Authors, and Institutions and Agencies

by

Lawrence S. Thompson

Entries 13514-15803

Volume VI

The Whitston Publishing Company

Troy, New York

1979

Copyright 1979
Lawrence S. Thompson

Library of Congress Catalog Card Number 73-85960

ISBN 0-87875-159-9

Printed in the United States of America

Biblio.
Z
1201
T45
v. 6

PREFACE

When I came to Kentucky in 1948 I could recognize the names
of only two contemporary citizens of the Commonwealth, A. B.
("Happy") Chandler and Adolph Rupp, "the baron of basketball."
There was a rather vague knowledge of another expatriate North
Carolinian, Daniel Boone, and of Henry Clay. Irvin S. Cobb,
James Lane Allen, and John Fox, Jr., all gone to their reward
in some Blue Grass heaven, were familiar and delightful reading
from a transmontane pays lointain. And, of course, there were
Alcibiades, Man o' War, Gallant Fox, and others of the equine
breed known to anyone who looks at the headlines on Sunday after
Derby Day.

As a new professor of classics and, more pertinent for
bookish purposes, new university librarian, arrival in Lexington
on 1 September 1948 introduced me to a bibliophilic milieu probably unequalled in any other community in the South. The
University of Kentucky had just inherited the princely collection
of books and manuscripts of the late Samuel Mackay Wilson,
superlative for Kentuckiana, strong in Presbyterian history, the
Ohio and Mississippi Valleys, and books about books. In their
prime were the great Lincoln collector and raconteur, William H.
Townsend, and J. Winston Coleman, Jr., master of a library comparable in many respects to Wilson's and just completing a bibliography of Kentucky history that is still basic. Thomas D. Clark,
professor of American history at the University of Kentucky,
was the scholarly pole for the Lexington bookmen. He was just
beginning the monumental bibliography of travels in the Old and
New South, probably the most important of his numerous contributions to Southern history. Clark had also worked earnestly on
the development of the University of Kentucky Library, scouring
the backwoods for manuscripts and book collections and developing
friends for the library who are still dedicated supporters of
what is the best research collection in the crescent from Indiana
to Texas.

Clark had also developed close contacts with the major
midwestern booksellers, as well as the miserably few in the South
(including several antique dealers in whose shops many a valuable
book or manuscript may be included with other lots). Clark
acquired treasures for the University of Kentucky Library from
Wright Howes, Ernest Wessen, Richard E. Banta, Bill Smith of

Cincinnati, and John Wilson Townsend for prices that seem impossible today. (Alas, many were brutally perforated and assigned to the bookstack; but the perforating machine was being used as a doorstop by early 1949.) With Banta and Smith there was a special cameraderie. Dick Banta came down from his beloved Crawfordsville, Ind., two or three times a year and sold, traded, and talked books, with a climactic two or three hour lunch cum Bourbon at the dignified and genteel old Lafayette Hotel.

Bill Smith, from whom Banta learned much, sold books in Cincinnati for three-quarters of a century. Some of the finest Americana in midwestern collections, private and institutional, passed through his hands. His catalogs carried a motto from his favorite Latin author, Flaxius, "Rare books are getting scarcer." Bill had a heart as warm and sympathetic for fellow bookmen as were his taste buds for J. W. Dant's product. He once offered a prime piece of Kentuckiana, the second edition of John Smith's General History of Virginia (remember, Kentucky, the New Commonwealth, was Kentucky County of the Old Commonwealth), for $400. The sternly honest old country schoolmaster, the late Herman Lee Donovan, then president of the University of Kentucky, required his prior personal approval for all book purchases of more than $50. All sorts of deception with noble purposes had to be used to evade this unrealistic policy. This time we paid a record low of $25 for the General History, bought some hundred more cats and dogs (but grist for the mill, to mix booksellers' and librarians' metaphors) at $3-$5 each. After celebrating his ninetieth birthday in gala and flowing style at the Netherland Plaza, Bill retired to his home across the river in Fort Thomas. I saw him for the last time en route home from a visit with the bookmen of Chillicothe (notably the late Col. David McC. McKell). Stopping by Fort Thomas to peer in, I saw Bill pouring over a catalog. He jumped up and shouted, "Come on in. Lemme give you a drink and tell you a dirty joke!"

A totally different personality was John Wilson Townsend of Lexington, inter alia, one of the many Kentuckians who never imbibed the Commonwealth's most famous product. John had been, variously, librarian, newspaperman, critic, anthologist of Kentucky literature, WPA bibliographical hack (and a first-rate one, well exploited), and bookseller. In the latter forties and until his death in 1968 he operated his Blue Grass Shop out of his homes on Lexington Avenue and, later, Bell Court. In the thirties his marvelous collection of Kentucky literature had gone to Eastern State Teachers' College (now University) in Richmond, largely through the perception of the same Herman Lee Donovan, then Eastern's president, who knew a bargain when he saw it. It is a crown jewel there, with most of the books in fine condition and a large proportion inscribed. The University of Kentucky had lost it through administrative blunders, and many of the titles were lacking in our collections. As one device to make up for this serious gap in our collections, I enlisted my future wife, Algernon Smith Dickson, a cataloger at the University, to secure with me a grant from the University Research Fund, to buy those novels we lacked for the preparation of our book on The Kentucky Novel. While conducting this bibliographical courtship, many was the time I sent John an urgent note to find new books so that I could have a legitimate excuse for dating an employee.

I learned very soon that John had to be "jewed down" (as he himself put it) for nearly every item. Fascinated with my subject, in love with the Blue Grass (and one of its loveliest daughters), I generally asked John if he had a second copy at an even lower price. Often he did, and here is the genesis of the Biblioteca Kentuckiensis Thompsoniana. The same applied to dealings with people such as Howes, Wessen, Banta, and Smith in the area of Kentuckiana, but their marked prices were firm. Once I pulled a book from Wright Howes' shelves in his apartment on the Near North Side, and it was obvious that a third digit was missing on the marked price. Howes said, "This is the marked price. It is on my shelves. Take it at this figure." I declined. A week later the book appeared on my desk with an invoice for the marked price.

John had all manner of other things needed by the University to catch up with the collection of what was then a little normal school library in the next county over. Often the copies he offered were in vastly better condition than our dog-eared, underlined, perforated, oversewn stack copies. The better copies were acquired for the nascent Rare Book Room. When our Research Fund grant ran out, I would often buy good copies with personal funds and, idealistically, trade them with the library for the execrable stack copy. Today I am going through the same process of replacing inferior copies with good ones for my personal collection, but the difference in prices is staggering. On the other hand, collectors of regional literature can often pick up good copies in localities where they are not particularly in demand. Thus the bulk of my James Lane Allen books, all fine copies, came from a lot purchased at a Kansas City antique shop for a half dollar per title.

Like most successful book scouts, John Townsend was reticent about his sources and the prices he paid. But he could not resist being the bibliographicus gloriosus when he acquired the third known and the best copy of Jesse Lynch Holman's

iii

The Prisoners of Niagara, or, The Errors of Education (Frankfort, Ky., 1810), the first, and possibly the worst novel printed west of the Appalachians. His asking price was $3,000. Unhappily, I could not get him down to a third of that figure, roughly what Seven Gables ultimately paid him to acquire it for C. Waller Barrett (and the University of Virginia). The University of Kentucky and this collector must be content with Will Fridy's modern reprint.

Dealers are and will remain the best source for the great rarities among printed books. Yet there are other devices for acquiring books, manuscripts, and other source materials for regional collections such as the one presented in this volume. Trading with dealers, libraries, and collectors is always productive. After Thomas D. Clark persuaded Centre College and the old Kentucky State Library to deposit their "Serial Sets" of U.S. documents at the University, there were hundreds of good duplicates for which Smith and Banta gave abundant credit. And many a solid piece came to the University of Kentucky as the result of trades with back files of the Register of the Kentucky Historical Society, the publications of the Kentucky Academy of Science, and the pre-1860 session laws and legislative journals which Clark used to bring in by the truckload.

The individual collector is more restricted in trading. If he is also associated with an institution, he must be meticulously careful not to add to his personal shelves anything that could be used by the library, even an unwanted duplicate which has an exchange value. Yet, when anyone, institutional representative or private collector, has a reputation as a perceptive and understanding bibliophile, these things inevitably drift in. The late Emmet F. Horine, Louisville cardiologist and master of a great library on the history of medicine, and J. Christian Bay, long-time librarian of the John Crerar in Chicago, left their collections to the University of Kentucky. During their life-times they always sent one copy of their many publications inscribed for the library, another inscribed for this compiler.

In 1965 the death of my wife three years earlier and the responsibility for three small children made it imperative for me to devote my time solely to teaching duties. I was on my own as a collector of Kentuckiana, but now the first copy came to me, the second, if any, to the library. While my primary objective has been to build a representative, practical collection of Kentuckiana, I have incorporated most anything of substantive value and many things of museum value only, yet valuable as cultural witnesses. Nearly everything in this volume can be found in the four or five major public collections of Kentuckiana within the Commonwealth. I have found, perforce, many new avenues for enriching a personal collection, but the lines followed by the institutional collector are still productive. For example, churches and civic groups almost always respond favorably to collectors who want their histories; but their cook books with all manner of Kentucky gourmet dishes are invariably for sale only (generally at quite low prices) to all comers. The big problem is to locate things like this in time, and often the individual has the advantage over the slow-moving institution. The cook book collection noted here is far from comprehensive, but it will provide an adequate sampling of what Kentuckians eat. Try and find the recipe for a Hot Brown in the cookery monographs of any other jurisdiction!

The exhaustive collection of Kentucky public documents is a job exclusively for libraries, but many items with Frankfort imprints are solid additions to a private collection. The Geological Survey, above all in the period under the directorship of the late Willard Rouse Jillson in the twenties, is rich in semi- or even non-technical material. Here again, it should have been picked up at the time of publication. Some of the Jillson-era publications now fetch rather hefty prices. The current monographs of the Legislative Research Commission contain much that is basic for Kentucky history, e.g., material on the vexed question of the Commonwealth's Constitution (more like a statute book than a foundation instrument). The various agencies concerned with education, civil rights, and race relations issue publications which may appear routine today, but they will ultimately be wanted by scholars. The selective bibliophile performs a valuable service by incorporating them in a tightly knit collection, where they are much more accessible than when scattered through a two-million-volume research library.

The empire-builders at the larger universities with their institutes, "seminars," bureaus, etc., publish all manner of things which a collector of Kentuckiana needs. The old Bureau of Government Research at the University of Kentucky is an egregious example. The collector should not scorn the unpretentious publications of the Agricultural Experiment Station and the Cooperative Extension Service. Among other things, they include well worth while material on the flora and fauna of the region. Annual or at least biennial visits to the Bulletin Office in the Experiment Station Building will yield many a significant piece that soon will go out of print. At the University of Kentucky the publications of the King Library Press, not included here because they are copyright, will be perhaps the most sought-after Kentucky imprints of the future, for they are typographically distinguished, textually significant, and in very small press runs.

Vandalism of a limited sort is an art which the collector of regional literature has to master. Many was the night on the University campus when I furtively removed a handbill calling for an anti-Red-River-Dam meeting, but it has achieved immortality in the large collection of materials on this basic ecological issue that attracted national attention. I dared not do the same at Brookside during the strike there, what with clubs and even shotguns obvious among the pickets, but a former student, then a striking miner, understood my motives and kept one copy of every crude handbill or folder he could find. The resurgent Klan, on which a file comparable to the Red River one is now being pulled together, is more cooperative. The necks of the Cyclopses of the seventies are as red as those of the Grand Dragons of the twenties, but they are vaguely aware of the need for P.R. and gladly furnish their crude broadsides when so requested. As one Kleagle explained: "We like to help good people. We even do good things for good niggers."

The importance of collecting, preserving, and bibliographically recording contemporary documents cannot be over-estimated. If the pamphlets of the English Civil War, the French Revolution, or the U.S. anti-slavery movement had not been brought together in a similar way by contemporaries, modern historians would be infinitely poorer. The apparently ephemeral things are often the sinews of scholarship.

Mentioned here are only a few facets and methods for the collector of regional literature. His primary qualities must be alertness to identify material of value for his collection and the will and ability to act promptly in acquiring it. It is a game that is, in many respects, more exciting than the one played by the well-heeled collector who has small concern for the price of his quarry before five figures are reached. Ingenuity, imagination, and resourcefulness are as valuable to the regional collector as a fat bank account. The historical manuscripts in the Wisconsin Historical Society and in the University of North Carolina would fetch millions if knocked down at auction today. Draper and Hamilton spent nothing beyond their own time, talent, and energy in acquiring them.

The present volume records a collection that is neither well rounded nor can be conceived as a general bibliography of Kentuckiana; but it is a contribution to the latter, and, as a developing collection, en route to better proportions. The compiler owns all but about a hundred titles in the original or in facsimile, and all are in the Lost Cause Press microfiche collection entitled "The Kentucky Culture Series". The compiler owns about twice as many Kentucky books which are not included here, mainly because the copyrights precluded microfiche reproduction. His collection is growing, and it is anticipated that another volume of The New Sabin will be dedicated to Kentuckiana in about seven or eight years.

J. Winston Coleman's Bibliography of Kentucky History (1949) with its 3,571 items is still the best work in the field; but the lacunae are very substantial, and much has been published in the last three decades. In a sense the present work supplements Coleman, since there is comparatively little overlap. But the time for a comprehensive bibliography of Kentucky history, literature, and imprints is long since overdue. Here is but one more fragment, but hopefully a useful one, which a student of Kentucky culture must search. Happily all of the titles here are in print in microform.

Inevitably a number of items relative to Kentucky and in the compiler's collection have been recorded in the first five volumes of The New Sabin. For the sake of completeness the numbers are listed here:

485	549	755	791	1243	1340	1359
1495	1799	1800	2004	2258	2592	2643
2682	2723	2784	2791	2829	2895	2937
2948	2952	3013	3014	3021	3110	3125
3175	3184	3210	3213	3240	3312	3359
3360	3380	3391	3412	3423	3426	3427
3433	3448	3468	3522	3526	3532	3595
3654	3714	3818	3869	3884	3916	3948
4012	4063	4073	4193	4225	4269	4370
4374	4382	4401	4403	4413	4425	4723
4807	4810	4848	4849	4913	4945	4965
4978	5006	5038	5196	5224	5259	5263
5272	5330	5407	5431	5442	5567	5642
5662	5699	5706	5743	6197	6289	6445
6446	6459	6461	6472	6655	6919	7093
7152	7153	7154	7155	7201	7276	7365
7378	7380	7804	8010	8186	8203	8217
8220	8221	8222	8330	8511	8512	8513
8515	8516	8656	9243	9553	9554	9555
9556	9557	9558	9932	10052	10098	10139
10140	10224	10225	10445	10265	10851	10953
11166	11506	11602	11795	12142	12248	12462

12554   12573   12953   13077   13122   13500

Lawrence S. Thompson
Lexington, Kentucky
November, 1978

To John Wilson Townsend
1885-1968

13514 Abernethy, Thomas Perkins, ed.
Journal of the First Kentucky Convention, Dec. 27,
1784-Jan. 5, 1785. Baton Rouge, La., 1935.
67-78 p.   27 cm.
Reprinted from The Journal of Southern History,
vol. I, no. 1, February, 1935. (Duplication of 14725)

13515. Adams, Randolph Greenfield, 1892-1951.
Two documents on the battle of King's Mountain.
Reprinted from the North Carolina Historical Review,
vol. VIII, no. 3, July, 1931. [Raleigh, N. C.,
1931]
348-352 p.   26½ cm.

13516 Addresses delivered at the inauguration of the professors
in the Danville theological seminary, October 13, 1853.
Printed at the request of the directors then present.
Cincinnati, Printed by T. Wrightson, 1854.
cover-title, 74 p.   23 cm.

13517 Ainslie, Hew, 1792-1878.
The Leddy Macmeeken. Louisville, 1870.
broadside.   28 x 12 cm.
Hummel, 781.
Poetry.
Original in Duke University Library.

13518 Album of Louisville. [n.p., n.d.]
[12] p.   illus.   14 x 15 cm.
No text; photographic views only.
This copy, possibly unique, has the words:
Compliments of (printed) The John C. Lewis Co.
(on a strip pasted over the original wrapper with
the word Chilton barely legible underneath)

13519 Alexander, Arabel Wilbur.
The life and work of Lucinda B. Helm, founder of
the Woman's parsonage and Home mission society of
the M. E. church, South. By Arabel Wilbur Alexander...

Nashville, Tenn., Publishing house of the Methodist
Episcopal church, South, 1898.
177 p., 1 ℓ. incl. plates. port. front. (port.)
20½ cm.

13520 Alexander, John.
The historic Opera House -- Can it be saved?
Lexington, Ky., 1973.
1 p. in 4 cols. illus.
Reprinted from Lexington Herald-Leader, 10 June
1973, p. 5.

13521 Alexander, John.
Railroad brings life to Midway. Lexington, Ky.,
1974.
broadside. illus. 52½ x 35 cm.
Includes article by Sue Napier, Boutiques, shops
make Midway a good place to browse.
Reprinted from Lexington Herald-Leader, 19 May 1974.

13522 Alexander, John.
[The Red Mile] Lexington, Ky., 1975.
2 p. illus. 29 cm.

13523 Alexander, John H
Needed: state aid for school building emergencies.
Frankfort, Ky., Legislative Research Commission,
1973.
78 p. tables. 29 cm. (Research report
no. 108, new series)

13524 Alexander, Paula.
A matter of honor. [Louisville, Ky.] 1974.
p. 28, 30. 29 cm.
Reprinted from Rural Kentuckian, v. 28, no. 10,
Oct. 1974.

13525 Allen, James Lane, 1849-1925.
The blue-grass region of Kentucky and other Kentucky
articles. New York and London, Harper and brothers,
1892.
322 p. illus. 22 cm.

13526 Allen, James Lane, 1849-1925.
The doctor's Christmas eve... New York, The Macmillan
company, 1910.
304 p. 20 cm.

13527   Allen, James Lane, 1849-1925.
            The emblems of fidelity, a comedy in letters...
        Garden City, N. Y., Doubleday, Page & company, 1919.
            219 p.   19½ cm.

13528   Allen, James Lane, 1849-1925.
            Fighting and drinking were county fair day features
        a century ago. Lexington, Ky., 1960.
            2 p.   illus.   57 x 38 cm.
            From Lexington Sunday Herald-Leader, 21 February
        1960, p. 26. Reprinted by permission from Harper's
        magazine, August, 1889.

13529   Allen, James Lane, 1849-1925.
            Flute and violin and other Kentucky tales and
        romances... Biographical edition. New York and
        London, Harper & brothers, publishers, 1899.
            308 p.   front. (port.)   20½ cm.

13530   Allen, James Lane, 1849-1925.
            The heroine in bronze, or, A portrait of a girl.
        A pastoral of the city. By James Lane Allen...
        New York, The Macmillan company, 1912.
            5 p.l., 281 p.   19 cm.

13531   Allen, James Lane, 1849-1925.
            A Kentucky cardinal. A story... New York, Harper
        & brother publishers [c1894]
            147 p.   illus.   16½ cm.

13532   Allen, James Lane, 1849-1925.
            A Kentucky cardinal. A story... New York and
        London, Harper & brothers, 1899.
            136 p.   illus.   18½ cm.

13533   Allen, James Lane, 1849-1925.
            A Kentucky cardinal, a story... New York,
        Macmillan, 1900.
            138 p.   illus.   17 cm.

13534   Allen, William Ray.
            A nature sketchbook. Twenty talks on the everyday
        life roundabout. Illustrated with photographs from
        the author's camera. Lexington, Department of
        University Extension, University of Kentucky, 1936.
            209 p.   illus.   24 cm.

3

13535 Allender, Phoebe Jo.
         Illuminated manuscripts from France, Italy and
         Spain (XIVth-XVIII centuries) Catalogue for an
         exhibition, compiled by Phoebe Jo Allender.
         Special Collections Gallery, University of Kentucky
         Libraries, 1-27 March 1978. [Lexington, 1978]
           2 p.l., [20] p.   28 cm.
         Foreword by Lawrence S. Thompson.

13536 Allison, Young Ewing, 1853-1932.
         The city of Louisville and a glimpse of Kentucky.
         [Louisville] Committee on industrial and commercial
         improvement of the Louisville board of trade, 1887.
           154, [2] p.   illus. [incl. ports.]   33 cm.

13537 Allison, Young Ewing, 1853-1932.
         The curious legend of Louis Philippe in Kentucky...
         Louisville, Ky., Priv. print., 1924.
           34 p.   24 cm.

13538 Allison, Young Ewing, 1853-1932.
         The Old Kentucky Home, immortalized by Stephen C.
         Foster. Its song and the story... Bardstown, Ky.,
         Published under the auspices of My Old Kentucky Home
         Commission, 1923.
           45 p.   illus., music.   35 cm.

13539 Almanac, for the year of Our Lord 1816, being bis-
         sextile, or leap year; and [after the 4th of July]
         the 41st of American independence. Calculated for
         the meridian of Lexington [Ky.] -- but may serve
         for any of the adjacent states, without any essential
         difference. By Thomas Henderson. Georgetown, Ky.,
         Printed and sold by Henderson and Reed, 1816.
           [24] p.   17 cm.

13540 A[lsterlund], B
         The Kentucky colonel: a study in semantics.
         [New York, 1947]
           3-8 p.   22 cm.
         Reprinted from American Notes & Queries, VII
         (no. 1, April, 1947), 3-8.

13541 Altsheler, Joseph Alexander, 1862-1919.
         Guthrie of the Times, a story of success, by
         Joseph A. Altsheler. Illustrated by F. R. Gruger.
         New York, Doubleday, Page & company, 1904.
           6 p.l., 338 p.   front., 3 pl.   20 cm.

4

13542 Altsheler, Joseph Alexander, 1862-1919.
     The Wilderness Road, a romance of St. Clair's
     defeat and Wayne's victory, by Joseph A. Altsheler...
     New York and London, D. Appleton-Century company,
     1940.
       vi, 379 p.   20 cm.

13543 [Amedeus, Father] 1872-
     The Right Reverend Dom M. Edmond Obrecht, O.C.S.O.,
     fourth abbot of Our Lady of Gethsemani (1852-1935);
     with a foreword by His Eminence Dennis cardinal
     Dougherty. [Trappist] Ky., Abbey of Our Lady of
     Gethsemani [c1937]
       335 p.   front., plates (1 fold.) ports.   23 cm.

13544 American Automobile Association.
     Tour book. Southeastern. Spring/summer 1971.
     Alabama, Georgia, Kentucky, Louisiana, Mississippi,
     North Carolina, South Carolina, Tennessee.
     [Washington, D.C.] 1971.
       424 p.   illus., maps.   24 cm.

13545 American book collector.
     Special Jesse Stuart number, v. 16, no. 6,
     February 1966. Chicago, 1966.
       40 p.   illus.   28 cm.
     Inscribed by Jesse Stuart.
     Tipped in at end is poem by Stuart, "Old Christmas,"
     in the Wheel Horse (Lexington, Ky., Rotary Club),
     v. XXVIV[!], no. 24, 21 Dec. 1972.
     Partial contents. Jesse Stuart, a critical biblio-
     graphy [bibliographical survey in narrative form],
     by Hensley C. Woodbridge. Five short stories by
     Jesse Stuart: The snow storm. Professor Zeke and
     the Simpson Clan. Three who made high on the test.
     The Clear Creek incident. Big Charlie had a party.
     Review of Stuart's Daughter of the legend, by Mary
     Washington Clarke.

13546 American Council of Learned Societies. Committee on
     Linguistics and National Stocks in the Population
     of the United States.
     Surnames in the United States census of 1790.
     An analysis of national origins of the population.
     Washington, American Historical Association, 1932.
       103-441 p.   24 cm.   (American Historical
     Association, Annual report, 1931, pp. 103-441)

Contains references to Kentucky on p. 110, 114, 115, 118, 120, 122, 123, 124-125, 126, 197, 199, 252-253, 270, 296-298, 304-305, 307, 378-379.

13547 The American farmer's almanac, for the year of Our Lord 1815; being the third after bissextile, or leap year and [after the 4th of July] the 40th of American independence. Calculated by Thomas Henderson. Containing, besides the usual matter of an almanac, some of the most important naval victories achieved during the American revolution, and a variety of useful and entertaining articles. Lexington, Sold by W. Essex & son, and H. C. Sleight [1814]
   [36] p.   19 cm.

13548 American Legion. Kentucky Department.
   Souvenir book, third annual convention, American Legion of Kentucky, September 1 and 2, 1921, Lexington, Ky., Auspices Lexington Post no. 8, American Legion of Kentucky. [Lexington, 1921]
   unpaged.   illus.   21 x 27½cm.
   Included article by Ulric Bell, Two years of sticking together; some realities and some recollections concerning the Kentucky Department, the American Legion.
   Includes numerous photographs of prominent Kentucky legionnaires.

13549 Anchorage, Ky., High School. Genealogical Society.
   History of the Old Stone Inn, by the Anchorage Genealogical Society, Anchorage High School. Edited by Sally Byrne. Printed by Peggy Schneidt- miller. Sponsored by Edith Wood. [Anchorage] 1947.
   18 p.   29 cm.

13550 Anderson, Charles, 1814-
   A funeral oration on the character, life, and public services of Henry Clay. Cincinnati, Ben Franklin office print, 1852.
   38 p.   23 cm.

13551 Anderson, Edward Lovell, 1842-
   Riding and driving. Riding, by Edward L. Anderson... Driving; hints on the history, housing, harnessing and handling of the horse, by Price Collier. New York, The Macmillan company; London, Macmillan & co.,

ltd., 1905.
xiii, 441 p.   front., plates.   21 cm.

13552   Anderson, James Blythe.
The nameless hero and other poems... New York,
A. Wessels company, 1902.
73 p. $20\frac{1}{2}$ cm.

13553   Anderson, Margaret Steele, 1867-1921.
The flame in the wind, by Margaret Steele Anderson,
with foreword by George Madden Martin. Third
printing. Louisville, Ky., John F. Morton & company,
1930.
[12], 71 p.   21 cm.

13554   Andover and Danville. A reply to an article in the
Biblioteca sacra for October, 1859. Containing a
review of Breckinridge's theology. Louisville, Ky.,
Hull & Brother, 1859.
cover-title, 15 p.   22 cm.

13555   [Andrews, Israel Ward]
Kentucky, Tennessee, Ohio: their admission into
the Union. [n.p., 1887?]
306-316 p. $24\frac{1}{2}$ cm.

13556   Appalachian coal miners want decent working conditions.
Duke Power Co. says - "No!" [n.p., 1974?]
8 p.   illus. $29\frac{1}{2}$ cm.

13557   Appalachian Kentucky Health Manpower Service.
County health contacts. Lexington, 1975.
52 p.   29 cm.

13558   Appalshop, Inc., Whitesburg, Ky.
Appalbrochure 1975. [Whitesburg] 1975.
28 p.   illus. $27\frac{1}{2}$ cm.

13559   Ardery, Julia Spencer.
Biographical index to Perrin's History of Bourbon,
Scott, Harrison, Nicholas counties, Kentucky.
[n.p., n.d.]
20 p.   29 cm.

13560   Ardery, W   B
He was a dead game sport. [Lexington, Ky., 1974]
2 p.   illus., port.   41 cm.

Includes Herman W. Knickerbocker's funeral oration
for Riley Grannan at Rawhide, Nev., 3 April 1908.

13561 Ardery, W   B
       John Fox, Jr., still popular with the over-50 set
       of Kentuckians. Lexington, Ky., 1973.
       1 p.   illus.
       From Lexington Herald-Leader, 11 March 1973, p. 5.

13562 Ardery, W   B
       A Kentucky Derby legend -- Col. E. R. Bradley.
       [Lexington, 1972]
       broadside.   30 cm.
       Reprinted from Sunday Herald-Leader, Lexington, Ky.,
       April 30, 1972, p. 5.

13563 Armstrong, Moses Kimball.
       The early empire builders of the great west...
       Compiled and enlarged from the author's early history
       of the Dakota territory in 1866... St. Paul, Minn.,
       E. W. Porter, 1900.
       x, 456 p.   illus.   23 cm.
       Kentucky: p. 420-423.

13564 Arnett, Maralea.
       A pictorial history of Henderson County, 1775-1950.
       Compiled by Maralea Arnett, Katheryn Basket, J. W.
       Duncan. Henderson, Ky., Published for Henderson's
       Bicentennial Committee by Gleaner Print Shop, Inc.,
       1974.
       [40] p.   illus., maps.   30 cm.

13565 Arnold, W   P
       Age and youth; or, A fast old widow. A comedy in
       four acts... Leitchfield, Ky., Isaac E. McClure,
       printer and publisher, 1881.
       24 p.   20 cm.

13566 Art work of Louisville... Chicago, The Charles Madison
       company, 1897.
       53 pl.   35 cm.

13567 Arts Club, Louisville, Ky.
       The Arts Club fourth poetry contest, Louisville,
       Kentucky, January 29, 1925. [Louisville, 1925]
       [20] p.   21 cm.
       The prize poem is "East of Eden" by William H.
       Field. Other poems are by W. H. McCreary, Mary

Lanier Magruder, Fanny Brandeis, Isabel McLennan
McMeekin, Norman Ware, Ella Vonnegut Stewart,
Frances Barton Fox, Ainslie Hewett, Maude Blanc
Harris, Jacqueline Embry, Maria Lindsey, and Elsie
McLennan Woodward.

13568 Ashland, Ky. Centennial Committee.
A history of Ashland, Kentucky, 1786 to 1954.
Published by the Ashland Centennial Committee for
the celebration of its centennial, October 1, 2 and
3, 1954.
128 p.   illus.   29½ cm.

13569 The Ashland melodies.   Written by "An old coon"...
[illegible text] J. L. Dimmock, esq. president of
the Boston Clay Club. Boston, Published by Henry
Prentiss [n.d.]
4 ℓ.   cover illus., music.   36 cm.
Includes words.
The original of this text was in the possession of
Elliott Shapiro, 118 West 70th Street, New York, in
February 1943. The original can not be located.
The present "photostatic" copy, possibly now unique,
is in the private library of Lawrence S. Thompson,
Lexington, Kentucky. At head of text: "Here's to
you, Henry Clay."

13570 Ashley, David H
An analysis of retirement and benefit plans for
Kentucky state employees, prepared by David H. Ashley,
Legislative Research Commission staff, and Meidinger
and Associates, Inc., consulting actuaries, Louisville,
Ky., under the direction of the Advisory Committee
on the Retirement Systems Study... Frankfort, Ky.,
Legislative Research Commission, 1975.
various pagings.   27 cm.   (Research report,
no. 128)

13571 Atcher, Charles L
Frederick M. Vinson, profile and papers.
[Paducah, 1975]
15-16 p.   23 cm.
Reprinted from Kentucky Library Association
Bulletin, v. 39, no. 4, 1975.

13572 Audubon, John James, 1785-1851.
The birds of America, from drawings made in the
United States and their territories... New York,

J. J. Audubon; Philadelphia, J. B. Chevalier,
1840-44.
   7 v.   illus., 500 col. pl.   27 cm.

13573 Austin, Thomas R
     The well-spent life. A brotherly testimonial to
the masonic career of Robert Morris... Louisville,
Ky., 1878.
     48 p.   front. (port.)

13574 Axon, James R
     Evaluation of the "two-story" trout fishery in
Lake Cumberland. [Frankfort, Ky., Department of
Fish and Wildlife Resources] 1974.
     2 p.l., 69 l.   (Kentucky fisheries bulletin, 60)
     Cover illus.
     "This project was financed partially with federal
aid in fish restoration funds, Kentucky project
F-32 (1-7)"

13575 Ayres & Givens, firm, Louisville, Ky.
     Eastern Kentucky, a field for profitable investment.
Louisville, Courier-Journal co., 1889.
     24 p.   23½ cm.

B

13576 Babcock, Jan Victor.
     Endangered plants and animals in Kentucky [by]
Jan V. Babcock... Photographs courtesy of Albert
G. Westerman. Lexington, Institute for Mining and
Minerals Research, University of Kentucky, 1977.
     128 p.   illus., maps.   22 x 28 cm.
     (IMMR25-GR4-77)

13577 Bachofen, Johann Jacob.
     Walls: res sanctae/res sacrae. A passage from
"Versuch ueber die Graebersymbolik der Alten",
translated by B. Q. Morgan & with a note on J. J.
Bachofen by Lewis Mumford. Lexington, Ky.,
Stamperia del Santuccio, 1961.
     5 l.   29 cm.

13578 Bailey, Clay Wade.
     Judge Gus Thomas, colorful and homey. [Lexington,

Ky., 1974]
     1 p.   port.   56 cm.
     Reprinted from Sunday Herald-Leader, Lexington, Ky.,
     3 February 1974, p. G8-G9.

13579 Bailey, G   S
          The great caverns of Kentucky: Diamond Cave,
     Mammoth Cave, Hundred Dome Cave. Chicago, Church
     & Goodman [1863]
          1 p.l., 63 p.   14½ cm.

13580 [Baird, Robert] 1798-1863.
          View of the valley of the Mississippi, or the
     emigrant's and traveller's guide to the west. A
     general description of that entire country; and also
     notices of the soil, productions, rivers and other
     channels of intercourse and trade: and likewise of
     the cities and towns, progress of education, &c. of
     each state and territory... Second ed. Philadelphia,
     Published by H. S. Tanner, 1834.
          ix, [4], 14-372 p.   maps (part fold.), tables.
     18½ cm.

13581 Baker, Lindsey, 1868-1949.
          Little old sod shanty, by Lindsey Baker and Bud
     Hatten. Catlettsburg, Ky., 1975.
          broadside.   port.   22 x 38 cm.
          Reprinted from The Press-Observer, Catlettsburg,
     Ky., 11 September 1975.

13582 Baldwin, Thomas, 1750?
          Narrative of a massacre, by the savages, of the
     wife and children of Thomas Baldwin, who, since
     the melancholy period of the destruction of his
     unfortunate family, has dwelt entirely alone...
     in the extreme western part of the state of Kentucky.
     New-York, Martin & Perry, 1836.
          24 p.   fold. col. front.   23 cm.

13583 *This number was skipped in preparation of copy.*

13584 The ballad of Black Bess. [Lexington, Ky., 1958]
          [4] p.   illus.   20½cm.
          Typed note at end: "By Bruce F. Denbo,
     Director, University of Kentucky Press, February
     1958."

13585   Ballingall, Neal.
        The life and confession of Neal Ballingall, who
        was convicted of counterfeiting and sentenced to the
        Kentucky penitentiary for eight years. Fleming
        County, Ky., 1855.
        20 p.   19 cm.

13586   Bancroft, A   C
        The life and death of Jefferson Davis, ex-president
        of the southern confederacy. Together with comments
        of the press, funeral sermons, etc., etc. Ed. by
        A. C. Bancroft. New York, J. S. Ogilvie [c1889]
        256 p.   incl. front., illus., port.   19 cm.

13587   Bangs, S   K
        Ripples on the stream of poesy. Louisville, Ky.,
        1882.
        31 p.   29 cm.
        Typed copy of original.

13588   The Bank dinner, an exposé of the court party in
        Kentucky, and the curtain drawn from the holy alliance
        of America, by Patrick Henry [pseud.]... Frankfort,
        A. Kendall and company, 1824.
        vii, [1], [9]-80 p.   19½ cm.

13589   Banks, Henry.
        The vindication of John Banks, of Virginia,
        against foul calumnies published by Judge Johnson,
        of Charleston, South Carolina, and Doctor Charles
        Caldwell, of Lexington, Kentucky. Also, the vindi-
        cation of Henry Lee, of Virginia. With sketches
        and anecdotes of many revolutionary patriots and
        heroes... Frankfort, Ky., The author, 1826.
        88 p.   21½ cm.

13590   Banks, Mrs. Nancy Huston.
        Oldfield,; a Kentucky tale of the last century,
        by Nancy Huston Banks. New York, London, The
        Macmillan company, 1902.
        ix, 431 p.   19½ cm.

13591   Banks, Mrs. Nancy Huston.
        Round Anvil Rock; a romance, by Nancy Huston
        Banks... New York, The Macmillan company;
        London, Macmillan & co., ltd., 1903.
        xi, 356 p.   front., 5 pl.   20 cm.

13592   Bannockburn for sale, on the splendid and desirable
        farm belonging to Jas. R. Skiles, Esq., will be sold
        at auction, on Monday 26 May, next... William B.
        Loving, John B. Helm, commissioners. Bowling Green,
        Ky., Green River gazette, 1845.
            broadside.   28 x 37 cm.
            Hummel, 716.
            Original in Western Kentucky University Library.

13593   Banquet in honor of the Honorable H. Church Ford.
        Lexington, Ky., June 10, 1935.
            [3] p.   22½ cm.

13594   Banta, Richard Elwell.
            Benjamin Fuller and some of his descendants,
        1765-1958. Crawfordsville, Ind., 1958.
            143 p.   25 cm.

13595   Baptist, Leona.
            Daniel Boone. South Hills, Charleston, W. Va.,
        The Children's Theatre press [1940]
            51 p.   illus.   23 cm.

13596   Bardstown, Ky. Woman's Club.
            Bardstown cook book. [Bardstown] Department of
        Home Economics of the Woman's Club [1913?]
            46 p.   23 cm.

13597   Barker, Elihu.
            Kentucky, reduced from Elihu Barker's large map.
        [n.p., n.d.]
            24½ x 50 cm.

13598   Barker, Henry Stites, 1850-1928.
            A selection of speeches and other writings by the
        second president of the University of Kentucky,
        Henry Stites Barker. With an introduction by
        Ezra L Gillis & with a foreword by H. L. Donovan.
        [Lexington] University of Kentucky press [1956]
            93 p.   front. (port.)   23 cm.

13599   Barker, T   F
            The cross road store, or The evils of a dram-shop.
        The history of a Kentucky village. A novel.
        Founded on facts. By T. F. Barker. Lexington, Ky.,
        E. D. Veach, 1892.
            165 p.   front. (port.)   19½ cm.

13600 Barker, W   M
        Memoirs of Eld. J. N. Hall, the peerless defender
        of the Baptist faith, by W. M. Barker, assisted by
        Mrs. J. N. Hall. Fulton, Ky., Baptist flag print,
        1907.
        vi, [7]-349, [1] p.   2 port. incl. front.
        22½ cm.

13601 *(This number was skipped in preparation of copy)*

13602 Barkley, Alben William, 1877-1956.
        Early military history of Kentucky. On July 20,
        1934, Senator Alben W. Barkley delivered an address
        at Fort Knox, Kentucky... [n.p., 1934?]
        cover-title, 8 p.   23 cm.

13603 Barkley, Alben William, 1877-1956.
        Henry Clay, an address... at the dedication of
        Ashland as the Henry Clay Memorial, April 12, 1950.
        Lexington, Ky., The Henry Clay memorial foundation
        [1950?]
        30 p.   front. (port.)   17 cm.

13604 Barkley, Alben William, 1877-1956.
        The War revenue bill. Speech of Hon. Alben W.
        Barkley of Kentucky in the Senate of the United
        States, February 23, 1944. [Washington, D. C., 1944]
        7 p.   24½ cm.
        The occasion of Roosevelt's famous "Dear Alben"
        letter.

13605 Barkley, Archibald Henry, 1872-1956.
        Kentucky's pioneer lithotomists, by A. H. Barkley...
        Cincinnati, O., C. J. Krehbiel & company, 1913.
        159 p. incl. plates, ports., facsims.   21 cm.
        Contents. - Ephraim McDowell. - Benjamin Winslow
        Dudley. - James Mills Bush. - Robert Peter. -
        Absolom Driver, the janitor of Transylvania university
        medical hall.
        Inscribed by author.

13606 Barnes, James C
        Questions on the sacred scriptures, for the use of
        Bible classes and Sabbath schools. Lancaster, Ky.,
        1820.
        50 p.

13607   Barr, Stephen A
        The family of Adam and Mary Claycomb/Barr,
        particularly the branch of George and Nancy
        Beauchamp/Barr, by Stephen A. Barr. [Louisville,
        Ky., 1977]
        141, 11, A1-A8, B1-B9, C1-C2, D1-D16, E1-E12,
        F1-F21, G1-G1b, H1, J1-J8, M1-M6, 48 p.   illus.,
        maps, facsims.   23 cm.

13608   Barren River Area Development District, Bowling Green,
        Ky.
        Area agency handbook on aging.   June 1974...
        [Bowling Green, Ky.] 1974.
        cover-title, [10], 57 p.   map.   23 cm.

13609   Barren River Area Development District, Bowling Green,
        Ky.
        City of Munfordville, initial housing element,
        November 1973...   [Bowling Green, Ky.] 1973.
        [8], 34 p.   map, tables.   28 cm.

13610   Barren River Area Development District, Bowling Green,
        Ky.
        1974 data book. Bowling Green, Ky., 1974.
        [4], 78 p.   maps, diagrs., tables.   28 cm.

13611   Barren River Area Development District, Bowling Green,
        Ky.
        Parks and playgrounds - city and county facilities.
        A review of local government recreational sites in the
        Barren River Area Development District. Compiled
        by Rick Starks. [Bowling Green, Ky.] 1975.
        [32] p.   illus.   28 cm.
        "Photographs for this report were taken by
        Tim Miskell."

13612   Barren River Area Development District, Bowling Green,
        Ky.
        A solid waste inventory for the Barren River Area
        Development District...   July, 1974. [Bowling Green,
        Ky.] 1974.
        [10], 59 p.   illus., maps, diagrs., tables.
        28 cm.

13613   Barren River Area Development District, Bowling Green,
        Ky.
        The year 2000, a long-range plan. Project director,
        Gerald Romsa...   Bowling Green [197-?]

ii, 90 p.   illus., maps (3 fold. in pocket at end)
28 cm.

13614 Barrow, Asa C
       Scholl's Station. By Asa C. Barrow, Schollsville.
       Transcribed by George F. Doyle, M.D., F.A.C.S.
       [Winchester, Ky., Clark County Historical Society,
       n.d.]
       2 l., 17 p.   28 cm.

13615 Barry, William Taylor.
       Speech of William T. Barry, Esq., on the death of
       Adams, Jefferson, and Shelby; delivered in Lexington,
       on Tuesday, fifteenth August, 1826. Lexington, Ky.,
       Printed by John Bradford -- Gazette Press, 1826.
       24 p.   port.   23½ x 14½ cm.

13616 Bartlett, Elisha, 1804-1855.
       A brief memoir of Dr. Elisha Bartlett, with
       selections from his writings and a bibliography of
       the same. Providence, S. S. Rider, 1878.
       71 p.   21 cm.
       Privately printed. An edition of 300 copies.
       Contents. - Brief memoir of Elisha Bartlett. -
       Hippocrates by the dying bed of Pericles; an extract
       from a discourse. - The head and the heart, or The
       relative importance of intellectual and moral
       education... a lecture. - Chronological list of the
       published writings of Dr. Elisha Bartlett.

13617 Bartlett, Elisha, 1804-1855.
       A brief sketch of the life, character, and
       writings of William Charles Wells, M.D., F.R.S.
       An address delivered before the Louisville Medical
       Society, December 7th, 1849... Louisville, Ky.,
       Prentice and Weissinger, 1849.
       32 p.   23 cm.

13618 Barton, William Eleazar, 1861-
       A hero in homespun, a tale of the loyal South...
       Boston [etc.] Lamson, Wolffe and company, 1897.
       393 p.   illus.   21 cm.
       On cover: Illustrated by Dan Beard.

13619 Barton, William Eleazar, 1861-
       Pine Knot, a story of Kentucky life... Illustrated
       by F. T. Merrill. New York, D. Appleton and company,

16

1900.
    360 p.   illus.   20 cm.

13620 Bateman, Charlotte.
    Restoration sparks Dr. Goldsmith interest. Danville,
Ky., 1973.
    1 p.   illus.   58 cm.
    Reprinted from Kentucky Advocate (Danville, Ky.),
15 April 1973.

13621 Battaile, Elizabeth Kinkead, 1887-
    Out of the kitchen into the house. Compiled by
Matilda B. Moore. [Lexington, Ky., 1971]
    cover-title, 7 ℓ., 53 p.   front. (port.)   23 cm.

13622 Bauder, Ward W
    Objectives and activities of special-interest
organizations in Kentucky. Lexington, Kentucky
Agricultural Experiment Station, 1956.
    43 p.   tables.   24 cm.   (Kentucky Agricultural
Experiment Station, Bulletin, 639)

13623 Baugher, Ruby Dell.
    Chips of cedar, by Ruby Dell Baugher... Lexington,
The Kernel press, University of Kentucky, 1943.
    60 p.   21½ cm.
    Poems.

13624 Baugher, Ruby Dell.
    Doorways, candles, and morning, by Ruby Dell Baugher.
Cynthiana, Ky., The Hobson book press, 1945.
    [iii]-viii, [6], 180 p.   21 cm.
    Poems.

13625 Baugher, Ruby Dell.
    Kites over Spring Grove, by Ruby Dell Baugher...
Lexington, The Kentucky Kernel Press, University of
Kentucky, 1941.
    62 p.   21 cm.
    Poems.

13626 Bay, Jens Christian, 1871-1962.
    The fortune of books. Essays, memories and
prophecies of a librarian... Chicago, Walter M.
Hill [1941]
    442 p.   illus.   25 cm.

13627 Bay, Jens Christian, 1871-1962.
       Onkel Toms hytte efter hundrede aar. Med tvende
       exkurser... Julen 1950. [Skjern, Denmark, Simon
       Gullander, 1950]
       [37] p.   22 cm.

13628 Baylor, Orval W
       J. Dan Talbott, champion of good government.
       A saga of Kentucky politics from 1900 to 1942.
       Louisville, Kentucky printing corporation, 1942.
       477 p.   illus.   23 cm.   (Kentucky political
       series)

13629 Bean, Dottie.
       In reference to... Roger Barbour. Paducah, Ky.,
       1974.
       22-24 p.   port.   24 cm.
       Reprinted from Kentucky Library Association
       Bulletin, v. 32, no. 4, 1974.

13630 Bear, John W   1800-
       The life and travels of John W. Bear, "the Buckeye
       blacksmith". Baltimore, D. Binswanger & co.,
       printers, 1873.
       299 p. incl. front. (port.)   19½ cm.

13631 Beard, James A
       Ham, the pride of Kentucky. Washington, D.C.,
       1974.
       broadside.   illus.   25 x 22 cm.

13632 Beard, Richard, 1799-1880.
       Brief biographical sketches of some of the early
       ministers of the Cumberland Presbyterian church.
       By Richard Beard, D.D. Nashville, Tenn., Southern
       Methodist publishing house, for the author, 1867.
       vi, 7-319 p.   19 cm.
       A "second series" appeared in 1874.

13633 Beard, Richard, 1799-1880.
       Brief biographical sketches of some of the early
       ministers of the Cumberland Presbyterian church.
       Second series. By Richard Beard, D.D. Nashville,
       Tenn., Cumberland Presbyterian board of publication,
       1874.
       4, v-vi, 7-408 p.   19 cm.

13634   Beardsley, Frank Grenville, 1870-
            A history of American revivals... Boston, New York
        [etc.] American tract society [c1904]
            3 p.l., 324 p.   20½ cm.

13635   Beauchamp, Jereboam O
            The Beauchamp tragedy in Kentucky, as detailed in
        the Confession of Jereboam O. Beauchamp. To which is
        added a biographical sketch of Col. Solomon P. Sharp,
        and a historical account of the old court and new
        court controversy, etc.... New York, Dinsmore & co.,
        1858.
            x, 134 p.   front.   17 cm.

13636   Beauchamp, Jereboam O
            The confession of Jereboam Beauchamp [written by
        himself] who was executed at Frankfort, Ky., for the
        murder of Col. Solomon P. Sharp, a member of the
        legislature and late attorney-general of Ky. To which
        is added some poetical pieces written by Mrs. Ann
        Beauchamp, who voluntarily put a period to her existence
        on the day of the execution of her husband, and was
        buried in the same grave with him. Kentucky, H. T.
        Goodsell [1854]
            1 p.l., 7-100 p.   23½ cm.

13637   ... Beaumont Inn. [Gettysburg, Pa., 1974]
            1 p.   illus.   30 cm.
        At head of title: Famous inns of Kentucky.
        Reprinted from American motorist, Bluegrass edition,
        v. 42, no. 4, Oct. 1974, p. 7.

13638   Beckner, Lucien.
            Advantages of Winchester described in brief,
        by Lucien Beckner [Winchester, Ky., Winchester
        Democrat, Oct. 15, 1915]
            3 p.   28 cm.

13639   Beckner, Lucien.
            Clark County in the Texan Revolution, by Lucien
        Beckner. Read before the Clark County Historical
        Society, December 12, 1921. Transcribed by George
        F. Doyle [n.p., n.d.]
            1 p.l., 6 typewritten l.   23 cm.

13640   Beckner, Lucien.
            Eskippakithiki, the last Indian town in Kentucky.

Louisville, Ky., The Filson Club, 1932.
355-382 p.   28 cm.

13641 Beckner, Lucien.
         History of Boonesboro. [n.p., n.d.]
         16 p.   15 cm.
         Mounted in galley proof; not known whether article
       was actually published.

13642 Beckner, Lucien.
         Samuel Mackay Wilson, an address delivered on the
       anniversary of the Battle of Blue Licks, August 19,
       1947. [Lexington] University of Kentucky Library,
       1949.
         8 p.   29 cm.

13643 Beckner, Marie Warren.
         Early history of Winchester. [Winchester, Ky.,
       1915]
         2 p.   28 cm.
         Reprinted from Winchester Democrat, 15 October 1915.

13644 Beckner, W   M
         Hand-book of Clark County and the city of Winchester,
       Kentucky... Chicago, The Arkansaw traveler publishing
       co., 1889.
         34 p.   illus.   36 cm.

13645 Beckner, W   M
         Indian Fields. Transcribed by George F. Doyle,
       M.D., F.A.C.S. [Winchester, Ky., Clark County
       Historical Society, n.d.]
         6 p.   21½ cm.

13646 Beers, D   G
         Atlas of Bourbon, Clark, Fayette, Jessamine and
       Woodford Counties, Ky. From actual surveys and
       official records. Compiled and published by D. G.
       Beers & co. D. G. Beers, J. Lanagan. Philadelphia,
       D. G. Beers & co., 1877.
         [77] p. maps.   36 cm.
         All copies examined are so tightly bound that the
       middle section of maps on facing pages is partially
       lost.

13647 Beers, Howard Wayland, 1905-
         Kentucky designs for her future. Edited by
       Howard W. Beers. Photographic editor, W. Brooks

Hamilton. Lexington, University of Kentucky press, 1945.
    323 p.   illus.   24 cm.

13648 [Beers, Howard Wayland] 1905-
         A report on public welfare.   [n.p.] Committee for
       Kentucky [194-]
         30 p.   illus.   24 cm.

13649 [Begley, Michael J   ]
         This land is home to me; a pastoral letter on
       powerlessness in Appalachia by the Catholic bishops
       of the region.   [Paintsville, Ky., Kentucky Highlands
       Publishing Co., 1975?]
         12 p.   illus.   58 x 40 cm.

13650 Belew, Pascal Perry.
         My old Kentucky home, or, Experiences from life...
       Kansas City, Mo., Nazarene publishing house [n.d.]
         48 p.   front. (port.)   20½ cm.
         Autobiography of a minister of the Church of the
       Nazarene.

13651 Bell, Eleanora May, 1901?-
         Poems by Eleanora May Bell. Georgetown, Ky., 1911.
         [14] p.   18 cm.
         "The poems in this little book were written by
       Eleanora May Bell at the age of ten years."

13652 Benedict, Jennie C
         The blue ribbon cook book, being a third publication
       of "One hundred tested receipts," together with many
       other which have been tried and found valuable, by
       Jennie C. Benedict...   Louisville, Ky., Standard
       printing co. [1904]
         138 p.   22½ cm.

13653 Benedict, Jennie C
         The road to Dream Acre [by] Jennie C. Benedict.
       Louisville, Ky., The Standard Printing Co., 1928.
         115 p.   illus.   23 cm.

13654 Berea College. Library.
         Mountain fiction from Addington to Zugsmith...
       924 works of fiction by Southern Appalachian
       authors, or with Southern Appalachian settings.
       A part of the 6,000 volume Weatherford-Hammond
       Mountain Collection of Berea College. Revised and

enlarged with the addition of 164 more titles
acquired since a similar 1970 list. Berea, Ky.,
Hutchins Library, 1972.
23 p.   29 cm.

13655   Bergstrom, Bill.
Whiskey running still thrives throughout state.
Harlan, Ky., 1974.
2 p.   28 cm.
Reprinted from The Harlan, Ky., Daily Enterprise,
Sunday, 18 August 1974.

13656   Berry, Carrie Williams.
Joel Tanner Hart. [n.p., n.d.]
48 p.   ports., illus.   18 cm.

13657   Berry, Wendell, 1934-
A tribute [to Thomas B. Stroup] Lexington, Ky.,
1973.
12-14 p.   23 cm.
Reprinted from Amanuensis, v. 2, no. 1, Spring
1973.

13658   Best, Edna Hunter.
The historic past of Washington, Mason County,
Kentucky. Cynthiana, Ky., The Hobson Book Press,
1944.
xi, 117 p.   illus.   27 cm.

13659   Best, Edna Hunter.
Sketches of Washington, Mason County, Kentucky...
Honoring the 150th anniversary of the establishing
of Washington as a town, 1786-1936. [n.p.] 1936.
cover-title, 12 p.   23 cm.

13660   Best, Robert.
Tables of chemical equivalents, incompatible
substances, and poisons and antidotes; with an
explanatory introduction. Collected and arranged
by Robert Best, A.M., lecturer on pharmaceutical
chemistry in Transylvania University. Lexington,
Ky. Printed by W. W. Worsley, corner of Main and
Mill streets, January, 1825.
74 p.   tables. $21\frac{1}{2}$ cm.

13661   Bevins, Ann.
Scott County Sally Ward became most talked of
belle of the century. [Lexington, Ky., 1968]

22

2 p.   illus.   30 cm.
Reprinted from the Sunday Herald-Leader, Lexington, Ky., 14 January 1968.
Sally Ward, born in Scott County, Kentucky, married T. Bigelow Lawrence on 5 December 1848; Dr. Robert P. Hunt; Verne Armstrong; and George F. Downs.

13662   Bibliographical Society of America.
Preliminary finding list on writings on the Kentucky book trade. Charlottesville, Va., 1949.
7 p.   29 cm.

13663   Bibliography; Kentuckyana library founded by Susan Steele Sampson, 1931. Located in the Executive mansion. Frankfort, Ky., State journal co., 1931.
cover title, 25 p.   24 cm.

13664   Binkerd, Adam D
Pictorial guide to the Mammoth Cave, Kentucky. A complete historic, descriptive and scientific account of the greatest subterranean wonder of the western world. Cincinnati, Press of G. P. Houston, 1889.
112 p.   illus. $19\frac{1}{2}$ cm.

13665   The biographical encyclopaedia of Kentucky of the dead and living men of the nineteenth century. Cincinnati, J. M. Armstrong & company, 1878.
792 p.   illus.   28 cm.

13666   Biographical sketch of General John Adair. Washington, Printed by Gales & Seaton, 1830.
23 p.   21 cm.

13667   Birch, Thomas E
The Virginian orator; being a variety of original and selected poems, orations, & dramatic scenes; to improve the American youth in the ornamental and useful art of eloquence & gesture... Second edition. Lexington, Ky., Printed by William Gibbes Hunt, 1823.
xv, 304 p.   18 cm.

13668   Bishop, Judson Wade, 1831-1917.
The story of a regiment; being a narrative of the service of the Second regiment, Minnesota veteran volunteer infantry, in the civil war of 1861-1865...

St. Paul, 1890.
2 p.l., 256 p.   front., port.   20½ cm.

13669 Bishop, Robert Hamilton, 1777-1855.
    Another voice from the tomb; being a funeral
    sermon, occasioned by the death of Joseph Cabell
    Breckenridge, esq. secretary of state: Delivered
    in M'Chord's Church, Lexington, Ky., sabbath after-
    noon, February 8th, 1824... Lexington, Printed by
    Thomas T. Skillman, 1824.
    26 p.   20½ cm.

13670 Bishop, Robert Hamilton, 1777-1855.
    A discourse occasioned by the death of Rev'd
    James M'Chord; Delivered in Market-Street church,
    Lexington, Ky., sabbath, 13th August, 1820. To
    which is added the address delivered at his inter-
    ment. By Robert H. Bishop, A.N. prof. of Nat.
    Philosophy and Hist. Trans. university. Lexington,
    Printed by Thomas T. Skillman, 1821.
    20, [1] p. 22 cm.

13671 Bishop, Robert Hamilton, 1777-1855.
    An introductory to a course of lectures on history...
    Printed at the request of the seniors and juniors
    of 1823-24. Lexington, Ky., William Tanner, Printer,
    1823.
    16 p.   17½ cm.

13672 Black Hawk Army.
    [Commission of Stephen M. Peaslee as brigade
    inspector, 1st brigade of the Black Hawk Army.
    Louisville, Ky., 1843]
        broadside.   30 x 25 cm.
    Accompanied by manuscript letter signed by Jn. D.
    Shepherd, Brigadier General, Black Hawk Army, with
    orders to Peaslee, dated 10 March 1843.

13673 Blake, Thaddeus C
    The old log house, a history and defense of the
    Cumberland Presbyterian Church, by T. C. Blake, D.D.
    Nashville, Tenn., Cumberland Presbyterian Publishing
    House, 1878.
    293 p.   front.   15½ cm.

13674 [Blanton, Alice Rogers Clay]
    Historical map, Bourbon County, Ky. [Paris, Ky.?]

1934.
        map.   30 x 30 cm.

13675 Blazer, Paul G
         "E pluribus unum!" "One out of many." An oil
       company grows through acquisitions. New York,
       The Newcomen Society in North America, 1956.
         28 p.   24 cm.

13676 Bledsoe, Jesse.
         An introductory lecture, preparatory to a course
       of instruction on common and statute law, delivered
       in the chapel of Transylvania University, on Monday,
       November 3d, 1823... Published by request of the
       class. Lexington, Ky., William Tanner, printer,
       1823.
         24 p. $17\frac{1}{2}$ cm.

13677 Blevins, Billy.
         In reference to... J. Winston Coleman, Jr.
       Kentucky's greatest "amateur" historian, the
       "Squire of Kentucky History." Paducah, Ky., 1974.
         25-29 p.   port.   23 cm.
         Reprinted from Kentucky Library Association
       Bulletin, v. 38, no. 2, Spring 1974.

13678 Blood-Horse.
         Silver anniversary edition... [Lexington, Ky.]
       1941.
         256 p.   illus. $26\frac{1}{2}$ cm.

13679 [Bodley, Edith Fosdick]
         An historical sketch of the First Unitarian
       Church of Louisville in the state of Kentucky.
       Souvenir of the one hundredth anniversary celebration,
       November 20-23, 1930. [Louisville, 1930]
         42 p.   front., ports., illus.   20 cm.
         "Compiled, with the help of many friends of the
       church, by Edith Fosdick Bodley and Gustav Breaux."

13680 Bodley, Temple, 1852-1940.
         History of Kentucky, the Bluegrass state.
       Volume I, by Temple Bodley. Volume II, by Samuel
       M. Wilson... Chicago and Louisville, The S. J.
       Clarke publishing company, 1927.
         unpaged.   illus.   32 cm.
         A prospectus for the complete work.

13681   Bodley, Temple, 1852-1940.
        History of Kentucky. Chicago and Louisville,
        the S. J. Clarke publishing company, 1928.
        4 v.   illus.   28 cm.
        Contents. v. 1. Before the Louisiana Purchase in
        1803, by Temple Bodley. v. 2. From 1803 to 1928, by
        Samuel M. Wilson. v. 3, 4. Biographical sketches.

13682   Bogardus, Carl R
        The early history of Gallatin County, Kentucky,
        1798-1948. Austin, Ind., 1948.
        cover-title, [11] p.   24 cm.
        Reprinted from Gallatin County News, Warsaw, Kentucky.
        In double columns.

13683   Bogardus, Carl R
        Shantyboat. Austin, Scott County, Indiana, 1959.
        21 p.   illus., facsim.   24 cm.

13684   Bolin, Daniel Lynn.
        The First United Methodist Church of Irvington,
        Ky., 1895-1974. A brief history. Hawesville, Ky.,
        Printed by Bruner Facing Slip Co., 1974.
        36 p.   illus.   22½ cm.

13685   Bolin, Daniel Lynn.
        On the Texas, a sketch of a railroad town.
        Irvington, Kentucky. [Irvington] Irvington Woman's
        Club, 1974.
        cover-title, [8] p.   illus., map.   26½ cm.

13686   Bond, Mrs. Lydia Kennedy.
        History of the Pierian Club, Lawrenceburg, Ky....
        1905-1944. [Lawrenceburg? 1944?]
        19 p.   cover illus.   24 cm.

13687   Booker, Anton S
        Carry Nation of Kansas, who fought the liquor
        traffic with a hatchet. By Anton S. Booker.
        Girard, Kansas, Haldeman-Julius publications [n.d.]
        24 p.   21 cm.
        Carry Nation was born in Garrard County, Ky.

13688   [Bookstaver, James N   ]
        Indian massacres and tales of the red skins: an
        authentic history of the American Indian from 1492
        to the present time. New York, A. D. Porter, 1895.
        256 p.   illus. (incl. ports.)   19 cm.

13689 Boone, Daniel, 1734-1820.
    [Letter to Judge John Coburn mentioning his petitions
to the Kentucky Legislature and to the Congress for
return of his Kentucky lands] [Frankfort, Kentucky
Historical Society, n.d.]
    manuscript, 1 ℓ.   29 x 22½ cm.

13690 Booth, Mrs. Charles.
    God lives in Kentucky. Lexington, Ky. 1968
    broadside.   19 x 16 cm.
    Reprinted from Lexington Herald, 21 February 1958.

13691 Booth, Richard M
    Spatial patterns of religious attitudes and levels
of economic development in Southern Appalachia. A
research proposal submitted to the faculty of the
Department of Geography of the University of Kentucky.
December 19, 1972. [Lexington, 1972]
    15 p.   29 cm.

13692 Booz, Allen and Hamilton.
    Program evaluation survey. Kentucky Commission on
Public Education... from the report by Booz, Allen
and Hamilton, management consultants. October 1961.
[Lexington, Ky., Bureau of School Service, University
of Kentucky, 1961?]
    2 v.   tables, graphs.   23 cm.
    Contents. v. 1. Section on general administration
of public schools in Kentucky (including historical
background) Divisions I and II. v. 2. Section on
teacher education (including chapters on compensation
and tenure) Divisions III, IV and V.

13693 Bostrom, Rob.
    Scott Mountain chess master. Lexington, Ky., 1975.
    broadside.   port.   43 x 10 cm.
    Reprinted from Lexington Herald-Leader,
9 November 1975.

13694 Boswell, Ira Matthews.
    Recollections of a red-headed man... Cincinnati,
The Standard publishing company [1915]
    144 p.   20 cm.

13695 Bourbon County, Ky. Bourbon County 175th Birthday
Celebration, Inc.
    ... A record of the celebration of the one
hundred seventy-fifth anniversary of the founding

27

of Bourbon County, Kentucky, May 13-20, 1961...
[Paris, Ky.? 1961]
100 p.   illus., map on t.-p.   26½ cm.
At head of title: Historical scrap book.
"Compiled by the History Committee: Mrs. Wm.
Breckenridge Ardery, Mrs. Brooks C. Buckner,
Miss Lorine Letcher Butler, Mrs. Cassius M. Clay,
Miss Helen Ferry Hunter, Mr. Robert J. Smart,
Mrs. Wade Hampton Whitley, Mr. Henry Lee Williams."
Mrs. Ardery and Mrs. Whitley were the principal
authors.

13696   Bower, William Clayton.
Robert Milton Hopkins, Christian statesman.
Lexington, Ky., College of the Bible, 1963.
45 p.   23 cm.

13697   Bowling Green and Warren County. Immigration Society,
Bowling Green, Ky.
A condensed, accurate, and fair description of
the resources and development of the city & county...
Bowling Green, Park City Daily Times print, 1885.
54 p.   illus.   23½ cm.

13698   [Bowmar, Daniel M   ]
Second National Bank and Trust Company celebrating
75 years of service to Lexington and central Kentucky.
[Lexington, 1958]
24 p.   illus.   22½ cm.

13699   Boyd County, Ky. Homemaker's Club.
Boyd County Homemaker's Club cook book. [n.p.,
ca. 1940]
cover-title, [28] p.   24½ cm.
Printed by Religious book and publishing company,
Huntington, W. Va.

13700   Boyd, Mrs. Lucinda [Joan] Rogers, 1840-
The sorrows of Nancy... Richmond, Va., O. E.
Flanhart printing company, 1899.
95 p. incl. front., plates.   18½ cm.

13701   Boyden, Henry Paine.
The beginnings of the Cincinnati southern railway;
a sketch of the years, 1869-1878... Cincinnati,
The R. Clarke co., 1901.
v p., 1 ℓ., 5-122 p.   24 cm.

13702　Bradley, Daniel.
　　　　Journal of Capt. Daniel Bradley.　An epic of the
　　　Ohio frontier.　With copious comment by Frazer E.
　　　Wilson.　Greenville, Ohio, Frank H. Jobes & son,
　　　1935.
　　　　76 p.　　illus., maps, facsims.　　19 cm.

13703　Bradley, Robert M
　　　　A sketch of Granny Short's barbecue, and the general
　　　statutes of Kentucky.　By Robt. M. Bradley...
　　　Vol. I - Granny Short's barbecue.　Louisville,
　　　Bradley & Gilbert, 1879.
　　　　vii, [9]-103 p.　　23 cm.

13704　Brady, Cyrus Townsend, 1861-1920.
　　　　Border fights & fighters;　stories of the pioneers
　　　between the Alleghenies and the Mississippi and in
　　　the Texan republic...　With maps, plans & many
　　　illustrations by Louis Betts, Howard Giles, J. N.
　　　Marchard, Roy L. Williams, Harry Fenn & A. de F.
　　　Pitney.　New York, McClure Phillips & co., 1902.
　　　　382 p. incl. maps, plates.　　front., plates.
　　　21 cm.

13705　Bramlette, Thomas Elliott, 1817-
　　　　Speech of Gov. Thomas E. Bramlette, of Kentucky,
　　　at the meeting held at Frankfort on Monday,
　　　September 19th, 1864, to ratify the nomination of
　　　of Gen. George B. McClellan for president, and
　　　George H. Pendleton for Vice-President of the U.S.
　　　[Frankfort, Ky., Osborne & co.] 1864.
　　　　15 p.　　23½ cm.

13706　Branson, Branley A
　　　　List of amphibians and reptiles from Tight Hollow
　　　in East-Central Kentucky.　[By] Branley A. Branson,
　　　Donald L. Batch, and Charles J. Moore.　[n.p.] 1970.
　　　　73-78 p.　　map, tables, diag.　　23 cm.
　　　Reprinted from Transactions of the Kentucky
　　　Academy of Science, v. 31, nos. 3-4, 1970.

13707　Branson, Branley A
　　　　Spiders (Arachnida:　Araneida) from northern
　　　Kentucky with notes on phalangids and some other
　　　localities.　[By] Branley A. Branson and Donald L.
　　　Batch.　[n.p.] 1970.
　　　　84-98 p.　　23 cm.

Reprinted from Transactions of the Kentucky
Academy of Science, v. 31, nos. 3-4, 1970.

13708 Breckenridge, Mrs. Issa [Desha] comp.
       "The work shall praise the master", a memorial
       to Joel T. Hart, the Kentucky sculptor, from the
       women of the Blue grass, selected and arranged by
       Issa Desha Breckenridge and Mary Desha. Cincinnati,
       Press of R. Clarke & co., 1884.
       80 p. incl. front. (port.)   illus., pl.   24 cm.

13709 Breckinridge, John Bayne, 1913-
       Federal Judge Mac Swinford, plumed knight of the
       Kentucky bar. [Washington, D.C., 1975]
       E773-E774 p.   29 cm.
       Reprinted from Congressional Record, 27 February
       1975.

13710 Breckinridge, Robert J
       From soups to nuts. Third edition. Old time
       recipes that have made Kentucky and Louisiana foods
       and liquids famous. Dinner service, celebrations,
       toasts and helpful hints. [Lexington, Ky.] Kentucky
       Cardinal Dairies, 1936.
       39 p.   illus.   24 cm.
       Includes the recipe for burgoo by J. T. Looney
       ("The Burgoo King"), anecdotes about Kentucky ham
       and chitterlings, baked possum, "The recipe for the
       mint Julep" by J. Soule Smith, and various recipes
       of Tandy Ellis for "camp cooking" (turtle soup,
       squirrel soup, "jole" and greens, baked ground-hog,
       and baked shitepoke, all humorous).

13711 Breckinridge, Sophonisba Preston.
       Madeleine McDowell Breckinridge, a leader in the
       new south... Chicago, University of Chicago [1921]
       275 p.   illus.   21 cm.

13712 Breckinridge, William Campbell Preston, 1837-1904.
       Address at the unveiling of the monument erected
       to the memory of Joseph Lewis Young. Delivered in
       Machpelah cemetery, Mt. Sterling, Ky., on October 2,
       1879, by Wm. C. P. Breckinridge. Cincinnati,
       Robert Clarke & co., 1879.
       20 p.   23 cm.

13713 Bremer, Fredrika, 1801-1865.
       The homes of the New World; impressions of America...

Translated by Mary Howitt... New York, Harper &
brothers, 1853.
2 v.   21¼ cm.

13714 Bridwell, Margaret Morris.
The story of Mammoth Cave National Park, Kentucky.
A brief history. Drawings by the author. [Mammoth
Cave, Ky., 1952]
63 p.   illus.   21 cm.

13715 A brief history of Berea College. Berea, Ky.,
Berea College [197-?]
42 p.   illus., ports., facsims.   28 cm.
In pocket at end: Folders and flyers, some illus.,
on Berea College, Friends of Berea College Library,
Churchill Weavers (Berea), Civil War musical drama
"Wilderness Road", Settlement institutions of
Appalachia, Kentucky's White Hall state shrine
(Madison County), Frontier Nursing Service (Hyden,
Ky.), Buckhorn (Ky.) Children's Center, Hindman (Ky.)
Settlement School, Appalachian South Folklife Center;
print of reading room of Berea College Library,
1879, by J. H. Cornelison.

13716 A brief history of the Kentucky Derby 1875-1958...
Lexington [1958]
broadside.   25 x 40 cm.

13717 Briscoe, Vera.
Safeguarding Kentucky's natural resources, by
Vera Briscoe, James W. Martin, and J. E. Reeves.
Lexington, Published for the Bureau of Business
Research and the Bureau of Government Research by
the University of Kentucky, 1948.
224 p.   24 cm.

13718 Bronson, Harry.
[Prostitution in Lexington, Ky.] Lexington, 1975.
unpaged.   size varies.
Five articles from Lexington Herald, 21-25 July
1975.

13719 The Brookside strike, 1973-74. Twenty-three documents
in facsimile with introductory note by Lawrence S.
Thompson. Lexington, Ky., 1974.
2 1., 23 facsims.   size varies.

13720   Browder, John Caldwell.
        Nisi prius. New York, The Neale publishing
        company, 1912.
        275 p.   19½ cm.

13721   Brown, John Mason, 1837-1890.
        The political beginnings of Kentucky. A narrative
        of public events bearing on the history of that
        state up to the time of its admission into the
        American Union... Louisville, John P. Morton and
        company, printers to the Filson Club, 1889.
        263 p.   31 cm.
        Later designated as Filson Club Publication no. 6.

13722   Brown, John Thomas, 1869-
        Bruce Norman. By John T. Brown. Author, Churches
        of Christ at the beginning of the twentieth century,
        etc. Louisville, Ky., Jno. T. Brown pub. house,
        1901.
        219 p.   20 cm.
        Autographed by author.

13723   Brown, John Thomas, 1859-   , ed.
        Churches of Christ; a historical, biographical,
        and pictorial history of churches of Christ in the
        United States, Australasia, England, and Canada...
        Introduction by John W. McGarvey... Louisville,
        Ky., J. P. Morton and company, 1904.
        683 p. incl. front., illus., ports.   26½ cm.

13724   Brown, Leland A
        Early philosophical apparatus at Transylvania
        College. Lexington, Ky., Transylvania College
        press, 1959.
        117 p.   illus.   24 cm.

13725   Brown, Theodore M
        Introduction to Louisville architecture.
        Louisville, Ky., Louisville Free Public Library
        [c1960]
        38 p.   illus.   26 cm.

13726   Brown, Thomas.
        Brown's three years in the Kentucky prisons,
        from May 30, 1854, to May 18, 1857. Indianapolis,
        Courier company print, 1857.
        21 p.   22 cm.
        Brown was convicted on a charge of aiding slaves to escape.

13727 Brown, Thomas, b. 1778.
    The philosophy of mind according to Thomas Brown,
M.D. Transylvania University, January, 1826.
[Lexington, Ky., T. Smith, printer, 1826]
    broadside.   33½ x 33 cm.
Contains a chart, enclosed in 2 double-rule border,
with the caption "Physiology of the Mind & Ethics
and Theology."

13728 Browning, Graeme.
    Utilization of television in Kentucky higher
education. Part A: Review and analysis of educational
television facilities and programs, prepared by
Graeme Browning and Donald Van Fleet, Legislative
Research Commission staff. Part B: Report on
educational television in higher education, prepared
by Council on Public Higher Education. Frankfort,
Ky., Legislative Research Commission, 1975.
    A-85, B-25 p.   tables, diagrs.   28 cm.
(Research report, no. 129)

13729 Bryan, George.
    Rev. John D. Shane's interview with George Bryan.
The State historical society of Wisconsin. Draper
mss. 22 C 16. Transcribed from copy made by the
Society for Jesse P. Crump, Kansas City, Mo., by
George F. Doyle, M.D., F.A.C.S. [Winchester, Ky.,
n.d.]
    43 p.   26½ cm.

13730 Buchanan, Joseph, 1785-1829.
    The philosophy of human nature... Richmond,
Ky., Printed by John A. Grimes, 1812.
    336 p.   23 cm.

13731 Buck, Charles Neville, 1879-
    The battle-cry... Illustrations by Douglas Duer.
New York, Grosset & Dunlap [1914]
    356 p.   illus.   20 cm.

13732 Buck, Charles Neville, 1879-
    The call of the Cumberlands, by Charles Neville
Buck... Illustrations by Douglas Duer. New York,
Grosset & Dunlap [1913]
    3 p.l., 348 p.   front., 3 pl.   20 cm.

13733 Buck, Charles Neville, 1879-
    The portal of dreams... Illustrated by Frank Snapp.

New York, W. J. Watt & company [1912]
vi p., 1 ℓ., [5]-303 p.   front., 3 pl.   20 cm.

13734　[Buckner, G　　　D　　　　]
To the worshipful grand lodge of Kentucky.
[Lexington? 1870?]
7 p.   23 cm.

13735　Buckner, Simon Bolivar, 1823-1914.
... To the freemen of Kentucky: One year ago I
addressed you from Russellville... [n.p., 1862]
broadside.   28 x 15 cm.

13736　Buford, Thomas.
Address of Thomas Buford, delivered on the fourth
of July, 1846, at Midway, Woodford County, Ky.
Lexington, Ky., Printed at the Observer and reporter
office, 1846.
8 p.   20½ cm.

13737　Bull, Jacqueline Page, 1911-
The Samuel M. Wilson Library. [Frankfort, Ky.,
1949]
3 p.   26½ cm.
Reprinted from the Kentucky Historical Society
Register, January 1949.

13738　Bullock, Waller Overton.
Dr. Benjamin Winslow Dudley, by Waller Overton
Bullock... New York, Paul B. Hoeber [c1935]
cover-title, 201-213 p.   27½ cm.
Reprinted from Annals of Medical history,
new series, vol. 7, no. 3.

13739　Bumgardner, Helen A　　　　, comp.
Index. The border settlers of northwestern
Virginia from 1768 to 1795, embracing the life of
Jesse Hughes, by Lucullus Virgil McWhorter...
Tacoma, Washington, 1961.
[41] ℓ.   22 cm.

13740　Burgheim, Max.
Cincinnati in Wort und Bild. Nach authentischen
Quellen bearbeitet und zusammengestellt von Max
Burgheim. Mit zahlreichen Illustrationen.
Cincinnati, Verlag von M. & R. Burgheim [c1888]
604 p.   illus.   29 cm.

34

13741 Burgheim, Philip.
         The Ashland march, composed and dedicated to the
       Hon. Henry Clay (of Kentucky) by Philip Burgheim.
       Baltimore, Published by F. D. Benteen [n.d.]
         3 p.   music.   30 cm.
         The original of this text was in the possession
       of Elliott Shapiro, 118 West 79th Street, New York,
       in February 1943. The manuscript note by Henry Clay
       was faded at the time of copying. The original
       cannot now be located. The present "photostatic"
       copy, possibly now unique, is in the private library
       of Lawrence S. Thompson, Lexington, Kentucky.

13742 Burke, Clyde T
         Vignettes of Kentucky history; six little known
       facets of Kentucky history, by Clyde T. Burke.
       [Lexington, Ky., 1976]
         2 p.l., 29 p.
         "Introduction" by J. Winston Coleman, Jr.: p. l.

13743 Burkett, W   Keith.
         Low incomes of rural people: the nature and
       extent of the problem in a south-central Kentucky
       area. By W. Keith Burkett and James F. Thompson.
       Lexington, Agricultural Experiment Station, University
       of Kentucky, 1965.
         52 p.   map, tables.   24 cm.   (Kentucky
       Agricultural Experiment Station, Bulletin, 697)

13744 Burns, James Anderson.
         The crucible, a tale of the Kentucky feuds. By
       Burns of the mountains. Oneida, Ky., The Oneida
       Institute, 1928.
         126 p.   front. (port.), illus.   24 cm.
         Mounted at the end of this copy is Malcolm Stallons,
       Oneida Institute emphasizes character as well as
       learning, Lexington Herald-Leader, 23 Feb. 1975,
       p. E-4, with three photographs.

13745 Burr, Aril Bond.
         Panther Rock... Illustrated by Helen M. Burr.
       Cincinnati, Printed for the author by the Ruter
       press [1931]
         186 p.   illus.   21 cm.
         Inscribed by author.

13746 Burroughs, Wilbur Greeley, 1886-
         The geography of the Kentucky Knobs; a study of

the influence of geology and physiography upon the
industry, commerce, and life of the people...
Frankfort, Ky., The Kentucky geological survey, 1926.
284 p.   illus., maps, diagrs.   24 cm.
(Kentucky geological survey, ser. VI, geologic reports,
v. 19)
Bibliography: p. 267-277.

13747 Burton, Karen Sue.
The story of Dr. Walker's cabin. Frankfort,
Kentucky Historical Society, 1967.
1 p.   illus.   28 cm.
Reprinted from Kentucky heritage, v. 8, no. 1,
Fall 1967.

13748 Burton, Lewis William, bp., 1852-1940.
Catechism of the Diocese of Lexington with a map
of the Diocese; prepared by the Rt. Rev. Lewis W.
Burton... on the basis of a report of the subject
by a committee of the diocesan council. Lexington,
Ky., Press of J. L. Richardson & co., 1911.
27 p.   front. (fold. map)   22 cm.

13749 Butler, Mann, 1784-1852.
A history of the Commonwealth of Kentucky...
Louisville, Published for the author by Wilcox,
Dickerman & co., 1834.
396 p.   front.   20½ cm.

13750 Butler, Mann, 1784-1852.
A history of the Commonwealth of Kentucky, from
its exploration and settlement by the whites, to
the close of the northwestern campaign in 1813;
with an introduction, exhibiting the settlement of
western Virginia... in 1736, to the treaty of
Camp Charlotte... in 1774. By Mann Butler.
2d ed.; rev. and enl. by the author. Cincinnati,
J. A. James and Co.; Louisville, The author, 1836.
lxxii, 551 p.   plates.   19½ cm.

13751 Butler, Mann, 1784-1852.
Valley of the Ohio... Edited with a biographical
and bibliographical essay by G. Glenn Clift and
Hambleton Tapp. Frankfort, Kentucky Historical
Society, 1971.
302 p.   23 cm.

13752 Caldwell, Charles, 1772-1853.
        An address to the Philadelphia medical society,
        on the analogies between yellow fever and true
        plague, delivered, by appointment, on the 20th of
        February, 1801. By Charles Caldwell, M.D. Phila-
        delphia, Printed by Thomas & William Bradford,
        booksellers and stationers, no. 8, South Front
        street, 1801.
        viii, 44 p.   21½ cm.

13753 Caldwell, Charles, 1772-1853.
        Analysis of fever. An analysis of fever, by
        Charles Caldwell, M.D., professor of the institutes
        of medicine and clinical practice in Transylvania
        University. Lexington, Ky., Printed for the author,
        by Thomas T. Skillman, 1825.
        viii, 97 p.   22 x 13½ cm.

13754 Caldwell, Charles, 1772-1853.
        Elements of phrenology... Lexington, Ky., Printed
        for the author by Thomas T. Skillman, 1824.
        viii, 100 p.   20½ cm.

13755 Caldwell, Charles, 1772-1853.
        Elements of phrenology. (Second edition, greatly
        enlarged)   With a preliminary discourse in vindication
        of the science; against an attack on it by Francis
        Jeffrey Esq.; and with a concluding essay in proof
        of its usefullness, as the true philosophy of the
        human intellect, and applicable to the most important
        purposes of life. By Charles Caldwell, M.D.,
        professor of the institutes of medicine and clinical
        practice, in Transylvania University. Lexington,
        Ky., Printed by A. G. Meriwether, 1827.
        viii, 279 p.   24½ x 15 cm.

13756 Caldwell, Charles, 1772-1853.
        ... An essay upon the nature and sources of the
        malaria or noxious miasma, from which originate the
        family of diseases usually known by the denomination
        of bilious diseases; together with the best means
        of preventing the formation of malaria... Offered
        as a "prize essay", according to the conditions
        prescribed by "The Medical and surgical faculty of
        Maryland, at their annual convention held in the

city of Baltimore, on the 7th and 8th of June,
1830"... By Charles Caldwell... Philadelphia,
Carey & Lea, 1831.
  80 p.   22 cm.
  At head of title: Prize essay.
  "Appendix" (p. 69-80) is a criticism of Dr.
Macculloch's essay on malaria.

13757 Caldwell, Charles, 1772-1853.
      Essays on malaria, and temperament. By Charles
    Caldwell, M.D., professor of the institutes of
    medicine and clinical practice in Transylvania
    University. Lexington, Ky., Printed by N. L.
    Finnell & J. F. Herndon, 1831.
      300 p.   20 x 12 cm.

13758 Caldwell, Charles, 1772-1853.
      An eulogium on Caspar Wistar, M.S., professor of
    anatomy, by Charles Caldwell... delivered by
    appointment, before the members of the Philadelphia
    medical society; and published at their request.
    Philadelphia, T. Dobson and son, 1818.
      28 p.   22 cm.

13759 Caldwell, Charles, 1772-1853.
      An eulogium to the memory of Dr. Samuel Cooper,
    delivered, by appointment, before the Philadelphia
    medical society. On the fourth day of March, 1799.
    By Charles Caldwell... Philadelphia, Printed by
    Henry Tuckniss, for Mathew Carey, no. 118, Market-
    street, 1799.
      48 p.   20½ cm.
      "Appendix. Last will and testament of Dr. Samuel
    Cooper": p. [45]-48.

13760 Caldwell, Charles, 1772-1853.
      An eulogium to the memory of Mr. George Lee,
    delivered by appointment, to the Philadelphia
    medical society, on the 24th day of Feb. 1802 by
    Charles Caldwell, M.D. Philadelphia, Printed by
    Thomas and William Bradford, 1802.
      34 p.   21½ cm.

13761 Caldwell, Charles, 1772-1853.
      Extract from an eulogium on William Shippen, M.D.,
    delivered by Charles Caldwell, M.D., in the Medical
    college. Philadelphia, Printed for the publisher, 1818.
      20 p.   21½ cm.

13762   Caldwell, Charles, 1772-1853.
        Introductory address on independence of intellect...
        Lexington, Ky., Printed at the Office of the
        Kentucky whig, 1825.
        49 p.   21½ cm.

13763   Caldwell, Charles, 1772-1853.
        Medical & physical memoirs, containing, among other
        subjects, a particular enquiry into the origin and
        nature of the late pestilential epidemics of the
        United States. By Charles Caldwell, M.D.   Phila-
        delphia, Printed by Thomas & William Bradford,
        booksellers and stationers, no. 8, South Front
        street, 1801.
        8 p.l., 296 p., 2 l., [305]-348 p.   22 cm.
        "An address to the Philadelphia medical society,
        on the analogies between yellow fever and true
        plague" has special t.-p.
        Contents. - A physical sketch of the city of Phila-
        delphia, interspersed with general remarks, applicable
        to all large and populous cities. - Facts and
        observations, relative to the origin and nature of
        the yellow fever, addressed to the citizens of
        Philadelphia, in ten numbers. - On the winter retreat
        of swallows. - Strictures on "A memoir concerning
        the disease of goitre, as it prevails in different
        parts of North America. By Benjamin Smith Barton,
        M.D." - An address to the Philadelphia medical
        society, on the analogies between yellow fever and
        true plague.

13764   Caldwell, Charles, 1772-1853.
        Medical & physical memoirs, by Charles Caldwell,
        M.D., professor of the institutes of medicine and
        clinical practice, in Transylvania University.
        Lexington, Ky., Printed at the office of the
        Kentucky Whig, 1826.
        [4], 224 p.   21 x 12½ cm.

13765   Caldwell, Charles, 1772-1853.
        Memoirs of the life and campaigns of the Hon.
        Nathaniel Greene, major general in the army of the
        United States, and commander of the Southern
        department, in the war of the revolution. By
        Charles Caldwell... Philadelphia, Published by
        Robert Desilver, no. 110 Walnut street, and
        Thomas Desilver, no. 2, Decatur street, J. Maxwell,
        printer, 1819.

xxiii, [1], 452 p.   front. (port.)   2 fold.
facsim.   21½ cm.

13766 Caldwell, Charles, 1772-1853.
       New views of penitentiary discipline, and moral
       education and reform. By Charles Caldwell, M.D.
       Philadelphia, W. Brown, printer, 1829.
          viii, 52 p.   21½ cm.   [Prison discipline
       pamphlets, v. 7, no. 6]

13767 Caldwell, Charles, 1772-1853.
       An oration commemorative of the character and
       administration of Washington, delivered before the
       American Republican Society of Philadelphia, on the
       22d day of February, 1810. By Charles Caldwell...
       Philadelphia, Bradford and Inskeep, 1810.
          37 p.   22½ cm.
       "Published at the request of the society."

13768 Caldwell, Charles, 1772-1853.
       An oration on the causes of the difference, in
       point of frequency and force, between the endemic
       diseases of the United States of America, and those
       of the countries of Europe, delivered, by appointment,
       to the "Philadelphia medical society," on the fifth
       day of February, 1802. By Charles Caldwell, M.D.,
       &c. &c. Philadelphia, Printed by T. and William
       Bradford, booksellers and stationers, no. 8, South
       Front street, 1802.
          46 p.   19 cm.

13769 Caldwell, Charles, 1772-1853.
       Outlines of a course of lectures on the institutes
       of medicine. By Charles Caldwell, M.D., professor
       of the institutes of medicine and clinical practice,
       in Transylvania University. Lexington, Ky.,
       Printed by William Tanner, 1823.
          x, 188 p.   23½ x 14 cm.

13770 Caldwell, Charles, 1772-1853.
       A semi-annual oration, on the origin of pestilential
       diseases, delivered before the Academy of medicine
       of Philadelphia, on the 17th day of December, 1798.
       By Charles Caldwell... Philadelphia, Printed by
       T. and S. F. Bradford, 1799.
          xii, [13]-59 p.   20½ cm.

13771   Caldwell, Charles, 1772-1853.
        Thoughts on quarantine and other sanitary systems,
        being an essay which received the prize of the
        Boylston medical committee, of Harvard university
        in August, 1834. By Charles Caldwell... Boston,
        Marsh, Capen & Lyon, 1834.
        72 p.   23½ cm.

13772   Caldwell, Charles, 1772-1853.
        Thoughts on schools of medicine, their means of
        instruction, and models of administration, with
        references to the schools of Louisville and
        Lexington... Louisville, Ky., Prentice and
        Weissinger, 1837.
        31 p.   21 cm.

13773   Caldwell, Charles, 1772-1853.
        Thoughts on the original unity of the human race.
        2d ed.: with additions and improvements. By
        Charles Caldwell, M.D. Cincinnati, J. A. and U. P.
        James, 1852.
        xv, [17]-165 p.   19½ cm.

13774   Call, Richard Ellsworth, 1856-1917.
        La cartographie de Mammoth Cave (Kentucky)
        [Paris?] 1897.
        [12]-22 p.   maps.   26½ cm.
        "Extrait du Bulletin de la Société de Spéléologie,
        Janvier-Mars et Avril-Juin 1897."

13775   Call, Richard Ellsworth, 1856-1917.
        The life and writings of Rafinesque... Louisville,
        Ky., John P. Morton and co., 1895.
        227 p.   front. (port.), facsims.   32 cm.
        At head of title: Filson Club publication no. 10.

13776   [Call, Richard Ellsworth] 1856-1917.
        Mammoth Cave, Kentucky... [Louisville, Ky.,
        Louisville & Nashville r.r., 1897?]
        [12] p. incl. illus., map.   24 cm.

13777   Call, Richard Ellsworth, 1856-1917.
        The Mammoth Cave, Kentucky. A sketch...
        Published by the Mammoth Cave estate. [Louisville,
        Courier-Journal job printing co., 189-?]
        [32] p. incl. illus., map.   17 cm.

13778   Camp Nelson's long and varied history is beginning
        a new chapter. Lexington, Ky., 1973.
          1 p. in 8 cols.
          Reprinted from Lexington Herald-Leader, 3 June
        1973, p. 61.

13779   Campbell, Alexander, 1788-1866.
          A debate between Rev. A. Campbell and Rev. N. L.
        Rice, on the action, subject, design and administration
        of Christian baptism; also, on the character of
        spiritual influence in conversion and sanctification,
        and on the expediency and tendency of ecclesiastic
        creeds, as terms of union and communion: held in
        Lexington, Ky., from the fifteenth of November to
        the second of December, 1843, a period of eighteen
        days. Reported by Marcus T. C. Gould, stenographer
        assisted by A. Euclid Darpier, stenographer, and
        amanuensis. Published, Lexington, Ky., by A. T.
        Skillman & son; Cincinnati, Wright and Swormstedt,
        J. A. James; Louisville, D. S. Burnett; New York,
        R. Carter; Pittsburgh, Thomas Carter, 1844.
          912 p. $21\frac{1}{2}$ x $13\frac{1}{2}$ cm.

13780   [Campbell, John P   ]
          The southern business directory and general
        commercial advertiser... Vol. I.   Charleston,
        Press of Walker & James, 1854.
          404, 171, [1] p.   22 cm.

13781   Cann, Marion Stuart.
          On Skidd's branch, a tale of the Kentucky
        mountains. By Marion Stuart Cann. Scranton, Pa.,
        Printed in the Republican job rooms, 1884.
          56 p. $14\frac{1}{2}$ cm.

13782   Carlisle, George William Frederick Howard, 7th earl
        of, 1802-1864.
          Travels in America. The poetry of Pope. Two
        lectures delivered to the Leeds Mechanics' Institution
        and Literary Society, December 5th and 6th, 1850.
        By the Right Honorable, the Earl of Carlisle
        (Lord Morpeth)   New York, G. P. Putnam, 1851.
          135 p.   19 cm.
          "The poetry of Pope": p. [87]-135.
          Kentucky: p. 63-65.

13783   Carpenter, Sandra.
          History - preserved by a church. Frankfort,

Kentucky Historical Society, 1967.
2 p.   illus.   28 cm.
Reprinted from Kentucky heritage, v. 8, no. 1,
Fall 1967.

13784   Carpenter, Stanley B
Kentucky coffee tree. Lexington, Cooperative
Extension Service, University of Kentucky [n.d.]
2 p.   map.   29 cm.   (FOR-8)

13785   Carrier, A   H
Monument to the memory of Henry Clay... Cincinnati,
W. A. Clarke, 1858.
516 p.   front. (port.)   21 cm.

13786   Carroll, Chuck.
Johnson County in his honor; Kentucky's first
native politician. Frankfort, Kentucky Historical
Society, 1967.
2 p.   illus.   28 cm.
Reprinted from Kentucky heritage, v. 8, no. 1,
Fall 1967.

13787   Carter, Tom.
History mirrored in county names. [Lexington,
Ky., 1974]
2 p.   43 cm.
Reprinted from Sunday Herald-Leader, Lexington,
Ky., 3 February 1974, p. G8-G9.

13788   Carter, Tom.
History of Kentucky, State Theater reflects
ups and downs of downtown shopping area. Lexington,
1976.
broadside.   illus.   42 x 28 cm.
Reprinted from Lexington Herald-Leader, 11 April
1976.

13789   Cartwright, Peter, 1785-1872.
Fifty years as a presiding elder. Ed. by Rev.
W. S. Hooper. Cincinnati, Hitchcock and Walden;
New York, Carlton and Lanahan, 1871.
281 p.   front. (port.)   19½ cm.

13790   Cass, Norma.
Kentucky progress magazine. Index to volumes
1-7, 1928-1936. Prepared by Norma Cass and
Jacqueline Bull... Lexington [University of Kentucky

Library] 1943.
      58 p.   28 cm.

13791 Cassidy, Samuel M
        The story of a log house, written at the prodding
        of my sons, Samuel and Charles, as they and their
        families want to know the background of this nearly
        200-year-old log house, built by their ancestor,
        Robert Boggs, and as I know more about its history
        than any living person. [By] Samuel M. Cassidy...
        Fayette County, Ky., 1976.
          20 p.   illus., plans, geneal. table.   21½ cm.

13792 Cassiodorus, Flavius Magnus Aurelius, Senator, ca. 487-
        ca. 583.
        ... Of scribes... Lexington, Ky., 1958.
          8 ℓ.   28 cm.

13793 Catalogue of books, maps, statuary, &c. belonging to
        Georgetown college, Kentucky. Cincinnati, Printed
        by E. Shepard, 1848.
          76, [1] p.   front.   19 cm.

13794 A catalogue of the officers and students of Transylvania
        university, Lexington, Ky., January, 1823.
        [Lexington, 1823]
          16 p.   21 cm.

13795 Caudill, Rebecca ("Mrs. James S. Ayars")
        The high cost of writing... A centennial publication.
        Cumberland, Ky., Published by the Southeast Community
        College, University of Kentucky, 1965.
          22 p.   illus.   23 cm.

13796 Cave, Sally Bullock, 1865-1958.
        Inland voices, by Sally Bullock Cave.   Boston,
        The Christopher publishing house [n.d.]
          viii, 9-63 p.   20 cm.
        Inscribed by author.

13797 Cave, Sally Bullock, 1865-1958.
        Stoneholt... Boston, Christopher publishing
        house [195-]
          372 p.   21 cm.

13798 Cawein, Madison Julius, 1865-1914.
        Days and dreams, poems by Madison Cawein...
        New York and London, G. P. Putnam's sons,

The Knickerbocker press, 1891.
vi, 173 p.   18½ cm.

13799 Cawein, Madison Julius, 1865-1914.
The giant and the star; little annals in rhyme,
by Madison Cawein. Boston, Small, Maynard &
company [1909]
vi, 173 p.   20 cm.

13800 Cawein, Madison Julius, 1865-1914.
Imitations of the beautiful and poems, by Madison
Cawein. New York and London, G. P. Putnam's sons,
The Knickerbocker press, 1894.
vii, [1], 208 p.   18½ cm.

13801 Cawein, Madison Julius, 1865-1914.
Kentucky poems... with an introduction by
Edmund Gosse. London, Grant Richards, 1902.
264 p.   18½ cm.

13802 Cawein, Madison Julius, 1865-1914.
Moods and memories, poems... New York, G. P.
Putnam's sons, 1891.
310 p.   front.   17 cm.

13803 Cawein, Madison Julius, 1865-1914.
The poet and nature, and The morning road, by
Madison Cawein... Louisville, Ky., John P. Morton
& company [1914]
xiv, 241 p.   18 cm.

13804 Cawein, Madison Julius, 1865-1914.
The republic, a little book of homespun verse,
by Madison Cawein. Cincinnati, Stewart & Kidd
company [1913]
98 p.   19 cm.

13805 Cawein, Madison Julius, 1865-1914.
The vale of Tempe, poems by Madison Cawein.
New York, E. P. Dutton and company, 1911.
x, [2], 275 p.   19½ cm.

13806 Centennial of Presbyterianism in Kentucky [1783-1883]
Addresses delivered at Harrodsburg, Kentucky,
October 12, 1883. Louisville, The Courier-Journal
printing co. [1883]
98 p.   23½ cm.

13807   Centre College of Kentucky.
        A quietly dynamic experience. Danville, Ky.,
        1975.
            56 p.   illus., map.   24 cm.

13808   Century's record of Winchester's post office.
        Who were postmasters and the time they served,
        1803-1896. Transcribed by George F. Doyle.
        [n.p., n.d.]
            5 typewritten ℓ.   31 cm.

13809   Chalkley, Lyman.
        Before the gates of the Wilderness Road. The
        settlement of southwestern Virginia. [Richmond,
        Va., 1922]
            183-202 p.
        Reprinted from the Virginia magazine of history
        and biography, v. 30, no. 2, April 1922.

13810   Chamberlain, Leo Martin, 1896-1968.
        The University of Kentucky project at Bogor
        in its fourth year 1961. Lexington, 1961.
            64 p.   cover illus.   29 cm.

13811   Chambers, T   Bell.
        A Kentucky belle, a comedy in three acts.
        Philadelphia, Penn Publishing company, 1923.
            35 p.   18 cm.

13812   Chandler, Woodruff T   1852-
        Rustic rhymes, by W. T. Chandler, M.D....
        Louisville, Ky., Published for the author by
        John P. Morton and company, 1883.
            325 p.   19½ cm.
        Inscribed by author.

13813   Chandley, Juanita K
        From saddlebags to shelves: a history of the
        Clinton County Public Library. [Paducah, Ky., 1977]
            9-16 p.   23 cm.
        Reprinted from Kentucky Library Association
        Bulletin, vol. 41, no. 4, fall 1977.

13814   Chapman, George Thomas.
        Sermons upon the ministry, worship, and doctrines
        of the Protestant Episcopal Church and other
        subjects. By G. T. Chapman, D.D. Rector of
        Christ Church, Lexington. Lexington, Ky., Printed

by Smith and Palmer, 1828.
viii, 399 p.   23 x 14 cm.

13815 Charless' Kentucky, Tennessee, and Ohio almanac for
the year 1806... Lexington, Printed by Joseph
Charless [1805]
[26] p.   17½ cm.

13816 Charless' Kentucky, Tennessee, and Ohio almanac for
the year 1807... Lexington, Printed by Joseph
Charless [1806]
[36] p.   17 cm.

13817 Charleston, Max.
The oldest town in Kentucky, 1774.   [Harrodsburg,
Ky., D. M. Hutton, 1929]
23 p.   24½ cm.

13818 Charter and by-laws of the Polytechnic society of
Kentucky. Louisville, J. P. Morton and company,
1892.
24 p.   19½ cm.

13819 Chenault, Robert.
Inheritance and estate taxation in Kentucky.
Prepared by Robert Chenault, research attorney
[and] Dr. Abdul Rahman, research analyst.
Frankfort, Legislative Research Commission, 1961.
viii, 89 p.   29 cm.   (Research report, no. 6)

13820 Cherry, Henry Hardin.
A greater Kentucky. A discussion of the
Declaration of principles and aims adopted by the
Kentucky Educational Association. This address
was delivered at the Warren County Farmers'
Chautauqua held at Mt. Pleasant, 1913. Frankfort,
Department of Education, 1913.
19 p.   21 cm.
Inscribed by author.

13821 Cherry, Thomas Crittenden.
Kentucky, the pioneer state of the west, by
Thomas Crittenden Cherry. With introduction by
Irvin S. Cobb. Boston [etc.] D. C. Heath and
company [1935]
[viii], 374 p.   illus., ports., maps (1 fold.)
18½ cm.

13822 Christ Church, Louisville, Ky.
    In memoriam. Rev. John Nicholas Norton, D.D.,
    late associate rector, Christ church, Louisville...
    By the wardens and vestry of the parish...
    [Louisville, Ky.] J. P. Morton and company, 1881.
    32 p.   port.   25½ cm.

13823 Christiansen, John R
    Social security and the farmer in Kentucky, by
    John H. Christiansen, C. Milton Coughenour,
    Louis J. Ducoff, and A. Lee Coleman. Lexington,
    Kentucky Agricultural Experiment Station, Univer-
    sity of Kentucky, 1958.
    52 p.   illus., map, tables, graph.   24 cm.
    (Kentucky Agricultural Experiment Station, Bulletin
    654)

13824 Churchill, Winston, 1871-1947.
    The crossing... with illustrations by Sydney
    Adamson and Lilian Bayliss. New York and London,
    Macmillan, 1904.
    498 p.   20½ cm.

13825 Cincinnati. Public Library.
    Catalog of the Inland rivers library, with a
    foreword by Captain Frederick Way, Jr., compiled
    by Clyde N. Bowden, curator. Based on the collection
    of the Sons and daughters of pioneer rivermen.
    Cincinnati, Public library of Cincinnati and
    Hamilton county, Rare book room, 1968.
    154 p.   illus.   29 cm.

13826 The Cincinnati pioneer. Edited and published by
    John D. Caldwell. Cincinnati, 1873-1885.
    6 nos.   illus.   22 cm.

13827 Cist, Henry M
    ... The Army of the Cumberland... New York,
    Charles Scribner's Sons, 1882.
    284 p.   maps.   20 cm.
    At head of title: Campaigns of the Civil War.
    VII.

13828 Cistercian contemplatives. Monks of the strict
    observance at Our Lady of Gethsemani, Kentucky;
    Our Lady of the Holy Ghost, Georgia; Our Lady
    of the Holy Trinity, Utah. A guide to Trappist
    life. [Trappist, Kentucky, Our Lady of Gethsemani,

1968]
62 p.   illus.   24 cm.

13829 Civil War battlefields, 1861-65. [n.p.] Historical
documents co., 1961.
map.   39 x 35 cm.

13830 Clark, Billy.
... Stub Toe the champion. A heap o' love. Fur
in the hickory. Pride o' the jug. Lexington,
1953.
43 p.   20 cm.
At head of title: Phi Beta Kappa, University of
Kentucky. Award for outstanding undergraduate
writing, number 1.

13831 Clark, Charles Eugene.
The early settlement of Kentucky... [Covington?
Ky., 1913]
9 p.   20 cm.

13832 Clark, Thomas Dionysius, 1903-
Americana in a state university library. Lexington,
1963.
11 p.   23 cm.   (Kentucky. University. Library.
Bulletin XXIII)

13833 Clark, Thomas Dionysius, 1903-
Athens of the west; tiny fort is seed for new,
important Lexington. [Lexington, Ky., 1976]
12 p.   illus.   58 cm.
Reprinted from Lexington Herald-Leader, 13 June
1975, a bicentennial supplement captioned "200 years
of history".
Other articles in this supplement: John Alexander,
Cassius Clay, model for rebellion; Burton Milward,
Under Henry Clay, House becomes 'All-Potent' power
at the nation; Kenn Johnson, Duels save honor;
Charles Case, Travel requires nerve, strength,
especially with new stagecoach on new road; Ambrose
Boston, Smile on her face means money in the concert
till [on Anna Chandler Goff, impressario of Artist
Concert Series in Lexington, 1918-mid-1930];
Lexington home of strongest of banks [on Northern
Bank of Kentucky, 1835-1898]; John Hunt Morgan yearns
for chance to use his military skills; W. B. Ardery,
John C. Breckinridge; Darlene Bowden, William
'King' Solomon, he stays to bury cholera victims;

Carol Cropper, Surveyor with no print experience,
establishes first newspaper in state; Ambrose
Boston, Here comes the circus; Ezra Medlinson,
Hippodrome home of vaudeville; Ambrose Boston,
Ada Meade Saffarans excels in opera, musical comedy;
Barry Bronson, Pleasure could be found at orderly,
disorderly 'Belle's Place' [on Belle Breezing,
Lexington madame]; Robert Horine, Kentucky religion:
Like politics, it produces controversy [includes
notes on James Moore, Barton W. Stone, Adam Rankin,
London Ferrill, Benjamin B. Smith, and the churches
and slavery]

13834 Clark, Thomas Dionysius, 1903-
            A history of Kentucky... New York, Prentice Hall, 1937.
            702 p.   map.   22 cm.

13835 Clay, Cassius Marcellus, 1810-1903.
            Speech of Cassius M. Clay, against the annexation
        of Texas to the United States of America, in reply
        to Col. R. M. Johnson and others, in a mass meeting
        of citizens of the 8th congressional district, at
        White Sulphur, Springs, in Scott County, Ky., on
        Saturday, Dec. 30, 1843. Lexington, Ky., Printed
        at the Observer and reporter office, 1844.
            22 p.   21 ½ cm.

13836 Clay, Cassius Marcellus, 1846-1913.
            Speech of Hon. C. M. Clay, jr., of Bourbon County,
        delivered in the House of Representatives, Thursday,
        February 15th, 1872, on the proposition to incor-
        porate the mandatory clause into the charter of the
        Frankfort, Paris, and Big Sandy railroad. Frankfort,
        Ky., A. G. Hodges, printer, 1872.
            12 p.   24 cm.

13837 Clay, Cassius Marcellus, 1846-1913.
            The speeches, addresses and writing of Cassius
        M. Clay, Jr. Including a biographical sketch by
        James K. Patterson... New York, The Winthrop
        press, 1914.
            178 p.   front. (port.)   25 cm.

13838 Clay, Henrietta.
            Bits of family history... Paper read before
        the John Bradford Club, Lexington, Kentucky,
        December 8, 1932. [Lexington? 1932]
            12 p.   24 cm.

13839 Clay, Henry, 1777-1852.
    An address of Henry Clay to the public, containing
    certain testimony in refutation of the charges
    against him made by General Andrew Jackson,
    touching the presidential election in 1825.
    Lexington, Ky., Reprinted by E. Bryant, Intelligencer
    office, 1837.
    66 p.   23 cm.

13840 Clay, Henry, 1777-1852.
    The beauties of the Hon. Henry Clay. To which is
    added, a biographical and critical essay... New York,
    E. Walker, 1839.
    [11]-235 p.   16 cm.

13841 Clay, Henry, 1777-1852.
    [Letter from Henry Clay to James Taylor, 26 May
    1800, indicating Clay's effort to secure public
    office] [Frankfort, Kentucky Historical Society,
    n.d.]
    manuscript. 1 l.   29 x 22½ cm.

13842 Clay, Henry, 1777-1852.
    The life and speeches of Henry Clay... New York,
    Greeley & McElrath, 1843.
    2 v.   fronts., port., fold. facsim.   23 cm.

13843 Clay, Henry, 1777-1852.
    The life and speeches of Henry Clay. New York,
    Greeley & McElrath, 1844.
    2 v.   illus., facsim.   23 cm.

13844 Clay, Henry, 1777-1852.
    Mr. Clay's speech, at the dinner at Noble's Inn,
    near Lexington, July 12, 1827. [Lexington, 1827]
    14 p.   24 x 15½ cm.

13845 Clay, Henry, 1777-1852.
    Mr. Clay's speech, delivered at the mechanics'
    dinner, in the Appollonian garden, Cincinnati, on
    the third of August 1830. Baltimore, Printed and
    for sale at the Baltimore patriot office, 1830.
    12 p.   21½ cm.

13846 Clay, Henry, 1777-1852.
    Speech of Mr. Clay, of Kentucky, delivered
    June 27, 1840, on the occasion of a public dinner,

given in compliment to him, at Taylorsville, in his
native county of Hanover, in the state of Virginia.
[n.p., 1840]
    11 p.   22 cm.

13847   Clay, Mrs. John M
        Uncle Phil, a novel... Second and revised edition.
New York, The Abbey press [1901]
    271 p.   front. (port.)   21 cm.

13848   Clay, Maurice A   , ed.
        A report of the Kentucky Association for Health,
Physical Education and Recreation. Fall workshop
held at Cumberland Falls, Kentucky, on the occasion
of the fiftieth anniversary, November 6-7-8, 1959.
[n.p., 1959?]
    46 p.   22 cm.

13849   Clay, William Marion.
        A field manual of Kentucky fishes. Frankfort,
Kentucky Dept. of Fish and Wildlife Resources, 1962.
    vii, 147 p.   illus., maps.   22 cm.
    "Dingell-Johnson act, Federal aid in fisheries.
Kentucky project F-7-R. Contribution no. 55 from
the Department of Biology of the University of
Louisville."
    Bibliography: p. 139-141.

13850   Cleland, Thomas.
        Unitarianism unmasked; its anti-Christian
features displayed; its infidel tendency exhibited;
and its foundation shewn to be untenable. By
Thomas Cleland, D.D. [one line Latin quotation]
[four lines Shakespeare quotation] Lexington, Ky.,
Printed by Thomas T. Skillman, 1825.
    184 p.   17 x 10 cm.

13851   Clement, J   , ed.
        Noble deeds of American women, with biographical
sketches of some of the more prominent... with an
introduction by Mrs. L. H. Sigourney. Boston,
Lee and Shepard, 1869.
    480 p.   20 cm.

13852   Clift, Garrett Glenn, 1909-1970.
        ... Bibliography of the House and Senate journals,
Commonwealth of Kentucky, 1792-1966. Frankfort,
Kentucky Historical Society, 1967.

58 p.   29 cm.
At head of title: Kentucky Historical Society,
Research contribution no. 3.

13853 Clift, Garrett Glenn, 1909-1970.
       ... Civil War engagements, skirmishes, etc. in
Kentucky, 1861-1865. A finding list designed for
use by researchers, speakers, and students during the
Civil War Centennial, 1861-1965... compiled for the
Kentucky Civil War Centennial Commission. [Frankfort,
1959?]
       29 p.   28½ cm.
At head of title: Kentucky Historical Society
Research contribution no. 2.

13854 Clift, Garrett Glenn, 1909-1970.
       History of Maysville and Mason County [Kentucky]
Volume one. Lexington, Ky., Transylvania printing
company, 1936.
       461 p.   23 cm.
V. 2 never published.

13855 Clift, Garrett Glenn, 1909-1970.
       John Bradford, "The Caxton of Kentucky": a
bibliography. [New York, 1948]
       35-41 p.   22 cm.
Reprinted from American Notes and Queries, VIII
(No. 3, 1948)

13856 Clutter, William, defendant.
       A concise statement of the trial and confession
of William Clutter, who was executed on Friday the
8th June, 1810, at Boone Court-House, Kentucky
for the murder of John Farmer. To which is prefixed
a short sketch of his life. Cincinnati, J. W.
Browns, 1810.
       8 p.   21 cm.

13857 Clyne, Patricia Edwards.
       The deadly lesson of Sand Cave. [Houston, Tex.,
Baroid Division, National Lead Industries, 1975]
       22-29 p.   illus.   23 cm.
Reprinted by permission from Baroid news bulletin,
v. 26, no. 2, summer 1975.

13858 Cobb, Ann.
       Kinfolks. Kentucky mountain rhymes. Boston and
New York, Houghton Mifflin company, 1922.

82 p.   20½ cm.
Includes two clippings at end, from an unidentified
periodical, the second from Outlook and Independent,
with additional poems.

13859 Cobb, Irvin Shrewsbury, 1876-1944.
        "Speaking of operations--"... Illustrations by
        Tony Sarg. New York, George H. Doran company, 1915.
        64 p.   illus.   20 cm.

13860 Cochran, Andrew McConnell, 1854-1934.
        Introductory addresses at the sesquicentennial
        celebration of the Battle of the Blue Licks, held at
        Blue Licks Battle-Field Park (Kentucky State Park,
        no. 5) on Friday, August 19, 1932. Lexington, 1932.
        13 p.   port.   26 cm.

13861 Cochran, Louis, 1899-
        The frolic; the courtship of Raccoon John Smith.
        Lexington, Ky., College of the Bible, 1964.
        52 p.   23 cm.

13862 Cockrill, W   Willard.
        A BRADD weather report; weather and climate of the
        Barren River Area Development District, by W. Willard
        Cockrill... Mike LeHeureux, research assistant.
        Bowling Green, Ky., Barren River Area Development
        District, 1975.
        ` 1 l., 29 p.   maps, diagrs., tables.   28 cm.

13863 Coe, Escar Olin, 1899-
        Escar Coe on the Upper Cumberland; reminiscences
        of a river pilot [edited by] Winton S. Smith
        [Bowling Green, Ky., 1974]
        59-83 p.   port.   23½ cm.
        Reprinted from Kentucky folklore record, v. 20,
        no. 3, July-Sept. 1974.

13864 Coffman, Edward, 1890-
        The story of Logan County... Nashville, Tenn.,
        The Parthenon press [1962]
        303 p.   23 cm.

13865 Coffman, Edward, 1890-
        The story of Russellville. A short history of
        the town of Russellville, Logan County, Ky.
        Russellville, Ky., The News-Democrat print, 1931.
        71 p.   24 cm.

13866 Coleman A   Lee.
        The Negro population of Kentucky: status and
        trends, 1970. By A. Lee Coleman and Dong I. Kim.
        Lexington, Kentucky Agricultural Experiment Station,
        University of Kentucky, 1974.
        71 p.   maps, tables, diagrs.   24 cm.
        (Kentucky Agricultural Experiment Station, Bulletin,
        714)

13867 Coleman, A   Lee.
        The Negro population of Kentucky at mid-century,
        by A. Lee Coleman, Albert C. Pryor, Jr., and John R.
        Christiansen. Lexington, Kentucky Agricultural
        Experiment Station, University of Kentucky, 1956.
        43 p.   maps, tables, diagrs.   24 cm.
        (Kentucky Agricultural Experiment Station, Bulletin,
        643)

13868 Coleman, John Winston, 1898-
        An autobiographical sketch, with a list of writings...
        Lexington, Ky., Winston Press, 1954.
        31 p.   front. (port.)   22 cm.
        In pocket at end: Bettye Lee Mastin, "Checking
        Kentucky lore with Winston Coleman is pleasant job,"
        Lexington Sunday Herald-Leader, 22 June 1958, p. 43.

13869 Coleman, John Winston, 1898-
        Assassination of President Lincoln and the capture
        of John Wilkes Booth... An address delivered before
        the Chevy Chase Coffee club, Lexington, February 10,
        1969. Lexington, Ky., Privately printed, 1969.
        10 p.   front. (port.)   24 cm.
        Front. is port. of author.

13870 Coleman, John Winston, 1898-
        The Beauchamp-Sharp tragedy. An episode of Kentucky
        history during the middle 20's. Frankfort, Roberts
        printing co., 1950.
        77 p.   illus.   23 cm.

13871 Coleman, John Winston, 1898-
        The British invasion of Kentucky, with an account
        of the capture of Ruddell's and Martin's Stations,
        June, 1780... Lexington, Winburn Press, 1951.
        30 p.   24 cm.

13872 Coleman, John Winston, 1898-
        The Casto-Metcalfe duel; an affair of honor in

Bracken County, Kentucky, May 8th, 1862. Lexington,
Winburn Press, 1950.
22 p.   25 cm.
Bibliographical references included in "Notes"
(p. 20-22)

13873 Coleman, John Winston, 1898-
A centennial history of Sayre School, 1854-1954...
Lexington, Ky., Winburn Press, 1954.
59 p.   illus., facsim.   24 cm.

13874 Coleman, John Winston, 1898-
The collected writings of J. Winston Coleman, Jr.
... Introduction by Dr. Holman Hamilton...
Lexington, Winburn Press, 1969.
112 p.   illus.   20 cm.

13875 Coleman, John Winston, 1898-
The College of Engineering, University of Kentucky.
Lexington, University of Kentucky Centennial
committee, 1965.
38 p.   illus.   24 cm.

13876 Coleman, John Winston, 1898-
Death at the court-house; an account of the mob
action in Lexington, Kentucky, on February 9, 1920,
and the events leading up to it. Lexington,
Winburn Press, 1952.
28 p.   24 cm.

13877 Coleman, John Winston, 1898-
The Desha-Kimbrough duel, an affair of honor in
Scott County, Kentucky, March 26th, 1866. Lexington,
Winburn Press, 1951.
14 p.   25 cm.
Bibliographical references included in "Notes"
(p. 13-14)

13878 Coleman, John Winston, 1898-
Kentucky rarities. A check list of one hundred
and thirty-five fugitive books and pamphlets
relating to the Bluegrass state and its people...
Lexington, Winburn Press, 1970.
34 p.   front. (port.)   23 cm.

13879 Coleman, John Winston, 1898-
Lafayette's visit to Lexington. An account of
the General's sojourn in the Bluegrass, May, 1825.

Lexington, Ky., Winburn Press, 1969.
16 p.   front. (port.)   illus.   24 cm.

13880   Coleman, John Winston, 1898-
Last days, death and funeral of Henry Clay, with
some remarks on the Clay monument in the Lexington
Cemetery. Lexington, Ky., Henry Clay Memorial
Foundation, 1951.
30 p.   facsim.   24 cm.   (Ashland monograph,
no. 4)

13881   Coleman, John Winston, 1898-
Lexington during the Civil war. Lexington, Ky.,
1968.
48 p.   illus.   18½ cm.

13882   Coleman, John Winston, 1898-
Old Kentucky watering places. Louisville,
The Filson club, 1942.
26 p.   28 cm.   (Filson Club history quarterly,
XVI, no. 1, 1942)

13883   Coleman, John Winston, 1898-
One hundred and fifty years of freemasonry in
Lexington, Kentucky, 1788-1938. By J. Winston
Coleman, Jr. ... Lexington, Service print shop,
1938.
8 p.   front. (port.)   24½ cm.

13884   Coleman, John Winston, 1898-
A preacher and a shrine; Rev. Jesse Head and the
Lincoln marriage temple, by J. Winston Coleman, Jr.
Harrogate, Tenn., Lincoln Memorial University, 1944.
8 p.   illus.   26½ cm.

13885   Coleman, John Winston, 1898-
Retribution at the court-house. An account of
the mob action in Lexington, Kentucky, on July 10th
1858, and the events leading up to it... Lexington,
Winburn Press, 1957.
15 p.   illus.   24 cm.

13886   Coleman, John Winston, 1898-
The Rowan-Chambers duel, an affair of honor in
Nelson County, Kentucky, February 3rd, 1801.
Lexington, Winburn Press, 1953.
25 p.   25 cm.

13887 Coleman, John Winston, 1898-
       Scarce Kentuckiana, a check list of one hundred
       uncommon and significant books and pamphlets relating
       to the Bluegrass state and its people... Lexington,
       Winburn Press, 1970.
       24 p.   front. (port.)   23 cm.

13888 Coleman, John Winston, 1898-
       Steamboats on the Kentucky River. Lexington,
       Winburn Press, 1960.
       41 p.   illus.   25 cm.

13889 Colerick, E   Fenwick.
       Adventures of pioneer children; or Life in the
       wilderness. A portrayal of the part performed by
       the children of the early pioneers in establishing
       homes in the wilderness... Cincinnati, R. Clark
       & co., 1888.
       xv, 236 p.   front., plates, port.   20 cm.

13890 Collier, Robert Lee, 1933-1960.
       Education, religion and the Kentucky Court of
       Appeals. Lexington, 1960.
       149 p.   front. (port.)   23 cm.

13891 Collings, Lindon W
       History of the Burks Branch Baptist Church,
       1801-1951. Shelbyville, Ky., Burks Branch Baptist
       Church, 1951.
       23 p.   illus.   22 cm.

13892 Collins, Lewis, 1797-1870.
       Collins' historical sketches of Kentucky.
       History of Kentucky: by the late Lewis Collins...
       rev. and enl.... by his son, Richard H. Collins...
       Frankfort, Kentucky Historical Society, 1966.
       2 v.   illus., facsims., fold. map.   26½ cm.
       Offset reprint of 1874 ed.

13893 Collins, Richard H   , 1824-1889.
       Memorial about Collins' History of Kentucky [to the
       General Assembly of Kentucky of 1871-2] [n.p., 1872?]
       14 p.   23 cm.

13894 Collins, Richard H   , 1824-1889.
       Memorial to the General Assembly of Kentucky of
       1871-72. [Frankfort, Ky.? 1871?]
       14 p.   24 cm.

13895 Collins, Stephen Foster, 1826-1860.
... My old Kentucky home, good night. Foster's
plantation melodies no. 20 as sung by Christy's
minstrels... New York [etc.] Published by Firth,
Pond & co. [n.d.]
5 p. music. 34 cm.
At head of title: Tenth edition.

13896 Collot, Georges Henri Victor, 1752-
Voyage dans l'Amérique Septentrionale, ou
Description des pays arrosés par le Mississippi,
l'Ohio, le Missouri y autres rivières affluentes...
Avec un atlas de 36 cartes, plans, vues et figures.
Paris, A. Bertrand, 1826.
2 v. 21 cm. and atlas of 36 pl. [incl.
11 fold. maps, 15 plans] 34 cm.

13897 Colonial Dames of America. Kentucky society.
Register of the National society of the Colonial
Dames of America in the Commonwealth of Kentucky.
[Louisville, 1947?]
179 p. 22½ cm.

13898 Colton, Calvin.
The life and times of Henry Clay... New York,
A. S. Barnes & co., 1946.
2 v. illus. 24½ cm.

13899 Columbia, Ky. Columbia Christian Church.
Columbia Christian Church of Columbia, Kentucky,
founded 1868. [n.p., 1943]
26 p. illus. 23 cm.
On cover: Seventy-fifth anniversary celebration.

13900 Combs, Leslie, 1793-1881.
A reply to General Andrew Jackson's letter,
of the 31st October, 1828. Published in the
Nashville Republican... [Nashville, 1828]
8 p. 23 cm.

13901 Combs, Sidney Sayre.
Old homes of the Blue grass. A photographic
review by Richard Garrison, with an introduction
by Sidney S. Combs and a commentary by J. Winston
Coleman, Jr. Lexington, The Kentucky society,
1950.
85 p. illus. 23 cm.

13902 Combs, Sidney Sayre.
  Our proud heritage. [Lexington, Ky., Real Estate
Dept., Security Trust Co., 1957]
  49 p. illus. 22 cm.
  Cover title.
  Facsimile reproduction of ms. copy.

13903 Committee for Kentucky.
  Blueprint for a greater Kentucky. [n.p., 1949?]
  104 p. illus. 24 cm.

13904 Complimentary dinner tendered to the Hon. Thomas Asbury
Combs, acting governor of Kentucky. [Lexington,
Transylvania Printing Company, 1916]
  11 p. front. (port.) 27 cm.

13905 Conclin, George.
  ... Conclin's new river guide, or A Gazetteer
of the towns on the western waters: containing
sketches of the cities, towns and countries...
on the Ohio and Mississippi rivers, and their
principal tributaries... with their population...
commerce, &c. in 1848... With forty-four maps.
Cincinnati, H. S. & J. Applegate, 1849.
  128 p. incl. front., illus. maps. 23 cm.

13906 Conder, Josiah, 1789-1855.
  A popular description of America: geographical,
historical and topographical. Illustrated by
maps and plates. By Josiah Conder... London,
James Duncan [n.d.]
  2 v. in 1. front. (fold. map) illus. $15\frac{1}{2}$ cm.
  "Kentucky": v. 2, p. 272-279.

13907 The confession of Jereboam O. Beauchamp, who was
hanged at Frankfort, Ky. on the 7th day of July,
1826. For the murder of Col. Solomon P. Sharp.
[n.p., 1826?]
  144 p. 20 cm.

13908 Conkwright, Bessie Taul.
  Captain Billy Bush. [Winchester, 1915]
  2 p. 20 cm.
  Reprinted from The Winchester Democrat, 15 October
1915.

13909 Conkwright, Bessie Taul.
  Indian Old Field. By Bessie Taul Conkwright.

Read before the Clark County Historical Society,
February 13, 1922. Transcribed by George F. Doyle,
M.D., F.A.C.S. [Winchester, Ky., Clark County
Historical Society, 1922]
    8 p.   21½ cm.

13910 Conkwright, Bessie Taul.
        Little tours among history shrines in and about
        Lexington, by Bessie Taul Conkwright. Sesqui-
        centennial ed., rev. [Lexington, Ky.] Lexington
        public library, 1925.
            16 p.   23½ cm.
        Portrait and illustration on p. [2] and [3] of cover.

13911 Conkwright, S   J
        Bush settlement of pioneer days... Clark County,
        Kentucky, by S. J. Conkwright and S. H. Rutledge
        [n.p., n.d.]
            1 (fold.) map.   23 cm.

13912 Conkwright, S   J
        History of the churches of Boone's Creek Baptist
        association of Kentucky. With a brief history of
        the Association... Winchester, Ky., 1923.
            192 p.   front., illus., maps (part fold.)   23½ cm.

13913 Connelly, Emma M
        Tilting at windmills, a story of the Blue Grass
        country; by Emma M. Connelly... Boston, D. Lothrop
        company [1888]
            439 p. incl. front.   19 cm.

13914 Conner, Eugene H
        A bibliography of Emmet Field Horine, M.D. ...
        on the occasion of the publication of Daniel Drake,
        M.D. ... Louisville, Ky., 1961.
            8 ℓ.   21½ cm.
        Cover is reproduction of jacket for Dr. Horine's
        Daniel Drake (1785-1852), pioneer physician of the
        midwest (University of Pennsylvania Press, 1961).
        All source materials for this book are in the
        University of Kentucky Library.

13915 Conover, Charlotte Reeve.
        A memoir with letters of Mrs. Horatio G. Phillips,
        "Kitt" Patterson, a pioneer woman. Dayton, Ohio,
        Press of the N.C.R. Co., 1914.
            48 p.   illus.   23½ cm.

13916   The constitution of the United Societies of Believers
        [called Shakers] containing sundry covenants and
        articles of agreement definitive of the legal
        grounds of the institution... Watervliet, Ohio [?]
        1833.
        [138] p.   18 cm.

13917   Cook, Marlow W
        [Pioneer Weapons Hunting Area and Zilpo Recreation
        Area in Daniel Boone National Forest, Kentucky.
        Washington, D.C., 1973]
          8 p.   28 cm.
        Appended at end is two-page news release on pertinent
        legislation.
        Reprinted from Congressional record, v. 119,
        no. 202 (Senate)
          Exhibit 1:   Jim Hayes, Kentucky's happiest hunting
        ground. Exhibit 2:   Harold Barber, The wild turkey
        under siege. Exhibit 3:   The Pioneer Weapons Hunting
        Area: background. Exhibit 4:   Taxpayers aren't
        really outsiders at Cave Run (from Louisville Courier-
        Journal, 16 October 1973)   Exhibit 5:   Concrete and
        nature don't mix (from Louisville Courier-Journal,
        30 October 1973)   Exhibit 6:   Impact of the proposed
        action on other agency projects (statement from
        Louisville district office of the Corps of Engineers)
        Exhibit 7:   Letter to Corps of Engineers from Reid Love,
        president, League of Kentucky Sportsmen, 15 October
        1973.

13918   Cooke, John Esten, 1783-1853.
        Answer to the review of an essay on the invalidity
        of Presbyterian ordination published in the January
        number of the Biblical Repertory & Theological Review,
        of Princeton, New Jersey. By John E. Cooke, M.D.
        Lexington, Ky., Printed at the Reporter office,
        1830.
          136 p.   23$\frac{1}{2}$ x 15 cm.

13919   Cooke, John Esten, 1783-1853.
        Essays on the autumnal and winter epidemics.
        By John Esten Cooke, M.D., professor of the theory
        and practice of medicine in Transylvania University.
        [Lexington] Transylvania press, Printed by J. G.
        Norwood, printer to the university, 1829.
          [4], 248 p.   20$\frac{1}{2}$ x 13 cm.
        Contains four essays: "An essay on autumnal
        epidemics," pages 1-68; "An essay on winter

epidemics," pages 69-84; "An essay on typhus fever,"
pages 85-121; "An essay on cholera infantum,"
pages 122-140.

13920 Cooke, John Esten, 1783-1853.
A treatise on pathology and therapeutics. By John
Esten Cooke, M.D. Professor of the theory and
practice of medicine in Transylvania University.
In three volumes. Lexington, Ky., 1828.
3 v. [?]   22½ x 13 cm.
Volume I, viii, 566 p.; volume II, iv, 522, iv p.;
there is no record of a third volume. On page ii
of volume I appears the note following: "It is but
just to state that notwithstanding this work is
published in Lexington, the first two volumes (except
the last forty or fifty pages) were printed in
Winchester, Virginia, in the office of Mr. Samuel H.
Davis, to whose great care and attention I am
indebted for the handsome dress in which they appear.
J.E.C."

13921 Cooke, Mary-Frances.
Story of early Louisville [by] Mary-Frances Cooke.
Louisville, Ky., Press of Theodore Ahrens trade
school, 1931.
29 p.   25 cm.

13922 Cooper, W   L
Stuart Robinson School and its work. A study in
meeting the needs of our school community and plans
for future service. Nashville, Tennessee, The
Parthenon press [1936]
124 p.   20 cm.

13923 Copeland, Lewis C
Survey of travel in Kentucky, 1968. For the
Tourist and Travel Division, Department of Public
Information, Commonwealth of Kentucky... Frankfort,
1968.
31 p.   tables.   28 cm.

13924 Corwin, Thomas, 1794-1865.
Life and speeches of Thomas Corwin, orator,
lawyer and statesman. Ed. by Josiah Morrow.
Cincinnati, W. H. Anderson & co., 1896.
477 p.   24 cm.

13925   Cotterill, Robert Spenser, 1884-
        History of pioneer Kentucky... Cincinnati,
        Johnson & Hardin, 1917.
        254 p.   fold. maps.   24 cm.

13926   Cotterill, Robert Spenser, 1884-
        Winchester in 1812-14, by R. S. Cotterill.
        [Winchester, Ky., Winchester Democrat, Feb. 26, 1915]
        2 p.   28 cm.

13927   Cotton, Nancy Jo.
        Teacher education and certification. Part 1.
        Special education: teachers of exceptional children.
        Prepared by Nancy Jo Cotton. Part 2. Vocational
        education: teachers of trades and industry.
        Prepared by John H. Alexander. Frankfort, Ky.,
        Legislative Research Commission, 1973.
        128 p.   tables.   29 cm.   (Research report
        no. 107, new series)

13928   Coulter, Ellis Merton, 1890-
        The Civil war and readjustment in Kentucky.
        Chapel Hill, N.C., University of North Carolina
        press, 1926.
        468 p.   facsims.   24½ cm.
        Facsimiles of one, five, ten, twenty, fifty,
        and hundred dollar Confederates notes in pocket
        at end.

13929   Covi, Madeline.
        Madison Cawein. Louisville, Ky., 1962.
        broadside.   port.   33 x 37 cm.
        Reprinted from the Courier-Journal, 6 May 1962,
        section 4, p. 6.
        With this are reprints of articles on Cawein in
        Dictionary of American biography, suppl., v. 2,
        and Oxford Companion to American Literature, and the
        section of Cawein entries in Library of Congress
        catalog.

13930   Covington, Ky. Charters.
        Charter of the city of Covington, and amendments
        thereto to March 1, 1874, and sundry local and
        general laws relating to municipal affairs.
        Compiled, by order of the city council, by John P.
        Harrison, city attorney. Covington, Ky., Published
        by order of the city council, 1874.
        174 p.   23½ cm.

13931   Cowan, John W
        The life and confession of John W. Cowan, who
        murdered his wife and two children on the 10th of
        October, 1835, in the city of Cincinnati. Written
        by himself and arranged for the press and published
        by James Allen. Cincinnati, Printed for the
        publisher by Kendall and Henry, 1835.
            23 p.   21 cm.

13932   [Cox, Millard F   ], 1856-
        The legionaries, by Henry Scott Clark [pseud.]
        A story of the great raid. Second edition. Illus-
        trated. Indianapolis, Indiana, The Bowen-Merrill
        company [1899]
            385 p.   illus.   20 cm.

13933   [Crabb, Alfred Leland, jr.] ed.
        ... Literary landmarks of Kentucky, a project of
        the Research and Publications Committee of the
        Kentucky Council of Teachers of English...
        [Lexington, 1961]
            48 p.   23 cm.
        At head of title: Kentucky English bulletin.
        Volume II, fall, 1961, number 1.

13934   Craik, James.
        The past and present position of the church.
        An address delivered on the occasion of laying the
        corner-stone of Christ Church, Lexington, Ky.
        on Wednesday, the 17th of March, 1847, by the
        Rev. James Craik, Rector of Christ Church, Louisville.
        [three lines quotation] Lexington, Scrugham & Dunlop,
        1847.
            23 p.   21 cm.

13935   Crandall, Albert R
        ... The coals of the Big Sandy valley, south of
        Louisa and between Tug Fork and the headwaters of
        the north fork of Kentucky river... Louisville,
        Printed by Geo. G. Fetter co., 1905.
            141 p.   illus., maps (part fold.)   27 cm.
        (Kentucky geological survey, Bulletin no. 4)

13936   Crandall, Albert R
        ... Coals of the Licking Valley region and some
        of the contiguous territory, including also an
        account of Elliott County and its dikes...
        Louisville, Continental printing company, 1910.

[xviii], 90 p.   illus., maps (1 fold. in pocket
at end), diags. (part fold.), tables (part fold.)
26½ cm.
At head of title: Kentucky Geological Survey,
Charles J. Norwood, director, Bulletin no. 10.

13937 Crawford, Charles.
        An essay on the propagation of the gospel; in which
    there are numerous facts and arguments adduced to
    prove that many of the Indians of America are des-
    cended from the ten tribes... The 2d ed. Philadelphia,
    Printed and sold by James Humphreys, 1801.
        154 p., 1 ℓ.   19 cm.

13938 Crawford, Dean.
        High Bridge. Lexington, Ky., 1973.
        broadside.   illus.   40 x 28 cm.
        Reprinted from The Kentucky Kernel, 24 January 1973.

13939 Crawford, Thomas J
        Compilation of coal and petroleum production data
    for Kentucky. Lexington, Ky., 1958.
        43 p.   maps, diags., tables.   24 cm.
    (Kentucky Geological Survey, Series X, Report of
    investigations, 1)

13940 Creason, Joe C   , 1919-1974.
        Kentucky, a land of firsts. [Louisville, Ky.?]
    The Courier-Journal [n.d.]
        5 ℓ.   illus.   21½ cm.

13941 Crider, A   F
        Coals of the Nortonville quadrangle. [Frankfort,
    Ky., State Journal company, printers to the Common-
    wealth, 1915]
        182 p.   fold. maps, tables.   27 cm.   (Kentucky
    Geological Survey, ser. IV, v. 3, pt. 1)
        Also includes sections on coals of the Drakesboro
    quadrangle, the Dunmor quadrangle, and the Little
    Muddy quadrangle.

13942 Crider, A   F
        The fire clays and fire clay industries of the
    Olive Hill and Ashland districts of northeastern
    Kentucky. [Frankfort, Ky., State Journal company,
    printers to the Commonwealth, 1913]
        589-1216 p.   tables.   27 cm.   (Kentucky
    Geological Survey, ser. IV, v. 1, pt. 2)

13943 Crismon, Leo T
       The Boone family and Kentucky Baptists, by
       Leo T. Crismon. Louisville, Kentucky Baptist
       Historical Society, 1946.
         31 p.   22 cm.   (Kentucky Baptist Historical
       Society. [Publication] no. 4)

13944 Crittenden, George Bibb, 1812-1880.
         Proclamation. Division headquarters, Mill Springs,
       Kentucky, January 6, 1862. To the people of
       Kentucky... [n.p.] 1862
         broadside.   32 x 21 cm.
         On verso, and continued on recto, is a letter of
       24 [January?] 1862, from Lebanon, Kentucky, from
       one Peter [Givins? Gwinne?] to his father. He states,
       "I found this paper in Zollicoffer's camp..."
       It was probably printed in Lebanon.
         G. B. Crittenden, son of J. J. Crittenden, the
       brother of Gen. Thomas Leonidas Crittenden of the
       Unionist Army, was badly defeated by the northerners
       at Mills Springs (Logan's Crossroads), resigned his
       commission, re-enlisted, and served through the
       remainder of the War without rank.
         Original in Emory University Library.

13945 Crittenden, John Jordan, 1787-1863.
         The union, the Constitution, and the laws. Speech
       of the Hon. John J. Crittenden, at Louisville, Ky.
       ... August 2, 1860. Published by order of the
       National union executive committee, Washington, D.C.
       W. H. Moore, printer, 1860.
         16 p.   24½ cm.

13946 Crockett, G   F   H
         An essay on the divinity of Jesus Christ; proving
       him to be the incarnate Son of God; co-equal,
       co-essential, and co-eternal with God the Father:
       intended to establish the doctrine of the Sacred Trinity.
       Lexington, Ky., Printed by T. T. Skillman, 1818.
         62 p.   21 cm.

13947 Crockett, Ingram, 1856-
         A brother of Christ; a tale of western Kentucky,
       by Ingram Crockett... illustrated in colors by
       Hartman. New York, Broadway publishing company
       [1905]
         3 p.l., 309 p.   col. front., 3 pl.   19½ cm.

13948 Crockett, Ingram, 1856-
    A year book of Kentucky woods and fields, by
    Ingram Crockett... Illustrated by the author.
    Buffalo, Charles Wells Moulton, 1901.
        112 p.   illus.   18½ cm.

13949 Cromwell, Emma Guy.
    Citizen, a manual for voters. Frankfort, Ky.
    [1920]
        68 p.   24 cm.

13950 Cross, James Conquest.
    An inaugural discourse on the value of time, and
    the importance of study to the physican... Lexington,
    Ky., Finnell & Zimmerman, printers -- Observer and
    reporter office, 1837.
        34 p.   20½ cm.

13951 Crouch, Ron.
    Medical assistance in Kentucky, prepared by Ron
    Crouch. Frankfort, Ky., Legislative Research
    Commission, 1975.
        iv, 175 p.   tables.   27 cm.   (Kentucky.
    Legislative Research Commission, Research report
    no. 124)

13952 Crozier, Robert Hoskins.
    The Confederate spy: or, Startling incidents of
    the War between the States. A novel... Fifth
    edition. Louisville, Printed by John P. Morton &
    company, 1885.
        406 p.   20 cm.

13953 Cull, William H
    Kentucky corrections: the case for reform.
    Frankfort, Ky., Legislative Research Commission,
    1973.
        163 p.   29 cm.   (Research report no. 102,
    new series)

13954 Cull, William H
    Mentally retarded offenders in adult and juvenile
    correctional institutions. Part I: Adult offenders,
    prepared by William H. Cull. Part II: Juvenile
    offenders, prepared by George L. Reuthebuck [and]
    Nancy Pope. Frankfort, Ky., Legislative Research
    Commission, 1975.

A-123, B-70 p.   tables.   28 cm.   (Research report, no. 125)

13955 Cumberland Gap. [Louisville, 1972]
          3A, 4A p.   illus.   29 cm.
          Reprinted from Rural Kentuckian magazine, v. 26, no. 9, Sept. 1972.

13956 Cuming, Fortescue, 1762-1828.
          ... Cuming's tour to the western country (1807-1809) Cleveland, The A. H. Clark company, 1904.
          4 p.l., [7]-377 p.   24½ cm.   (Early western travels, 1748-1846... ed. ... by Reuben Gold Thwaites ... vol. IV)
          A reprint, including facsimile t.-p. of the author's Sketches of a tour to the western country... Pittsburgh, 1810.

13957 Curtiss, Daniel S
          Western portraiture, and emigrants' guide: a description of Wisconsin, Illinois, and Iowa; with remarks on Minnesota, and other territories...
          New York, J. H. Colton, 1852.
          xxx, [31]-351 p.   front. (fold. map)   18 cm.
          "Mr. Thompson's letters," p. 306-342.

                                    D

13958 Daingerfield, Foxhall, 1887-1933.
          Bryan Station, a play in four acts. Lexington, Ky., Press of J. L. Richardson & co., 1908.
          28 p.   23 cm.

13959 Daingerfield, Foxhall, 1887-1933.
          The southern cross, a play in four acts...
          Produced at the Opera House, Lexington, Ky., April 13, 1909, for the benefit of the Morgan Monument.
          Lexington, Ky., Press of J. L. Richardson & co., 1909.
          62 p.   22 cm.

13960 Danforth, Edward F   , 1893-1963.
          Old Man Henry. [Lexington, Ky., 1962]
          1 p.   38 cm.
          Reprinted from Lexington Herald, 25 Dec. 1962, p. 13.

13961   Daniel Boone; or, The hero of Kentucky. A story of the
        "dark and bloody ground". By the author of "Crackskull
        Bob" ... New York, Ornum & company [18-?]
        [7]-99 p.   illus.   16½ cm.

13962   Danville, Kentucky, cradle of the Commonwealth. Danville,
        Bluegrass printing company [n.d.]
        map.   illus.   26 x 38 cm.

13963   Danville artist draws praise. Washington, D.C., 1976.
        6-8 p.   illus.   29 cm.
        Reprinted from Ties, v. 30, no. 2, Mar.-Apr. 1976.
        On paintings of Mrs. Louis Cross (Bernadine Cross)
        of Danville, Ky.

13964   Danville Literary and Social Club.
        "Anaconda." History and semi-centennial celebration,
        December 27, 1889. 1839-1889. [Danville, Ky.,
        Advocate printing company, 1889]
        3 p.l., 5-76 p.   mounted pl., ports. [1 mounted]
        20 cm.

13965   Danville's historic McDowell House.
        [Gettysburg, Pa. 1975]
        [2] p.   illus.   29 cm.
        Reprinted from the Bluegrass edition of American
        motorist, v. 43, no. 8, November 1975.

13966   Darnell, Ermina Jett.
        After the manner of the oak; a study of the growth
        of the Frankfort Christian Church. Frankfort, Ky.,
        1935.
        74 p.   23 cm.

13967   Darnell, Ermina Jett.
        South Frankfort Kentucky. Frankfort, Ky.,
        Roberts Printing Company, 1947.
        15 p.   23 cm.

13968   Darnell, Jacob C
        The first fifty years of the Choateville Christian
        Church, Route 4, Frankfort, Ky. A brief historical
        study prepared by Rev. Jacob C. Darnell for the 50th
        anniversary homecoming, June 16, 1946. [n.p., 1946]
        22 ℓ.   cover illus.   28 cm.
        Mimeographed.

13969 Daughters of Colonial Wars. Kentucky.
       Kentucky pioneers and their descendants. [Compiled
       by Ila Earle Fowler for the Kentucky Society,
       Daughters of Colonial Wars] [Frankfort, Ky.]
       Kentucky Society, Daughters of Colonial Wars, 1941-
       1950 [1951]
           460 p.   23 cm.
           Inscribed by author.

13970 Daughters of the American Revolution, 20th continental
       congress, Washington, D.C., 17-22 April 1911.
       Special souvenir programme of the presentation of
       a portrait bust of Governor Isaac Shelby as Kentucky's
       gift to Memorial Continental hall at the Twentieth
       continental congress of the National Society of the
       Daughters of the American Revolution, April 17 to 22,
       1911, Washington, D.C. [Lexington, Ky? 1911?]
           [5] ℓ.   illus.   21 cm.

13971 Daughters of the American Revolution, Kentucky.
       D.A.R. Souvenir [in honor of the twelfth annual
       state conference of the Daughters of the American
       Revolution of the State of Kentucky] Lexington, 1908.
           30 p.   illus.   35 cm.

13972 Daughters of the American Revolution. Frankfort, Ky.,
       Chapter.
       What's cooking in Frankfort; a book of traditional
       recipes by Frankfortians past and present. Issued
       by the Frankfort Chapter, National Society of the
       Daughters of the American Revolution. Compiled by
       Violet C. Sutterlin... [Frankfort] 1949.
           82 p.   24 cm.

13973 David Têtu de les raiders de Saint-Alban. Episode de la
       guerre américaine 1864-1865. Deuxième édition.
       Québec, N. S. Hardy, libraire éditeur, 1891.
           187 p.   front. (port.)   17 cm.

13974 Davidson, Robert, 1808-1876.
       History of the Presbyterian church in the state
       of Kentucky; with a preliminary sketch of the churches
       in the valley of Virginia... New York, Robert Carter,
       58 Canal Street, Pittsburgh, 56 Market Street.
       Lexington, Ky., Charles Marshall, 1847.
           xii, [13]-371 p.   23½ cm.

13975 Daviers, William Watkins.
       Transfusion. Louisville, Ky., John P. Morton &

company, 1923.
56 p.   26 cm.
Inscribed by author.

13976 Daviess, Maria Thompson, 1872-
The elected mother, a story of woman's equal rights,
by Maria Thompson Daviess. Indianapolis, The Bobbs-
Merrill company [1912]
31 p.   18½ cm.

13977 Daviess, Maria Thompson, 1872-
Under silken skies, by Maria Thompson Daviess.
[n.p.] 1914.
481-490 p.   illus.   22 cm.
Reprinted from The Century, v. 88, Aug. 1914.
"Picture by Martin Justice."

13978 Davis, Beverly.
... Cubism and atonality. An art of our own.
Sculpture for architecture. Lexington, 1953.
18 p.   20 cm.
At head of title: Phi Beta Kappa, University of
Kentucky. Award for outstanding undergraduate
writing, number II.

13979 Davis, Darrell Haug, 1879-
The geography of the Blue grass region of Kentucky;
a reconnaissance study of the distribution and
activities of man in the area of ordovician outcrop
embraced by the Commonwealth... Frankfort, Ky.,
The Kentucky Geological Survey, 1927.
215 p.   front., illus., maps, diags.   24 cm.
(Kentucky Geological Survey, ser. VI, Geologic
reports, v. 23)
General bibliography: p. [207]-212.

13980 Davis, Garrett Morrow, 1851-1872.
Hugh Darnaby; a story of Kentucky, by Garrett
Morrow Davis. Washington, D.C., Gibson bros., 1900.
253 p.   19 cm.

13981 Dazey, Charles T
... In old Kentucky. Foreword by Barrett H. Clark...
Detroit, 1937.
147 p.   illus.   20 cm.

13982 Declaves, Alonso, pseud.
New travels to the westward; or, Unknown parts

of America, being a tour of almost fourteen months...
A new edition. Lexington, Ky., Printed for John
Willoughby Brush, 1802.
  36 p.   14 cm.

13983 DeGroot, Alfred Thomas, 1903-
  The literature of the Disciples of Christ [by]
A. T. DeGroot and E. E. Dowling. Advance, Ind.,
Hustler print, 1933.
  4 p.l., 78 p.   24 cm.
  "Limited edition (approximately one hundred copies),"
- Pref.
  "Revision of a bulletin published by Dr. W. E.
Garrison in 1923." - Explanatory note.

13984 De Jong, Gordon F
  Kentucky's Negro population in 1960. By Gordon J.
De Jong and George A. Hillery, Jr. Lexington,
Agricultural Experiment Station, University of
Kentucky, 1965.
  32 p.   maps, tables, diags.   24 cm.
  (Kentucky Agricultural Experiment Station, Bulletin,
704)

13985 De Jong, Gordon F
  The population of Kentucky: changes in the number
of inhabitants, 1950-60. Lexington, University of
Kentucky, Agricultural Experiment Station, Department
of Rural Sociology, 1961.
  26 p.   maps, graph, tables.   24 cm.

13986 Delta Kappa Gamma.
  Well-spring in the wilderness... project pioneer
women teachers. Kentucky. Edited by representatives
of Alpha, Beta and Zeta chapters. Louisville, Ky.,
Gibbs Inman co., 1955.
  68 p.   26½ cm.

13987 Delta Sigma Theta.
  Delta Sigma Theta presents debutantes of 1973.
A lovely package. April 13, 1973. 8:00 P.M.
Phoenix Hotel. Lexington, Ky. [Lexington, 1973]
  41 p.   illus.   23 cm.

13988 Democratic Party. Kentucky.
  An address to the people and Congress of the
United States. Louisville, Printed at the office
of the Democrat, 1863.

73

27 p.   20½ cm.
Signed: W. A. Dudley, Nat Wolfe [etc.] Committee
on behalf of the Democratic party.

13989   Democratic Party. Kentucky.
Rules of the Democratic Party adopted by the
Democratic state convention held in Lexington, Ky.,
May 14, 1924. [Lexington? 1924]
22 p.   15½ cm.

13990   Democratic Society of Kentucky.
Fellow-citizens. The Democratic society of Kentucky
have directed us to transmit to you the address and
remonstance which accompany this lecture...
Lexington, John Bradford, 1793.
broadside.   20 x 35 cm.

13991   Democratic Society of Kentucky.
To the inhabitants of the United States west of
the Allegheny and Apalachian mountains. Fellow-
citizens, the Democratic society of Kentucky, having
had under consideration the measures necessary to
obtain the exercise of your right to the free navigation of the Mississippi, have determined to address
you upon that important topic... Lexington, John
Bradford, 1793.
broadside.   31½ x 39½ cm.

13992   Democratic Society of Kentucky.
To the President and Congress of the United States
of America. The remonstrance of the citizens west
of the Allegheny mountains. Respectfully sheweth.
That your remonstrants are entitled by nature and by
stipulation, to the undisturbed navigation of the
river Mississippi, and it a right inseparable from
their prosperity... Lexington, John Bradford, 1793.
broadside.   22 x 55 cm.

13993   The Democratic woman's journal, published monthly by
the Democratic Woman's Club of Kentucky. v. 1-
1928-   . Louisville.
v.   24 cm.
Library has v. 2, no. 1, June 1929.
This issue contains articles by Samuel M. Wilson,
"The paramount political need is not a new party
but a new personality," p. 6-8, and by Mrs. John L.
Woodbury, "Kentucky history," p. 9-11.

13994 [De Moss, John C   ]
       A short history of the soldier-life, capture and
       death of William Francis Corbin, captain Fourth
       Kentucky cavalry, U.S.A. [n.p., 1897]
       32 p.   incl. port.   22 cm.

13995 Denson, Jesse.
       The chronicle of Andrew; containing an accurate and
       brief account of General Jackson's victories in the
       South, over the Creeks. Also his victories over the
       British at New-Orleans. With a biographical sketch
       of his life... Lexington, Ky., Printed for the author,
       1815.
       35 p.   17½ cm.

13996 Deppen, U. L., haberdasher, Louisville, Ky.
       ... Clothing and gents' furnishing goods...
       Louisville, 1872.
       broadside.   27 x 22 cm.
       Printed on both sides.
       Envelope addressed to Jno. S. Humphries, Bardstown,
       Ky., attached to recto.

13997 De Peyster, John Watts, 1821-1907.
       The affair at King's Mountain, 7th October, 1780.
       By J. Watts de Peyster... New York and Chicago,
       A. S. Barnes & Co. [1880]
       cover-title, p. [401]-424.   front. (port.)
       illus. (plan)   24½ cm.
       Reprinted from the Magazine of American history
       for Dec., 1880.

13998 Deutsch-Amerikanischer Hecker Denkmal-Verein,
       Cincinnati.
       Friedrich Hecker und sein Antheil an der Geschichte
       Deutschlands und Amerikas... Cincinnati, Gedruckt
       von Heinrich Siebel, 1881.
       84 p.   front. (port.)   19½ cm.

13999 Devers, Samuel.
       To the public. The following letter received by me
       from Alfred Jones, a tailor of this place, is laid
       before the public, in order that they may correct
       opinion of his character... signed at end: Samuel
       Devers. Lexington, Ky., Dec. 30th, 1828.
       broadside.   26 x 25½ cm.

14000　Dewees, Mrs. Samuel ("Mrs. Mary Coburn Dewees"), fl. 1787.
　　　　Journal of a trip from Philadelphia to Lexington
　　　　in Kentucky kept by Mary Coburn Dewees in 1787.
　　　　Crawfordsville, Ind., R. E. Banta, 1936.
　　　　6, 16, iii p.　　23 cm.

14001　Dining at the crossroads. [Lousville, Ky., 1977]
　　　　　　14-15, 26 p.　　illus.　　29 cm.
　　　　Reprinted from Rural Kentuckian, v. 31, no. 7,
　　　　July, 1977.

14002　Diocese of Lexington (Kentucky) Woman's Auxiliary.
　　　　　　In memoriam: Miss Mary E. Harrison, first president
　　　　of the Woman's Auxiliary in the Diocese of Lexington...
　　　　Lexington, Diocesan Council, 1915.
　　　　　　25 p.　　front. (port.)　　21½ cm.

14003　Disturnell, John, 1801-1877, comp.
　　　　　　Disturnell's guide through the middle, northern,
　　　　and eastern states; containing a description of the
　　　　principal places, canal, railroad, and steamboat
　　　　routes; tables of distances, etc. Compiled from
　　　　authentic sources... New York, J. Disturnell, 1847.
　　　　　　80 p.　　fold. map.　　15 cm.

14004　[Dixon, Samuel Houston]
　　　　　　Robert Warren, the Texan refugee. A thrilling story
　　　　of field and camp life during the late Civil War.
　　　　New York, United States Book company [1879?]
　　　　　　viii, 568 p.　　20 cm.
　　　　A Texas unionist's adventures with the northern
　　　　army at Somerset, Donelson, Shiloh, and elsewhere in
　　　　Kentucky and the middle South.

14005　Dollars for Duke Power. Hell for Harlan County.
　　　　[n.p., 1974?]
　　　　　　8 p.　　illus.　　22½ x 22½ cm.

14006　Donohue, James T
　　　　　　Milton Hannibal Smith, his life and achievements.
　　　　Address before the Filson Club, Louisville, Ky.,
　　　　April 4, 1949. [Louisville? 1949?]
　　　　　　[13] p.　　28 cm.
　　　　In double columns.

14007　Donovan, Herman Lee.
　　　　　　At the threshold of greatness! University of Kentucky...
　　　　New York, San Francisco, Montreal, The Newcomen

Society in North America, 1955.
28 p.   illus.   24 cm.

14008   Dorris, Jonathan Truman, 1883-
A glimpse at historic Madison county and Richmond,
Kentucky... endorsed by the Daniel Boone centennial
commission, issued by the Richmond Chamber of Commerce,
incorporated, the Madison County Historical Society,
incorporated, Richmond, Kentucky. Richmond, printed
by the Richmond daily register co., 1934.
3 p.l., 65 p.   illus. (incl. ports., map, plan)
23½ cm.
Includes short biographies.

14009   Dowden, Darnall.
The contrast: a tale of facts. Designed to show
the advantages of religious over irreligious education
in the family. By Darnall Dowden, Brandenburg, Ky.
Louisville, A. G. Caperton & co., 1880.
240 p.   19 cm.

14010   Down-home cooking. [Lexington, Ky., 1978?]
broadside (r. & v.)   illus.   28 cm.
Includes recipes for mint julep, country ham, burgoo,
beaten biscuits, sweet potatoes, corn pudding,
and chess pie.

14011   Drake, Daniel, 1785-1852.
Dr. Daniel Drake's letters on slavery to Dr. John C.
Warren of Boston. Reprinted from The National
Intelligencer, Washington, April 3, 5 and 7, 1851.
With an introduction by Emmet Field Horine, M.D.,
of Louisville, Ky. New York, Schuman's, 1940.
69 p.   front. (port.)   26 cm.

14012   Drake, Daniel, 1785-1852.
An inaugural discourse on medical education
delivered at the opening of the Medical College of
Ohio in Cincinnati, Ohio, 11 November 1820...
with an introduction by Emmet Field Horine. New York,
Henry Schuman, 1951.
33 p.   front. (port.)   26 cm.

14013   Drake, Daniel, 1785-1852.
Pioneer life in Kentucky. A series of reminiscential
letters from Daniel Drake... to his children. Ed.
with notes and a biographical sketch by his son,
Charles D. Drake. Cincinnati, R. Clarke & co.,

77

1870.
    4 p.l., [v]-xlvi, 263 p.   front. (port.)   24 cm.

14014 Drake, Daniel, 1785-1852.
        A systematic treatise, historical, etiological, and
    practical on the principal diseases of the interior
    valley of North America, as they appear in the
    Caucasian, African, Indian, and Esquimaux varieties
    of its population. By Daniel Drake, M.D. Ed. by
    S. Hanbury Smith... and Francis C. Smith... 2d ser.
    Philadelphia, Lippincott Grambo & co., 1854.
        xix, [17]-985 p. incl. tables.   24 cm.

14015 Drake, Leah Bodine.
        This tilting dust, by Leah Bodine Drake...
    Francestown, N. H., The Golden Quill press [1955]
        61 p.   20½ cm.

14016 Drake, Richard B
        Documents relating to the broad form deed.
    Lexington, Ky., 1974.
        6 p.   24 cm.
        Reprinted from Appalachian notes, v. 2, no. 1, 1974,
    with addition of six articles from Lexington Herald
    7, 8, 18 and 29 March, 17 and 30 April 1975, and one
    from the Kentucky Kernel, 18 April 1975, relative to
    the Court of Appeals affirmative decision on consti-
    tutionality of the 1974 law requiring surface owner's
    consent for strip mining.

14017 Drake, Samuel Gardner, 1798-1875.
        Tragedies of the wilderness; or, True and authentic
    narratives of captives who have been carried away by
    the Indians from the various frontier settlements
    in the United States, from the earliest to the present
    time. Illustrating the manner and customs, barbarous
    rites and ceremonies, of the North American Indians,
    and their various methods of torture practised upon
    such as have from time to time fallen into their hands.
    Boston, Antiquarian bookstore and institute, 1841.
        vi, 7-360 p. incl. illus. pl. front.   19 cm.

14018 Drake, Mrs. William Preston.
        Kentucky in retrospect. Noteworthy personages and
    events in Kentucky History, 1792-1942. By Mrs.
    William Preston Drake, Judge Samuel M. Wilson, Mrs.
    William Breckenridge Ardery. Editors, Mrs. William
    Breckenridge Ardery, Harry V. McChesney. [Frankfort]

Sesquicentennial Commission, Commonwealth of Kentucky, 1942.
205 p.   illus.   25 cm.

14019   Drane, Maude Johnston.
History of Henry County, Kentucky. [n.p., 1948]
274 p.   illus.   23½ cm.

14020   Draper, Lyman Copeland, 1815-1891.
Lyman C. Draper's notes of his interview with John Scholl. Draper MSS. 22 S 269-74. Transcribed from the copy made by the Society for Jesse P. Crump, Kansas City, Mo., by George F. Doyle. [n.p., n.d.]
1 p.l., 4 typewritten l.   28 cm.

14021   Draper, Lyman Copeland, 1815-1891.
Lyman C. Draper's notes of his interview with Joseph Scholl. Draper MSS. 24 S 205-22. Transcribed from the copy made by the Society of Jesse P. Crump, Kansas City, Mo., by George F. Doyle. [n.p., n.d.]
10 p.   28 cm.
Error in pagination.

14022   Draper, Lyman Copeland, 1815-1891.
Lyman C. Draper's Notes of his interview with Samuel Boone. Draper MSS. 22 S 241-68. Transcribed from copy made by the Society for Jesse P. Crump, Kansas City, Mo., by George F. Doyle. [n.p., n.d.]
17 p.   28 cm.

14023   Duff, Jeffrey M
Preliminary inventory of the records of the Department of Agriculture, Commonwealth of Kentucky [by] Jeffrey M. Duff and Martha L. Hall. Frankfort, Division of Archives and Records, Department of Library and Archives, 1977.
iv, [1], 13 p.   28 cm.

14024   D[ugan], F[rances] L   S[mith]
The bluegrass of Kentucky. [New York, 1948]
83-88 p.   22 cm.
Reprinted from American Notes & Queries, VIII (no. 1, September, 1948)

14025   Dugan, Frances L   Smith.
Rainfall harvest: Gilbert Hinds King and the

79

Lexington hydraulic & manufacturing company.
Lexington, Ky., Published privately, 1953.
Inscribed by author.

14026 Duke, Basil Wilson, 1838-1916.
Reminiscences of General Basil W. Duke, C.S.A. ...
Garden City, N. Y., Doubleday, Page & company, 1911.
512 p.   24 cm.

14027 Dunlap, Boutwell.
Augusta County, Virginia, in the history of the
United States, by Boutwell Dunlap. Frankfort,
The Kentucky state historical society, 1918.
73 p. incl. port.   22½ cm.

14028 Dunlavy, John, 1769-1826.
The manifesto, or A declaration of the doctrines
and practice of the church of Christ. Pleasant Hill,
Ky., P. Bertrand, printer, 1818.
vi, 520 p.   22 cm.

14029 Dunn, R   I
A condensed military pocket manual, for volunteer
and militia officers, non-commissioned officers and
privates. Agreeable to the system laid down for the
United States Army. [ten lines describing contents
in very small print] By Major R. I. Dunn, professor
of military tactics and the swords, and teacher of
military schools in different parts of the United
States, for twenty-five years. Price one dollar.
Second edition, revised and corrected. Lexington,
Ky., J. Cunningham, printer, 1841.
88 p.   16 x 9½ cm.

14030 Dupre, Huntley.
Rafinesque in Lexington, 1819-1826. Lexington,
Ky., Bur press, 1945.
99 p.   front. (port.)   21 cm.

14031 Durrett, Reuben Thomas, 1824-1913, ed.
... Bryant's Station and the memorial proceedings
held on its site under the auspices of the Lexington
chapter, D.A.R., on August 18th, 1896, in honor of
its heroic mothers and daughters... Louisville,
J. P. Morton and company, printer, 1897.
vii p., 1 ℓ., 277 p.   front., plates, ports.
32½ x 24½ cm.   (Filson Club publications, no. 12)

14032 Durrett, Reuben Thomas, 1824-1913.
    ... The centenary of Louisville, a paper read
before the Southern Historical Association, Saturday,
May 1st, 1880, in commemoration of the one hundredth
anniversary of the beginning of the City of Louisville
as an incorporated town, under an act of the legislature
of Virginia... Louisville, John P. Morton and
company, 1893.
    200 p.   illus. $27\frac{1}{2}$ cm.
At head of title: Filson Club publication no. 8.

14033 Durrett, Reuben Thomas, 1824-1913.
    An historical sketch of St. Paul's Church,
Louisville, Ky., prepared for the semi-centennial
celebration, October 6, 1889... Louisville,
John P. Morton and company, 1889.
    75 p.   illus. $27\frac{1}{2}$ cm.
In subsequent lists of Filson Club publication
recorded as no. 5.

14034 Durrett, Reuben Thomas, 1824-1913.
    John Filson, the first historian of Kentucky.
An account of his life and writings, principally from
original sources. Prepared for the Filson Club and
read at its meeting, in Louisville, Ky., June 26, 1884...
Louisville, Printed for the Filson Club by John P.
Morton & co., 1884.
    132 p.   front. (port.) facsim.   30 cm.
(Filson Club publication, no. 1)

14035 Durrett, Reuben Thomas, 1824-1913.
    ... Traditions of the earliest visits of foreigners
to North America, the first formed and first inhabited
of the continents... Louisville, John P. Morton &
company, 1908.
    xxii, 179 p.   illus., map. $27\frac{1}{2}$ cm.
At head of title: Filson Club publication no. 23.

E

14036 Early history of Covington. [Covington, Printing
Department, Holmes High School, ca. 1958]
    [4] p.   23 cm.

14037　Earth changes:　past, present, future.　[Virginia
　　　　　Beach, Association for Research and Enlightenment
　　　　　Press, 1963]
　　　　　　61 p.　　3 maps.　　23 cm.　　(Professional study
　　　　　series, no. 1)
　　　　　　Cover title.
　　　　　　"Originally published in January 1939 under the
　　　　　title:　A psychic interpretation of some late-
　　　　　cenozoic events compared with selected scientific
　　　　　data.　It has been revised and augmented."
　　　　　　Bibliography:　p. 47-51.

14038　East Kentucky rock asphalt co., inc., Lexington, Ky.
　　　　　　Prospectus.　[Lexington?　n.d.]
　　　　　　16 p.　　23 cm.

14039　Eastern Kentucky State Teachers College, Richmond.
　　　　　　Three decades of progress.　Eastern Kentucky State
　　　　　Teachers College, 1906-1936.　Prepared by members of
　　　　　the faculty.　Richmond, Ky., 1936.
　　　　　　365 p.　　illus., tables, graphs.　　(Eastern
　　　　　Kentucky Review, vol. XXIX, May, 1936, no. 1)

14040　Eaton, Clement, 1898-
　　　　　　Kentucky colonel - new vintage... Lexington,
　　　　　Privately printed, 1942.
　　　　　　11 p.　　front. (port.)　　$22\frac{1}{2}$ cm.
　　　　　　"Reprinted from The Southern Literary Messenger,
　　　　　Richmond, Virginia, March, 1941."

14041　Eberhard, Carl A
　　　　　　A brief history of the First Evangelical Lutheran
　　　　　Church of Louisville, Ky., 1878-1928.　[Louisville]
　　　　　Published by the Congregation for the golden jubilee,
　　　　　1928.
　　　　　　[16] p.　　illus., ports.　　24 cm.
　　　　　　Cover title.

14042　Eberhardt, Frederick William, 1864-1971.
　　　　　　The heart of old Kentucky, by Frederick W. Eberhardt...
　　　　　[Paris, Ky.?　195-?]
　　　　　　[20] p.　　illus.　　19 cm.
　　　　　　Poetry.

14043　Eckdahl, Andrew.
　　　　　　Coldstream Farm.　[Lexington, Ky., 1957]
　　　　　　[4] p.　　illus.　　24 cm.
　　　　　　Reprinted from Lexington Herald, 25 January 1957.

14044　Eckdahl, Andrew.
　　　　Henry Ward's "Recollections" cover 45 years of
　　　　public service. [Lexington, 1974]
　　　　　　broadside.　　illus.　　57 cm.
　　　　Appended to the broadside is an illustrated article
　　　　from the Sunday Herald-Leader, Lexington, Ky.,
　　　　23 June 1974, and correspondence between Ward and
　　　　Lawrence S. Thompson concerning the biography.

14045　Edwards, Georgie Hortense.
　　　　Historic sketches of the Edwards and Todd families
　　　　and their descendants, 1523-1895. Springfield, Ill.,
　　　　H. W. Rokker, printer and binder, 1894.
　　　　　　37 p.　　29 cm.　　(Kentucky. University. Library.
　　　　Kentucky reprints, III. 1964)

14046　Edwards, John Ellis, 1814-
　　　　Life of Rev. John Wesley Childs: for twenty-three
　　　　years an itinerant Methodist minister... Richmond,
　　　　Va., and Louisville, Ky., J. Early for the Methodist
　　　　Episcopal church, South, 1852.
　　　　　　295 p.　　19½ cm.

14047　Edwards, Sharon.
　　　　From wilderness to wildlife sanctuary. Self-
　　　　taught naturalist Carr made transformation in only
　　　　two years. Lexington, Ky., 1969.
　　　　　　broadside.　　illus.　　60 x 40 cm.　　(Sunday
　　　　Herald-Leader, 2 February 1969)

14048　Ehmann, William D
　　　　The Walltown, Kentucky, meteorite, by William D.
　　　　Ehmann and Jack R. Busche. [Lexington] 1968.
　　　　　　6-7 p.　　illus., table.　　23 cm.
　　　　Reprinted from Transactions of the Kentucky Academy
　　　　of Science, v. 29, nos. 1-4, 1968.

14049　Elam National Tercentennial Association.
　　　　Addresses and proceedings of the Elam National
　　　　Tercentennial held at Lexington, Ky., August 13-14,
　　　　1938. [Lexington] 1938.
　　　　　　32 p.　　23 cm.
　　　　Cover title: "The next meeting of the Elam National
　　　　Tercentennial will be held at Lexington, Ky., July 4-5,
　　　　1943."

14050　Elizabethtown, Ky. Memorial United Methodist Church.
　　　　History of Memorial United Methodist Church

1791-1968. Compiled by The Historical Committee of
the Memorial United Methodist Church, Elizabethtown,
Ky., in 1968. Members of the Committee: Elizabeth
Beeler, Chairman, W. H. Marriott, John Behen.
[Elizabethtown, Ky. n.d.]
25 p.   24 cm.

14051   Eller, Ronald D
Dissertations on the Appalachian South. Lexington,
Ky., Erasmus Press, 1975.
6 p.   24 cm.
Reprinted from Appalachian notes, v. 3, no. 1, 1975.

14052   Elliott, Charles, 1792-
Sinfulness of American slavery; proved from its
evil sources... Ed. by Rev. B. F. Tefft...
Cincinnati, L. Swormstedt & J. H. Power, 1850.
2 v.   18 cm.

14053   Elliott, Harrison.
Songs from "Call of the Cumberlands," first
American folk opera. [Louisville, 1937]
2-12 p.   illus.   24 cm.
Reprinted from Dixieana, v. 1, no. 4, April 1937.

14054   Elliott, J   M
To the people of Kentucky. Fellow-citizens:
I am informed that the Provisional Council of
Kentucky have [!] recently convened, and...
authorize [!] an election... for representatives
from Kentucky to the Congress of the Confederate
States. Richmond, Va., January 1, 1864.
broadside.   31 x 26 cm.

14055   Ellis, James Tandy, 1868-
Sycamore Bend, by James Tandy Ellis...   Macon, Ga.,
The J. W. Burke company, 1923.
90 p.   18½ cm.

14056   Ellis, Joseph.
Old timers hearken!!! Gila Bend, Arizona, 4 July
1867.
broadside.   32 x 26 cm.
Incipit: We are camping on the trail and there's
but a few of us left. Explicit: Now, boys, whoop'em
up for Joseph or the Jews'll get him, catch him where
the hair's short!
Advertisement for an itinerant peddler, whose goods

included twelve barrels of "wet goods" produced in Robinson County, Kentucky, before the war (1846) and known as "Joe Blackburn".

14057 Ellison, Sherry Sue.
A young historian encounters "The Falls". Frankfort, Kentucky Historical Society, 1967.
2 p.   28 cm.
Reprinted from Kentucky heritage, v. 8, no. 1, Fall 1967.

14058 Elmwood Inn. [Gettysburg, Pa., 1976]
broadside.   30 x 23 cm.
Reprinted from Kentucky edition of The American Motorist, v. 44, no. 9, January 1976.

14059 Ely, William.
The Big Sandy Valley. A history of the people and country from the earliest settlement to the present time... Catlettsburg, Ky., Central Methodist, 1887.
500 p.   illus.   20 cm.

14060 [Emlyn, Thomas] 1663-1741.
An humble enquiry into the Scripture account of Jesus Christ: or, a short argument concerning his deity and glory, according to the gospel... London-printed; Frankfort, Kentucky, re-printed by James M. Bradford, 1803.
viii, 53 p. $22\frac{1}{2}$ cm.
"A sketch of the life and character of Mr. Emlyn": p. [iii]-viii.

14061 Ennemoser, Franz Joseph.
Eine reise vom Mittelrhein: Mainz über Cöln, Paris, und Havre nach den nordamerikanischen Frei-staaten... 10. durchgesehene und mit einem anhange vermehrte aufl. Kaiserslautern, G. J. Tascher, 1865.
160 p. $19\frac{1}{2}$ cm.

14062 Errett, Isaac, 1820-1888.
Life and writings of George Edward Flower, edited by Isaac Errett. Cincinnati, Standard publishing company, 1865.
338 p.   front. (port.) $21\frac{1}{2}$ cm.

14063 Evans, Nancy.
       Old Stone Inn [Simpsonville, Ky.] [n.p., 1974]
       1 ℓ.   illus.   28½ cm.
       Reprinted from American Motorist (Blue Grass
       edition), v. 42, no. 12, p. 7 (April, 1974)

                              F

14064 Fackler, Calvin Morgan.
       A chronicle of the old First (Presbyterian church,
       Danville, Kentucky) 1784-1944. Louisville, The
       Standard printing co., 1946.
       99, [2] p.   plates, ports.   23 cm.

14065 Fackler, Calvin Morgan.
       Early days in Danville. Louisville, The Standard
       printing co., 1941.
       283 p.   map, illus.   24 cm.

14066 A famous Kentucky shrine. McDowell house and apothecary
       shop... [Danville, Ky., n.d.]
       12 p.   in folding leaflet.   illus.   21 cm.

14067 The farmer's almanac for the year of Our Lord 1822...
       Calculated for the meridian of Lexington, Ky., and
       will serve, without any sensible variation, for the
       states of Ohio, Indiana, Illinois, Tennessee, and
       Missouri. Lexington, Printed and published by James W.
       Palmer [1821]
       36 p.   18½ cm.

14068 The farmer's almanac, for the year of Our Lord 1823...
       Calculated for the meridian of Lexington, Ky. And
       will serve, without any sensible variation for the
       states of Ohio, Indiana, Illinois, Tennessee and
       Missouri. By James W. Palmer. Lexington, Printed
       by James W. Palmer, for self, W. W. Worsley, & W. C.
       Hunt [1822]
       36 p.   18½ cm.

14069 The farmer's almanac for the year of Our Lord 1824...
       Calculated for the meridian of Lexington, Ky. And
       will serve without any sensible variation, for the
       states of Tennessee, Ohio, Indiana, Illinois and
       Missouri. By James W. Palmer. Lexington, Printed

by James W. Palmer, for self & W. G. Hunt [1823]
36 p.   19½ cm.

14070   Farmers' Bank and Capital Trust Co., Frankfort, Ky.
        A century of progress with Frankfort. [Frankfort,
        Ky., 1949?]
        67 p.   illus.   38 cm.

14071   Farmers' Bank and Capital Trust Co., Frankfort, Ky.
        Radius 100 years. A sketch of the period cir-
        cumscribed by the life of Farmers Bank & Capital
        Trust Co. [Frankfort, 1955?]
        45 p.   illus.   23 cm.

14072   Farmington and Locust Grove: two historic Louisville
        homes. [Gettysburg, Pa., 1976]
        broadside.   illus.   29½ x 45 cm.
        Reprinted from American motorist (Bluegrass
        edition) v. 44, no. 12, April 1976.

14073   Farnsley, Sally, 1938-
        "Dear Miss Bettie." Louisville, Ky., 1962.
        .4 p.   illus., facsims.   37 cm.
        Reprinted by permission from the Courier-Journal
        Magazine, 17 June 1962.

14074   Farrell, Edward P
        The Law and Order league... Written in the fall
        of 1904. [Lexington, Ky.? n.d.]
        5 ℓ.   28 cm.

14075   Farrington, E[dmond] F
        A full and complete description of the Covington and
        Cincinnati suspension bridge, with dimensions and
        details of construction... Cincinnati, J. P.
        Lindsay & co., printers, 1867.
        17 p.   15½ cm.

14076   Faulconer, J   B
        The Keeneland story. A quarter-century of racing
        in the finest tradition. [Lexington, Ky., n.d.]
        111 p.   illus., maps.   29 cm.

14077   Faux, William.
        ... I. Memorable days in America... III. A visit
        to North America and the English settlements in
        Illinois. By Adlard Welby. Edited with notes,
        introductions, index, etc., by Reuben Gold Thwaites...

Cleveland, The Arthur H. Clark company, 1904-1905.
2 v.   illus.   25 cm.   (Early western travels,
1748-1846, v. XI)
At head of title: Early western travels.

14078   Fayette County Bar, Lexington, Ky.
Addresses delivered in honor of John Marshall Day,
by members of the Fayette County Bar, February 4, 1901.
Lexington [1901?]
89 p.   front. (port.)   25 cm.

14079   Fayette County Bar, Lexington, Ky.
Proceedings at presentation of portrait of
Colonel John Rowan Allen to the Fayette county bar.
Fayette circuit court room, Lexington, Ky. Friday,
May 18, 1945, 10:30 o'clock A.M. [Lexington, Ky.?
1945?]
20 p.   front. (port.), illus.   27 cm.

14080   Federal Writers' Project. Kentucky.
Lexington and the Bluegrass country. Lexington,
E. M. Glass, publisher, 1938.
168 p.   illus., maps.   20 cm.

14081   Federal Writers' Project. Kentucky.
... Old capitol and Frankfort guide, compiled and
written by the Federal Writers' Project of the Works
Progress Administration in the state of Kentucky.
Sponsored by the Kentucky Historical Society,
Frankfort. [Frankfort] Harry McChesney [1939]
98 p.   illus. (plan)   20½ cm.   (American
guide series)

14082   Fee, John Gregg, 1816-1901.
[Letter to Rev. James R. Fairchild, 17 August 1872,
from Berea, Kentucky concerning his son, Burritt;
postal card to Rev. G. F. Wright, Lawrence, Mass.,
20 Dec. 1880, concerning Rev. Wright's ministry
and publications]
4 ℓ.   29½ cm.
Manuscripts in Oberlin College archives.

14083   Ferguson, Nora Young.
History of the Old Green river union meeting house
at Richardsville, Warren county, Ky.... [Bowling
Green, Ky.] 1960.
[8] p.   19 cm.

14084   Fernow, Berthold.
        The Ohio Valley in colonial days. By Berthold
        Fernow... Albany, N. Y., Joel Munsell's sons, 1890.
        299 p.   23 cm.

14085   A few reflections of a cool minded man on the present
        judiciary question of Kentucky. [n.p., 1825]
        12 p.   23½ cm.
        Signed "A Cool Minded Man."

14086   Field, Thomas Parry, 1914-
        ... A guide to Kentucky place names... [Lexington]
        College of Arts and Sciences, University of Kentucky
        [1961]
        264 p.   22 cm.   (Kentucky Geological Survey,
        Special publication, 5)

14087   Field, Thomas Parry, 1914-
        Index to the map of Kentucky and the Southwest
        Territory 1794. [Lexington, Ky.] 1966.
        48 p.   fold. map.   29 cm.

14088   Field, Thomas Parry, 1914-
        Kentucky and the Southwest Territory 1794.
        A map illustrating the documented geographical
        references through statehood for Kentucky and
        Tennessee... Lexington, Dept. of Geography, Uni-
        versity of Kentucky, 1965.
        col. map.   51 x 85 cm.

14089   Field, Thomas Parry, 1914-
        Religious place-names in Kentucky. [n.p.] 1972.
        26-46 p.   maps, tables.   24½ cm.
        "Reprinted from Names, volume 20, number 1,
        March 1972."

14090   Figgins, Jesse Dade, d. 1944.
        Birds of Kentucky... Lexington, University of
        Kentucky Press, 1945.
        366 p.   illus.   26 cm.

14091   Filson, John, 1753-1768.
        Kentucke and the adventures of Col. Daniel Boone
        [by] John Filson with an introduction by Willard
        Rouse Jillson... A facsimile reproduction of the
        original Wilmington edition and an exact reprint of
        the first map of 1784. Louisville, John P. Morton
        & company, 1934.

[13] p., 118 p. of facsim.   front. (map)   22 cm.
Fold. map in pocket at end.
"Issued... under the sponsorship of the Boone
Bicentennial Commission of Kentucky, as Document No. 2
of its Boone Publications..."

14092 Filson Club, Louisville, Kentucky.
        The centenary of Kentucky. Proceedings at the
celebration by the Filson Club, Wednesday, June 1,
1892, of the one hundredth anniversary of the
admission of Kentucky as an independent state into
the Federal Union. Louisville, John P. Morton &
company; Cincinnati, Robert Clarke & company, 1892.
        200 p.   27 cm.
In subsequent lists of Filson Club publication
recorded as no. 7.

14093 Filson Club, Louisville, Kentucky.
        The Filson Club, its future. [Louisville? 1926?]
        23 p.   ports., plans., facsim.   25 cm.

14094 Finck, Edward Bertrand, 1870-
        Shadows on the wall, by Bert Finck... Louisville,
John P. Morton & company, 1922.
        [8], 110 p.   18½ cm.
        Contents. - Shadows on the wall. - The poet. -
The house of tragedy. - The unwelcome visitor. -
Remorse. - Adversity.

14095 Finley, Alexander C
        The history of Russellville and Logan county, Ky.,
which is to some extent a history of western Kentucky.
By Alex. C. Finley... Russellville, Ky., O. C. Rhea,
1878.
        3 pts. in 1 v.   22½ cm.

14096 Finley, Isaac J
        Pioneer record and reminiscences of the early
settlers and settlement of Ross County, Ohio. By
Isaac J. Finley and Rufus Putnam. Cincinnati,
Printed for the authors by Robert Clarke & co.,
1877.
        148 p.   22½ cm.
        Contains material on early history of Ohio and
Kentucky.

14097 First Presbyterian Church, Lexington, Ky.
        A Presbyterian celebration, the 175th anniversary,

90

1784-1959. Lexington, Ky., 1959.
63 p.   illus.   20 cm.

14098 Fisher, Elwood, 1808-1862.
... Lecture on the North and the South, delivered
before the Young Men's Mercantile Library Association
of Cincinnati, Ohio, January 16, 1849. By Elwood
Fisher. Cincinnati, Chronicle book and job rooms,
1849.
64 p.   21 cm.
Kentucky: p. 10-11 et passim. Virginia and
Kentucky provide nearly all the data relative to
the South.

14099 Fitch, Joseph B
A brief history of the Bardstown Christian Church...
Material collected and prepared by Joseph B. Fitch,
minister. Bardstown, Ky., 1946.
18 p.   illus., ports.   24 cm.

14100 Five million endowment scheme. Fifth and last concert
for the benefit of the Public Library of Kentucky.
On Friday, July 31, 1874. Twenty thousand cash
gifts. $2,500.00. Last chance for an easy fortune...
[Louisville? 1874?]
broadside.   illus.   43 x 26 cm.
Hummel, 764.
Original in Western Kentucky University Library.

14101 The Flag. Extra. Flemingsburg, Sept. 28, 1847.
Flemingsburg, Ky., 1847.
broadside.   44 x 17 cm.

14102 Flanagan, James, 1820-1906.
The Asiatic cholera in Winchester in 1833. Memories
of the terrible epidemic. By Judge James Flanagan.
Transcribed by George F. Doyle, M.D., F.A.C.S.
[Winchester, Ky., Clark County Historical Society,
n.d.]
11 p.   28 cm.

14103 Flanagan, James, 1820-1906.
Falling of the stars; the remarkable phenomenon
that scared everybody to prayers in 1833; Donaldson's
long trumpet, and what he did with it; M. Firitz
proclaims himself the Angel Gabriel, by Judge James
Flanagan. Transcribed by George F. Doyle.

91

[Winchester, Ky., n.d.]
4 typewritten ℓ.   31 cm.

14104 Flanagan, James, 1820-1906.
History of Canewood, the seat of the Gist family
and home of Governor Charles Scott. By Judge James
Flanagan. Transcribed by George F. Doyle, M.D.,
F.A.C.S. [Winchester, Ky., Clark County Historical
Society, n.d.]
6 p.   28 cm.

14105 Flanagan, James, 1820-1906.
The Kentucky Militia in early days, by Judge James
Flanagan. Transcribed by George F. Doyle, M.D.,
F.A.C.S. [Winchester, Ky., Clark County Historical
Society, n.d.]
6 p.   28 cm.

14106 Flanagan, James, 1820-1906.
Noted suit in 1847 to set aside the will of Joel T.
Quisenberry. Large estate involved. History of the
trial. By Hon. James Flanagan. Transcribed by
George F. Doyle, M.D., F.A.C.S. [Winchester, Ky.,
Clark County Historical Society, n.d.]
6 p.   28 cm.

14107 Flanagan, James, 1820-1906.
Recollections of a famous will contest of nearly half-
century ago. By Judge James Flanagan. Transcribed by
George F. Doyle, M.D., F.A.C.S. [Winchester, Ky.,
Clark County Historical Society, n.d.]
5 p.   28 cm.

14108 Flanagan, James, 1820-1906.
Winchester, by Judge James Flanagan. Transcribed by
George F. Doyle. [Winchester, Ky., n.d.]
1, 14 typewritten ℓ.   30½ cm.

14109 Fleenor, Creedmore.
In passing through, by Creedmore Fleenor.
Author's edition. Limited. Bowling Green, Ky.,
Courier pub. co., 1898.
1 ℓ., 132 p.   16 cm.
Poetry.

14110 Flexner, Anne Crawford.
Mrs. Wiggs of the Cabbage Patch, a dramatization
in three acts, by Anne Crawford Flexner, from the
novel, "Mrs. Wiggs of the Cabbage Patch," by Alice

Hegan Rice... New York, Samuel French; London,
Samuel French, ltd. [1924]
96 p.   illus., diagrs.   19½ cm.

14111 Flexner, Bernard, 1865-
Mr. Justice Brandeis and the University of Louisville,
by Bernard Flexner. Louisville, Ky., University of
Louisville, 1938.
3 p.l., 86 p.   front. (mounted port.) facsims.
24 cm.

14112 Flint, James.
Letters from America... Edited with notes, introductions, index, etc. by Reuben Gold Thwaites...
Cleveland, The Arthur H. Clark company, 1904.
333 p.   illus.   25 cm.   (Early western
travels, 1748-1846, v. IX)

14113 Flint, Timothy, 1780-1840.
The first white man of the West: or, The life and
exploits of Col. Dan'l Boone, the first settler of
Kentucky; interspersed with incidents in the early
annals of the country. By Timothy Flint. Cincinnati,
Conclin, 1849.
252 p.   incl. front., illus.   18½ cm.

14114 Foerste, August F
... Report on the value of the Dix river as a source
of water power... Field work done in 1910-'11.
[Frankfort, Ky.?] Interstate publishing co., 1912.
63 p.   graphs, tables.   25 cm.
At head of title: Kentucky Geological Survey...
Bulletin 21, Serial 28)

14115 Foerste, August F
... The Silurian, Devonian and Irvine formations
of east-central Kentucky, with an account of their
clays and limestones... Louisville, Geo. G. Fetter
co., 1906.
369 p.   illus., maps, tables, graphs.   26½ cm.
At head of title: Kentucky Geological Survey,
Charles J. Norwood, director, Bulletin no. 7.

14116 Fohs, F   Julius.
... Coals of the region drained by the Quicksand
Creeks in Breathitt, Floyd, and Knott Counties...
Field work done in 1910. [n.p.] Printed by the
Interstate publishing co., 1912.

[xvi], 79 p.   maps, diags.   26½ cm.
At head of title: Kentucky Geological Survey,
Charles J. Norwood, director, Bulletin no. 18,
Serial no. 25.

14117 Fohs, F   Julius.
        ... Fluorspar deposits of Kentucky, with notes on
        the production, mining and technology of the mineral
        in the United States. Also some data concerning
        barite deposits... Louisville, Globe printing co.,
        1907.
        [x], 296 p.   illus., maps (1 fold.), tables,
        graphs.   26½ cm.
        At head of title: Kentucky Geological Survey,
        Charles J. Norwood, director, Bulletin no. 9.

14118 Foreman, Anthony.
        Old homes - the pride of Lexington. Frankfort,
        Kentucky Historical Society, 1967.
        2 p.   illus.   28 cm.
        Reprinted from Kentucky heritage, v. 8, no. 1,
        Fall 1967.

14119 Ft. Thomas, Ky. Highland Methodist Church.
        1830-1900-1950: Highland Methodist Church anniversary
        celebration, September 24-27, 1950. [Ft. Thomas,
        Ky., 1950]
        16 p.   illus., ports.   29 cm.
        Cover-title.
        "A brief history of Highland Methodist Church,
        1830-1900": p. 1-10.

14120 Fortune, Alonzo Willard.
        The Disciples in Kentucky... [Lexington?] Published
        by the Convention of the Christian churches in
        Kentucky [c1932]
        415 p.   illus.   23 cm.

14121 Forwood, William Stump, 1830-1892.
        An historical and descriptive narrative of the
        Mammoth cave of Kentucky. Philadelphia, J. B.
        Lippincott & co., 1870.
        xi, 13-225 p.   front., plates.   19½ cm.

14122 Foster Hall. A reminder of the life and work of
        Stephen Collins Foster, 1826-1864. Indianapolis,
        Josiah Kirby Lilly, 1933.
        12 p.   illus., facsims.

94

Mounted at end are clippings from the Washington Post, 25 July 1957, and from Louisville Courier-Journal, 10 August 1957, concerning censorship of Collins' songs.

14123 Foster, Stephen Collins, 1826-1864.
... Massa's in de cold ground, as sung by Christy's minstrels... New York [etc.] Published by Firth, Pond & co. [n.d.]
5 p.   music.   34 cm.
At head of title: Fifth edition.

14124 Foster, Stephen Collins, 1826-1864.
... My old Kentucky home, good night, Foster's plantation melodies, no. 20, as sung by Christy's minstrels... piano... guitar. New York, Firth, Pond & co. [etc., etc.] [n.d.]
[5] p.   music.   36 cm.
At head of title: Tenth edition.

14125 Foster, Stephen Collins, 1826-1864.
... Old Dog Tray, sung by Christy's minstrels... New York [etc., etc.] Published by Firth, Pond & co. [n.d.]
5 p.   music.   34 cm.
At head of title: Foster's American melodies, no. 21.

14126 Foster, Stephen Collins, 1826-1864.
Songs of Stephen Foster. Prepared especially for the armed forces by the staff of the Foster Hall Collection of the University of Pittsburgh. Pittsburgh, University of Pittsburgh, 1952.
24 p.   24 cm.

14127 Foster, Stephen Collins, 1826-1864.
Songs of Stephen Foster prepared for schools and general use. Edited and arranged by Will Earhart and Edward B. Birge. Pittsburgh, University of Pittsburgh press, 1944.
109 p.   front. (port.) music.   28½ cm.

14128 Fowler, Ila Earle.
Down in west Kentucky and other poems... Cynthiana, Ky., The Hobson book press, 1944.
65 p.   22 cm.

14129 Fox, Elma.
The house that two sheep built. [Gettysburg, Pa.

1974]
    broadside.   illus.   29 x 21 cm.
    Reprinted from American motorist (Lexington, Ky. ed.)
    v. 42, no. 9, Jan. 1974.

14130   Fox, John, 1862-1919.
    Personal and family letters and papers, compiled by
    Elizabeth Fox Moore. Lexington, University of
    Kentucky Library Associates, 1955.
    91 p.   front. (port.)   28 cm.

14131   Fox, John William, 1863-1919.
    Crittenden, a Kentucky story of love and war...
    New York, Charles Scribner's sons, 1900.
    256 p.   20 cm.

14132   Fox, John William, 1863-1919.
    The Kentuckians... illustrated by W. T. Smedley.
    New York and London, Harper & brothers publishers,
    1898.
    228 p.   illus.   30 cm.

14133   Fox, Oliver E
    The trail of the lonesome pine. A description of
    the setting for John Fox Jr.'s romantic story.
    A plea for authentic road markings. By Oliver E.
    Fox. Winchester, Ky., Winchester Sun, 1936.
    8 p.   28 cm.
    Newspaper clippings mounted.

14134   Frankfort, Ky. Christian Church.
    Centennial, 1832-1932. Birthday dinner program,
    centennial program, and history of the church.
    [Frankfort? 1932]
    [18] p.   plates, ports.   24 cm.

14135   Frankfort's 175th anniversary. Frankfort, Ky., The
    State Journal, 1961.
    108 p.   illus.   56 x 40 cm.
    Special issue of The State Journal, Sunday, 4 June
    1961.

14136   Franklin, Joseph, 1834-
    The life and times of Benjamin Franklin, by Joseph
    Franklin, and J. A. Headington. St. Louis, J. Burns,
    1879.
    xv, 508 p.   front. (port.) $19\frac{1}{2}$ cm.

14137 Freedman, Greg.
        Solid waste: the third pollutant. Frankfort, Ky.,
        Legislative Research Commission, 1973.
        79 p.   29 cm.   (Research report no. 106,
        new series)

14138 Freedman, Gregory A
        Insurance agents: licensing and regulations,
        prepared by Gregory A. Freedman. Frankfort, Ky.,
        Legislative Research Commission, 1977.
        iv, 80 p.   28 cm.   (Research report no. 131)

14139 Freemasons. Kentucky. Grand Lodge.
        Proceedings of the Grand Lodge of Kentucky, at a
        grand annual communication, in the town of Lexington,
        August, 1826. Lexington, Ky., Printed by John Bradford,
        Gazette Press, 1826.
        64 p.   24 cm.

14140 Free Suffrage, pseud.
        The Constitution shown to be consistent with a new
        election, by Free Suffrage. [Lexington? Ky., 1816?]
        39 p.   20 cm.
        Urging a new election, on the succession of the
        lieutenant governor, Gabriel Slaughter, to the
        governorship of Kentucky, vacated by the death of
        Governor Madison on October 14, 1816.

14141 Freiberg, Lewis.
        Kentucky tax policy: suggested considerations.
        Prepared by Lewis Freiberg and Don M. Soule...
        Frankfort, Ky., Legislative Research Commission,
        1972.
        87 p.   tables, diagrs.   29 cm.   (Research
        report, no. 69)

14142 Freitag, Christina.
        Back in 1830 Kentucky ranked no. 3 in iron.
        Louisville, 1975.
        [2] p.   illus.   29 cm.
        Reprinted from Rural Kentuckian, v. 29, no. 12,
        December 1975.

14143 Freitag, Christina.
        Two centuries and still in the family.   Louisville,
        1976
        [2] p.   illus.   28 cm.
        Reprinted from Rural Kentuckian, v. 30, no. 5, May, 1976.

14144 Frost, James Marion, 1849-1916.
Our church life; serving God on God's plan...
[by] J. M. Frost... Nashville, Tenn., Sunday school
board, Southern Baptist Convention [c1909]
269 p.   front.   18½ cm.   [The Eva Garvey
publishing fund, sixth book]

14145 Frost, John, 1800-1859.
Heroic women of the West; comprising thrilling
examples of courage, fortitude, devotedness, and
self-sacrifice, among the pioneer mothers of the
western country... Philadelphia, A. Hart, 1854.
vi, 7-348 p.   front., plates.   19 cm.

14146 Frost, John, 1800-1859.
Life of Major General Zachary Taylor; with notices
of the war in New Mexico, California, and in
southern Mexico; and biographical sketches of officers
who have distinguished themselves in the war with
Mexico... New York, D. Appleton & co.; Philadelphia,
C. S. Appleton, 1847.
346 p.   front., illus. (incl. maps, plan, chart)
plates, ports.   20 cm.

14147 Fry, James Barnet, 1827-1894.
Operations of the army under Buell from June 10th
to October 30th, 1862, and the "Buell Commission" ...
New York, D. Van Nostrand, 1884.
201 p.   front. (port.) fold. map.   18½ cm.

14148 Fugate, George W   , jr.
Geology of the area of Smith Mills North Geneva
oil pools, Henderson County, Kentucky. Lexington,
Ky., 1956.
27 p.   map, tables, graphs.   24 cm.
(Kentucky Geological Survey, Series IX, Bulletin,
no. 18)

14149 Fulling mill. The society called Shakers, in Logan
County, Ky., continue their fulling mill in operation...
South Union, Jasper Spring, Sept. 12th, 1815.
Russellville, Printed at the Office of the Weekly
messenger, 1815.
broadside.   38 x 17 cm.
Hummel, 760.
Original in Western Kentucky University Library.

14150   Fulton-South Fulton Chamber of Commerce.
         Ken-Tenn-o-rama. Historical program booklet.
         July 19-25, 1959. [Fulton, Ky., 1959]
         unpaged.   illus.   28½ cm.

14151   Funkhouser, William Delbert, 1881-1948.
         Ancient life in Kentucky; a brief presentation
         of the paleontological succession in Kentucky coupled
         with a systematic outline of the Commonwealth, by
         W. D. Funkhouser... and W. S. Webb... Frankfort,
         The Kentucky Geological Survey, 1928.
         349 p.   illus., maps, diags.   cm.   (Kentucky
         Geological Survey, ser. VI, geologic reports, v. 34)
         Bibliography: p. 335-341.

14152   Funkhouser, William Delbert, 1881-1948.
         An eccentric egocentric, by W. D. Funkhouser, 1930.
         [Lexington, Ky., 1940]
         cover-title, 23 p.   20½ cm.
         "Reprinted 1940. The one hundredth anniversary of
         the death of Rafinesque."

14153   Funkhouser, William Delbert, 1881-1948.
         Kentucky snakes, by W. D. Funkhouser. Lexington,
         University of Kentucky, Dept. of University Extension,
         1945.
         cover-title, 31 p.   23 cm.

14154   Funkhouser, William Delbert, 1881-1948.
         Portraits of Kentuckians. Brief studies in
         anthropology. Some thumbnail sketches of early
         Kentuckians who were interesting but are not famous.
         Lexington, 1943.
         102 p.   24 cm.

14155   Funkhouser, William Delbert, 1881-1948.
         Primitive magic. A study of cultural anthropology...
         Lexington, 1946.
         38 p.   24 cm.

14156   Funkhouser, William Delbert, 1881-1948.
         Who's who in Kentucky [by] W. D. Funkhouser...
         [Lexington? 1945]
         55 p.   23 cm.
         "A series of radio talks [on animal life and habits]
         presented from the studios of the University of
         Kentucky during November and December, 1944."

14157 Funkhouser, William Delbert, 1881-1948.
        Wild life in Kentucky. The reptiles, birds and
mammals of the Commonwealth, with a discussion of
their appearance, habits and economic importance...
Frankfort, The Kentucky Geological Survey, 1925.
        385 p.   col. front., illus., maps, diags.   24 cm.
(Kentucky Geological Survey, ser. VI, Geologic reports,
v. 16)
        Copy inscribed by author to Dr. F. L. McVey (president
of the University of Kentucky).

14158 Furman, Lucy, 1870-1958.
        The glass window. A story of the quare women...
Boston, Little, Brown and company, 1926.
        287 p.   20 cm.

14159 Furman, Lucy, 1870-1958.
        Mothering on Perilous... with illustrations by
Mary Lane McMillan and F. R. Gruger. New York,
The Macmillan company, 1915.
        310 p.   illus.   20½ cm.

14160 Fuson, Henry Harvey, 1876-1964.
        Just from Kentucky (a second volume of verse)
by Henry Harvey Fuson... Louisville, J. P. Morton
& company, incorporated, 1925.
        6 p.l., 149 p.   front.   19½ cm.

14161 Fuson, Henry Harvey, 1876-1964.
        These hills. By Henry Harvey Fuson... Frankfort,
Ky., Roberts Printing Co., 1951.
        37 p.   24½ cm.
        Poetry.

14162 Futch, Ladell J
        A keyhole peep into the past. [Louisville, Ky.]
1974.
        5-7 p.   illus.   29 cm.
        Reprinted from Rural Kentuckian, v. 28, no. 9,
Sept. 1974.

14163 Futch, Ladell J
        Old Fort Harrod, birthplace of Kentucky. Louisville,
1973.
        14-16 p.   illus.   29 cm.
        From Rural Kentuckian Magazine, v. 27, no. 3,
March 1973.

Also contains "The Mystery of the Beautiful Belle"
(at the Harrodsburg Spa).

G

14164 G.A.R. Souvenir sporting guide. [n.p.] Wentworth
       publishing house, 1895.
          29 p.   18 cm.
          A guide to the houses of ill fame for the 1895
       encampment of the Grand Army of the Republic in
       Louisville, 1895.
          Two folding facsimiles at end: (1) Obituary of
       Belle Breazing [!] from Time, 26 August 1940, and
       (2) a sheet containing "The Ballad of Dynamite Dun,"
       noted Lexington prostitute, and another on "The
       Banning of 'Dixie'".

14165 Gagliardini, Elise Chenault Bennett.
          From my journal; random thoughts. New York, 1858.
          107 p.   illus.   26½ cm.
          Inscribed and annotated by author and contains
       letter of author.

14166 Gaines, B   0
          The B. 0. Gaines history of Scott county [Kentucky]
       [Georgetown, Ky.] 1905.
          2 v.   illus.   28 cm.
          Continuous pagination; 558 pp. in all.

14167 Gaines, Joe.
          Cypress Boardwalk Nature Trail, Reelfoot Lake
       State Park, Tiptonville, Tennessee. Written by
       Joe Gaines. Illustrated by Ruth Dillard.
       [Nashville, Tenn., Tennessee Conservation Department,
       Parks Division, 197-]
          15 p.   illus.   21 cm.

14168 Gaines, William H
          Virginia history in documents, 1621-1788.
       Richmond, Virginia State Library, 1974.
          84 p., facsims. of 10 documents in portfolio.
       23 cm.
          Until 1792 Kentucky County (and other counties into
       which it was divided) were part of Virginia.

14169   Gaitskill, Laurence R
        State regulation of political parties. Frankfort,
        Ky., Legislative Research Commission, 1962.
        22 p.   diagr.   19 cm.   (Research report no. 13)

14170   Galloway, Juliet.
        Lexington began life as a corporation 141 years ago.
        [Lexington, Ky., 1973]
        1 p.   illus.   29 cm.
        Reprinted from Sunday Herald-Leader, 4 February 1973.

14171   Galloway, Robert E
        Rural manpower in eastern Kentucky. A study of
        underemployment among rural workers in economic
        area 8. Lexington, Kentucky Agricultural Experiment
        Station, University of Kentucky, 1955.
        32 p.   map, tables, diags.   24 cm.   (Kentucky
        Agricultural Experiment Station, Bulletin, 627)

14172   The Galt House, Louisville, Kentucky, 1869-1914.
        [Louisville, 1914?]
        34 p.   illus.   14½ cm.

14173   Gardner, James H
        ... Clays in several parts of Kentucky, with some
        account of sands, marls and limestones. I. Kaolins
        and plastic clays on the eastern rim of the western
        coalfield; notes on clays in the western, lead,
        zinc and spar district (F. J. Fohs); clays and sands
        of Jackson's Purchase; clays in the Red River Valley,
        by James H. Gardner. II. Clays of Silurian, Devonian,
        Waverly and Irvine formations. By Aug. F. Foerste.
        III. Analyses of miscellaneous Kentucky clays...
        Louisville, Printed by the Geo. G. Fetter co., 1905.
        xii, 223 p.   illus., tables, graphs.   26½ cm.
        At head of title: Kentucky Geological Survey,
        Charles Norwood, director, Bulletin no. 6.

14174   Gardner, James H
        ... The economic geology of the Hartford quadrangle...
        and on the soils of the same quadrangle, by S. C.
        Jones, field work done in 1910. Louisville, Interstate
        publishing co., 1912.
        33 p.   tables, maps.   27 cm.   (Kentucky
        Geological Survey, Bulletin no. 29, Serial no. 27)

14175   Garr, Elizabeth Headley ("Mrs. Amos Lawrence")
        The history of Kentucky courthouses, an illustrated

story of courthouse and county historical data...
[Frankfort, Liberty Hall, Inc., 1972]
   166 p.   illus., fold. maps.   29½ cm.
   Ms. in pocket at end, including permission to copy
in microform. Photograph of author and review precedes
title-page.

14176 Garrett, Betty.
       An Appalachian author describes his life style.
[Washington, D.C., 1973]
   24-28 p.   illus.   29 cm.
   Reprinted from Appalachia, December 1972-January
1973.
   Inscribed by Mr. Stuart.

14177 Gartin, Michael.
       McGuffey's school. Gettysburg, Pa., 1973.
   1 p.   illus.   29 cm.
   Reprinted from American Motorist, v. 42, no. 2,
July 1973.

14178 Gaskin, E   R
       Folk tales of the Kentucky hills. [Wartburg,
Tenn., 1968]
   96 p.   29 cm.
   This film was made from a dimly typed ms., and the
pencilled annotations are sometimes difficult to read.

14179 Gatz, Carolyn.
       Old Episcopal Cemetery; historic landmark born
during 1833 epidemic.
   broadside.   illus.   38 x 19 cm.
   Reprinted from Lexington Herald-Leader, 28 September
1975, Section D, p. 1.

14180 Gay times. [Lexington, Ky., Gay Liberation Movement
of the University of Kentucky, 1973] v. 1, 1973-
   illus.
   Library has v. 1, no. 2.
   At end is article by Ken Briggs, "Gay church
movement still grows, despite traditionalists'
opposition," The Courier-Journal & Times, Sunday,
May 13, 1973.
   This periodical, not officially sponsored by the
University of Kentucky, was printed without permission
on equipment belonging to the University of Kentucky
and created considerable discussion in the press in
the spring of 1973.

14181 Geer, Curtis Manning, 1864-
... The Louisiana purchase and the westward movement
... Philadelphia, Printed for subscribers only by
G. Barrie & sons [c1904]
xxii, 500 p.   col. front., plates, ports. (part
col.) maps, facsims.   23 cm.

14182 Geis, Edna Kirker.
Poems from Taylor Manor. [Versailles, Ky., 1972]
[8] p.   15 cm.

14183 A general map of the new settlement called Transilvania.
[n.p., n.d.]
map.   27½ x 53½ cm.   (Kentucky. University.
Library. Kentucky map facsimile, no. 4)
Originally printed, November, 1776.
Includes Virginia, North Carolina, South Carolina,
Tennessee, and parts of adjacent states.

14184 General Roger W. Hanson, 1827-1863. Lexington, Ky.,
1967.
8 p.   port.   27 cm.

14185 Gibson, William.
An address by William Gibson, late general super-
intendent of the Baltimore and Ohio Railroad before
the junior and senior classes. College of Mechanical
and Electrical Engineering, State University of
Kentucky, October 1910. Pittsburgh, Printed by
Myers and Shinkle co. [1910]
cover-title, 14 p.   23 cm.
Author's presentation copy.

14186 Gibson, William.
James Kennedy Patterson... an appreciation of the
College of Engineering of the University of Kentucky.
[n.p., 1923?]
cover-title, 15 p.   23 cm.

14187 Gilleland, J   C
The Ohio and Mississippi pilot, consisting of a
set of charts of those rivers... to which is added
a geography of the states and territories west and
south of the Allegheny mountains... Pittsburgh,
R. Patterson & Lambdin, 1820.
xii, 13-274 p.   maps.   12 cm.

14188 [Gillis, Ezra L]
    The University of Kentucky: its history and
    development. Series of charts depicting some of
    the more important data 1866-1950. Lexington, 1950.
    32 p.   23 cm.

14189 [Gillis, Ezra L]
    The University of Kentucky. Its history and
    development. A series of charts depicting the more
    important data, 1862-1955. Lexington, Ky.,
    August 1956.
    32 p.   tables.   24½ cm.   (Kentucky.
    University. Libraries. Bulletin XVI)

14190 Gilmore, James Roberts, 1822-1903.
    A mountain-white heroine, by James R. Gilmore
    (Edmund Kirke [pseud])... New York and Chicago,
    Belford, Clarke and company, 1889.
    240 p.   20 cm.

14191 Giltner, Hellen Fairleigh.
    Westport. Louisville, Ky., Press of Mayes
    Printing Co. [c1947]
    15 p.   illus., maps.   25 cm.

14192 Giovannoli, Harry.
    Kentucky Female Orphan School, a history...
    Midway, Ky., 1930.
    210 p.   illus.   24 cm.

14193 Glenn, L   C
    ... A geological reconnaissance of the Tradewater
    river region, with special reference to the coal
    beds. Embracing parts of Union, Webster, Hopkins,
    Crittenden, Caldwell and Christian counties...
    Prepared for publication in 1910.   [n.p.] Interstate
    publishing co., 1912.
    75 p.   tables (part fold.)   27 cm.   (Kentucky
    Geological Survey, Bulletin no. 17, Serial no. 24)

14194 Glynn, William C
    The capitol quick step, composed and adapted to
    the piano forte by William C. Glynn. Respectfully
    dedicated to the Hon. Henry Clay of Kentucky.
    Boston, Henry Prentiss [n.d.]
    3 ℓ.   cover illus., music.   36 cm.
    The original of this text was in the possession
    of Elliott Shapiro, 118 West 79th Street, New York,

in February 1943. The original cannot now be located.
The present "photostatic" copy, possibly now unique,
is in the library of Lawrence S. Thompson, Lexington,
Kentucky.

14195   Godbey, Edsel T
        The governors of Kentucky and education 1780-1852.
        Lexington, Bureau of School Service, University of
        Kentucky, 1960.
        · 122 p.   23 cm.   (Kentucky. University.
        Bureau of School Service. Bulletin, XXXII, no. 4,
        June 1960)
        Portraits of all governors during period covered
        on cover.

14196   Godbey, W   B
        Baptism: mode and design. By Rev. W. B. Godbey,
        A.M., of the Kentucky Conference. Louisville,
        Pentecostal publishing co. [1883]
        101 p.   17 cm.

14197   Goddard, Mrs. Glave.
        Special recipes. Compiled by Mrs. Glave Goddard.
        Revised by Mrs. T. Curry Dedman. Harrodsburg, Ky.,
        Beaumont Inn [194-?]
        11 p.   16½ cm.
        Cover illus.

14198   Goebel assassination nearly lead to civil war.
        [Louisville, 1974]
        12-13 p.   illus.   27 cm.
        Reprinted from Rural Kentuckian magazine, v. 28,
        no. 1, Jan. 1974.

14199   Goff, John.
        Notes from Indian Field. By Rev. John Goff.
        (Written December 8, 1923)   Transcribed by George
        F. Doyle, M.D., F.A.C.S. [Winchester, Ky., Clark
        County Historical Society, n.d.]
        1 ℓ., 3 p.   24 cm.

14200   Gooden, Elmer Clayton, 1921-
        The life and times of Antioch Christian Church,
        Fayette County, Kentucky, by Clayton Gooden, 125th
        anniversary, 1827-1952. [n.p., 1952?]
        8, [1] ℓ.   25 cm.
        Mimeographed.
        Initials on last page: E.C.G.

14201 Goodloe, Green Clay.
... General orders, no. 2. Whereas the rebels
occupied this portion of the State they treated with
disrespect all evidences of loyalty... this camp
shall bear the name of that young lady "ELLA BISHOP."
Lexington, Ky., October 28th, 1862.
broadside. 29 x 23 cm.
At head of title: Head-quarters, 1st brigade, 2nd
division, Camp Ella Bishop, Lexington, Ky., October 28th,
1862.
This copy, presumably an unicum in the personal
library of Lawrence S. Thompson, was poorly printed,
and some parts of the text are obliterated by ink
smears.

14202 Goodman, Clavia.
Bitter harvest; Laura Clay's suffrage work...
Lexington, Ky., Bur press, 1946.
73 p. illus. 21 cm.

14203 Gospel news, or, A brief account of the revival of
religion in Kentucky, and several other parts of the
United States... Baltimore, 1801.
24 p. 21 cm.

14204 [Gottschall, Amos H   ] 1854-
Travels from ocean to ocean, and from the lakes
to the gulf; being a narrative of a twelve years'
ramble, and what was seen and experienced... By the
author of "The Chippewa's last turn"... 4th ed.
Harrisburg, Penn., A. H. Gottschall, 1894.
viii, 9-286 p. $17\frac{1}{2}$ cm.
Notes on Mammoth Cave: p. 264-274.

14205 Government Guides, Inc., Madison, Tenn.
Governmental guide 1973. [Kentucky ed.] Madison,
Tenn., 1973.
128 p. illus., map, diagrs.
Pictorial map of Kentucky on front cover.

14206 Gracchus, pseud.
Shall we have a convention? Citizens of Kentucky...
[Lexington? 1798]
22 x 28 cm.

14207 Grafton, Thomas W
Alexander Campbell, leader of the great reformation
of the nineteenth century. With an introduction by

Herbert L. Willett. St. Louis, Christian publishing
company, 1897.
xiv p., 1 ℓ., 17-234 p. front. (port.) 20½ cm.

14208 Graham, C   C
Pioneer life. William Whitley. [Louisville, 1879]
193-199 p. 26½ cm. (Louisville monthly
magazine, v. 1, no. 4, April 1879)

14209 Graham, Roscoe William.
... Charles Harold Dodd, 1884-1973. A bibliography
of his published writings... Lexington, Ky.,
Lexington Theological Seminary, 1974.
26 p. 23 cm.
At head of title: Lexington Theological Seminary
Library. Occasional studies.

14210 Grant, Anne.
A Clark County spot that was Strode's Station.
Frankfort, Kentucky Historical Society, 1967.
2 p. illus. 28 cm.
Reprinted form Kentucky heritage, v. 8, no. 1,
Fall 1967.

14211 Grant, Philip A
The Kentucky Press and the 1938 Democratic
senatorial primary. Lexington, 1974.
49-58 p. 24 cm.
Reprinted from Appalachian notes, v. 2, no. 4, 1974.

14212 Graves, George T
The sun shines bright. Kentucky scenes. Photographs
by George T. Graves; verses by Helen Howard.
Paris, Ky., Press of the Kentuckian-Citizen [1940]
[92] p. illus. 28 cm.

14213 Gray, John Thompson.
A Kentucky chronicle, by John Thompson Gray.
New York and Washington, The Neale Publishing Company,
1906.
590 p. 19½ cm.

14214 Great sale of real estate. Six tracts of land within
4 to 5 miles of Bowling-Green... October 10, 1842.
Henry Grider, com'r. [Bowling Green, Ky.? 1842?]
broadside. 41 x 28 cm.
Hummel, 705.
Original in Western Kentucky University Library.

14215 Greater Lexington Committee.
     Greater Lexington... A report of the Greater
     Lexington Committee... April 1955. [Lexington, Ky.,
     1955]
       223 p.   map, graphs, tables.   29 cm.

14216 Green, Harold Everett.
     Towering pines, the life of John Fox, Jr. ...
     Boston, Meador publishing company [1943]
       186 p.   front. (port.)
     This biography confuses John Fox, Jr., with other
     individuals.

14217 [Green, Warren]
     A Blue-grass thoroughbred; a novel by Tom Johnson
     [pseud.] Chicago, New York, Belford, Clarke & co.
     [etc., etc. c1889]
       216 p.   19½ cm.

14218 Greene, Nancy Lewis.
     Ye olde Shaker bells, by Nancy Lewis Greene.
     Records furnished by Margaret Buckner Clark.
     Lexington, Ky., 1930.
       83 p.   illus.   23½ cm.

14219 Greene, Talbot.
     The bivouac; or, Life in the Central army of
     Kentucky. By Talbot Greene, O.M.S., 26th Tennessee
     Regiment. In 10 numbers. - No. 1. Bowling-Green,
     Ky., Samuel F. Wilson, Publisher, 1861.
       41 p.   22 cm.
     No more published?
     "To the soldiers of the South," by Virginius
     Hutchen, of the Fourth Kentucky regiment, p. 41.
     At present the only known work other than broadsides
     published in any part of Kentucky under the juris-
     diction of the Confederate States of America.

14220 Greene, W   P   , ed.
     The Green River country from Bowling Green to
     Evansville, its traffic, its resources, its towns
     and its people. Embracing a history of the Green
     and Barren Rivers, and a description of the minerals
     and coal measures of the counties bordering on
     these streams. Illustrated. Edited and compiled
     by W. P. Greene. Evansville, Ind., Published by
     J. S. Reilly, 1898.
       164 p.   illus.   27 cm.

14221 Greer, Michael.
       Atlas of Kentucky licensed professions, prepared
       by Michael Greer and Nathaniel Haynes. Frankfort,
       Legislative Research Commission, 1977.
       ii, 56 p.   maps.   35 x 21½ cm.   (Informational
       bulletin, 122)

14222 Grider, George W
       Pharmacy, medicine and the Battle of Perryville,
       Kentucky, by George W. Grider and Norman H. Franke.
       [n.p.] 1862.
       2 p.   30 cm.
       Reprinted from The Kentucky pharmacist, v. 25, no. 3,
       March 1962, p. 12, 23.

14223 Griffin, Bill.
       Printing the old ways. [Louisville, Ky., 1977]
       12-13, 17 p.   illus.   27½ cm.
       Reprinted from Rural Kentuckian, v. 31, no. 1,
       December 1977.
       On the Mennonite settlement in Brockett, in
       northwest corner of Morgan County, Ky.

14224 Griffing, B   N
       An atlas of Nelson & Spencer cos., Kentucky,
       from actual surveys under the direction of B. N.
       Griffing. Philadelphia, D. J. Lake & co., 1882.
       unpaged.   maps.   38 cm.

14225 Griffith, Dorothy Amburgey.
       Amburgey ancestry in America (Amburgey ancestral
       register, indexed)   Compiled by Dorothy Amburgey
       Griffith. [St. Louis, Mo., Saint Louis Genealogical
       Society] 1976.
       xix, 208 p.   ports.   22 cm.
       Reprinted with author's permission.

14226 Griffith, Dorothy Amburgey, ed.
       1860 & 1880 U.S. censuses. Letcher Co., Kentucky.
       Transcribed and indexed by Dorothy Amburgey Griffith.
       St. Louis, Mo., Genealogical Research and Productions,
       1977.
       ii, 50, [13] p.   28 cm.
       Reprinted by permission of editor.

14227 Griswold, Thomas.
       Management of Kentucky's water resources.
       Prepared by Thomas Griswold, Judy Marlowe, Alan

McElhaney of Spindletop Research, Inc. Edited by
Brooks Talley. Frankfort, Ky., Legislative Research
Commission, 1973.
    79 p.   29 cm.   (Research report no. 110, new
series)

14228 Guerrant, Edward Owings, 1838-1916.
        The soul winner, by Rev. Edward O. Guerrant.
    Lexington, Ky., J. B. Morton & co. [1896]
        252 p.   front. (port.)   20 cm.

14229 ... A guide through Lexington and the Blue Grass.
    Famous horses and great estates. Tours, places of
    interest, highways, schools, churches, streets of
    Lexington and environs. [Lexington, Ky., 193-]
        cover-title, 64 p.   15 cm.   (Little Kit Carson,
    VI)
        Signed, p. 4: Robert J. Breckinridge.

14230 Guide to Kentucky. Bicentennial '74-'76. [Shelbyville,
    Ky., Landmark Community Newspapers, 1974?]
        unpaged.   illus., maps.   41 cm.
        Contains historical sketches of each of the 120
    counties, one to a page.

14231 Gullion, Carroll Hanks.
        Small town tales. [n.p., n.d.]
        86 p.   16 cm.

14232 Guthrie, J   D
        ... Granger axes... [Louisville? 187-]
        broadside.   27 x 18½ cm.

                            H

14233 Hackensmith, Charles William, 1906-
        Ohio Valley higher education in the nineteenth
    century, by Charles William Hackensmith. Lexington,
    Bureau of School Service, College of Education,
    University of Kentucky, 1973.
        132 p.   24 cm.   (Bureau of School Service
    Bulletin, v. 45, no. 3, March 1973)

14234 Haedens, Kléber.
        Salut au Kentucky. Roman. [Paris] Robert Laffont,

1947.
318 p.   20 cm.

14235   Hale, John Peter, 1824-
Daniel Boone: some facts and incidents not hitherto
recorded. Lexington, Ky., 1969.
12 p.   27 cm.

14236   Hale, John Peter, 1824-
Daniel Boone. Some facts and incidents not hitherto
published. His ten or twelve years' residence in
Kanawha county. Wheeling, L. Baker & co., printers
[188-]
cover-title, 18 p.   22½ cm.

14237   Hale, Will T
Early history of Warren County... McMinnville,
Tenn., Printed by Standard Printing Co., 1930.
60 p.   23½ cm.

14238   (Omitted)

14239   (Omitted)

14240   Hall, James, 1793-1868.
The Catholic question, to which are annexed
Critical notices of A plea for the west. From the
Western monthly magazine for 1835... Cincinnati
[Catholic telegraph office] 1838.
32 p.   18 cm.

14241   Hall, James, 1793-1868.
The Harpe's head; a legend of Kentucky. By
James Hall... Philadelphia, Key and Biddle, 1833.
256 p.   19 cm.

14242   Hall, James, 1793-1868.
The soldier's bride and other tales. By James
Hall... Philadelphia, Key and Biddle, 1833.
272 p.   19 cm.
Contents. - The soldier's bride. - Cousin Lucy
and the village teacher. - Empty pockets. - The
captain's lady. - The Philadelphia dun. - The
bearer of dispatches. - The village musician. -
Fashionable watering places. - The useful man. -
The dentist. - The bachelor's elysium. - Pete
Featherton. - The billiard table.

112

14243　Hall, James, 1793-1868.
　　　　　Tales of the border, by James Hall... Philadelphia,
　　　　Harrison Hall, 1835.
　　　　　276 p.　　19 cm.
　　　　　Contents. - The pioneer. - The French village. -
　　　　The spy. - The Capuchin. - The silver mine. - The
　　　　dark maid of Illinois. - The new moon.

14244　Hall, R　　　　Clifford.
　　　　　Progress report on a study of forest conditions in
　　　　Kentucky. By R. Clifford Hall, forest assistant,
　　　　Forest Service. December, 1909. [Frankfort? 1909?]
　　　　　124 p.　　tables (part fold.)　　24 cm.

14245　Hall, William Scott, 1905-
　　　　　Kentucky manufacturing, an initial report...
　　　　[Frankfort] Department of Revenue [1941]
　　　　　92 p.　　24 cm.　　(Kentucky. Department of Revenue.
　　　　Special report, 4)

14246　[Hall, William Scott] 1905-
　　　　　A report on manufacturing.　[n.p.] Committee for
　　　　Kentucky [194-]
　　　　　24 p.　　illus., map, graphs.　　24 cm.

14247　Hamill, Howard Melancthon, 1847-1915.
　　　　　The old south, a monograph.　Nashville, Tenn.,
　　　　Confederate veteran, 1905.
　　　　　79 p.　　plates, ports.　　17 cm.

14248　Hamilton, Anne, ed.
　　　　　Inside Kentucky.　Containing a bibliography of
　　　　source materials on Kentucky.　Frankfort, Kentucky
　　　　Department of Education, 1974.
　　　　　189 p.　　illus., front. (port.)　　24 cm.

14249　Hamilton, Holman, 1910-
　　　　　Kentuckians opposed presidential power.　Lexington,
　　　　Ky., 1975.
　　　　　broadside.　　ports.　　46 x 37 cm.
　　　　　Reprinted from Lexington Herald-Leader, 1 Jan.
　　　　1975.

14250　Hamilton, Holman, 1910-
　　　　　The Kentucky Civil War Round Table.　[n.p.] 1972.
　　　　　4 p.　　illus.　　29 cm.
　　　　　Reprinted from the Civil War Times, v. XI, no. 5,
　　　　August 1972.

14251 Hamilton, Holman, 1910-
Through public spirit of many, we are able to
rededicate cherished monument. Lexington, Ky., 1976.
broadside. illus. 22 x 37 cm.
Reprinted from Lexington Herald, 6 August 1976.
Appended to this are clippings concerning the
restoration of the Clay monument in the Lexington
Cemetery from the Kentucky Kernel, 29 October 1975;
Lexington Herald-Leader, 16 March 1975; Lexington
Herald-Leader, 17 March 1975; Lexington Herald,
10 June 1975 and 11 June 1975.

14252 Hamilton, Thomas, 1789-1842.
Men and manners in America. By Thomas Hamilton...
A new ed., with a protrait of the author, and letters
written by him during his journey through the United
States. Edinburgh and London, William Blackwood and
sons, 1843.
xxxvi, 454 p. 19½ cm.
Louisville: p. 325-327.

14253 Hamlett, Barksdale.
... History of education in Kentucky. Frankfort,
Kentucky department of education, 1914.
330, iv p. illus. 23½ cm.
At head of title: Bulletin of Kentucky department of
education, volume 7, July, 1914, Number 4.

14254 Hammer, Bonaventura, 1842-1917.
Der Apostel von Ohio. Ein Lebensbild des hochw.
Eduard Dominik Fenwick... Freiburg im B., Herder;
Wien, B. Herder, 1890.
ix p., 1 ℓ., 168 p. incl. front. [port.] 20 cm.

14255 Hammer, Bonaventura, 1842-1917, ed.
Unsere Bischöfe. Kurze Schilderungen aus dem Leben
und Wirken der verstorbenen Bischöfe der Vereinigten
Staaten. Gesammelt und als Prämie zum VII. Jahrgang
des Katholischen Glaubensboten herausgegeben von p.
Bonaventura Hammer... Louisville, Ky., Verlag des
"Katholischen Glaubensboten," 1872.
146 p. 16½ cm.

14256 Hamon, J Hill.
The saga of Shitty Smith, by J. Hill Hamon. [Frankfort,
Ky., Whippoorwill Press, 1971]
2 p.l., 15, [2]p. 8 x 6 cm.

"A limited edition of 100 copies bound in boards;
this is copy number 24."

14257 The hands. Prose writing class, 1955. Berea, Kentucky,
Berea College Press, 1955.
46 p.   24 cm.

14258 Hanly, Edith Sheldon.
An alluring little footpath and other Kentucky poems,
by Edith Sheldon Hanly. Illustrations by Frances
Johnson Taylor [Shouse] Louisville, Press of C.T.
Dearing printing co., 1927.
35 p.   illus.   23 cm.

14259 Hardee, Joseph Gilbert.
Town-country relations in special interest organiza-
tions, four selected Kentucky counties. By Joseph
Gilbert Hardee and Ward W. Bauder. Lexington, Kentucky
Agricultural Experiment Station, University of Kentucky,
1952.
36 p.   tables, diags.   24 cm.   (Kentucky
Agricultural Experiment Station, Bulletin, 586)

14260 Hardin, Bayless.
Lieutenant Samuel Woodfill, Kentucky's outstanding
World War soldier. Frankfort, Ky., Kentucky State
Historical Society, 1939.
2 p.   27 cm.
Describes mural by George Gray portraying Woodfill's
action at Cunel, France, 12 October 1918.

14261 Hardin, Bayless.
Sesquicentennial of Kentucky, 1792-1942. Map
showing the nine counties formed by Virginia before
Kentucky was admitted to the Union, June 1, 1792, with
their country seats and present counties with dates
of formation & early stations. Frankfort, Ky., 1942.
map.   39 x 72 cm.

14262 Hardin County, Kentucky. Fiscal court.
Important to land holders!! Attend to your titles!!
Below is a list of deeds not recorded, lying in the
clerk's office of the Hardin County court. [Elizabeth-
town, Ky.? n.d.]
broadside.   48   29 cm.
Original in Duke University Library.

115

14263   Hardin County Historical Society.
          Bulletin, v. 1, no. 1-   January 1962-
        Elizabethtown, Ky.
          Library has v. 1, no. 1.
          No more published?
          V. 1, no. 1, contains articles by John F. Blackburn,
        Hardin Countians in the Orphan Brigade and Margaret
        S. Richardson, Samuel Haycraft, Jr.

14264   Harding, Benjamin.
          A tour through the western country, A. D. 1815 &
        1819. New London, Printed by Samuel Green, for the
        author, 1819.
          2 p.l., [3]-17 p.   22½ cm.

14265   Harding, Chester.
          Letter to Governor William Owsley concerning his
        portrait of Daniel Boone. [Frankfort, Kentucky
        Historical society, n.d.]
          manuscript.   1 ℓ.   29 x 22½ cm.

14266   Hardwick, Elizabeth.
          Morning song. [Louisville, 1937]
          17-19 p.   24 cm.
          Reprinted from Dixieana, v. 1, no. 5, May 1937.
          A reverie beside the now non-existent pond in front
        of the Engineering Building of the University of Kentucky.

14267   Hare and Hare, City Planners, Landscape Architects,
          Site Planners, Kansas City, Missouri.
            Master plan of campus, University of Kentucky,
        Lexington, Ky., June 1958.
            map.   39 x 69 cm.

14268   Hargis, Thomas Frazier, 1842-1903.
          A patriot's strategy. [A novel] By Thomas F. Hargis.
        Louisville, C. T. Dearing, 1895.
          291 p.   19½ cm.

14269   Harlan labor news, v. 1, no. 1, August 1974. [Harlan,
          Ky.] 1974.
          7 p.   28 cm.
          No more published.

14270   Harris, Alfred W
          History. The progressive spirit of Parkland Lodge no.
        638 F. & A. M., 1888-1918, including the Parkland High

Twelve Club, 1911-1918, and Bright Star Chapter, no. 16,
O.E.S., 1902-1918... Compiled, enlarged and arranged by
Alfred W. Harris, P.S., P.T. [Louisville? 1918?]
149 p.   ports.   24 cm.

14271   Harris, Charles G   1869-
McDaniel family record; family of Stephen McDaniel,
sr., compiled by Charles G. Harris... assisted by Miss
Hettie C. O'Connor... Louisville, The Franklin printing
company, incorporated [1929]
1 p.l., 5-179 p. incl. ports.   22 cm.
Blank pages for "Birth record, Marriage record,
Death record" (162-179)

14272   Harris, Credo, Fitch, 1874-
Where the souls of men are calling; A love story
out of the war zone, by Credo Harris. With frontispiece
by John R. Neill. New York, A.L. Burt company [1918]
298 p.   front.   20 cm.

14273   Harris, Credo Fitch, 1874-
Toby; a novel of Kentucky, by Credo Harris. Boston,
Small, Maynard and company [1912]
4 p.l., 367 p.   19½ cm.

14274   Harris, Rufus Carrollton.
The conservation of education resources. 92nd
annual commencement, University of Kentucky. [Lexington,
1957]
10 p.   23 cm.

14275   Harrison, Ellanetta.
The stage of life; a Kentucky story, by Ellanetta
Harrison. Cincinnati, the Robert Clarke company, 1903.
iv, 252 p.   front., pl.   19 cm.

14276   Harrod, James, 1742-1793.
[Four documents by or relating to James Harrod.
Harrodsburg, 1775-1791]
Contents. Will of James Harrod, dated 28 November
1791. - Promissory note to John Slack, dated 2 October
1790. - Promissory note to Michael Cresap, dated 23
February 1775. - Warrant for James Harrod, accusing him
of trespassing on the land of William Caldwell,
dated 17 March 1787.

14277   Harrodsburg, Danville bicentennial map & guide.
         [Harrodsburg?] Harrodsburg, Danville, Burgin and
         Perryville Lions Clubs [1975?]
             map.   illus.   71 x 51 cm.

14278   Hart, Charles Henry.
             Jouett's Kentucky children.   [New York, 1900]
             51-56 p.   ports.   24 cm.
             Reprinted from Harper's new monthly magazine,
         v. 101, June 1900.

14279   Hart, Charles Henry.
             Kentucky's master-painter.   Matthew Harris Jouett,
             1788-1827.   [New York, 1899]
             [914-921] p.   illus.   24 cm.
             Reprinted from Harper's new monthly magazine, v. 98
         (1899)

14280   Hart, Lochie.
             The Kentucky Lane story, by Lockie Hart,
             Helen Hodges, Evalie Fisher, Ann Knight, Nora McGee,
             Sidney Snook Haman, Ella Rena Martin.   Illustrated
             by Dorothy H. Moore.   Paducah, Leake printing
             company [n.d.]
             51 p.   illus., map, music.   24 cm.

14281   Hart and Mapother, Civil Engineers, Louisville, Ky.
                 City of Lexington, Fayette co., Ky., 1855.   Louisville,
             Lith of Robyn Co. [1855?] Reprinted, Lexington,
             Ky., Haag and sons, engineers, 1939.
             map.   310 x 210 cm.

14282   Harvey, Prentice
             Driver licensing in Kentucky, prepared by Prentice
             Harvey.   Frankfort, Ky., Legislative Research Commission,
             1977.
             viii, 60 p.   27½ cm.   (Research report, no. 139)

14283   Harvey, Prentice A
             The multiplicity of local governments in Jefferson
             County, prepared by Prentice A. Harvey.   Frankfort,
             Ky., Legislative Research Commission, 1977.
             iii, 57 p.   map, table.   27½ cm.   (Research
             report, no. 130)

14284   Hasse, Adelaide Rosalia, 1868-1953.
             Index of economic material in documents of the United

118

States: Kentucky, 1792-1904. Prepared for the
Department of Economics and Sociology of the Carnegie
Institution of Washington... [Washington] Carnegie
Institution of Washington, 1910.
452 p. 29 cm. (On verso of t.p.: Carnegie
institution of Washington. Publication no. 85
[Kentucky]

14285 Hatcher, Mattie Austin.
Letters of an early American traveller. Mary
Austin Holley, her life and her works, 1784-1846...
Dallas, Southwest press [1933]
216 p. illus. 24½ cm.

14286 Havana scheme. Library Association Co. Lottery of
Kentucky... To be drawn in Covington, Ky., on
Tuesday, Oct. 31st, 1865... [n.p., 1865?]
broadside. 25½ x 21½ cm.

14287 Havana scheme. Shelby College lottery of the state
of the State of Kentucky... to be drawn in Covington,
Ky., on Friday, March 31, 1865... [n.p., 1865?]
broadside. 25½ x 21½ cm.

14288 Haviland, Mrs. Laura [Smith] 1808-1898.
A woman's life-work: labors and experience of
Laura S. Haviland. Cincinnati, Printed by Walden &
Stowe, 1882.
2 p.l., 520 p. front. [port.] plates. 19½ cm.

14289 [Hawks, Francis Lister] 1798-1866.
The adventures of Daniel Boone, the Kentucky
rifleman. By the author of "Uncle Philip's con-
versations". New York, D. Appleton & co. [etc.]
1850.
174 p. incl. front. 15½ cm.

14290 Hawley, J   F
Cholera in Lexington [letter to four Lexington
physicians, 14 June 1833] Lexington, University of
Kentucky Library, 1963.
cover-title, 4 l., facsim. 26 cm. (University
of Kentucky Library Associates, Keepsake no. 12)
Commentary by Kurt W. Deuschle.

14291 Haycraft, Samuel, 1795-1878.
          Haycraft's History of Elizabethtown, Kentucky, by
       R. Gerald McMurtry... a supplement to the first and
       second editions. [Elizabethtown? n.d.]
          [12] p.   illus.   22 cm.

14292 Haynes, Donald, ed.
          Virginiana in the printed book collections of the
       Virginia State Library, edited by Donald Haynes.
       Richmond, Virginia State Library, 1975.
          2 v.   31 cm.
          Includes Kentucky to 1792.

14293 Haynes, Nathaniel.
          County government in Kentucky (revised 1976)
       Prepared by Nathaniel Haynes, Jr. Edited by Gary
       W. Luhr. Frankfort, Legislative Research Commission,
       1976.
          viii, 164 p.   27 cm.   (Informational bulletin,
       no. 115)

14294 Hazard, Ky. Bowman Memorial Methodist Church. Woman's
       Society of Christian Service.
          Hazard cook book. Hazard, 1942.
          115 p.   22 cm.

14295 Hazard, Ky., Christian Church. Mildred Faulkner
       Auxiliary.
          Ideal cook book. Compiled and published by the
       Mildred Faulkner Auxiliary of the Christian Church,
       Hazard, Kentucky. Second edition. Hazard, The
       Hazard Leader print, 1927.
          75 p.   23 cm.

14296 Hazelrigg, John T
          Historical address upon the occasion of the
       centennial anniversary of the Declaration of
       American independence, July 4, 1876, by John T.
       Hazelrigg... West Liberty, Ky., Morgan county publ.
       co., 1913.
          2 p.l., 16 p.   23 cm.

14297 Healy, George Peter Alexander, 1813-1894.
          Reminiscence of a portrait painter, by George
       P.A. Healy. Chicago, A.C. McClurg and company, 1894.
          ix p., 1 l., [13]-221 p.   21 port. (incl. front.)
       19½ cm.

Contents. - pt. 1. A sketch of my life. - pt. 2.
My friends and my sitters: Thomas Couture. Crowns and
coronets. American statesmen. French statesmen. Men
of letters.

14298 Heck, Earl L   W
James Lane Allen, a classical tragedian. [Frankfort,
Ky., 1932]
31, 47 p.   port., illus.   28½ cm.
Reprinted from Kentucky progress magazine, v. 4,
no. 10, p. 31, 47, June 1932.

14299 Heger, Herbert K   , ed.
Urban education, Kentucky style, Lexington, Bureau
of School Service, University of Kentucky, 1973.
72 p.   illus.   23 cm.   (Bureau of School
Service, Bulletin, XLV, 4)

14300 Heikel, Felix, 1844-1921.
Från Förenta Staterna. Nitton bref jemte bihang.
Helsingfors, Hufvudstadsbladet [1973]
184 p. (facsim.), xix p.   port.   20 cm.
"Felix-Heikel — en Finlandssvensk liberal," by
Torsten Steinby, p. i-xix.
Contents. - 1. Öfverfarten. - 2. Ytan af New York.
Färd till Boston. - 3. Från Boston till Washington via
Hartford och Baltimore. - 4. Undervisningsväsendet. - 5.
Ett besök i en folkskola, jemte ett p.s. om Newton.
-6. Ett folkbibliothek. - 7. Ett fängelse. - 8. Staten
och religionen. - 9. Lowell och Lawrence samt arbetarens
samhallsställning och vilkor. - 10. Qvinnans rättigheter.
-11. State House och litet politik. - 12. City hall
och town meeting. - 13. Från Castle Garden till Niagara.
-14. Allting och ingenting från Ohio. - 15. Kentucky
och Tennessee samt något om tillståndet i Södern.
-16. Prairierna och Chicago. - 17. Michigan och
hushållningen med publikt land. - 18. Slutfest i en
high school, magisterpromotion m.m. - 19. Familjelif
och gästfrihet.

14301 Helay, George Peter Alexander, 1813-
Reminiscences of a portrait painter... Chicago,
A.C. McClurg and company, 1894.
[13]-221 p.   21 port. [incl. front.]   19½ cm.

14302 Helm, Benjamin.
Allie in Beulah land, or, Swanannoa camp-meeting.

A Kentucky story... Louisville, Pentecostal
publishing co. [1901]
284 p.   illus.   22 cm.

14303 Henderson, Archibald, 1877-1963.
The conquest of the old southwest; the romantic
story of the early pioneers into Virginia, the
Carolinas, Tennessee, and Kentucky, 1740-1790. New
York, Century, 1920.
395 p.   front., fold.   map.   20 cm.
Inscribed by author

14304 Henderson, Archibald, 1877-1963.
Isaac Shelby, Revolutionary patriot and border
hero. Raleigh, N.C., 1917.
cover-title, 109-188 p.   front. (port.)   24 cm.
Reprinted from the North Carolina booklet, xvi, no. 3,
January, 1917.
Cover title reads: Part I. - 1750-1780. Part II
never published?

14305 Henderson, Archibald, 1877-1963.
Memorial celebration in honor of the Transylvania
Company and the founding of Henderson at Henderson,
Kentucky, October 11, 1929 [Henderson, Ky., 1929]
cover-title, [16]p.   illus.   23½ cm.

14306 Henderson, Archibald, 1877-1963.
The Transylvania company and the founding of
Henderson, Ky., by Archibald Henderson... [Henderson?
Ky., 1929]
cover-title, 2 p.l., 15 p.   illus., ports.
25 x 19½ cm.
Portrait on cover.

14307 Henderson, Mrs. S   E
Jelard [a novel] By Mrs. S. E. Henderson. Logansport,
Ind., Longwell & Cummings, 1892.
554 p.   20 cm.

14308 Henderson, Thomas.
An easy system of the geography of the world; by way
of question and answer. Principally designed for schools.
By Thomas Henderson... Lexington, Ky. Printed by
Thomas T. Skillman, 1813.
213 p.   17 cm.
Signatures: A-R^6, S^5 (last verso blank) Each signature

marked on only 1st and 3d leaf, the latter being signed
A2, B2, etc.
Advertisement written at "Great Crossing academy,
Scott county, Ky."
Appendix (p. [161]-213) devoted mainly to the Mississippi
valley, with a chapter on the British possessions in
North America.

14309 Henry Clay's first biographer. Fort Wayne, Ind., 1974.
       4 p.   port.   29 cm.   (Lincoln lore, no. 1631)

14310 Henry, Josephine K
       Musings in life's evening, by Josephine K. Henry,
       Versailles, Ky. [n.d.]
       18 p.   16½ cm.

14311 Henshall, James Alexander, 1844-1925.
       Book of the black bass, comprising its complete
       scientific and life history together with a practical
       treatise on angling and fly fishing and a full
       description of tools, tackle and implements...
       Cincinnati, Robert Clarke & co., 1881.
       436 p.   illus.   20 cm.

14312 Herndon, James.
       A selective bibliography of materials in state
       government and politics, compiled and edited by
       James Herndon, Charles Press [and] Oliver P. Williams.
       Lexington, Ky., Bureau of Government Research,
       University of Kentucky, 1963.
       143 p.   18 cm.
       Kentucky: p. 48-50.

14313 Herndon, William Henry, 1818-1891.
       Abraham Lincoln; Miss Ann Rutledge. Pioneering,
       and the poem. [Springfield, Ill.? 1866]
       42½ x 60 cm.
       In eight columns.

14314 Herndon, William Henry, 1818-1891.
       Lincoln and Herndon— religion and romance.
       Lexington, University of Kentucky Library Associates,
       1959.
       3 p.   facsim.   34 cm.   (Keepsake, no. 6)
       Two facsimiles of lectures by Herndon, "Lincoln's
       religion" ("State Register, Supplement") and Abraham

Lincoln. Miss Ann Rutledge. New Salem. Pioneering, and The Poem."

14315 Herndon, William Henry, 1818-1891.
Lincoln's religion. [n.p., n.d.]
In eight columns.
At head of title: State register, supplement.

14316 Herrmann, Jesse, 1884-1953.
James McChord - a portrait, by Jesse Herrmann...
Lexington, Ky., Transylvania Press, 1940.
vii, 70 p. incl. front. (port.) illus. 21 cm.

14317 Hersey, Dr.
An oration delivered in Greensburg, Pennsylvania,
by Dr. Hersey, at the celebration of the anniversary
of the Declaration of Independence, July 4th, 1808.
Danville, Ky., Thomas P. Moore, printer, 1814.
20 p.
On p. 9-19: War the work of the Lord, and the
coward cursed; a sermon by Joshua Lacy Wilson.

14318 Hewett, John B
The Kentucky gentleman... dedicated to Henry Clay,
the farmer of Ashland... New York, John F. Nunns [n.d.]
2 ℓ., 4-7 p. cover port., music. 36 cm.
Includes words.
The original of this text was in the possession of
Elliott Shapiro, 118 West 79th Street, New York, in
Februrary 1943. The original connot now be located.
The manuscript note by Henry Clay was faded at the
time of copying. The present "photostatic" copy,
now possibly unique, is in the private library of
Lawrence S. Thompson, Lexington, Ky.

14319 Heywood, John Healy, 1818-1902.
Judge John Speed and his family. A paper prepared
for the Filson club, and read at its meeting, June 4,
1894. Louisville, J. P. Morton & company, 1894.
35 p. 22 cm.

14320 Heywood, Robert, 1786-1868.
A Journey to America in 1834, by Robert Heywood...
[Cambridge, Eng.] Priv. print., 1919.
viii, 112 p. 22 cm.
Cover-title: Diary of a journey to America in 1834.
"One hundred copies printed for the editor by J. B.

Peace, M.A., at the University press, Cambridge."
Edited by Mrs. Mary (Heywood) Haslam.

14321　Hickman County [Ky.] Gazette. 100th anniversary edition.
Thursday, 30 April 1953. Clinton, Ky., 1953.
140 p.　illus.　54 x 40 cm.

14322　Hightower, Raymond Lee.
Joshua L. Wilson, frontier controversialist.
[n.p., 1934]
16 p.　27 cm.

14323　Hightower, Ted.
History of Broadway Methodist Church, Paducah,
Kentucky, 1834-1945, by Rev. Ted Hightower...
[Paducah, Ky.] Broadway Methodist Church, 1945.
115 p. incl. plates, ports.　$22\frac{1}{2}$ cm.

14324　Hill, Jerry D
Climate of Kentucky. Lexington, Ky., University of
Kentucky, Agricultural Experiment Station [1976]
88 p.　maps, tables.　28 cm.

14325　Hill, Joseph D
The Macedonia Christian Church. Lexington, Ky., 1938.
51 p.　plates, ports.　$23\frac{1}{2}$ cm.

14326　Hill Richard H
The Filson Club's seventy-fifth anniversary (1884-
1959). Louisville, 1959.
187-194 p.　24 cm.
In The Filson Club history quarterly, vol. 33, no. 3,
July 1959. The entire issue is reprinted here, with
permission of the Director of the Filson Club, since
it contains supporting information on Mr. Hill's article.

14327　Hillery, George A
Population growth in Kentucky, 1820-1960. By George
A. Hillery, Jr. Lexington, Kentucky Agricultural
Experiment Station, University of Kentucky, 1966.
54 p.　maps, tables, diags.　24 cm.　(Kentucky
Agricultural Experiment Station, Bulletin, 705)
Errata sheet at end.

14328　Hirsch, Nathaniel David Mttron, 1896-
... An experimental study of the east Kentucky
mountaineers; a study in heredity and environment,

125

from the psychological laboratories of Harvard
university and Duke university, by Nathaniel D.
Mttron Hirsch... Worcester, Mass., Clark university,
c1928.
   3 p.l., p. [189]-244.   25 cm.   (Genetic psychology
monographs... vol. III, no. 3)

14329 Historical catalogue of Georgetown college, 1829-
       1917... Georgetown, Ky., The Georgetown news press
       [1917]
          111 p.   19½ cm.

14330 History of Cincinnati and Hamilton County, Ohio; their
       past and present, including early settlement and
       development; antiquarian researches; their aboriginal
       history; pioneer history; political organization;
       agricultural, mining and manufacturing interests; a
       history of the city, villages and townships; religious,
       educational, social, military and political history;
       statistics; biographies and portraits of pioneers
       and representative citizens, etc. Illustrated.
       Cincinnati, S. B. Nelson & co., 1894.
          1056 p.   illus.   27 cm.

14331 History of the Ohio falls cities and their counties, with
       illustrations and biographical sketches. Cleveland,
       O., L.A. Williams & co., 1882.
          2 v.   plates, ports., 2 maps [incl. front.: v. 2]
       facsim.   28 cm.

14332 Hitchcock, Champion Ingraham.
          The dead men's song: being the story of a poem and
       a reminiscent sketch of its author, Young Ewing
       Allison, together with a browse through other gems
       of his and recollections of older days, by his friend
       and associate Champion Ingraham Hitchcock. Louisville,
       Ky., 1914.
          93 p.   25 cm.
          In pocket at end are facsimiles of three letters
       written by Allison and three letters from Allison
       to Frederick Gronberg.
          Inscribed by Hitchcock and Allison.

14333 Hobbs, E   D
          City of Louisville and its enlargements in 1832.
       Drawn by E. E. Hobbs, city surveyor; for Prentice &
       Buxton & R. W. Otis. Engraved by Doolittle & Munson.

[Louisville? 1832]
map.   40 x 53 cm.
Originally drawn to accompany The Louisville
directory for the year 1832... (Louisville, 1832),
but no known copy of the book contains this map.
The original of the photograph, from which this
Microcard edition was made, was once in the Filson
Club but cannot presently be located there. No
other copy is known.

14334   Hockersmith, Lorenzo Dow, 1833-
Morgan's escape. A thrilling story of war times.
A true history of the raid of General Morgan and
his men through Kentucky, Indiana and Ohio... Madison-
ville, Ky., Glenn's graphic print, 1903.
iv, [5]-54 p. incl. port., plan.   22cm.

14335   Hodge, Fronza Gail.
The story of Boonesborough. Frankfort, Kentucky
Historical Society, 1967.
1 p.   28 cm.
Reprinted from Kentucky heritage, v. 8, no. 1,
Fall 1967.

14336   Hodge, James M
Coals of the North Fork of Kentucky River in
Breathitt and Perry Counties. [Frankfort, Kentucky,
State Journal company, printers to the Commonwealth,
1915]
[xvi], 409 p.   tables.   27 cm.   (Kentucky
Geological Survey, ser. IV, v. 3, pt. 3)

14337   Hodge, James M
... Report on the coals of the three forks of the
Kentucky River, beginning at Troublesome Creek on
North Fork; at Beginning Branch on Middle Fork; at
Sexton Creek on South Fork; and extending to the
heads of the respective forks... Louisville, The
Continental printing company, 1910.
[xx], 280 p.   illus., tables, graphs, fold. map in
pocket at end.   27 cm.
At head of title: Kentucky Geological Survey,
Charles J. Norwood, director, Bulletin no. 11.

14338   Holing, J   B
... Oil and gas sands of Kentucky... Louisville,
Printed by the Geo. W. Fetter co., 1905.

233 p.   illus., fold. map.   27 cm.   (Kentucky
geological survey, Bulletin no. 1)

14339 Holladay, Harriett MacDonald.
A wild flower book, with ten woodcuts by Harriett
MacDonald Holladay. [Lexington, n.d.]
[14]p.   illus.   24½ cm.
Introduction by Rena Niles.

14340 Holley, Horace, 1781-1827.
A discourse occasioned by the death of Col. James
Morrison, delivered in the Episcopal church,
Lexington, Kentucky, May 19th, 1823. Lexington,
Printed by J. Bradford, 1823.
37 p.   21½ cm.

14341 Holliday, Fernandez C   1814-1888.
Life and times of Rev. Allen Wiley, A. M. ...
Edited by Rev. D. W. Clark. D. D. Cincinnati, L.
Swormstedt & A. Poe, for the Methodist Episcopal
church, 1853.
291 p.   18½ cm.

14342 Holman, Jesse Lynch, 1784-1842.
The prisoners of Niagara, or, Errors of education...
[Berea, Ky., Kentucky imprints, 1973]
367 p.   23½ cm.
"Introduction to the 1973 edition, " by Will
Fridy, p. 363-366.

14343 Holmes, Daniel Henry, 1851-1908.
Under a fool's cap: songs, by Daniel Henry Holmes.
Portland, Maine, Printed for Thomas B. Mosher and
published by him, 1914.
xvi, 101 p.   18 cm.
"Foreword" by T. B. M. [Thomas Bird Mosher]:
p. xi-xvi.

14344 Hopkins, Patricia M
Court of justice; a look at Kentucky's new judicial
systems, prepared by Patricia M. Hopkins.
Frankfort, Ky., Legislative Research Commission, 1977.
iii, 14 p.   maps.   21 cm.

14345 Hopkins, Porter H
KEA. The first hundred years. The history of an
organization, 1857-1957... For the centennial of the

Kentucky education association. Louisville, 1957.
95 p.   24 cm.

14346   Hopkins, Robert Milton.
          Dr. Hopkins, the mission leader, by Robert M.
        Hopkins, jr. [Lexington, Ky., 195-?]
          7 p.   28 cm.   .
        cover-title with port.

14347   Horine, Emmet Field, 1885-1964.
          Cincinnatian unique: Daniel Drake. [1952]
          23 p.   illus., ports.   26 cm.
        "...address before the Academy of Medicine of
        Cincinnati, Ohio, May 27, 1952. Reprinted from the
        Daniel Drake Memorial Edition of the Cincinnati
        Journal of Medicine," v. 33, May, 1952.

14348   Horine, Emmet Field, 1885-1964.
          Daniel Drake and his contributions to education.
        Louisville, 1941.
          11 p.   25 cm.
        Bibliographical footnotes.
        Reprinted from Bibliographical Society of America.
        Papers. [Portland, Me., 1940] v. 34, p. 303-314.

14349   Horine, Emmet Field, 1885-1964.
          Daniel Drake and his medical classic. Bowling
        Green, Ky., Kentucky State Medical Association, 1952.
          [14] p.   illus.   27 cm.
        Bibliographical footnotes.
        Reprinted from the Journal of the Kentucky State
        Medical Association, v. 50, p. 68-79, Feb. 1952.
        Inscribed by author.

14350   Hough, Emerson, 1857-1923.
          The way to the West, and the lives of three early
        Americans, Boone -- Crockett -- Carson... with
        illustrations by Frederic Remington. Indianapolis,
        The Bobbs-Merrill company [1903]
          5 p.l., 446 p.   front., plates. $19\frac{1}{2}$ cm.

14351   Hough, Emerson, 1868-1923.
          The way out; a story of the Cumberlands to-day,
        by Emerson Hough... Illustrated by J. Henry. New
        York, London, D. Appleton and company, 1918.
          6 p.l., 3-213, 1 p.   front., plates. $19\frac{1}{2}$ cm.

14352   The House of Belle Breezing (a lament for that historic
        monument destined soon for destruction in Lexington's
        program of urban renewal)   Lexington, Ky.   May, 1961.
          Poem signed "Anonymous", but it is believed that the
        author may be identified in the University of Kentucky
        Library archives.
          Appended: Article from Kentucky Kernel (University of
        Kentucky student newspaper), vol. LIII, no. 62, 9 Feb.
        1962, p. 1-2, entitled: "Citizens oppose razing of
        Belle Breezing house."

14353   Houston, F   W
          Joel T. Hart. A chapter from his early life; the
        nadir and zenith of his glory. Lexington, Ky., 1940.
          7 p.   29½ cm.
          Typed copy of article in Paris (Ky.) True Kentuckian,
        4 April 1877.

14354   Hovey, Horace Carter, 1833-1914.
          Mammoth Cave of Kentucky; an illustrated manual,
        by Horace Carter Hovey... and Richard Ellsworth Call.
        Louisville, J. P. Morton and company, 1899.
          v, [1],111, [1] p.   13 pl. [incl. front. map.]
        22 cm.

14355   Howard, H[enry] Clay.
          ...Caleb Powers, appellant, vs. The Commonwealth of
        Kentucky, appellee. Brief for appellant on validity of
        pardon... Lexington, Ky., Press of Jas. E. Hughes [n.d.]
          32 p.   27 cm.
          At head of title: Kentucky Court of Appeals.

14356   Howard, Mrs. Virginia Webb.
          Bryan Station heroes and heroines; being a historical
        sketch of Bryan Station from 1779 to 1932, including
        pen sketches of the heroes and heroines... [Lexington,
        Ky., Press of the Commercial print. co., 1932]
          168 p.   illus.   24 cm.

14357   Howlett, William Joseph, 1848-
          A review of Father O'Daniel's estimate of the early
        secular missionaries of Kentucky... [Louisville? n.d.]
          24 p.   23 cm.

14358   Hoyt, R   D
          An annotated list of fishes from the upper Salt River,
        Kentucky. [By] R.D. Hoyt, S.E. Neff, and L.A. Krumholz.

[n.p.] 1970.
51-63 p.   map., diags.   23 cm.
Reprinted from Transactions of the Kentucky Academy of Science, v. 31, nos. 3-4, 1970.

14359 Huddleston, Eugene L
Place names in the writings of Jesse Stuart.   [n.p.]
California Folklore Society, 1972.
169-177 p.   24 cm.
At end: Letter form Mr. Stuart about Kentucky place names.

14360 Huddleston, Walter Dee.
Dr. Robert R. Martin.   [Washington, D. C., 1976]
S12423-S12424 p.   28 cm.
Reprinted from Congressional record, Senate, 26 July 1976.

14361 Huddleston, Walter Dee.
Henderson, Ky. - A great place to live.   Washington, D. C., 1976.
S6018-S6019 p.   28 cm.
Reprinted from the Congressional record, Senate, 27 April 1976.

14362 Hughes, Paul.
Prototype of a Kentucky gentleman.   [Louisville, 1953]
broadside.   prot., illus.   42 x 40 cm.
Reprinted from Louisville Courier-Journal, 6 Sept. 1953.
Attached to this are obituaries of Judge O'Rear from the Lexington Herald, Lexington Leader, Louisville Courier-Journal for 13 Sept 1961 and on his 97th and 98th birthdays from the Lexington Herald for 3 Feb. 1960 and 3 Feb. 1961.

14363 Hughes, William Joseph Leander, 1844-
The Hughes family and connections, especially the Gass, Ward and Boze families.   By W. J. L. Hughes.
Owensboro, Ky., 1911. Reprinted, Evansville, Ind., Unigraphic, Inc., 1974.
xvii p., [5], 19-89 p.   ports.   22 cm.
Index, p. 165-196, added to this ed.

14364 Hulme, Thomas.
...I. Journal of a tour in the west... II. Letters from Lexington and the Illinois... by Richard Flower.   III.

Letters from Illinois, 1820-21, by Richard Flower.
IV. Two years' residence in the settlement on the
English prairie, in the Illinois country... by John
Woods. Edited with note, introductions, index, etc.
by Reuben Gold Thwaites... Cleveland, The Arthur H.
Clark company, 1904.
357 p.   illus.   24 cm.   (Early western travels,
1748-1846, v. X)
At head of title: Early western travels.

14365   Hume, Edgar Erskine, 1889-1952.
Lafayette in Kentucky... With an introduction by
His Excellency M. André de Laboulaye, ambassador of
France in Washington. Frankfort, Ky., Published by
Transylvania College and the Society of the Cincinnati
in the State of Virginia, 1937.
115 p.   front. (port.)   26½ cm.

14366   Humphreys, Charles.
A compendium of the common law in force in Kentucky,
to which is prefixed a brief summary of the laws of
the United States. By Charles Humphreys. Lexington,
Ky., Printed by William Gibbes Hunt, 1822.
xi, 594 p.   20 cm.

14367   Hunt, William Gibbes, 1791-1833.
An appeal to the public, in consequence of an attack
by Rev. Nathan H. Hall, made in the Argus of western
America, on the 4th of February, 1824, in an anonymous
article signed Spectator... Lexington [Ky.] Printed
at the office of the Western monitor, 1824.
15 p.   21½ cm.

14368   Hunter Ham; or, The outlaw's crime.
New York, Beadle and Adams [1870]
102 p.   16½ cm.
Attributed to J. Edgar Iliff, 1825-

14369   Hussey, John.
... Report on the botany of Barren and Edmonson
counties... with an introduction by N. S. Shaler.
[Frankfort, n.d.]
32 p.   27½ cm.
At head of title: Geological survey of Kentucky.
N. S. Shaler, director. (Part II, vol. 1, second series)

14370 Hutchins, Thomas, 1730-1789.
       A topographical description of Virginia, Pennsylvania,
       Maryland, and North Carolina; reprinted from the
       original edition of 1778; edited by Frederick Charles
       Hicks. Cleveland, The Burrows brothers company, 1904.
       143 p.   fold. map [in pocket] 2 plans, fold.
       facsim., fold. tab.   25 cm.

14371 Hutton, Daniel Mac-Hir.
          Ephraim McDowell. [Harrodsburg, Ky., 1960]
          36 p.   illus.   21 cm.
          "Second edition".

14372 Hutton, Daniel Mac-Hir.
          The garb of the pioneer influenced by that of the
       Indian; how the skins of animals were employed as
       substitutes for cloth. Harrodsburg, Ky. [n.d.]
          cover-title, [6]p.   illus.   24 cm.

14373 Hyland, Peggy.
          Physician man power in Kentucky: supply and
       distribution, prepared by Peggy Hyland. Frankfort,
       Ky., Legislative Research Commission, 1977.
          viii, 88 p.   maps, tables.   28 cm.   (Research
       report no. 133)

14374 Hymns and spiritual songs, for the use of Christians;
       including a number never before published. Lexington,
       Ky., Printed and sold by Joseph Charless, 1803.
          246, 6 p.   12½ cm.

                              I

14375 Imlay, Gilbert, ca. 1754-1828?
          A topographical description of the western
       territory of North America... The third ed., with
       great additions. London, Printed for J. Debrett, 1797.
          598, [28] p.   fold. maps.   22½ cm.

14376 Imordes, Inc., Louisville, Ky.
          Louisville in 1873, a reminiscence. [Louisville, n.d.]
          [8] p.   17 cm.
          cover title (illus.)

                            133

14377   In Kentucky. [Frankfort, Department of Public Relations,
        n.d.]
            32 p.   illus., map.   28 cm.
            An album made up from illustrations in the Department's
        periodical, In Kentucky.

14378   In memoriam. Curtis Field Burnam. Printed privately.
        [Louisville, Ky., Press of J.P. Morton & company,
        incorporated, 19--?]
            48 p., front. [port.]   27½ cm.

14379   In memoriam. Proceedings of the Lexington bar and certain
        memorial resolutions adopted on the occasion of the death
        of John Todd Shelby... Lexington, Ky. [Press of the
        Westerfield-Bonte company, Louisville, Ky.] 1920.
            52 p.   port.   23½ cm.
            cover-title: In memoriam John Todd Shelby, a tribute
        by the Lexington bar.

14380   Index of names to History of county of Christian,
        Kentucky. Historical and biographical. Edited by
        William H. Perrin. Chicago and Louisville, F. A.
        Battey Publishing Co., 1884. [Evansville, Ind.?
        Unigraphic, Inc., 1973?]
            17 p.   25 cm.

14381   Inman, Henry, 1837-1899.
            A pioneer from Kentucky; an idyl of the Raton Range
        [by] Colonel Henry Inman. Topeka, Kan., Crane &
        company, 1898.
            2 p.l.,   3-160 p.   front.   18 cm.

14382   International Banana Festival links the Americas.
        Fulton, Kentucky, and South Fulton, Tennessee, bridge
        the miles from Latin America with annual festival.
        [n.p., 1973]
            2 p.   illus.   28 cm.
            Reprinted from Holiday Inn International Magazine,
        July/August, 1973, p. 61-62.

14383   Irvin, Helen Deiss.
            Hail Kentucky! A pictorial history of the University
        of Kentucky... with an introduction by Holman Hamilton.
        [Lexington] Published for the University of Kentucky
        Centennial committee by the University of Kentucky

press [1965]
103 p.   illus., facsims.   29 cm.

14384   Irvin S. Cobb, the man with a cigar. [Frankfort, Ky.
Department of the Public Relations, 1957]
22-24 p.   port.   28 cm.
Reprinted from In Kentucky, v. 19, no. 5, Summer
1957.

14385   Irvine, Donald V
Bondage of midnight. [n.p., n.d.]
4 p.   20 cm.

14386   [Isenberg, James L   ] comp.
Harrodsburg's national historic pre-eminence.
Harrodsburg, Ky., Published by the Harrodsburg
Herald [n.d.]
[9] p.   23cm.

J

14387   J.R. Golladay's thirty-first monthly drawing.
Lebanon, Ky., January 24th, 1870... net proceeds are
for the purpose of a paper in raised letters for the use
of the blind... Bowling Green, Ky. [1870?]
broadside. 54 x 20 cm.
Hummel, 760.
Original in Western Kentucky University Library.

14388   J.R. Golladay's thirty-eighth monthly drawing.
Elizabethtown, Kentucky, August 22, 1870...
Golladay & Smith, dealers in books and pianos,
Bowling Green, Ky. Bowling Green, Democrat print
[1870?]
broadside.   13 x 53 cm.
Hummel, 759.
Original in University of Alabama Library.

14389   Jackson, Margaret A
Memoirs of the Rev. William Jackson, first
rector of St. Paul's church, Louisville... with
an introduction by the Right Rev. William Meade...
New York, Protestant Episcopal society for the

promotion of evangelical knowledge [n.d.]
xx, 408 p.   front. (port.)   20 cm.

14390 Jackson, W   E
Kentucky forest trees and how to know them, by W. E.
Jackson, James A. Newman, and Stanley B. Carpenter.
Lexington, University of Kentucky, College of
Agriculture, Cooperative Extension Service [n.d.]
89 p.   illus.   23½ cm.   (Circular 532)

14391 Jansen, William Hugh.
The rationale of the dirty joke. Lexington, Ky.,
1975.
13-15 p.   illus.   29 cm.
Reprinted from the Kentucky alumnus, v. 45, no. 2,
Spring 1975.
Distinguished Professor Lecture at the University
of Kentucky, 1974.

14392 Jefferson, Wade Hampton.
The bicentennial polka. Lexington, Ky., 1975.
7 p.   music.   31 cm.
Reprinted by permission of the author.
At end is Buckley Hills Audubon Society Newsletter,
July-August 1976 (1 p.) with photograph of author.

14393 Jennings, Walter Wilson.
Transylvania, pioneer university of the west.
New York, Pageant press [1955]
321 p.   24 cm.

14394 [Jett, Ann Searcy] 1843-
A Kentucky girl; or, A question unanswered, by Ann
Se Arcy [pseud.] Berea, Ky., Printing department,
Berea College, 1909.
4 p.l., 7-111 p.   front. (port.) pl.   20 cm.

14395 Jewell, James William, 1889-
Biting tales of rattlesnakes and men. [Frankfort, Ky.,
1949]
cover-title, 48 p.   23 cm.

14396 Jewell, James William, 1889-
End of the feud and other Kentucky legends, by
James W. Jewell. New York, Exposition press
[1952]

80 p.   22 cm.
Reprinted with author's permission.

14397   Jewell, James William, 1889-
Folklore: love: verse. A survey of folklore love
rhymes in more than forty states, and the development
of these love rhymes into full fledged poems plus
many original love poems, by James William Jewell.
Frankfort, Ky., 1951.
170 p.   28 cm.

14398   Jewell, James Willaim, 1889-
Girls behind the man from 1905 to 1945, by James
W. Jewell. Frankfort, Ky., Roberts Printing Company,
1955.
35 p.   23 cm.

14399   Jewell, James William, 1889-
Kentucky days. Lexington, Ky., Lang co., 1950.
92 p.   28 cm.

14400   Jewell, James William, 1889-
Kentucky mountian melodies, by James William Jewell.
[Lexington, Ky., The Lang Company, 1950]
266 p.   music.   28 cm.

14401   Jewell, James William, 1889-
"Melee" (woman in command) [by] James William
Jewell. [Lexington, Ky., Lang co., 1951]
64 p.   28 cm.

14402   Jewell, James William, 1889-
My God and my country, by James William Jewell.
Frankfort, Ky., Roberts printing company, 1951.
90 p.   24 cm.
Poems.

14403   Jewell, James William, 1889-
My Kentucky, by James W. Jewell. Plain verse
of a mountain man from Old Kentucky. (With a
foreword by Dr. William M. Moore, associate
professor of journalism, University of Kentucky)
[Lexington, Ky., The Lang co., 195-]
123 p.   29 cm.

14404   Jewell, James William 1889-
My sojourn in that wonder state; simple verse on

137

distinctive Arkansas subjects, by James W. Jewell.
[Lexington, Ky., The Lang company, 1950]
[12] 135 p.   (Chapter headings unpaged)   28 cm.
"Foreword" by William M. Moore: p. [iii]

14405 [Jewell, James William] 1889-
Pastors versus poets (a reading for three)
[Frankfort, Kentucky, n.d.]
15 p.   19½ cm.

14406 Jewell, James William, 1889-
Selected speech rhymes, by James William Jewell...
Frankfort, Ky., Roberts printing company, 1951
109 p.   24 cm.

14407 Jewell, James William, 1889-
Unique life portraits portrayed in simple verse
[by] James W. Jewell. Lexington, Ky., The Lang
company [1951]
[10], 123 p.   28 cm.

14408 Jewell, James William, 1889-
Verse with news significance, by James William
Jewell. [Frankfort, Ky.?] 1951.
54 p.   24 cm.

14409 Jewert, Russell J
State-Federal income tax conformity in Kentucky.
Frankfort, Ky., Legislative Research Commission,
1961.
33 p.   29 cm.   (Research report no. 8)

14410 The Jill Raymond case. [Lexington, Ky., 1975-1976]
Portfolio of fifty-three clippings from Lexington
Herald and Kentucky Kernel between 14 March 1975 and
5 May 1976 and of three broadsides relative to
incarceration of Jill Raymond for refusal to answer
Grand Jury questions.
"Introduction" by Lawrence S. Thompson.

14411 Jillson, Willard Rouse, 1890-1975.
The advance of geology in Kentucky during one
hundred and thirty-four years (1784-1918) [by]
Willard Rouse Jillson. [Louisville, Ky.? 1965]
48-57 p.   23 cm.
Reprint from Transactions of the Kentucky Academy
of Science, v. 25, nos. 1-2, 1965.

14412   Jillson, Willard Rouse, 1890-1975.
        The answering silhouettes: an historical geological
        apostrophe, by Willard Rouse Jillson, 'state geologist
        of Kentucky. Frankfort, Kentucky Geological survey,
        1931.
        [6]p.   illus.   23 cm.   (Kentucky. Geological
        Survey, 1920-   Ser. VI. Pamphlet no. 27)

14413   Jillson, Willard Rouse, 1890-1975.
        A bibliography of Bath County, Kentucky. Citations
        of printed and manuscript sources touching upon its
        history, cartography, geology, paleontology, and
        mineral resources with annotations (1791-1961) by
        Willard Rouse Jillson... Frankfort, Roberts printing
        co., 1966.
        27 p.   23 cm.

14414   Jillson, Willard Rouse, 1890-1975.
        A bibliography of Clark County, Kentucky.
        Citations of printed and manuscript sources touching
        upon its history, geology, calcite, barite, fluorite,
        galenite, sphalerite, pyrite, oil and gas with brief
        annotations, by Willard Rouse Jillson... Frankfort,
        Roberts printing co., 1963.
        15 p.   23 cm.

14415   Jillson, Willard Rouse, 1890-1975.
        A bibliography of Henry County, Kentucky.
        Citations of printed and manuscript sources touching
        upon its history, geology, paleontology, calcite,
        barite, fluorite, sphalerite, galenite, pyrite, oil
        and gas with annotations (1751-1962), by Willard
        Rouse Jillson... Frankfort, Roberts printing co.,
        1963.
        26 p.   23 cm.

14416   Jillson, Willard Rouse, 1890-1975.
        A bibliography of Knox County, Kentucky.
        Citations of printed and manuscript sources touching
        upon its history, geology, cartography, coal, salt,
        oil and gas with annotations (1750-1956) by Willard
        Rouse Jillson... Frankfort, The Perry publishing co.,
        1958.
        34 p.   23 cm.

14417   Jillson, Willard Rouse, 1890-1975.
        A bibliography of Madison County, Kentucky.

Citations of printed and manuscript sources touching upon its history, cartography, geology, calcite, barite, fluorite, galenite, sphalerite, oil and gas (1750-1963), by Willard Rouse Jillson... Frankfort, Roberts printing co., 1964.
    35 p.   23 cm.

14418 Jillson, Willard Rouse, 1890-1975.
    A bibliography of Menifee County, Kentucky.
Citations of printed and manuscript sources touching upon its history, cartography, geology, paleontology and mineral resources (1818-1964) by Willard Rouse Jillson... Frankfort, Roberts printing co., 1967.
    30 p.   23 cm.

14419 Jillson, Willard Rouse, 1890-1975. .
    A bibliography of the Big Sandy valley.
Citations of printed and manuscript sources touching upon its history, geology, coal, oil, gas shale, clay, sandstone, limestone and mining industries with annotations by Willard Rouse Jillson... Frankfort, Roberts printing co., 1964.
    42 p.   34 cm.

14420 Jillson, Willard Rouse, 1890-1975.
    A bibliography of the Kentucky River valley.
Citations of printed and manuscript sources touching upon its history, geology, coal, oil, gas, calcite, barite, flourite, galenite, sphalerite and mining industries with annotations, by Willard Rouse Jillson... Frandfort, Roberts printing co., 1963.
    55 p.   23 cm.

14421 Jillson, Willard Rouse, 1890-1975.
    The coal industry in Kentucky, a review of the discovery, development, mining methods, qualities, markets, analyses, geology, correlations, locations, production statistics, and mine operators of the coals of Kentucky, including a complete bibliography. By Willard Rouse Jillson... Frankfort, Kentucky Geological Survey, 1924.
    [12], 164 p.   illus., map, tables. 22 cm.
(Ser. 6, v. 20)

14422 Jillson, Willard Rouse, 1890-1975.
    The coal industry in Kentucky, an historical sketch...

Frankfort, The State Journal company, 1922.
87 p.   illus.   21 cm.

14423 Jillson, Willard Rouse, 1890-1975.
Daniel Boone in Kentucky (a story)   Frankfort,
State journal co., 1939.
20 p.   illus.   21 cm.

14424 Jillson, Willard Rouse, 1890-1975.
Filson's map of Wilmington, Delaware, by
Willard Rouse Jillson. [Louisville, Ky., 1933]
[209]-213 p.   24 cm.
Reprinted from the Filson Club history quarterly,
v. 7, October 1933.

14425 Jillson, Willard Rouse, 1890-1975.
The flowering of Kentucky history; a chronology
of the life and times of Reuben Thomas Durrett,
1824-1913... Frankfort, Roberts Printing Company,
1946.
36 p.   front. (port.)   24 cm.

14426 Jillson, Willard Rouse, 1890-1975.
The founding of Harrodsburg; Old Fort Harrod,
by Willard Rouse Jillson... Frankfort, Ky.,
Kentucky state park commission, 1929.
14 p.   illus.   25½ cm.

14427 Jillson, Willard Rouse, 1890-1975.
Geologic map of Kentucky. Frankfort, Kentucky
geological survey, 1929.
map. 73 x 151 cm.   (Kentucky geological
survey, Series VI, 1929)

14428 Jillson, Willard Rouse, 1890-1975.
Geologic map of Kentucky and the adjoining states
showing the superficial distribution of oil and
gas producing formations in the Appalachian and
adjacent fields, adapted from P.P. 71, U.S.G.S.,
by W. R. Jillson. Lexington, Ky., 1918.
map.   22 x 29 cm.
Scale: 1:5,000,000.

14429 Jillson, Willard Rouse, 1890-1975.
The geology and mineral resources of Kentucky, a
brief description of the physiography, stratigraphy,
areal and structural geology, and mineral resources

141

of each of the counties comprising the Commonwealth...
Frankfort, Kentucky Geological Survey, 1928.
    xvi, 409 p.   illus., maps, diag.   24 cm.
(Kentucky Geological Survey, ser. VI, v. 17)

14430   Jillson, Willard Rouse, 1890-1975.
    Geology of the Camp Pleasant Branch Fault in
Franklin County, Kentucky. Frankfort, Ky., Roberts
printing co., 1962.
    21 p.   illus., map, tables.   24 cm.

14431   Jillson, Willard Rouse, 1890-1975.
    The glory of the hills, by Willard Rouse Jillson.
Frankfort, Ky., Frankfort Garden Club, 1933.
    cover-title, [4]p.   19 cm.
    Text on p. [3] of cover.
    Poem.

14432   Jillson, Willard Rouse, 1890-1975.
    The Kentucky Appalachian and lake states oil and gas
fields, by W. R. Jillson. Lexington, 1919.
    map.   24½ x 33 cm.
    "This map compiled from U.S.G.S., state geological,
and private reports corrected to Jan. 1919."

14433   Jillson, Willard Rouse, 1890-1975.
    Kentucky hemp: a history of the industry in a
commonwealth of the Upper South 1775-1942, by
Willard Rouse Jillson. An address delivered on the
occasion of the hemp celebration banquet of the Woodford
Chamber of Commerce. Versailles, Ky., 1942.
    cover-title, 8 p.   port.   23½ cm.

14434   Jillson, Willard Rouse, 1890-1975.
    Kentucky state parks, a brief presentation of the
geology and topography of some proposed state park areas
based upon original field investigation, by Willard
Rouse Jillson... Illustrated with thirty-four
photographs and maps. Presidential address, delivered
before the Kentucky academy of science at Lexington,
Ky,. May 10, 1924. Frankfort, Kentucky Geological
Survey, 1924.
    6 p.l., 92 p. incl. front., illus., maps.   20½ cm.

14435   Jillson, Willard Rouse, 1890-
    Kentucky tavern; a sketch of an old roadside inn, its
proprietor William Owen, and his family, 1787-1907,

by Willard Rouse Jillson. Frankfort, Ky.,
Roberts Printing Co., 1943.
42 p. incl. front.   23 cm.
"Documentary sources": p. 40-42.

14436 Jillson, Willard Rouse, 1890-1975.
The land title of Liberty Hall. Frankfort, Ky.,
State Journal Co., 1939.
9 p.   illus.   26 cm.
"Reprint from the Register of Kentucky State
Historical Society, April issue 1939."

14437 Jillson, Willlard Rouse, 1890-1975.
The lost letter of Aaron Burr, 1805, a tale of
early Lexington, by Willard Rouse Jillson. Frankfort,
Ky., Roberts printing co., 1946.
5 p.l., 18 p.   24 cm.
"This narrative was written for the entertainment
and delectation of the members and guests of the
Cakes and Ale Club of Lexington, Kentucky...
February 22, 1946." - Foreword.

14438 Jillson, Willard Rouse, 1890-1975.
Major General Edgar Erskine Hume, a biographical
sketch... Frankfort, Kentucky Historical Society,
1952.
15 p.   front. (port.)   27 cm.

14439 Jillson, Willard Rouse, 1890-1975.
Natural gas in eastern Kentucky; a summary account
of the occurrence of natural gas in the eastern part
of this commonwealth coupled with brief statements
as to the production and geology of each separate
field, by Willard Rouse Jillson... Louisville,
Standard printing co., 1937.
xviii, 237 p.   maps. $21\frac{1}{2}$ cm.

14440 Jillson, Willard Rouse, 1890-1975.
The next oil pool, a general consideration of some
of the undeveloped areas of outstanding merit in
Kentucky, by Willard Rouse Jillson... Lexington,
Transylvania press, 1932.
xiv, 116 p.   illus.   20 cm.

14441 Jillson, Willard Rouse, 1890-1975.
Oil and gas in the bluegrass region of Kentucky,
a preliminary report outlining the principal regional

geological features and controls, affecting exploratory
drilling, its history, present status, and prospect
with an adjacent to the area of the ordovician outcrop
of this commonwealth... Frankfort, The Kentucky
Geological Survey, 1931.
123 p.   illus., maps.   24 cm.

14442   Jillson, Willard Rouse, 1890-1975.
The oil and gas resources of Kentucky. A geological
review of the past development and the present status
of the industry in each of the one hundred and
twenty counties of the Commonwealth... Second
edition... Frankfort, Kentucky Geological Survey,
1920.
630 p.   illus., maps. (Kentucky Geological Survey
[reorganized April 1, 1920] Series VI. This book
published originally and now reprinted as Series five -
Bulletin one)

14443   Jillson, Willard Rouse, 1890-1975.
Pioneer Kentucky, an outline of its exploration
and settlement, its early cartography and primitive
geography coupled with a brief presentation of the
principal trails, traces, forts, stations, springs,
licks, fords and ferries used prior to the year 1800,
by Willard Rouse Jillson... Frankfort, The State
Journal company, 1934.
152 p.   front.   22 cm.

14444   Jillson, Willard Rouse, 1890-1975.
A rare iron conglomerate occurring in northeastern
Hardin County, Kentucky. Lingula nodularata, sp. nov.,
occurring in Powell County, Kentucky. A limestone
conglomerate occurring in the Eden of Clark County,
Kentucky. Fish coprolites in the Onandaga limestone
of eastern central Kentucky. [By] Willard Rouse
Jillson. [Louisville? 1966]
69-84 p.   illus.   23 cm.
Reprint from Transactions of the Kentucky Academy
of Science, v. 27, nos. 3-4, 1966.

14445   Jillson, Willard Rouse, 1890-1975.
Rebuke to Pandora... An address delivered at the
commencement of the Bridgeport High School, Bridgeport,
Kentucky, May 15, 1946. Frankfort, Ky., Roberts
Printing Co., 1946.
23 p.   24 cm.

14446 Jillson, Willard Rouse, 1890-1975.
         A selective bibliography of the American Indian,
      historic and prehistoric, in Kentucky, by Willard
      Rouse Jillson... Frankfort, Roberts printing co.,
      1964.
         42 p.   23 cm.

14447 Jillson, Willard Rouse, 1890-1975.
         The sixth geological survey, an administrative
      report of the several mineral resource and general
      geological investigations undertaken and completed
      in Kentucky during the biennial period 1920-1921, by
      Willard Rouse Jillson, director and state geologist.
      Presented with ten separate miscellaneous geological
      papers by George P. Merrill, Stuart Weller, Willard
      Rouse Jillson, Stuart St. Clair, and Charles Stevens
      Crouse... Frankfort, The Kentucky Geological Survey,
      1921.
         xii, 291 p.   illus., maps (part fold.), diags.,
      tables.   24½ cm.   (Kentucky Geological Survey,
      ser. VI, v. 6)

14448 Jillson, Willard Rouse, 1890-1975.
         Sketches in geology, a group of twenty-two separate
      papers on American geology by Willard Rouse Jillson...
      Louisville, Ky., C. T. Dearing printing co., 1928.
         [14], 158 p.   illus., maps.   23 cm.

14449 Jillson, Willard Rouse, 1890-1975.
         Some Kentucky obliquities in retrospect. Meade.
      Rafinesque. Wilkinson. ... Read before the Filson
      Club, Louisville, Kentucky, October 1, 1951.
      Frankfort, Ky., Roberts printing co., 1952.
         38 p.   front.   24 cm.

14450 Jillson, Willard Rouse, 1890-1975.
         Songs and satires, a chronology of youthful rhymes
      and verses, by Willard Rouse Jillson... Louisville,
      The C. T. Dearing company press, 1920.
         x, 58 p.   front.   20 cm.

14451 Jillson, Willard Rouse, 1890-1975.
         Tales of the dark and bloody ground. A group of
      fifteen original papers on the early history of
      Kentucky. By Willard Rouse Jillson... Louisville,
      C. T. Dearing printing company, 1930.
         16, 154 p.   illus., maps, facsims.   24 cm.

145

14452 Jillson, Willard Rouse, 1890-1975.
      The topography of Kentucky. A systematic study and
classification of all the prominent physical features
of Kentucky coupled with an indexed collection of
twenty-four separate papers on the geology and mineral
resources of the Commonwealth. Frankfort, Kentucky
Geological Survey, 1927.
      291 p.   illus., maps (1 fold. in pocket at end)
$22\frac{1}{2}$ cm.   (Kentucky Geological Survey, ser. VI, v. 30)

14453 John, Don D
      The diary of Eliza John, an historical and genealo-
gical record of the early Quakers in Northumberland
County, Penna., and what befell them. A paper read
before the Northumberland County Historical Society
on May 12, 1950. [n.p., 1950?]
      cover title, 49-70 p.   27 cm.
      "Reprinted from The Proceedings of the Northumberland
County Historical Society, Volume 19."

14454 Johnson, Eunice Tolbert.
      History of Perry County, Kentucky. Written and
published by Hazard Chapter, Daughters of the
American Revolution. [Hazard, Ky.? 1953]
      286 p.   illus., maps.   23 cm.

14455 Johnson, Gurney.
      Prolific Kentucky writer Billy C. Clark: an inter-
view.
      1 p.   illus.   41 cm.
      Reprinted from Sunday Herald-Leader, Lexington, Ky.,
May 20, 1973, p. 5.

14456 Johnson, Kenn.
      Country doctor: pacifist who will hit back.
Lexington, Ky., 1975.
      broadside.   port.   36 x 27 cm.
      Reprinted from Lexington Herald Leader, 26 October
1975, p. SC-7.
      Biography of W. E. Davis.

14457 Johnson, Kenn.
      Walnut Hill church, a historic memory rebuilt by
two church groups. Lexington, Ky., 1973.
      broadside.   56 x $14\frac{1}{2}$ cm.
      Reprinted from the Lexington Herald and the Lexington
Leader, 28 April 1973.

14458 Johnson, L   Frank, 1869-1931.
       The history of Franklin County, Ky., by L. F.
       Johnson, B.A., M.A. 1912. [Frankfort, Ky., Historical
       Frankfort Press, 1974]
       286, xviii, 23 p.   map.   22½ cm.

14459 Johnson, Leland R
       The Falls City engineers, a history of Louisville
       district, Corps of Engineers, United States Army.
       Louisville [1974]
       vii, 347 p.   illus., maps (incl. maps on lining
       papers)   25 cm.

14460 Johnson, Lewis Frank.
       Four miles up Kentucky River. [n.p., n.d.]
       23 p.   24 cm.

14461 Johnson, Lewis Franklin, 1859-1931.
       History of the Frankfort cemetery... Frankfort,
       Ky., Roberts printing co., 1921.
       74 p.   22½ cm.

14462 Johnson, Madison Conyers, 1807-
       Commonwealth of Kentucky, appellant, vs. Thomas C.
       Jones, appellee. Brief. [n.p.] 1875.
       49 p.   23 cm.
       Caption title.
       At head of title: Court of Appeals of Kentucky.
       Winter term, 1874-75.
       "This is an appeal from a judgement of the Franklin
       criminal court, sustaining a demurrer to an indictment
       against the appellee, charging him with the usurption
       and illegal holding of the office of the clerk of
       the Court of Appeals."
       Signed: M. C. Johnson.

14463 Johnson, Thomas, of Kentucky.
       O rare Tom Johnson, Kentucky's first poet, who,
       a century before Masters, wrote his own Spoon River
       anthology - The Kentucky miscellany... with an
       exasperating aside by John Wilson Townsend. Lexington,
       Bluegrass Bookshop, 1949.
       36 p.   23 cm.

14464 Johnson & Warner's Kentucky almanac, for the year of Our
       Lord 1810... Lexington, Published and sold wholesale
       and retail, at the book-store of Johnson & Warner

[1809]
[48] p.   15½ cm.

14465   Johnston, Alexander, ed.
Representative American orations to illustrate
American political history, edited, with introductions,
by Alexander Johnston...   New York & London, G. P.
Putnam's sons, The Knickerbocker press [1884]
3 v.   17 cm.
Contains orations by Henry Clay, "On the War of 1812,
House of Representatives, January 8, 1813," I, 170-195;
Henry Clay, "On the Compromise of 1850, United States
Senate, July 22, 1850," II, 118-134; John Jordan
Crittenden, "On Secession, border state opinion
(Unionist), in the United States Senate, December 4,
1860," III, 72-75; and Henry Clay, "On the American
system, in the United States Senate, February 2-6,
1832," III, 358-373.

14466   Johnston, Annie Fellows, 1863-1931.
Travelers five along life's highway. Jimmy,
Gideon Wiggan, the clown, Wexley Snathers, Bap.
Sloan... With a foreword by Bliss Carman. Frontispiece... by Edmund H. Garrett. Boston, L. C. Page &
company, 1911.
199 p.   illus.   20½ cm.

14467   Johnston, J   Stoddard.
... First explorations of Kentucky. Doctor Thomas
Walker's journal of an exploration of Kentucky in
1750, being the first record of a white man's visit
to the interior of that territory, now first published
entire, with notes and biographical sketch. Also
Colonel Christopher Gist's Journal of a tour through
Ohio and Kentucky in 1751, with notes and sketch...
Louisville, John P. Morton & co., 1898.
222 p.   32 cm.

14468   Johnston, Orramel.
The chartered rag light; or, An impartial view
of the banking system of the United States...
Maysville, Ky., Printed for the publisher by
A. Crookshanks, 1818.
10 p.   22½ cm.

14469   Joint Commission on Kentucky and Tennessee Boundary.
Report of the commissioners appointed to mark the

boundary line between the states of Kentucky and
Tennessee, to the governor of Kentucky. Frankfort,
Ky., Printed at the Yeoman office, 1860.
98 p.   maps.   24 cm.

14470 A joint patriotic celebration of the one-hundred and
forth-seventh anniversary of the Battle of Bunker Hill
by the Kentucky Society, Sons of the Revolution,
Ohio society, Sons of the Revolution, Ohio Society,
Colonial Wars, Kentucky Society, Colonial Wars,
Kentucky Society, Sons of the American Revolution,
Reserve Officers' Mess of Central Kentucky at
Lexington, Kentucky, Saturday, the 17th of June, 1922.
[Lexington, 1922]
[8] p.   19 cm.
Contains "The Battle of Bunker Hill," historical
note by General Emory Upton.

14471 Joliet, Louis, 1645-1700.
Joliet's map of New France in the years 1673 and
1674. Prepared by Joliet for Count Frontenac,
governor of New France. Issued in commemoration
of the tricentennial of the Joliet-Marquette expedition, 1973.   Iowa City, State Historical Society
of Iowa, 1973.
col. map.   32 x 24 cm.
From vol. 59 of Jesuit relations.
Kentucky and the Ohio River are shown near the
center of the map.

14472 Jonas, Edward Asher, 1865-
Matthew Harris Jouett, Kentucky Portrait painter
(1787-1827)   Louisville, Ky., J. B. Speed Memorial
Museum, 1938.
118 p.   illus.   26 cm.

14473 Jonas, Edward Asher, 1865-
A table for critics; portrait by Bethuel Moore.
Served by Edward A. Jonas. Louisville, Ky.,
J. P. Morton & company, incorporated, 1932.
4 p.l., 7-21 p.   front. (port.)   19½ cm.
"Privately printed and limited to 200 copies."
In verse.

14474 Jones, Edgar De Witt, 1876-1956.
Fairhope, the annals of a country church, by
Edgar De Witt Jones. Frontispiece by Herbert

Deland Williams. New York, The Macmillan company,
1917.
   5 p.l., 3-212 p.   front.   19½ cm.

14475 Jones, J   Catron.
       The Kentucky constitutional convention. [Louisville?
1931]
       4 pts. of 4 p. each, except pt. 3, a folder of 6 p.
20 cm.
       Excerpts from radio talks given over WHAS July 14,
21, and 28, and August 4, 1931.
       Parts 1, 2, and 3 appeared as supplements to
Kentucky City, September 19 and 23, 1931.

14476 Jones, Janie L
       Kentucky's kindergarten program: four years later,
prepared by Janie L. Jones. Frankfort, Ky.,
Legislative Research Commission, 1977.
       iv, 39 p.   28½ cm.   (Research report, no. 132)

14477 Jones, John Beauchamp, 1810-1869.
       ... The war path: a narrative of adventures in the
wilderness: with minute details of the captivity
of sundry persons; amusing and perilous incidents
during their abode in the wild woods; fearful
battles with the Indians; ceremony of adoption into
an Indian family; encounters with wild beasts and
rattlesnakes, &c. ... Philadelphia, J. B. Lippincott
& co., 1860.
       335 p.   illus.   19 cm.
       At head of title: Wild western scenes. - Second
series.

14478   *Omitted*

14479 Jones, Laban, 1796-
       A brief memoir of the Rev. Samuel Ayres Noel,
minister of the gospel of the Cumberland Presbyterian
church: with sermons on important practical
subjects. Louisville, C. C. Hull & brothers,
printers, 1846.
       436 p.   15 cm.

14480 Jones, Uriah James, 1818-1864.
       Simon Girty the outlaw, by U. J. Jones... with a
biographical sketch and notes by A. Monroe Aurand,
Jr. Harrisburg, Pa., The Aurand press, 1931.

vii p., 3 l., [3]-174 p.   29½ cm.
Reprint, including reporduction of t.-p. of original
edition, Philadelphia, 1846.
"Limited edition. 500 copies."
Bibliography: p. 174.

14481 Jones, William B[asil]
Wonderful curiosity; or, A correct narrative of the
celebrated Mammoth Cave of Kentucky; with incidents
and anecdotes. Russellville, Ky., Smith & Rhea,
printers, 1844.
87 p., 1 ℓ.   14 cm.

14482 Jordan, Jim.
Coal's future in Kentucky. Lexington, 1978.
4 p.   illus.   28-39 cm.
Reprinted from Lexington Herald, 30 April-3 May 1978.

14483 Joyce, John Alexander, 1842-1915.
A checkered life. By Col. John A. Joyce... Chicago,
S. P. Rounds, jr., 1883.
2 p.l., [7]-9 p., 3 l., 17-318, [1]p. incl. front.
(port.) illus., facsims.   20½ cm.
"Poetic waifs, by John A. Joyce": p. 301-318.

14484 Joyce, John Alexander, 1842-1915.
Truth... Chicago, Regan printing and publishing house
[1908]
191 p.   front. (port.)   19½ cm.

14485 Judd, R   D
A brief history of the Georgetown Baptist Church;
with related topics and notes by R. D. Judd.
Georgetown, Ky., 1965.
36 p.   illus., ports.
"Source materials": p. 24.

14486 Juettner, Otto.
...Daniel Drake and his followers; historical
and biographical sketches... Cincinnati, Harvey
publishing company [1909]
496 p.   illus.   26 cm.

14487 Junior League of Lexington, Ky.
Fiftieth year. 1973-1974. Lexington, 1974.
164 p.   illus. 20 cm.

14488 Junius, pseud.
        To the electors of Franklin county. Fellow
    citizens... May 1, 1798... [Frankfort? 1798]
        broadside.   20½ x 34½ cm.

                          K

14489 Kaufman, M
        To the voters of Lexington and Fayette county.
    Convincing facts and arguments in support of the
    local Democratic ticket. Full text local Democratic
    platform and list of Democratic nominees. Published
    by authority of the Fayette county Democratic campaign
    committee. [Lexington, Ky.] 1911.
        [20]p.   22½ cm.

14490 Kavanaugh, Mrs. Russell.
        Three brave men: a drama. [Louisville, 1879]
        218-223 p.   illus.   23 cm.   (Louisville
    monthly magazine, v. 1, no. 4, April 1879)

14491 Keeling, Larry Dale.
        Revived Appalachia reversing exodus. Lexington,
    Ky., 1945.
        [6]p. size varies.
        Reprint of four articles from Lexington Herald,
    28, 29, 30, 31 December 1975.

14492 Keen, John S
        Memoir of F. W. Henck, with notes and comments.
    Highway, Ky., Bible advocate print, 1899.
        3 p.l., 247 p.   front. [port.]   19½ cm.

14493 Keeneland association, Lexington, Ky.
        Opening, 1936. [Lexington? 1936?]
        78 p.   illus.   34 cm.
        Contains Henry W. Knickerbocker, Funeral oration
    of Riley Grannan, p. 72-73, 76-77.
        At end is a letter of the late Ed Penisten of
    Chillicothe, Ohio, transmitting a four-page commentary
    on Grannan.

14494 Keith, Charles A   ed.
        Jewels of verse, jingle and limerick. [Richmond,

                          152

Ky., 1955]
46 p.   24 cm.
Foreword by W. J. Moore.

14495   Kell, Jeffrey.
Final report on the Kentucky environmental and
economic development policy project. Prepared by
Jeffrey Kell. Frankfort, Ky., Legislative Research
Commission, 1975.
various pagings.   29 cm.   (Kentucky. Legislative
Research Commission. Informational Bulletin, no. 111)

14496   Kell, Jeffrey J
Off-track betting in Kentucky. Prepared by Jeffrey
J. Kell, Dr. John P. Nelson, Meg W. Anderson.
Frankfort, Ky., Legislative Research Commission, 1973.
143, 40, 36, 15, 23, 7, 4, 82 p.   tables, diagrs.
27 cm.   (Kentucky. Legislative Research Commission,
Research report no. 109)

14497   Kelley, Julielma M
Biographical record of Daniel and Mary (Jackson)
Williams, early Kentucky pioneers, including portraits
and biographies of their children: Thomas Williams,
Daniel Jackson Williams, John Williams, Elijah
Williams, Sarah Williams, Katharine (Williams) Orr,
Mary (Williams) Forsyth and their descendants.
1752-1898... Baltimore, Md., Published for the
author, 1898.
37 p.   29 cm.

14498   Kelsey, D   M
Our pioneer heroes and their daring deeds. The
lives and famous exploits of... hero explorers,
renowned frontier fighters, and celebrated early
settlers of America, from the earliest times to the
present. By D. M. Kelsey... Philadelphia and St.
Louis, Scammell & Company, 1887.
xviii, [19]-672 p.   incl. col. front., illus.,
ports.   23 cm.

14499   Kemp, Janet T
Retirement for non-certified school board
employees. Frankfort, Ky., Legislative Research
Commission, 1973.

30 p.   tables.   29 cm.   (Research report
no. 103, new series)

14500 Kemper, Andrew Carr.
A memorial of the Rev. James Kemper for the
centennial of the synod of Kentucky... [Louisville,
1899?]
24 p.   front. (port.)   23½ cm.

14501 Kemper, George Whitefield, 1870-   , ed.
Kentucky university alumni book, Lexington,
Ky. 1861-1896... Comp. and ed. by George Whitefield
Kemper. Lexington, Transylvania printing co.,
1896.
135 p.   incl. front., illus., plates, ports.
19½ cm.

14502 Kendall, Amos, 1789-1869.
Autobiography of Amos Kendall. Ed. by his son-in-law,
William Stickney. Boston, Lee and Shepard; New York,
Lee, Shepard, and Dillingham, 1872.
ix, 700 p.   front. (port.) plates, fold, facsim.
24 cm.

14503 Kennedy, H   C
A damphool in the Kentucky legislature, by H. C.
Kennedy. Chicago, W. B. Conkey company [1909]
190 p.   illus.   20½ cm.

14504 Kennedy, William Sloane, 1850-1929.
Wonders and curiosities of the railway; or,
Stories of the locomotive in every land... Chicago,
S.C. Griggs and company, 1884.
xvi, 254 p.   illus.   19½ cm.

14505 Kenton, Simon, 1755-1836.
[Promissory note signed by Kenton, 22 September
1786, in facsimile with printed commentary] [Lexington,
University of Kentucky Library associates, 1956]
2 p.   facsim.   15 cm.

14506 Kentuckians, to arms!!! Louisville, 1861.
broadside.   25 x 14 cm.
Hummel, 731.
Poetry (pro-Secessionist)
Original in Duke University Library.

14507 Kentucky. Adjutant-general's Office.
Report of the adjutant general of the state of
Kentucky. Soldiers of the war of 1812. Printed by
authority of the legislature of Kentucky. Frankfort,
E. P. Johnson, public printer, 1891.
2 p.l., 370 p., 1 ℓ. 31 x 25 cm.
Sam E. Hill, Adjutant general.

14508 Kentucky. Adjutant-general's Office.
State of Kentucky. General orders. November 24, 1808.
The governor and commander in chief, having received
instructions from the President of the United States
through the secretary of war... [Frankfort, 1808]
broadside. 30 x 44 cm.

14509 Kentucky. Blue Licks Battle-field Monument Commission.
The battle of the Blue Licks. Commemoration of the
145th anniversary of the battle. At Blue Licks, Ky.,
Friday, August 19, 1927. Celebration held under the
auspices of the Blue Licks Battle-field Monument
Commission. [Louisville, Westerfield-Bonte co.,
incorporated, 1927]
50 p. 23 cm.

14510 Kentucky. Blue Licks Battle-field Monument Commission.
Blue Licks Battle-Field Monument. Proceedings at
the unveiling and dedication of the monument on the
site of the battle of the Blue Licks, and exercises in
commemoration of the 146th anniversary of the battle.
At Blue Licks, Kentucky, Sunday, August 19, 1928.
Celebration held under the auspices of the Blue Licks
Battle-field Monument Commission. [Louisville, 1928]
88 p. front., map. 23 cm.

14511 Kentucky. Bureau of Agriculture, Horticulture, and
Statistics.
The resources and condition of the Commonwealth
of Kentucky, prepared by the state Bureau of
Agriculture, Horticulture and Statistics. For
general distribution. Frankfort, Ky., S. I. M.
Major, public printer, 1877.
2 p.l., 108 p. front. (fold. map) diagrs.
23½ cm.
p. 1-74 are reprinted from General account of the
Commonwealth of Kentucky prepared by the Geological
Survey, 1876.

14512   Kentucky.   Civil War Centennial Commission.
        The Civil War in Kentucky.
        map.   43 x 89 cm.   illus.   [Lexington, Ky.?
        1961]
        Text on verso.
        Map signed by Sandman.

14513   Kentucky.   Civil War Centennial Commission.
        Kentucky remembers.   Civil war centennial manual
        for use of county committees, schools, newspapers,
        tourists, civic and patriotic organizations and
        Kentuckians at large.   Lexington, Ky., 1961.
        24 p.   fold. map.   23 cm.

14514   Kentucky.   Commission, Louisiana Purchase Exposition.
        Kentucky at the World's fair, St. Louis, 1904.
        Being a report of the Commission authorized by an
        act of the General assembly to the governor of the
        Commonwealth.   [Frankfort?   1904?]
        142, [2] p.   plates, ports.   24 cm.

14515   Kentucky.   Commission on Human Rights.
        Kentucky's black heritage.   The role of the black
        people in the history of Kentucky from pioneer days
        to the present.   A supplement to current texts on
        Kentucky history.   Frankfort, 1971.
        iv, 162 p.   illus.   29 cm.

14516   Kentucky.   Commission on Negro Affairs.
        The report of the Kentucky Commission on
        Negro Affairs, November 1, 1945.   [Frankfort?   1945?]
        55 p.   29 cm.

14517   Kentucky.   Commission on Public Education.
        Curriculum Study Committee.
        Report.   Lexington, 1961.
        344 p.   tables, map.   22 cm.

14518   Kentucky.   Commissioners on the Boundary Line.
        Message of the acting governor to the House of
        representatives, communicating the correspondence
        between the Kentucky and Tennessee commissioners
        on the subject of the boundary line, with the reports
        of the Kentucky commissioners.   Frankfort, Printed by
        Kendall and Russell,   printers to the state, 1820.
        40 p.   21 cm.

14519 Kentucky. Committee on Functions and Resources of
State Government.
Final report. Finds and recommendations. Frankfort,
Ky., 1951.
63 p.   28½ cm.

14520 Kentucky. Committee to Study Intermittent Industry.
...A study of intermittent industry in Kentucky.
Submitted to the acting executive director by the
Commission to Study Intermittent Industry... Frankfort,
1941.
v, 40 numb. l.   incl. tables, diagr.   28 cm.
At head of title: Kentucky Unemployment Compensation
Commission.
Raymond Cella, chairman.

14521 Kentucky. Constitution.
The constitution, or form of government for the
state of Kentucky. Pub. by order of the Convention.
Frankfort, Printed by Hunter and Beaumont, printers
to the commonwealth, 1799.
30 p.   18½ cm.

14522 Kentucky. Constitution.
Constitution of Kentucky. Compiled by Ella
Lewis, secretary of state. [Frankfort, Ky.] 1928.
89 p.   22 cm.

14523 Kentucky. Constitution.
The constitution of Kentucky published, with an
explanatory essays by James T. Fleming. 7th ed.
Frankfort, Legislative Research Commission, 1973.
57 p.   cover illus.   27 cm.   (Informational
bulletin, no. 59)

14524 Kentucky. Constitution.
The constitution of Kentucky. With an
explanatory essay by James T. Fleming. Frankfort,
Legislative Research Commission, 1976.
xxi, 62 p.   27 cm.   (Informational bulletin,
no. 112)

14525 Kentucky. Constitution Revision Committee.
100 [One hundred] questions about a constitutional
convention. Frankfort, Ky., 1960.
cover-title, 37 p.   24 cm.

14526   Kentucky. Constitution Revision Committee.
          You and your constitution... Kentucky considers
        a convention. Frankfort, Ky., 1960.
          cover-title, [13]p.   illus.   23 cm.

14527   Kentucky. Constitutional Convention, 1792.
          Journal of the first Constitutional convention
        of Kentucky, held in Danville, Kentucky, April 2 to 19,
        1792. Published in commemoration of Kentucky's
        sesquicentennial anniversary, June 1, 1942, by the
        State Bar Association of Kentucky. Lexington, 1942.
          xii, 28 p.   illus. (facsims.)   23 cm.

14528   Kentucky. Constitutional Convention, 1799.
          Resolutions agreed to in committee of the whole.
        Frankfort, Hunter & Beaumont, 1799.
          broadside.   22½ x 29 cm.

14529   Kentucky Constitutional Convention, 1890.
          Rules of the Constitutional Convention, also,
        the Constitution of Kentucky, and standing committees
        of the convention of 1890. Frankfort, Ky., Capital
        Office, E. Polk Johnson, printer to the convention,
        1890.
          2 p.l., 64 p.   21 cm.

14530   Kentucky. Council of Defense.
          A statewide movement to make a record of Kentucky's
        part in the World war including military service
        records of fighting forces. War work done by
        civilians. Collection and preservation of other
        historical matter. Louisville, Kentucky Council of
        defense, 1919.
          24 p.   incl. tables.   16½ cm.

14531   Kentucky. Curriculum Study Committee.
          Abstract of the report of the Curriculum Study
        Committee to the Commission on Public Education.
        [Frankfort, 1961]
          iv, 91 p.   29½ cm.

14532   Kentucky. Daniel Boone Bicentennial Commission.
          ... Report of the Daniel Boone bicentennial
        commission to the 1936 General assembly of Kentucky
        and appendix... [Frankfort, 1936]
          1 p.l., 7-62 p.   illus., pl., port.   22½ cm.

At head of title: The Daniel Boone bicentennial.
"Appendix, addresses: 'Daniel Boone, 1734-1934,' by
Samuel M. Wilson; 'The Fame of Daniel Boone,' by
Dr. Louise Phelps Kellogg..."

14533 Kentucky. Dept. of Commerce.
       Commuting patterns of Kentucky counties.
       [Frankfort] Division of Research and Planning,
       Kentucky Department of Commerce, 1973.
       89 p.   29 cm.

14534 Kentucky. Dept. of Commerce.
       Financing industry. The Kentucky plan. [Frankfort]
       Division of Research and Planning, Kentucky Department
       of Commerce, 1973.
       28 p.   29 cm.

14535 Kentucky. Dept. of Commerce.
       Guidebook. Kentucky business regulations and
       industrial start-up checklist. [Frankfort]
       Division of Research and Planning, 1973.
       52 p.   29 cm.

14536 Kentucky. Dept. of Commerce.
       Industrial resources. Berea, Kentucky. Prepared
       by the Kentucky Department of Commerce in cooperation
       with the Berea Chamber of Commerce. [Frankfort]
       1972.
       31 p.   illus., maps.   29 cm.
       Three-page folder with map, "Berea industrial
       sites," in pocket at front.

14537 Kentucky. Dept. of Commerce.
       Industrial resources, Cadiz, Kentucky. Prepared
       by the Kentucky Department of Commerce in
       cooperation with the Cadiz-Trigg County Chamber of
       Commerce and the Trigg County Industrial Foundation.
       [Frankfort] 1972.
       27 p.   illus., tables. 29 cm.
       Four-page folder with map, "Cadiz industrial sites,"
       in pocket at front.

14538 Kentucky. Dept. of Commerce.
       Industrial resources, Hindman, Kentucky. Prepared
       by the Kentucky Department of Commerce in cooperation
       with the city of Hindman and the Knott County

Development Association. [Frankfort] 1972.
20 p.   maps.   29 cm.

14539   Kentucky. Dept. of Commerce.
        Industrial resources, Kentucky. [Frankfort]
        Division of Research and Planning, Kentucky Department
        of Commerce, 1974.
        29 p.   maps (8 fold. at end)   29 cm.

14540   Kentucky. Dept. of Commerce.
        Industrial resources, Lancaster, Kentucky.
        Prepared by the Kentucky Department of Commerce
        in cooperation with the Garrard County Chamber of
        Commerce. [Frankfort] 1972.
        26 p.   illus., maps.   29 cm.
        Three-page folder with map; "Lancaster
        industrial sites," in pocket at front.

14541   Kentucky. Dept. of Commerce.
        Industrial resources, McLean County, Kentucky.
        Prepared by the Kentucky Department of Commerce in
        cooperation with the Calhoun Industrial Development
        Cooperation, Livermore-Island Chamber of Commerce.
        [Frankfort] 1972.
        28 p.   maps.   29 cm.
        Six-page folder with maps, "Calhoun industrial
        sites," in pocket at front.

14542   Kentucky. Dept. of Commerce.
        Industrial resources, Madisonville, Ky.
        Prepared by the Kentucky Department of Commerce in
        cooperation with the Madisonville Chamber of Commerce.
        [Frankfort] 1972.
        27 p.   illus., maps.   29 cm.
        Three-page folder with map, "Madisonville
        industrial sites," in pocket at front.

14543   Kentucky. Dept. of Commerce.
        Industrial resources, Pike County, Kentucky.
        Prepared by the Kentucky Department of Commerce in
        cooperation with the Pike County Chamber of Commerce,
        Inc. [Frankfort] 1972.
        32 p.   illus., maps, tables.   29 cm.
        Four-pages folder, "Pike County industrial sites,"
        in pocket at front.

14544 Kentucky. Dept. of Commerce.
          Industrial resources, Richmond, Ky. Prepared by
       the Kentucky Department of Commerce in cooperation
       with the Richmond Chamber of Commerce. [Frankfort] 1972.
          34 p.   illus., map.   29 cm.
       Three-page folder with map "Richmond industrial
       sites," in pocket at front.

14545 Kentucky. Dept. of Commerce.
          Input. V. 1, 1969 - v. 3, 1972. Frankfort,
       1969-1972.
          3 v.   illus.   29 cm.
       No more published.

14546 Kentucky. Dept. of Commerce.
          Kentucky deskbook of economic statistics.
       [Frankfort] Division of Research and Planning,
       Kentucky Department of Commerce, 1973.
          52 p.   maps, diagrs., tables.   29 cm.

14547 Kentucky. Dept. of Commerce.
          Major river sites in Kentucky. [Frankfort] 1972.
          165 p.   illus., maps (1 fold.)   29 cm.

14548 Kentucky. Dept. of Commerce
          Maps and publications. Price list. [Frankfort]
       1974.
          54 p.   maps. (1 fold.)   25 cm.

14549 Kentucky. Dept. of Commerce.
          Transportation in Kentucky. [Frankfort] Research
       and Planning Division, Department of Commerce, 1973.
          35 p.   maps. (1 fold.), tables.   29 cm.

14550 Kentucky. Dept. of Conservation. Division of
          Forestry.
          Forest trees of Kentucky. How to know them.
       A pocket manual. [Frankfort] 1937.
          76 p.   illus.   24 cm.

14551 Kentucky. Dept. of Conservation. Division of
          publicity.
          [Report to... 1938 to 1943] Frankfort, Dept. of
       conservation, Division of publicity, 1943.
          1 p.l., 7,6,6,7,3p.   tables.   30 cm.

14552   Kentucky. Dept. of Economic Development.
        Industrial uses for limestone and dolomite with
        specific application to the Kentucky market for
        lime and fine-ground limestone. Frankfort, 1961.
        18 p.   maps.   29 cm.

14553   Kentucky. Dept. of Education.
        Advancing education in Kentucky. Challenges -
        processes - outcomes. 1956 - 1957 - 1958 - 1959.
        [Frankfort, 1959]
        819-976 p.   illus.   24 cm.
        Publisher indicated on cloth binding.

14554   Kentucky. Dept. of Education.
        A centennial exhibit of education in Kentucky,
        by Howard A. M. Henderson, superintendent of
        public instruction. Frankfort, Major, Johnston &
        Barrett, 1876.
        cover-title, 36 p.   23 cm.

14555   Kentucky. Dept. of Education.
        History of education in Kentucky, 1915-1940.
        [Frankfort, 1940?]
        145 p.   ports., tables.   22½ cm.

14556   Kentucky. Dept. of Education.
        Teacher's manual on the new Kentucky court system.
        [Frankfort] 1977.
        v, [1], 71 p.   illus., ports.   27½ cm.

14557   Kentucky. Dept. of Education.
        Units in conservation for Kentucky public schools
        for elementary and secondary schools. Prepared and
        distributed by cooperation of the Kentucky Division
        of game and fish, League of Kentucky sportsmen,
        Kentucky state Department of education, August,
        1941. [Frankfort, 1941]
        275 p.   illus.   23 cm.   (Educational
        bulletin, IX, No. 6, August 1941)

14558   Kentucky. Dept. of Finance. Division of the Budget.
        Kentucky state government. A progress report
        from Lawrence W. Wetherby, governor, 1950-1955.
        Frankfort, 1955.
        163 p.   illus., map, tables. 29 cm.

14559   Kentucky. Dept. of Fish and Wildlife Resources.
        Fishing & boating in Kentucky. Frankfort,
        [n.d.]
        32 p.   illus., map.   13 x 20 cm.

14560   Kentucky. Dept. of Fish and Wildlife Resources.
        Fisheries bulletins. Frankfort [1976]
        [5]p.   28 cm.

14561   Kentucky. Dept. of Fish and Wildlife Resources.
        The lure of fishing in Kentucky, a manual for
        Kentucky fishing. [n.p., n.d.]
        32 p.   illus.   14 x 22 cm.

14562   Kentucky. Dept. of Geology and Forestry.
        Map of Allen County [Ky.] Base by L. M. Sellier.
        Geology by A. M. Miller. [Frankfort, 191-?]
        map.   58 x 70 cm.
        Scale: 1 inch = 1 mile

14563   Kentucky. Dept. of Geology and Forestry.
        Map of the structural geology of Breathitt
        County, Ky., prepared under the direction of W. R.
        Jillson. Structural geology by I. B. Browning.
        [Frankfort] 1919.
        map.   56 x 70 cm.
        Scale: 1:62,500.

14564   Kentucky. Dept. of Geology and Forestry.
        Map of the structural geology of Knott County, Ky.,
        prepared under the direction of W. R. Jillson.
        Structural geology by I. B. Browning. [Frankfort]
        1919.
        map.   66 x 70 cm.
        Scale: 1:62,500.

14565   Kentucky. Dept. of Geology and Forestry.
        The mineral and forest resources of Kentucky,
        v. I, series V, no. 3. October 1, 1919. Frankfort,
        1919.
        147-396 p.   illus., maps (part fold.), tables
        (part fold.)   24 cm.
        Contains articles by Charles Butts, Willard Rouse
        Jillson, and Arthur McQuiston Miller.

14566 Kentucky. Dept. of Geology and Forestry.
       Oil and gas pool and pipeline map of Kentucky, by
       W. R. Jillson. April, 1919. [Frankfort, 1919]
       map.   24 x 46 cm.
       Scale: 1 inch = 20 miles.

14567 Kentucky. Dept. of Geology and Forestry.
       Sketch map showing oil and gas development in
       Warren County, Ky., by Willard R. Jillson.
       Frankfort, 1919.
       map.   43 x 40 cm.
       Scale not indicated.
       "Base adapted from map by J. E. McAdoo, 1891."

14568 Kentucky. Dept. of Highways.
       ...Historic Kentucky highways. [Frankfort, 1948]
       cover title, 56 p.   illus.   24 cm.
       At head of title: "The sun shines bright in the
       old Kentucky home."

14569 Kentucky. Dept. of Highways.
       Martin County, Kentucky. Inez, Ky., Inez Deposit
       Bank [n.d.]
       map.   45 x 63 cm.
       Current and historical photographs reproduced on
       edges of map.

14570 Kentucky. Dept. of Justice. Bureau of Training.
       Kentucky criminal law manual. [Richmond, Ky.,
       1976]
       321 p.   15½ cm.
       Loose-leaf; contains all revisions through 1976;
       some page numbers repeated as a, b, etc.

14571 Kentucky. Dept. of Mines and Minerals. Division of
       Geology.
       State parks, by the committee. Lexington, 1946.
       209-239p.   illus.   24 cm.   (Series VIII,
       Reprint 11)
       "Reprinted from the Bulletin of the Bureau of
       School Service, College of Education, University of
       Kentucky, Vol. 18, No. 2, December, 1945, pp.
       210-239, for the Department of Mines and Minerals."

14572 Kentucky. Dept. of Public Instruction.
       Programme and syllabus for the county institutes

of Kentucky, 1890. Frankfort, E. Polk Johnson, Public
printer and binder, 1890.
43 p.   15 cm.

14573 Kentucky. Dept. of Public Relations.
Kentucky facts. Frankfort [1957?]
16 p.   illus., map. 23 cm.

14574 Kentucky. Eastern Kentucky State Teachers College.
Three decades of progress, Eastern Kentucky
State Teachers College, 1906-1936. Richmond,
Kentucky. Prepared by members of the faculty,
Richmond, 1936.
365 p.   illus., tables, diagr.   23 cm.

14575 Kentucky. Educational Commission.
Public education in Kentucky, a report by the
Kentucky Educational Commission. Prepared under the
direction of the Commission by the General Education
Board. New York, General Education Board, 1921.
ix, 213 p.   illus., tables (port fold.),
diagrs. $20\frac{1}{2}$ cm.

14576 Kentucky. Efficiency Commission.
The government of Kenucky. Report of the
Efficiency commission of Kentucky. January 1, 1924.
[Frankfort, 1924]
2 v.   fold. tab.   24 cm.

14577 Kentucky. General Assembly.
Biographical sketch of the Hon. John L. Helm,
late governor of Kentucky... Frankfort, Ky.
Printed at the Kentucky Yeoman office, 1868.
144 p.   front. [port.] $23\frac{1}{2}$ cm.

14578 Kentucky. General Assembly.
Biographical sketch of the Hon. Lazarus W.
Powell [of Henderson, Ky.] governor of the state
of Kentucky from 1851-1855, senator in Congress
from 1859-1865... Frankfort, Ky., Printed at the
Kentucky Yeoman office, 1868.
134 p., 1 ℓ.   front. [port.] $23\frac{1}{2}$ cm.

14579 Kentucky. General Assembly
Mr. Rowan's motion, for an inquiry into the
conduct of Harry Innis, district judge of the United
States for the district of Kentucky. City of

Washington, A. & G. Way, printers, 1808.
54 p.   21 cm.

14580   Kentucky. General Assembly.
        Preamble and resolutions of the legislature, of
        Kentucky, in relation to the late decision of
        the Court of appeals on the replevin and endorsement
        laws, and of the Supreme court of the United States
        on the occupying claimant laws of said state.
        [Frankfort, Ky., 1824]
        28 p.   24 cm.

14581   Kentucky. General Assembly.
        Speeches and proceedings upon the announcement of
        the death of Hon. Jno. C. Breckinridge in the Senate
        and House of Representatives of Kentucky, Friday and
        Saturday, January 7th and 22d, 1876. Frankfort,
        Ky., Jas. A. Hodges. 1876.
        57, [2] p.   23½ cm.

14582   Kentucky. General Assembly.
        Speeches and proceedings upon the announcement
        of the death of the Hon. Linn Boyd, in the
        Senate and House of representatives of Kentucky,
        Tuesday, December 20, 1859. Frankfort, Ky.,
        Printed at the Yeoman office, 1860.
        52 p.   21 cm.

14583   Kentucky. General Assemlby.
        To the freemen of Kentucky. [Frankfort? 1825?]
        16 p.   22 cm.

14584   Kentucky. General Assembly. Committee on the Coal
        Trade and Iron Interests of Kentucky.
        Report of the Committee on the Coal Trade and
        Iron Interests of Kentucky.
        20 p.   23 cm.

14585   Kentucky. General Assembly. House of Representatives.
        Rules and regulations of the House of Representatives.
        [Lexington? John Bradford? 1798?]
        4 p.   33½ cm.

14586   Kentucky. General Assembly. House of Representatives.
        Selected committee on charges against Benjamin
        Sebastian. The report of the Select committee, to
        whom was referred the information communicated to the

House of representatives, charging Benjamin
Sebastian, one of the judges of the Court of
appeals of Kentucky, with having received a pension
from the Spanish government. Frankfort [Ky.]
From the press of J. M. Street, 1806.
27 p.   22½ cm.

14587 Kentucky. General Assembly. House of Representatives.
Select Committee on Charges against Humphrey
Marshall... Report of the Select Committee Appointed
to Investigate Certain Charges against Humphrey
Marshall. February 9, 1808. [Lexington? 1818]
27 p.   fold. plan.   23 cm.

14588 Kentucky. General Assembly. House of Representatives.
...Wednesday, Nov. 7, 1898. Mr. Breckenridge
gave notice that he would on tomorrow move the House
to go into a committee of the whole on the state
of the Commonwealth on that part of the governor's
address which relates to certain inconstitutional laws
passed at the last session of Congress... Frankfort,
Hunter & Beaumont, 1798.
broadside.   28 x 44 cm.

14589 Kentucky. Geological Survey.
Location of bench marks shown on maps of the upper
Big Sandy valley. [Frankfort? n.d.]
10 p.   23 cm.

14590 Kentucky. Geological Survey.
Map of Boyd, Carter and Greenup Counties, by
L. M. Sellier. [Frankfort] 1913.
map.   39 x 39 cm.
Scale: 1 inch = 3 miles.

14591 Kentucky. Geological Survey.
Map of Georgetown quadrangle, by L. M. Sellier.
[Frankfort] 1913.
map.   56 x 44 cm.
Scale: 1:62,500.

14592 Kentucky. Geological Survey.
Map of Pond and Blackberry Creeks, by L. M.
Sellier. [Frankfort] 1913.
map.   36 x 32 cm.
Scale not indicated; approximately 1:62,500.

14593   Kentucky. Geological Survey.
             Map of upper Big Sandy valley, by L. M. Sellier
         [Frankfort] 1913.
             map in 4 sheets.   63 x 75 cm.   (sheet 1)
         45 x 65.   (Sheet 2)   55 x 36 cm.   (sheet 3)
         70 x 70 cm.   (sheet 4)
             Scale: 1 inch = 1 mile.

14594   Kentucky. Geological Survey.
             Map of upper Licking valley, by L. M. Sellier.
         [Frankfort] 1913.
             map.   24 x 56 cm.
             Scale: 1 inch = 1 mile.

14595   Kentucky. Geological Survey.
             Memoirs of the Geological Survey of Kentucky.
         N. S. Shaler, director. Volume I. Cambridge,
         University Press, 1876.
             246 p.   illus.   32 cm.
             Contents. Pt. I. On the antiquity of the caverns
         and cavern life of the Ohio Valley, By N. S. Shaler,
         Pt. II. The American bisons, living and extinct, by
         J. A. Allen.

14596   Kentucky. Geological Survey.
             Reconnaissance geologic map of Barren County,
         Kentucky, surveyed in cooperation with the United
         States Geological Survey. By Charles Butts.
         [Frankfort] 1919.
             map.   61 x 46 cm.
             Scale: $\frac{1}{2}$ inch = 1 mile.
             "Base compiled from the following sources: an old
         road map made by private enterprise; river from
         Sellier's map of Allen County by the Kentucky
         Geological Survey; roads, streams, place names,
         and locations revised by Charles Butts and others."

14597   Kentucky. Geological Survey.
             Sketch map of a portion of Rowan County, by L. M.
         Sellier. [Frankfort] 1913.
             map.   43 x 24$\frac{1}{2}$ cm.
             Scale: 1 inch = 1 mile.

14598   Kentucky. Geological Survey.
             Timber and botany. B. Comprising seven reports on
         the forests and botany of different parts of the
         state. Frankfort, Kentucky, Stereotyped

168

for the Survey by Major, Johnston & Barrett,
Yeoman press, 1884.
    various pagination. tables. 26½ cm.

14599 Kentucky. Governor, 1808-1812. [Charles Scott]
    Freemen and soldiers of Kentucky! Your country
again calls upon you to rally round her standard...
Frankfort, September 17th, 1808.
    20½ x 33 cm.

14600 Kentucky. Governor's Commission on the Study of
    Public Higher Education.
    Report to the Honorable Bert T. Combs, governor
of the Commonwealth of Kentucky. Frankfort, Ky.,
1961.
    28 p.   maps, tables.   29 cm.

14601 Kentucky. Highway Dept.
    [General highway maps of the 120 Kentucky counties.
Frankfort, Ky., 1973?]
    120 maps.   29½ x 38 cm.

14602 Kentucky. Historical Events Celebration Commission.
    Kentucky's '74-'76 celebrations [Frankfort, 1973]
    [32] p.   illus., map, plan.   27½ cm.
    cover-title.
    Appended at end are Kentucky '74 bicentennial
calendar of events, July-December 1974 (Frankfort,
1974; 24 p., illus.) and Bourbon County Bicentennial
festival days, June 30-July 7, 1974 (Paris,
Bourbon County Bicentennial Commission; 4 p., illus.)

14603 Kentucky Historical Society.
    Catalogue. Prehistoric relics collected in
Kentucky and in other states of the Union by W. J.
Curtis. Ninth series. Frankfort, Kentucky State
Historical Society [1914?]
    16 p.   24 cm.

14604 Kentucky. Laws, statutes, etc.
    General Assembly action. Regular session, 1972.
Frankfort, Legislative Research Commission, 1972.
    74 p.   29½ cm.   (Informational bulletin, no. 98)

14605 Kentucky. Laws, statutes, etc.
    Militia laws: comprising the acts of Congress, with
the rules and articles of war; and the act of

169

Kentucky, passed in February 1815. With a complete
index to the whole. Published by authority.
Frankfort, Printed by Johnston and Buchanan, 1815.
x, [2], 94, [1] p.   17 cm.

14606   Kentucky. Legislative Research Commission.
        Bill drafting manual for the Kentucky General
        Assembly... Frankfort, 1976.
        [4], 43 p.   21 ½ cm.   (Informational bulletin,
        no. 117)

14607   Kentucky. Legislative Research Commission.
        Criminal procedure: history of the criminal code...
        Frankfort, 1959.
        iii, 10 p.   29 cm.   (Research publication, 69)

14608   Kentucky. Legislative Research Comission.
        Final reports of interim joint and special committees,
        1974-1975. Presented to the Legislative Research
        Commission and the 1976 General Assembly. Frankfort,
        Legislative Research Commission, 1975.
        249 p.   28½ cm.   (Informational bulletin,
        no. 109)

14609   Kentucky. Legislative Research Commission.
        Final reports of interim joint and special committees,
        1976-1977, presented to the Legislative Research
        Commission and the 1978 General Assembly. Frankfort,
        Ky., Legislative Research Commission, 1977.
        v, 157 p.   27½ cm   (Informational bulletin,
        no. 127)

14610   Kentucky. Legislative Research Commission.
        General Assembly action, regular session, 1976.
        A staff summary of legislative measures sent to the
        governor... April, 1976. [Frankfort, 1976]
        [4], 66 p.   29 cm.

14611   Kentucky. Legislative Research Commission.
        General Assembly action, regular session 1978.
        A staff summary of legislative measures sent to the
        governor. Frankfort, 1978.
        [96] p.   28 cm.   (Informational bulletin, no. 128)
        Arranged by numbers of Senate bills, House bills,
        and veto messages, and with lists of Senate and House
        members and a subject index.

14612 Kentucky. Legislative Research Commission.
       Historical development of Kentucky courts.
       Frankfort, 1958.
       29 p.   29 cm.   (Research publication, 63)

14613 Kentucky. Legislative Research Commission.
       Implementing Kentucky's new judicial system and
       other issues likely to confront the General Assembly
       at the 1976 special session. Prepared by members
       of the Legislative Research Commission staff, Edited
       by Gary W. Luhr, Frankfort, Legislative Research
       Commission, 1976.
       iii, 51, [9]p.   27 cm.   (Informational bulletin,
       no. 120)

14614 Kentucky. Legislative Research Commission.
       Legislative hearing on non-fault insurance before
       the interim joint committee on banking and insurance...
       Frankfort, Ky., Legislative Research Commission,
       1977.
       v, 33 p.   27½ cm.   (Informational bulletin,
       no. 125)

14615 Kentucky. Legislative Research Commission. Interim
       Joint Committee on Health and Welfare. Laetrile
       Study Subcommittee.
       Report... Frankfort, Ky., Legislative Research
       Commission, 1977.
       iii, 121 p.   27½ cm.   (Informational
       bulletin, no. 124)
       Representative Dottie Priddy, chairman; Legislative
       Research Commission staff, Richard D. Willis.

14616 Kentucky. Legislative Research Commission. Interim
       Study Commission on Computer-Stored Information
       and Personal Privacy.
       Personal information and privacy. Frankfort, 1977.
       xi, 267 p.   tables.   27½ cm.   (Research
       report, no. 145)

14617 Kentucky. Legislative Research Commission.
       Investment of life insurance funds in Kentucky.
       Frankfort, 1963.
       iii, 7 p.   29 cm.   (Informational bulletin, 35)

14618 Kentucky. Legislative Research Commission.
       Kentucky veterans bonus; estimated cost. Prepared

by Charles Zettlemoyer, budget analyst... Frankfort, Ky., 1960.
   34 p.   map, tables.   29 cm.

14619 Kentucky. Legislative Research Commission.
     Kentucky's constitutional development. [Frankfort, 196-]
     20 p.   illus.   24 cm.

14620 Kentucky. Legislative Research Commission.
     Kentucky's future transportation needs. Study supervised by Brian Kiernan... Frankfort, 1975.
     various pagings.   illus., maps (one fold. in pocket at end)   tables.   28 cm.   (Research report, no. 122)

14621 Kentucky. Legislative Research Commission.
     Legislative hearings on the proposed budget, 1976 extraordinary session. Conducted by Joint House and Senate Appropriations and Revenue Committee, December 6, 7, and 9, 1976. Frankfort, Legislative Research Commission, 1977.
     iii, 339 p.   28 cm.   (Informational bulletin, 123)

14622 Kentucky. Legislative Research Commission.
     The legislative process in Kentucky. Frankfort, 1955.
     244 p.   24 cm.   (Research publication, no. 43)

14623 Kentucky. Legislative Research Commission.
     Needs of children in Kentucky... [Frankfort, 1977]
     x, 175 p.   tables, diagrs.   27 cm.   (Research report, no. 138)

14624 Kentucky. Legislative Research Commission.
     Public higher education in Kentucky. Report to the Committee on Functions and Resources of State Government, prepared under the direction of the Division of Higher Education, U. S. Office of Education, Federal Security Agency... by a staff consisting of John Dale Russell [et al.] Frankfort [1951]
     vii, 185 p.   map, tables.   28 cm.   (Research publication, 25)

14625 Kentucky. Legislative Research Commission.
Public library services. Frankfort, The Commission,
1959.
83 p. 28 cm. (Research publication, no. 65)

14626 Kentucky. Legislative Research Commission.
Records management and state archives. Prepared
by the research staff, Legislative Research Commission.
Frankfort, 1957.
55 p. illus. 29 cm. (Research publication,
50)

14627 Kentucky. Legislative Research Commission.
Report of special committee to investigate education
to the House of Representatives of the Kentucky
General Assembly. March 10, 1960. Frankfort, 1960.
49 p. 29 cm.

14628 Kentucky. Legislative Research Commission.
Revision of Kentucky education statutes. Report
of subcommittee on Educational Statute Review...
Frankfort, Ky., 1977.
v, 41 p. 27½ cm. (Research report, no. 141)

14629 Kentucky. Legislative Research Commission. Special
Advisory Committee on Nuclear Waste Disposal.
Report... Frankfort, 1977.
x, 123 p. 27½ cm. (Research report, no.
142)

14630 Kentucky. Legislative Research Commission. Subcommittee
on Long Term Care of the Interim Joint Committee
on Health and Welfare.
Nursing Homes in Kentucky. Frankfort, 1977.
ix, 149 p. maps., diagrs., tables. 29 cm.
(Research report, no. 146)

14631 Kentucky. State Agent at Washington.
Report of the state agent for Kentucky at
Washington, made to the Governor, 1867-69. Frankfort,
J. H. Harney, public printer, 1869.
1 v. 22 cm.

14632 Kentucky. State Board for Vocational Education.
Suggested content and methods for a course in
homemaking for Kentucky high schools. Frankfort,
1931.

83 p.   24 cm.
"Revised 1931."

14633 Kentucky. State Dept. of Health.
       A new health philosophy - a new State Board of
       Health. Frankfort, 1973.
       27 p.   illus.   24 cm.   (Bulletin of the
       Kentucky State Department of Health, v. 46, no. 1,
       Jan., Feb., Mar. 1973)
       A history of the Department, with pictures of
       men prominent in its development and of former
       headquarters.

14634 Kentucky. State Forest Service.
       Forest trees of Kentucky. How to know them.
       A pocket manual. [Frankfort] Kentucky state forest
       service, in co-operation with the Forest service,
       U. S. Department of Agriculture, 1934.
       76 p.   23 cm.

14635 Kentucky. State Historical Society. Archives
       Dept.
       Death records, 1852-1862, Clark County, Kentucky.
       Transcribed from the original vital statistics
       in the Archives department of the Kentucky State
       Historical Society, Frankfort, by Mrs. Joseph
       Beard, Sr. & Mrs. H. K. McAdams [n.p., n.d.]

14636 Kentucky. State Industrial and Commercial Conference,
       Louisville, 1887.
       Kentucky towns and counties. Being reports of
       their growth, natural resources and industrial
       improvement made to the state Industrial and
       Commercial Conference at Louisville, October 4th,
       5th, and 6th, 1887. Frankfort, Capital book and
       job printing co., 1887.
       112 p.   tables.   24 cm.

14637 Kentucky. State Industrial and Commercial Conference,
       Louisville, 1887.
       Transportation systems, together with a review of
       transportation problems and opportunities to be
       developed. Frankfort, Capital printing co., 1887.
       66 p.   27 cm.

14638 Kentucky. State Park Board.
       The 1935 Kentucky state parks annual. Frankfort

[1935?]
48 p.   illus., map.   28½ cm.
No more published?

14639   Kentucky.   State Park Commission.
Biennial report of the Kentucky state park
commission.   May 1, 1928 - December 31, 1929.
[Frankfort, 1929?]
59 p.   illus., fold. map.   25 cm.

14640   Kentucky.   State Park Commission.
Biennial report...   January 1, 1929 - December
31, 1931.   [Frankfort, 1932?]
115 p.   illus.   25 cm.

14641   Kentucky.   State Park Commission.
Sesqui-centennial celebration of the battle of
the Blue Licks at Blue Licks Battlefield Park
(Kentucky State Park no. 5) Friday, August 19,
1932; report of proceedings, in the commemoration of
the 150th anniversary of the battle of August 19, 1782,
conducted under the auspices of the Kentucky state
park commission.   Lexington, 1932.
2 p.l., 125 p.   plates, 2 port.   (incl. front.)
map.   26 cm.

14642   Kentucky.   State Parks Division.
Blue Licks state park.   [n.p., n.d.]
unpaged.   illus., maps.   25 cm.

14643   Kentucky.   University.
Beginning a second century.   The University
of Kentucky academic program: curricula, policies,
and organization...   October, 1965.   [Lexington, Ky.,
1965]
220 p.   29 cm.

14644   Kentucky.   University.
Distinguished alumni.   [Lexington, Ky., 196-]
32 p.   illus.   29 cm.

14645   Kentucky.   University.
Five year plan, 1975-1980, University of
Kentucky.   [Lexington, 1975]
2 v.   maps, tables, diagrs.   22 x 30 cm.
Contents. - Vol. I.   Introduction.   Missions,

functions, and goals. Programs. - Vol. II. Land
use plan. Facilities plan. Financial plan.

14646 Kentucky. University.
      University of Kentucky. Lexington campus.
General development plan. Prepared by Crane &
Gorwic, planning design consultants, Detroit,
Michigan, in collaboration with Lawrence Coleman,
campus planner, University of Kentucky, June 1963.
Lexington, 1963.
      55 p.   maps (part fol.)   29½ x 29½ cm.

14647 Kentucky. University.
      University of Kentucky centennial preview,
1887-1965. [Lexington, 1964?]
      64 p.   illus., ports.   23 cm.

14648 Kentucky. University.
      University of Kentucky self-study. In cooperation
with the Southern Association of Colleges and
Secondary Schools. Lexington, April 1960.
      280, [3] p.   29½ cm.

14649 Kentucky. University.
      ...The unveiling of the replica of the statue
of the Honorable Alben W. Barkley. The speaker:
The Honorable Everett M. Dirksen. Tuesday, November
23, 1965... Lexington, [1965?]
      cover title.   [8] p.   illus.

14650 Kentucky. University. Alumni Association.
      The American political tradition. Addresses
presented at the First Annual Alumni Seminar,
July 30-August 2, 1958. Lexington, University of
Kentucky, 1959.
      78 p.   24 cm.
      Contents. I. A. D. Kirwan, The development of
the American political tradition. II. Herman E. Spivey,
American political tradition in American literature.
III. E. V. Murphree, The impact of the science
revolution on the American political tradition. IV.
Jesse W. Tapp, Industrialization and urban growth.
V. Amry Vandenbosch, The United States and world
leadership. VI. Frank G. Dickey, Closing remarks
at alumni seminar.

14651   Kentucky. University. Alumni Association.
        Communications, 1960: seeking a balance between
        freedom and responsibility. Transcript of the Third
        Annual Alumni Seminar, May 27-28, 1960. Lexington,
        1960.
        95 p.   22 cm.

14652   Kentucky. University. Bureau of Business Research.
        Kentucky tourist preferences. Lexington, 1962.
        57 p.   tables.   29 cm.

14653   Kentucky. University. Bureau of School Service.
        Kentucky's resources, their development and use.
        Revised edition... Lexington, 1958.
        347 p.   illus., tables, graphs, maps.   23 cm.

14654   Kentucky. University. Centennial Committee.
        The College of Commerce, University of Kentucky.
        Lexington, 1965.
        32 p.   24 cm.

14655   Kentucky. University. Centennial Committee.
        The College of Pharmacy, University of Kentucky.
        Lexington, 1965.
        14 p.   23 cm.

14656   Kentucky. University. Centennial Committee.
        University Extension, University of Kentucky.
        Lexington, 1965.
        24 p.   23 cm.

14657   Kentucky. University. Center for Developmental
        Change.
        A program for improving the quality of life in
        Appalachia... Lexington, 1972.
        40 p.   29½ cm.

14658   Kentucky. University. College of Adult and Extension
        Education.
        Living Kentucky composers. [Lexington] 1955.
        unpaged.   29 cm.

14659   Kentucky. University. College of Adult and
        Extension Education.
        Some Kentucky authors of the twentieth century.
        [Lexington, 1955]
        unpaged.   29 cm.

14660 Kentucky. University. College of Agriculture.
          Vitae. Lexington [1971]
          136 p.   ports.   29 cm.
          Biographical sketches of personnel, College of
       Agriculture, Agricultural Experiment Station, and
       Agricultural Extension Service.

14661 Kentucky. University. College of Education. Bureau of
          School Service.
          ...Kentucky's resources, their development and use,
       prepared under the direction of a core committee
       appointed by the commissioner of conservation and
       the superintendent of public instruction. Introduction
       by William Septimus Taylor... [Lexington, 1945]
          351 p.   illus., diag.   23 cm.   (Bulletin,
       xviii, No. 2, December, 1945)

14662 Kentucky. University. College of Law. Office of
          Continuing Legal Education.
          Index to reports of the proceedings of the
       continuing legal education seminars, University of
       Kentucky, College of Law. For CLE seminars 1974-
       1976. [Lexington, 1977?]
          33 p.   28 cm.

14663 Kentucky. University. College of Law. Office of
          Continuing Legal Education.
          Report on proceedings on Kentucky no fault
       insurance, October 25-26, 1974. [Lexington, 1974]
          206 p.   29 cm.

14664 Kentucky. University. College of Law. Office of
          Continuing Legal Education.
          Report of seminar, civil trial advocacy, January
       23-24, 1976. Presented by the Office of Continuing
       Legal Education, University of Kentucky, College of
       Law, in cooperation with the Kentucky Bar Association.
       [Lexington, 1976]
          81 p.   28 cm.

14665 Kentucky. University. College of Law. Office of
          Continuing Legal Education.
          Report of seminar, commercial law, February 20-21,
       1976. Presented by the Office of Continuing Legal
       Education, University of Kentucky College of Law,
       in cooperation with the Kentucky Bar Association.

[Lexington, 1976]
97 p.   28 cm.

14666   Kentucky. University. College of Law. Office of
        Continuing Legal Education.
        Report of seminar on criminal trial advocacy,
        March 19-20, 1976. Presented by the Office of
        Continuing Legal Education, University of Kentucky
        College of Law, in cooperation with the Kentucky
        Bar Association. [Lexington, 1976]
        74 p.   28 cm.

14667   Kentucky. University. College of Law. Office of
        Continuing Legal Education.
        Report of a seminar on domestic relations,
        February 22-23, 1974. Prepared by the Office of
        Continuing Legal Education, University of Kentucky
        College of Law in cooperation with the Kentucky
        Bar Association. [Lexington, 1974]
        77, [4], 4 p.   28 cm.
        Contents. - Henry H. Foster, Jr. No fault
        divorce - an overview. - Robert S. Petrilli,
        Kentucky's dissolution of marriage law. - S. J.
        Stallings, Kentucky procedure for dissolution of
        marriage. - William P. Mulloy, Child custody. -
        Stephen J. Vasek, Tax axpects of dissolution of
        marriage.

14668   Kentucky. University. College of Law. Office of
        Continuing Legal Education.
        Report of seminar on estate planning, July 19-20,
        1974. Presented by the Office of Continuing Legal
        Education, University of Kentucky College of Law,
        in cooperation with the Kentucky Bar Association.
        [Lexington, 1974]
        266 p.   28 cm.
        Contents. - Donald MacDonald, A trust officer views
        estate planning. - William B. Penden, Jointly
        held property. - Cynthia H. Camuel, Federal estate
        and gift taxes. - William P. Sturm, Kentucky
        inheritance tax. - William S. Dillon, Uses of trusts
        in estate planning. - J. E. Banahan, Estate planning
        for the farmer. - Edward A. Rothschild, Post mortem
        estate planning. - John Peter Frank III, Income
        taxation of trusts. - Richard S. Leventhal, The
        professional service corporation. - Michael Winston,

Qualified deferred compensation: profit sharing
and pension plans.

14669 Kentucky. University. College of Law. Office of
Continuing Legal Education.
Report of second annual seminar on estate
planning, July 18-19, 1975. Presented by the
Office of Continuing Legal Education, University of
Kentucky College of Law, in cooperation with the
Kentucky Bar Association. [Lexington, 1975]
115 p.   28 cm.

14670 Kentucky. University. College of Law. Office of
Continuing Legal Education.
Report of seminar on federal rules of evidence,
June 20-21, 1975. Presented by the Office of
Contintuing Legal Education, University of Kentucky
College of Law, in cooperation with the Kentucky Bar
Association. [Lexington, 1975]
92 p.   28 cm.

14671 Kentucky. University. College of Law. Office of
Continuing Legal Education.
Report of seminar on general practice review,
August 22-23, 1975. Presented by the Office of
Continuing Legal Education, University of Kentucky
College of Law, in cooperation with the Kentucky Bar
Association. [Lexington, 1975]
112 p.   28 cm.

14672 Kentucky. University. College of Law. Office of
Continuing Legal Education.
Report of seminar on juvenile law and procedure,
December 12-13, 1975. Presented by the Office of
Continuing Legal Education, University of Kentucky
College of Law, in cooperation with the Kentucky
Bar Association. [Lexington, 1975]
84 p.   28 cm.

14673 Kentucky. University. College of Law. Office of
Continuing Legal Education.
Report of seminar, Kentucky corporation law,
February 14-15, 1975. Presented by the Office of
Continuing Legal Education, University of Kentucky
College of Law, in cooperation with the Kentucky
Bar Association. [Lexington, 1975]
120 p.   28 cm.

14674 Kentucky. University. College of Law. Office of
       Continuing Education.
           Report of seminar on Kentucky penal code,
       September 26-27, 1974. Presented by the Office of
       Continuing Legal Education, University of Kentucky
       College of Law, in cooperation with the Kentucky Bar
       Association. [Lexington, 1974]
           243 p.   28 cm.

14675 Kentucky. University. College of Law. Office of
       Continuing Legal Education.
           Report of seminar on labor law, October 17-18, 1975.
       Presented by the Office of Continuing Legal Education,
       University of Kentucky College of Law, in cooperation
       with the Kentucky Bar Association. [Lexington, 1975]
           86 p.   28 cm.

14676 Kentucky. University. College of Law. Office of
       Continuing Legal Education.
           Report of seminar, law and medicine, April 24-26, 1975.
       Presented by the Office on Continuing Legal Education,
       University of Kentucky College of Law, in cooperation
       with the Kentucky Bar Association. [Lexington, 1975]
           iv, 140 p.   28 cm.

14677 Kentucky. University. College of Law. Office of
       Continuing Legal Education.
           Report of seminar on law and medicine - 1976.
       May 26-28, 1976. Presented by the Office of
       Continuing Legal Education, University of Kentucky
       College of Law, in cooperation with the Kentucky
       Bar Association. [Lexington, 1976]
           160 p.   28 cm.

14678 Kentucky. University. College of Law. Office of
       Continuing Legal Education.
           Report of the seminar on no fault insurance,
       October 25-26, 1974. Presented by the Office of
       continuing Legal Education, University of Kentucky
       College of Law, in cooperation with the Kentucky Bar
       Association. [Lexington, 1974]
           207 p.   28 cm.

14679 Kentucky. University. College of Law. Office of
       Continuing Legal Education.
           Report of seminar, Pension Reform Act, January 17-18,
       1975. Presented by the Office on Continuing Legal

Education, University of Kentucky College of Law,
in cooperation with the Kentucky Bar Association.
[Lexington, 1975]
    87 p.   28 cm.

14680 Kentucky. University. College of Law. Office of
       Continuing Legal Education.
          Report of seminar on professional responsibility,
       March 15, 1974. Presented by the Office of Continuing
       Legal Education, University of Kentucky College of
       Law, in cooperation with the Kentucky Bar Association.
       [Lexington, 1974]
          58, [3] p.

14681 Kentucky. University. College of Law. Office of
       Continuing Legal Education.
          Report of seminar on workmen's compensation,
       April 19-20, 1974. Presented by the Office of
       Continuing Legal Education, University of Kentucky
       College of Law, in cooperation with the Kentucky
       Bar Association. [Lexington, 1974]
          174 p.   28 cm.

14682 Kentucky. University. College of Law. Office of
       Continuing Legal Education.
          Report of workshop on law of debtor relief,
       September 19-20, 1975. Presented by the Office of
       Continuing Legal Education, University of Kentucky
       College of Law, in cooperation with the Kentucky Bar
       Association. [Lexington, 1975]
          83 p.   28 cm.

14683 Kentucky. University. College of Law. Office of
       Continuing Legal Education.
          Seminar on eminent domain held at the College of
       Law, University of Kentucky, Lexington, Kentucky,
       April 22-23, 1977. John K. Hickey, director of
       continuing legal education, presiding. [Lexington,
       1977]
          2 p.l., 118 p.   28 cm.

14684 Kentucky. University. College of Law. Office of
       Continuing Legal Education.
          Seminar on estate planning held at the College of
       Law, University of Kentucky, Lexington, Kentucky,
       July 22-23, 1977. Samuel Milner [of] Eblen, Milner,
       Rosenbaum and Wilson, Lexington, Kentucky, presiding.

[Lexington, 1977]
[4], 95 p.   28 cm.

14685   Kentucky. University. College of Law. Office of
        Continuing Legal Education.
        Seminar on mineral law held at the College of
        Law, University of Kentucky, Lexington, Kentucky,
        October 15-16, 1976.   [Lexington, 1976]
        100 p.   28 cm.

14686   Kentucky. University. College of Law. Office of
        Continuing Legal Education.
        Seminar on pension reform held at the College
        of Law, University of Kentucky, Lexington, Kentucky,
        November 19-20, 1976. Frederick W. Whiteside, Jr.,
        presiding. [Lexington, 1976]
        106 p.   28 cm.

14687   Kentucky. University. College of Law. Office of
        Continuing Legal Education.
        Seminar on prejudgment and post-judgment
        collections held at the College of Law, University
        of Kentucky, Lexington, Kentucky, September 9-10,
        1977. John K. Hickey, director of continuing legal
        education, College of Law, University of Kentucky,
        presiding. [Lexington, 1977]
        ii, 121 p.   28 cm.

14688   Kentucky. Univeristy. College of Law. Office of
        Continuing Legal Education.
        Seminar on public employee to labor relations held
        at the College of Law, University of Kentucky,
        presiding... [Lexington, 1977]
        [4], 114 p.   28 cm.

14689   Kentucky. University. College of Law. Office of
        Continuing Legal Education.
        Seminar on public service commission practice held
        at the College of Law, University of Kentucky,
        Lexington, Kentucky, September 24-25, 1976. William
        L. Matthews, Jr., presiding [Lexington, 1976]
        81 p.   28 cm.

14690   Kentucky. University. College of Law. Office of
        Continuing Legal Education.
        Seminar on workmen's compensation held at the
        College of Law, University of Kentucky, Lexington,

Kentucky, March 18-19, 1977. Shelby T. Denton,
Chairman... [Lexington, 1977]
   87 p.   28 cm.
   In cooperation with the Kentucky Bar Association.

14691 Kentucky. University. Dept. of Physical Education.
   Kentucky folk festival dances. University of
   Kentucky, April 4-5, 1952. [Lexington, 1952]
      vi, 54 p.   23 cm.

14692 Kentucky. University. Dept. of Political Science.
   Legislative and congressional redistricting
   in Kentucky. Lexington, Bureau of Government
   Research, College of Arts and Sciences, 1951.
      vii, 88 p.   maps, tables.   29 cm.

14693 Kentucky. University. Dept. of Printing.
   Printing guide. [Lexington, 1966]
      14 p.   21½ cm.

14694 Kentucky. University. Department of Zoology.
   ...The Zoological museum... Catalogue of exhibits...
   [Lexington, n.d.]
      [16] p.   22½ cm.
   Exhibits relate mainly to fauna of Kentucky.

14695 Kentucky. University. Library.
   Bulletin, nos. 1-25, 1949-1964. Lexington,
   1949-1964.
      25 nos.   23-26½ cm.
   "Writings on Kentucky history": nos. 1 (1948),
   2 (1949), 4 (1950), 5 (1951), 10 (1952), 13 (1953),
   14 (1954), 17 (1955), by Jacqueline Page Bull.

14696 Kentucky. University. Library.
   An exhibit of products from Stanbrook Abbey Press,
   1876-1966. End September - October 1966. [Lexington,
   1966]
      8 p.   23 cm.
   Introduction by J. G. Dreyfus.

14697 Kentucky. University. Library.
   Guide to the libraries. Lexington [1974]
      24 p.   illus., diagrs.   23 cm.

14698 Kentucky. University. Library.
   Guide to the University of Kentucky Libraries.

[Lexington, 1975]
28 p.   illus.   21½ x 26½ cm.   (Instructional
Services Department series, 4)

14699   Kentucky. University. Library.
A Hammer bibliography (1930-1952) Lexington,
Margaret I. King Library, 1952.
84 p.   29 cm.   (Occasional contribution, no.
48)

14700   Kentucky. University. Library.
Here's to you, Harry Clay! An exhibition of books,
manuscripts and memorabilia from the Department of
Special Collections in celebration of the two
hundredth anniversary of the birth of Henry Clay.
Gallery, Special Collections, University of Kentucky
Libraries, weekdays 8-5, Saturday 8-noon, March 1
through April 1. [Lexington, 1977]
[24]p.   22 cm.

14701   Kentucky. University. Library.
Library guide. Lexington, 1963.
40 p.   illus., plans.   21½ cm.

14702   Kentucky. University. Library.
Library notes. v. 1, nos. 1-3. Lexington,
1969-70.
3 nos.   illus., facsims.   29¼ cm.
No more issued.

14703   Kentucky. University. Library.
Lincoln facsimile. Nos. 1-22, Nov. 1959 - Sept.
1963.   Lexington, 1959-1963.
22 nos. incl. 13¼ and 14½. facsims.
29-39 cm.

14704   Kentucky. University. Library.
Subject guide to research. [Lexington, 1975]
9 nos.   29 cm.
Contents. Women's studies. - Geography. - American
history. - Elections. - Statistical sources. - City
plans. - Film - Modern European history. - Literature:
Beginning research.

14705   Kentucky. University. Woman's Club.
Hors d'oeuvres cookbook 1971. Appetite tempters.

　　　　[Lexington, 1971]
　　　　　cover-title.　　24 p.　　23 cm.

14706　Kentucky. The bluegrass state.　[n.p., n.d.]
　　　　　[98] p.　　illus., fold map.

14707　Kentucky.
　　　　　[Certificate issued to Simon Kenton for his services
　　　　as a captain on the 1785 expedition against the
　　　　Shawnee Indians]　[Frankfort, Kentucky Historical
　　　　Society, n.d.]
　　　　　manuscript 1 ℓ.　　29 x 22½ cm.

14708　Kentucky. (Provisional government, 1861-1865)
　　　　　Constitutional convention. Declaration of
　　　　independence and constitution of the Provisional
　　　　government of the State of Kentucky; together with
　　　　the message of the Governor.　Bowling Green, Ky.,
　　　　W. N. Holdeman, 1861 [Anchorage, Ky., 1961]
　　　　　1 p.l., facsim: 16 p.　　22 cm.
　　　　　cover title.
　　　　　Introd. signed: Philip Cloutier.

14709　Kentucky. Sights to see.　Lexington, 1977.
　　　　　32 p.　　illus.　　26½ cm.
　　　　　Supplement to Lexington Sunday Herald-Leader,
　　　　24 April 1977.
　　　　　Covers Western Kentucky beyond the Green River.

14710　Kentucky. Sights to see.　The Blue Grass and environs.
　　　　　[Lexington, 1977]
　　　　　32 p.　　illus.　　26½ cm.
　　　　　Supplement to Lexington Sunday Herald-Leader,
　　　　21 June 1977.

14711　The Kentucky almanac, for the year of Our Lord 1806...
　　　　Lexington, Printed by John Bradford [1805]
　　　　　[36]p.　　17 cm.

14712　The Kentucky almanac, for the year of Our Lord 1807...
　　　　Lexington, Printed by John Bradford [1806]
　　　　　[36]p.　　17 cm.

14713　The Kentucky almanac, for the year of Our Lord,
　　　　1815.　Being the third after bissextile, or leap-
　　　　year; and after the 4th of July, the 40th year of
　　　　American independence.　Calculated by James G.

Arnold, for the meridian of Maysville, in lat. 38, 27, 8.
Maysville, Printed at the "Eagle" press, and
sold there, and at the different stores in town [1814]
[36] p.   17 cm.

14714   The Kentucky almanac, for the year of Our Lord,
1816. Being bissextile, or leap-year; and after
the 4th of July, the forty-first year of American
independence. Calculated by James G. Arnold. For the
meridian of Maysville, in lat. 38, 27, 8. Maysville,
Ky., Printed at the Eagle Office, by J. H. & R.
Corwine [1815]
[24] p.   17 cm.

14715   The Kentucky almanac, for the year of Our Lord 1817:
being the first after bissextile of leap year. The
41st year of American independence after 4th of July...
Calculated for the meridian of Lexington, but will
serve without any essential difference, for the
states of Ohio and Tennessee, the western parts of
Virginia and the territories. Lexington, Printed
at the office of the Kentucky Gazette, by F.
Bradford, Jr. [1816]
[36] p.   17½ cm.

14716   The Kentucky almanac, for the year of Our Lord 1818:
being the second after bissextile or leap year. The
42nd year of American independence [after the 4th of
July] the 30th of the federal government -- and the 27th
of this commonwealth... Calculated for the meridian
of Lexington [Ky.] and will serve without any
sensible variation, the states of Ohio, Indiana,
Tennessee, and the western parts of Virginia.
Lexington, Printed at the office of the Kentucky
Gazette, by John Norvell & co. [1817]
[36] p.   18 cm.

14717   The Kentucky almanac, and astronomical ephemeris,
for the year of Our Lord 1819: being the
third after bissextile or leap year, the 43d
year of American independence [after the 4th of
July] the 31st of the federal government -- and the
28th of the Commonwealth, after the 1st day
of June... Calculated for the meridian of
Lexington, [Ky.] and will serve without any
sensible variations, the states of Ohio, Indiana,
Illinois, Tennessee, and Virginia. Lexington,

Printed at the office of the Kentucky gazette, by
John Norvell [1818]
[36] p.   18 cm.

14718   The Kentucky almanac, for the year of Our Lord 1820:
being bissextile, or leap year... Calculated for
the meridian of Lexington [Kentucky] and will serve
without any sensible alteration, the states of Ohio,
Indiana, Illinois, Tennessee, and Virginia. By
John Bradford, esq. Lexington, Printed at the
office of the Kentucky Reporter, by Thomas Smith
[1819]
36 p.   20 cm.

14719   The Kentucky almanac, for the year of Our Lord 1821:
(Being the first after bissextile or leap year)
The 45th year of American independence (after the
4th of July) the 33d of the federal government, and
the 29th of this Commonwealth... Calculated for the
meridian of Lexington, Ken., and will serve without
any sensible alteration for the states Ohio,
Indiana, Illinois, Tennessee and Virginia. By
John Bradford, esq. Lexington, Published by William
Worsley, T. Smith - Printer [1820]
36 p.   18 cm.

14720   The Kentucky almanac, for the year of Our Lord 1822...
Calculated for the meridian of Lexington, Ken. And
will serve without any sensible error, the states of
Ohio, Indiana, Illinois, Tennessee, and Virginia.
The astronomical calculations by James W. Palmer.
Lexington, Printed at the office of the Public
Advertiser [1821]
24 p.   17 cm.

14721   Kentucky ancestors. Published quarterly by the
Genealogical Committee of the Kentucky Historical
Society. v. 1, no. 1, July 1965-   Frankfort.
v.   illus., maps.   28 cm.
Library has v. 1, 1965-v. 10, 1974.

14722   Kentucky Baptist atlas. Baptists' beginning the
westward expansion. [Middletown, Ky., Kentucky
Baptist historical society in cooperation with
the Historical Commission of the Southern Baptist
convention and the Kentucky Baptist convention, 1964]
8 l.   illus., map.   29 cm.

14723   ...Kentucky bluegrass isn't either blue or native...
        Lexington, 1969.
            broadside.   illus.   60 x 42 cm.   (Reprinted
        from Sunday Herald-Leader, 2 February 1969)

14724   Kentucky Civil War Round Table.
            In memoriam: William Henry Townsend, 1890-
        1964. [Lexington, Kentucky, 1964]
            12 p.   port. on cover-title.
            Includes promotional note for Mr. Townsend's
        Hundred Proof; Salt River Sketches & Memoirs of the
        Bluegrass, an article in Lexington Herald, 22 September
        1964, on memorial services for Mr. Townsend at Kentucky
        Civil War Round Table, 21 September 1964.

14725   Kentucky County (Virginia) Convention of 1784/85.
            Journal of the first Kentucky Convention,
        Dec. 27, 1784 - Jan. 5, 1785. Edited by Thomas
        P. Abernethy. Baton Rouge, La., The Franklin press,
        1935.
            67-78 p.   27 cm.
            Reprinted from The Journal of southern history,
        v. 1, no. 1, Feb. 1935. (Duplication of 13514)

14726   Kentucky Education Association.
            Selected K. E. A. addresses of general interest.
        April 16-17-18, 1941. Lexington, Kentucky, The
        Hobson press, 1941.
            150 p.   21 cm.

14727   The Kentucky farmer's almanac, for the year 1812,
            being bissextile, or leap-year; and [after the
        4th of July] the 36th of American independence:
        containing, [exclusive of the astronomical
        calculations,] a variety of useful and entertaining
        matter. Calculated by Robert Stubbs. Lexington,
        Printed by W. W. Worsley, and sold wholesale and
        retail, by self, and Maccoun, Tilford & co. [1811]
            [36] p.   17 cm.

14728   The Kentucky farmer's almanac, for the year 1813,
            being the first after bissextile, or leap year and
        [after the 4th of July] the 37th of American
        independence. Containing [exclusive of the
        astronomical calculations,] a variety of useful and
        entertaining matter. Calculated by Robert Stubbs,
        philomath. Lexington, Printed by William W.

189

Worsley, and sold wholesale and retail by self,
and Maccoun, Tilford & co. [1812]
[36] p.   18 cm.

14729 The Kentucky farmer's almanac, for the year 1814,
being the second after bissextile, or leap-year;
and [after the 4th of July] the 39th of American
independence. Containing [exclusive of astronomical
calculations], a variety of useful and entertaining
matter. Calculated by Robert Stubbs, philomath.
Lexington, Printed by William W. Worsley, and sold,
wholesale and retail, by self, and Maccoun, Tilford
& co. [1813]
[34] p.   18½ cm.

14730 The Kentucky farmer's almanac, for the year 1815;
being the third after bissextile or leap year;
and [after the 4th of July] the 40th of American
independence. Calculated by Robert Stubbs.
Containing [exclusive of the astronomical calculations]
a variety of useful and entertaining matter. Lexington,
Printed and published by William W. Worsley [1814]
[36] p.   16 cm.

14731 The Kentucky farmer's almanac, for the year 1817,
being 1st after bissextile, or leap year; and
[after the 4th of July] the 42nd of American
independence. Containing [exclusive of the
astronomical calculation] a variety of useful
and entertaining matter. Calculated by T.
Henderson. Georgetown, Ky., Printed by Shellers
and Lyle [1816]
[36] p.   16 cm.

14732 The Kentucky farmer's almanac, for the year 1818,
being 2d after bissextile, or leap year; and
[after the 4th of July] the 43rd of American
independence. Containing [exclusive of the
astronomical calculation] a variety of useful and
entertaining matter. Calculated by T. Henderson.
Georgetown, Ky., Published by William Sebree, John
N. Lyle, printer [1817]
[36] p.   16 cm.

14733 Kentucky Health, Welfare and Salary-limit Amendment
Committee, Louisville.

Whose ox but yours? [Louisville? n.d.]
32 p.   graph.   24 cm.

14734   Kentucky Heritage Commission.
State-wide survey of historical sites in
Kentucky, prepared... in cooperation with the
Kentucky Program Development Office and National
Park Service, Department of Interior by Spindletop
Research, Inc. Lexington, Kentucky, March 1971.
various pagination.   maps, facsims.   28½ cm.

14735   Kentucky historical and genealogical magazine.
v. 1, no. 1-2, May-June, 1899. Lexington,
Polk & Peay, 1899.
2 nos.   24 cm.
No more published.

14736   The Kentucky Home Schools for Girls... Louisville,
Ky. Founded in 1865 by Miss Belle S. Peers.
1928-1929. [Louisville, 1929]
30 p.   illus.   21 cm.

14737   Kentucky Marijuana Feasibility Study, Inc., Lexington,
Ky.
Marijuana: a pot of money for Kentucky.
[Lexington, 1976?]
[4] p.   22½ cm.

14738   Kentucky North-Bend Agricultural Society.
Annual fair. Fourth exhibition of the Kentucky
North-Bend Agricultural Society, to be held on
Friday and Saturday, 9th & 10th of Sept. 1836,
at Burlington, Boone County, Ky. [n.p., 1836?]
broadside.   57 x 40 cm.

14739   Kentucky River soundings. Nos. 1-3, 5-6, April -
Dec., 1975. Camp Nelson, Ky., 1975.
5 nos.   illus.   29 cm.
No. 4 not published? No more issued.
At end is article by Sue Alexander, Camp Nelson
moves toward fulfilling dream, reprinted from
Lexington Herald-Leader, 9 November 1975.

14740   Kentucky state fair. History. [n.p., 1968]
cover-title.   64 p.   illus.   27 cm.

14741　Kentucky Utilities company, Lexington.
　　　　　Dix dam and Herrington lake. [Lexington, n.d.]
　　　　folder in octavo. illus., map.　41 x 58 cm.
　　　　　Appended are a letter by Lawrence S. Thompson to
　　　　the Lexington Herald dated 28 July 1972 and an
　　　　article by Joe Ward in the Louisville Courier-
　　　　Journal, 7 August 1972, "'Monster' reported
　　　　swimming in Herrington Lake."

14742　Kenys, Janet T
　　　　　Retirement for non-certified school board
　　　　employees. Frankfort, Ky., Legislative Research
　　　　Commission, 1973.
　　　　　30 p.　taples.　29 cm.　(Research report
　　　　no. 103, new series)

14743　Kerr, Charles, 1863-1950.
　　　　　An address delivered at Lexington, Kentucky,
　　　　June 4, 1930, on the occasion of the sesquicentennial
　　　　of Transylvania University, 1780-1930. [Lexington?
　　　　1930?]
　　　　　8 p.　24 cm.

14744　Kerr, Charles, 1863-1950.
　　　　　Address of Charles Kerr, delivered at Washington,
　　　　Mason County, Kentucky, on June 5, 1936, on the
　　　　occasion of the sesqui-centennial of the founding of
　　　　the town of Washington. [n.p., 1936?]
　　　　　cover-title, 15 p.　23 cm.

14745　Kerr, Charles, 1863-1950.
　　　　　An address on the occasion of the celebration
　　　　of the Sesqui-Centennial of the signing of the
　　　　constitution, held at Lexington, Kentucky, October 6,
　　　　1937, under the auspices of Transylvania College.
　　　　[Lexington, 1937?]
　　　　　cover title, 18 p.　23 cm.

14746　Kerr, Hazel Cary.
　　　　　Richard L. Cary, Jr. ("Hyder Ali") The story
　　　　of his life and his sporting ballads, by Hazel
　　　　Cary Kerr and John Wilson Townsend. [n.p.]
　　　　1927.
　　　　　5 p.　port.　30 cm.
　　　　　From an electrostatic copy of the only copy that
　　　　could be located, formerly in the University of
　　　　Kentucky Library but not now on the shelf.

14747   Kidder, D   P   ed.
          Frontier sketches. Selected and arranged by the
        author of "Dying hours," etc. New York, Lane &
        Scott, 1851.
          142 p.   15 cm.

14748   Killebrew, Joseph Buckner.
          Information for immigrants concerning middle
        Tennessee and the counties in that division traversed
        by or tributary to the Nashville, Chattanooga & Louis
        Ry... Nashville, Tenn., Marshall & Bruce co., printers,
        1898.
          148 p.   illus., map.

14749   King, Edward.
          The southern states of North America: a record
        of journeys in Louisiana, Texas, the Indian
        Territory, Missouri, Arkansas, Mississippi, Alabama,
        Georgia, Florida, South Carolina, North Carolina,
        Kentucky, Tennessee, Virginia, West Virginia and
        Maryland. By Edward King. Profusely illustrated
        from original sketches by J. Wells Champney.
        London, Blackie and son, 1875.
          806 p.   illus.   26 cm.

14750   King, Helen Galvin, 1904-
          Sparks from my Christmas tree, by Helen G.
        King. Lexington, Ky., The Kernel press [1936]
          16 p.   22 cm.
          Verse.

14751   King, Warren Raymond.
          The surface waters of Kentucky, a preliminary
        report descriptive of the stream flow and power
        resources of the Ohio, Big Sandy, Kentucky, Green
        and Cumberland Rivers in Kentucky... Frankfort,
        Kentucky Geological Survey, 1924.
          [12], 192 p.   illus., tables. $24\frac{1}{2}$ cm.
        (Kentucky Geological Survey, ser. VI, v. 14)

14752   Kinkead, Eleanor Talbot ("Mrs. Thompson Short")
          'Gainst wind and tide, by Nellie Talbot Kinkead.
        Chicago and New York, Rand McNally & company, 1892.
          214 p.   22 cm.

14753   Kinkead, Eleanor Talbot ("Mrs. Thompson Short")
          The invisible bond. New York, Moffat,

Yard & company, 1906.
513 p.   front.   20½ cm.

14754   Kinkead, Eleanor Talbot ("Mrs. Thompson Short")
        The spoils of the strong. New York, The James
        A. McCann company, 1920.
        308 p.   20 cm.

14755   Kinkead, Elizabeth Shelby.
        A history of Kentucky, by Elizabeth Shelby
        Kinkead. New York [etc.] American Book Company
        [1919]
        288 p.   illus., port., map.   18½ cm.
        "Constitution of the Commonwealth of Kentucky":
        p. 227-272.

14756   Kinkead, George Blackburn.
        Reminiscence of the Fayette bar by an old
        lawyer who recalls the impressions they made on
        him in his youth. An address... before the
        Kentucky state bar association held at Lexington,
        April 5, 1928. [n.p., n.d.]
        24 p.   23 cm.
        Inscribed by author.

14757   [Kinne, William Alfred]
        The gum tree story. [Stearns, Ky.? n.d.]
        [4] p.   illus.   23 cm.
        Signed by author.
        At end of this copy are mounted undated
        clippings from the McCreary County Record relative
        to Senator Kinne and his business and a photograph
        of the author on an election campaign card from
        around 1930.

14758   Kirby, Harriet Griswold.
        Barbesieu, or the troubador. A libretto by
        Harriet Griswold Kirby. Louisville, John P.
        Morton & company, 1913.
        [6], 21 p.   21¼ cm.

14759   Kirby, Harriet Griswold.
        Christmas gift, a play for small children in
        schools and Sunday schools, by Harriet G. Kirby.
        Louisville, Ky., John P. Morton & compnay, 1933
        [3], 12 p.   23 cm.

14760　Kirk, Charles D
　　　　　...Wooing and warring in the wilderness.　By
　　　　Chas. D. Kirk (Se De Kay)... New York, Derby &
　　　　Jackson; Louisville, Ky., F. A. Crump, 1860.
　　　　　288 p.
　　　　　At head of title:　A story of Canetuckey.

14761　Kniffin, Thomas Henderson.
　　　　　Kentucky of Kentucky, a romance of the Blue
　　　　Grass region, by T. Henderson Kniffin.　New York,
　　　　Cochrane publishing co., 1909.
　　　　　3 p.l., 5-163 p.　　incl. plates.　　19½ cm.

14762　Knight, Grant Cochran, 1893-1955.
　　　　　Bluegrass and laurel:　the varieties of Kentucky
　　　　fiction.　[n.p., 1945]
　　　　　12-13 p.　　ports.　　30 cm.
　　　　　Reprinted from The Saturday review, v. 28,
　　　　6 January 1945.

14763　Kinght, Grant Cochran, 1893-1955.
　　　　　James Lane Allen and the genteel tradition...
　　　　Chapel Hill, N. C., University of North Carolina
　　　　Press, 1935.
　　　　　313 p.　　front. (port.)　　23 cm.

14764　Knight, Grant Cochran, 1893-1955.
　　　　　The new freedom in American literature.
　　　　Edited with an introduction by Scott C. Osborn.
　　　　Volume III of The first phase of realism in
　　　　American literature...　Lexington, Ky., 1961.
　　　　　79 p.　　front. (port.)

14765　Knight, Grant Cochran, 1893-1955.
　　　　　The sealed well [by] Grant C. Knight.　New York,
　　　　The Fine editions press, 1943.
　　　　　32 p.　　19½ cm.
　　　　　Poems.
　　　　　Inscribed by author.
　　　　　Includes manuscript poem by author at end, a
　　　　clipping from Lexington Herald, 1 February 1945 on
　　　　Mr. Knight's election as distinguished professor
　　　　at University Kentucky, two undated clippings
　　　　reviewing The sealed well (one signed H.H.H.), and
　　　　a clipping on his College book of prose.

14766   Knight, Thomas A
         Country estates of the Blue Grass. [By] Thomas
         A. Knight [and] Nancy Lewis Greene. Lexington, Ky.,
         Henry Clay press, 1973.
         200 p.   illus.   24 x 31 cm.
         Reprint of 1905 edition.

14767   Knott, James Proctor, 1830-1911.
         Proctor Knott on Duluth. A reprint of the speech
         delivered in Congress by the Hon. J. Proctor Knott
         of Kentucky in eighteen seventeen-one. [Duluth,
         Minn.?] Convention tourist, & publicity bureau,
         Duluth Chamber of Commerce [n.d.]
         30 p.   illus., map.   18½ cm.

14768   Knott, James Proctor, 1830-1911.
         Proctor Knott's speech on Duluth, edited by
         Philip D. Jordan. [St. Paul, Minn., 1954]
         67-78 p.   illus.   26½ cm.
         Reprinted from Minnesota History, 1954.

14769   Knott, Sarah Gertrude.
         Kentucky lore. A gatherin' of mountain music,
         songs and dances. Frankfort, Ky., Kentucky
         Council of the Performing Arts and the Kentucky
         Department of Commerce, 1963.
         52 p.   29 cm.

14770   Knox College, Galesburg, Illinois.
         A catalogue of the Sang Collection of letters,
         books, manuscripts, documents and prints
         illustrating "the irrepressible conflict."
         An exhibit from the collections of Mr. and Mrs.
         Philip D. Sang, of River Forest, Illinois, held
         in Galesburg, Knox College, October 4-5-6-7, 1958,
         on the anniversary of the fifth Lincoln-Douglas
         debate [Galesburg? 1958?]
         52 p.   illus., facsims.   23 cm.
         Contains materials relative to slavery in
         Kentucky and Uncle Tom's cabin.

14771   Koenig, James B
         The petrography of certain igneous dikes of
         Kentucky. Lexington, 1956.
         57 p.   maps, tables.   24 cm.   (Kentucky
         Geological Survey, Series IX, Bulletin, no. 21)

14772 Kohler, Marianne Styles.
         Prehistoric mammals in Kentucky. [Louisville, 1973]
         12-14 p.   illus.   27½ cm.
         Reprinted from Rural Kentuckian magazine, v. 27,
         no. 9, September, 1973.

14773 Körner, Gustav Philipp, 1809-1896.
         Das deutsche Element in den Vereinigten Staaten
         von Nordamerika, 1818-1843. Cincinnati, A. E.
         Wilde & co., 1880.
         461, [2] p.   22½ cm.

14774 Kottenkamp, Franz Justus, 1806-1858.
         Die ersten Amerikaner im Westen. Daniel Boone
         und seine Gefährten [Die Gründung Kentucky's]
         Tecumseh und dessen Brüder. Zweite Ausgabe mit
         acht colorirten Bildern. Stuttgart, Verlag von
         Schmidt & Spring, 1858.
         xii, 540 p.   col. front.   22½ cm.

14775 Kruegel, David L
         Projected Kentucky population growth by age, sex
         and color groups: 1960 to 1970. By David L.
         Kruegel. Lexington,Kentucky Agricultural Experiment
         Station, University of Kentucky, 1965.
         23 p.   tables, diags.   24 cm.   (Kentucky
         Agricultural Experiment Station, Bulletin, 703)

14776 Kubala, Linda.
         Rising electricity rates: current issues.
         Prepared by Linda Kubala, Frankfort, Ky.,
         Legislative Research Commission, 1977.
         vi, 103 p.   27½ cm.   (Research report, no.
         136)

                              L

14777 La Bree, Benjamin, ed.
         Camp fires of the confederacy; a volume of
         humorous anecdotes, reminiscences, deeds of
         heroism, thrilling narratives, campaigns, hand-to-
         hand fights, bold dashes, terrible hardships
         endured, imprisonments... etc. Confederate
         poems and selected songs... Ed. by Ben La Bree...

Louisville, Courier-Journal job printing company,
1898.
   2 p.l., 560 p.   illus.   24½ cm.

14778   Lafayette [pseud.]
         Lafayette, To the People, (originally published
in the Kentucky Gazette) [text begins] [Lexington,
John Bradford, 1825]
         64 p.   19 x 11 cm.
         Caption title; no imprint. First advertised in
the Kentucky Gazette, July 1, 1825; "Just published,
and for sale at this office, Lafayette To the
People. Being a series of numbers published in
this paper and now collected and given in pamphlet
form..." The first article signed with this
pseudonym appeared in Bradford's paper February 24,
1825. There is no significance to the pseudonym
except that the writer, like the French hero who
was touring the United States at the time, is for
control of the government by the people.

14779   Lafayette Female Academy.
         Visit of General Lafayette to the Lafayette
Female Academy, in Lexington, Kentucky, May 16,
1825, and the exercises in honour of the Nation's
guest: Together with a catalogue of the instructers
[!] visiters [!], and pupils, of the academy.
Lexington, Printed by John Bradford, May, 1825.
         32 p.   21 x 13 cm.

14780   Lafferty, Maude (Ward) "Mrs. W. T. Lafferty"
         1869-
         Catalogue of Henry Clay items in Ashland, the
home of Henry Clay. 2d., rev. ed. [Lexington, Ky.]
The Henry Clay Memorial Foundation, 1950.
         9 p.   22 cm.

14781   Lafferty, Maude (Ward) "Mrs. W. T. Lafferty", 1869-
         Pageant of Kentucky's historic, past...
The celebration of the 150th anniversary of
Kentucky's first permanent settlement, Monday,
June 16, 1924, 2 P.M.-8 P.M., Graham Springs
Park, Harrodsburg, Ky. Directed by M. W. H.
McGreevy [and] Mrs. Neva Summers Burgess.
Music under direction of Professor Carl Lampert...
Auspices of Kentucky Pioneer Memorial Association...

[n.p., 1924]
64 p. illus. 28½ cm.

14782 Lafferty, Maude (Ward) "Mrs. W. T. Lafferty", 1869-
A pioneer railway of the west. [Lexington,
Ky., University of Kentucky, College of mechanical
and electrical engineering, 1916]
cover-title, 29 p. 21 cm.

14783 Lafferty, Maude (Ward) "Mrs. W. T. Lafferty," 1869-
Sesquicentennial stories... Published and
distributed by the Kentucky sesquicentennial
commission... Cynthiana, Ky., The Hobson press,
1942.
41 p. 24 cm.

14784 Lafferty, William Thornton, 1856-1923.
John Aker Lafferty and Francis Henry Lafferty, his
wife, during the Civil War. [Lexington, Ky.? 1921?]
52 typewritten l. 16 cm.

14785 Laflin, Bonny Dale.
A guide to 28 public fishing lakes, by Bonny
Dale Laflin and Peter W. Pfeiffer. Frankfort, Ky.,
Kentucky Department of Fish and Wildlife resources,
1972.
83 p. illus., maps., diagrs. 29 cm.

14786 Lampkins, G   W
Kentucky of today; its principal citities [!]
and towns, protective and commercial ability,
financial and trade resources, historical and
descriptive. [n.p.] Issued by the Kentucky Division
of the Travelers Protective Association of
America, 1896.
86 p. illus. 26 x 33 cm.

14787 Lancaster, Clay.
A guide to the location of houses standing in
1961 and included in Ante-bellum houses of the
Bluegrass by Clay Lancaster. Lexington, 1961.
map. 65 x 55 cm.

14788 Lander, Arthur B
Blue Licks Battlefield State Park. [Falls
Church, Va., 1976]
10-11 p. illus. 27 cm.

199

14789　Lander, Arthur B
　　　　　Perryville:　tribute to Civil war dead.
　　　　[Gettysburg, Pa., 1976]
　　　　　10-11, 15 p.　　illus.　　28 cm.
　　　　　Reprinted from American motorist (Bluegrass ed.),
　　　　v. XLV, no. 1, July 1976.

14790　Large, Mary Harriott.
　　　　　The twelfth juror, by Mary Harriott Large.
　　　　Boston, The C. M. Clark publishing company, 1908.
　　　　　3 p.l., 298 p.　　front.　　20 cm.

14791　Lawrence, Raymond E
　　　　　History of Crittenden Baptist Church of Jesus
　　　　Christ, 1856-1950, by Raymond E. Lawrence.
　　　　[n.p., 1950?]
　　　　　cover title,　54 p.　　illus., port., facsims.
　　　　23 cm.

14792　Lawson, Albert.
　　　　　The iron industries of Ironton, and the Hanging
　　　　Rock iron region of Ohio.　Comp. by A. Lawson,
　　　　for the Ironton Board of trade...　Cincinnati,
　　　　Bloch & co., 1871.
　　　　　cover-title, 26 p.　　21½ cm.

14793　Lawson, Norman W
　　　　　Circuit court redistricting...　Frankfort, Ky.,
　　　　Legislative Research Commission, 1971.
　　　　　46 p.　　maps.　　29 cm.　　(Research report, no. 59)

14794　League of Women Voters, Lexington, Ky.
　　　　　Housing in Lexington and Fayette County.　An
　　　　outline for study.　Lexington, League of Women
　　　　Voters, 1952.
　　　　　28 p.　　29 cm.

14795　Lee, Lucy C
　　　　　A historical sketch of Mason County, Kentucky,
　　　　by Lucy C. Lee...　Louisville, Press of Masonic
　　　　home journal [1928]
　　　　　1 p.l., [5]-46 p.　　21½ cm.

14796　LeMaster, J　　　　R
　　　　　Jesse Stuart's 'Album of destiny' - in
　　　　Whitman's eternal flow.　Normal, Ill., 1973.
　　　　　38-48 p.　　23 cm.

Reprinted from Illinois quarterly, v. 36,
no. 1, Sept. 1973.

14797 Lenroot, Katharine Frederica, 1891-
Sophonisba Preston Breckinridge, 1866-1948.
A supplementary statement read at the Illinois
Welfare Conference, resolutions by the American
Association of Welfare Workers, and articles by
May Estelle Cook and Katharine F. Lenroot.
[Chicago, 1949]
88-96 p.   ports.   24 cm.
"Reprinted from the Social Services Review, v. 23,
no. 1, March 1949."

14798 Lester, William Stewart.
The Transylvania colony... Spencer, Ind.,
Samuel R. Guard & co., 1935.
288 p.   20 cm.

14799 Lester, William Stewart.
The Transylvania colony. Abstract of dissertation.
A dissertation submitted in partial fulfillment of
the requirements for the degree of doctor of
philosophy at the University of Kentucky. Lexington,
1934.
13 p.   27 cm.

14800 Les Williams... a builder of time. [Louisville,
1976]
[2] p.   illus.   28 cm.
Reprinted from Rural Kentuckian, v. 30, no. 12,
December, 1976.

14801 Letters; a quarterly magazine published at the
University of Kentucky.
v. 1-5 (no. 1-20); Nov. 1927 - Aug. 1932.
[Lexington, Ky. 1927-32] Edited by the Department
of English language and literature, E. R. Farquhar,
editor.
No more published.

14802 Lewis, Annie R
Historical sketch, First Methodist Church,
1789-1939, Lexington, Kentucky. Lexington,
Byron-Page Printing Co., Printers [1939?]
32 p.   plates, ports.   24 cm.

14803   Lewis, Calien Crosby.
        History of Simpsonville Christian Church,
        compiled by Calien Crosby Lewis. [n.p., 1943?]
        20 p.   17 cm.

14804   Lewis, Ralph A
        Forests and forestry in Kentucky [by] Ralph A.
        Lewis. Lexington, University of Kentucky, College
        of Agriculture, Cooperative Extension Service [1974?]
        22 p.   illus., diagrs.   28 cm.   (For-4)
        Tipped in at end are James A. Newman, Yellow
        poplar - the state tree of Kentucky (2p.; FOR-2);
        James A. Newman, Weed control for walnut seedlings
        (2p.; FOR-3); James A. Newman, Growing trees for
        dollars (2p.; FOR-6); and O. M. Davenport, Seasoning
        lumber (5p., FOR-7)

14805   Lexington, Ky. Central Christian Church. Ladies'
        Aid Society.
        Cook book. Lexington [n.d.]
        66 p.   23½ cm.
        Manuscript title page.

14806   Lexington, Ky. Citizens.
        Taylor meeting. [Lexington, Serugham & Dunlop,
        printers, 1847]
        12 p.   22½ cm.

14807   Lexington, Ky. First Presbyterian Church.
        In memoriam. Reverend Robert Whitfield Miles,
        D. D. [Lexington, University of Kentucky Press,
        1952]
        25 p.   front. (port.)   15 cm.

14808   Lexington, Ky. Laws, statutes, etc.
        An act to incorporate the city of Lexington, and
        ordinances passed in pursuance thereof, regulating
        the interests and concerns of the city government.
        Published by authority. Lexington, Observer &
        reporter printing company, 1867.
        141 p.   23 cm.

14809   Lexington, Ky. Lexington-Fayette County Recreation,
        Tourist and Convention Commission.
        Historic Lexington. [Lexington, 1976]
        [8] p.   illus., maps.   23 cm.

14810 Lexington, Ky. Public Library.
       A catalogue of the books, belonging to the
       Lexington library company; to which is prefixed,
       a concise narrative of the origin and progress of
       the institution; with its charter, laws &
       regulations, Lexington, Printed by Thomas Smith,
       Jordan's Row, 1821.
       xiv, 172, [2] p.   23 x 14 cm.

14811 Lexington, Ky. St. Joseph Hospital.
       100 years of service to central Kentucky.
       [Lexington, 1977]
       17 p.   illus.   28 cm.

14812 Lexington, Ky. Sesqui-centennial jubliee
       celebration.
       ...Official souvenir program of Sesqui-centennial
       jubilee celebration of Lexington, Kentucky, May 31 -
       June 6, 1925. Published by the Citizen's general
       committee. Lexington, 1925.
       115 p.   illus. (incl. ports.)   23 cm.
       At head of title: 1775-1925.
       "The pageant of Lexington," by Mrs. W. T.
       Lafferty: p. 45-106.
       Advertising matter interspersed.

14813 Lexington, Ky. Woodland Christian Church. Ladies'
       Aid Society.
       The home economist... Lexington [n.d.]
       36 p.   26 cm.

14814 Lexington and Eastern Railway.
       Natural Bridge, being an illustrated description
       of this wonderful natural formation and its
       historical surroundings. Published by the
       Passenger department in 1899. Stanton, Ky.,
       Reprinted by the Powell County Lions Club, 1957.
       47 p.   illus.   21 x 25 cm.

14815 Lexington Chamber of Commerce.
       Map of Lexington and suburbs. Fayette
       County, Kentucky. Street guide and bus lines.
       [Lexington, 196-?]
       map.   64 x 56 cm.

14816 Lexington in a nutshell; a handbook for college
       1975/76. [n.p.] 1975.

84 p.   illus.   29 cm.
On cover: Compliments of U. K. Student Center
Board.
   Apparently a national publication with local
articles in addition to general ones and local
advertising. Includes "U. K. - Outside the
classroom," by Georgeann Rosenberg, p. 2-3.

14817 Lexington Junior League.
          1974 horse show. Lexington, Ky. 1975.
          271 p.   illus.   28 cm.

14818 Lexington 1969: Land of horses, tobacco, livestock,
          colleges, culture, industry. Lexington, Kentucky,
          1969.
            2 p.   illus.   32 x 42 cm.   Reprinted from
          Sunday Herald-Leader, 2 February 1969.

14819 Lexington Roller Mills Co., Lexington, Ky.
          A few famous recipes by an old Kentucky cook...
          The Lexington twins... [Lexington, n.d.]
          [12] p.   illus.   24 cm.
          Title on p. [3]: Lexipep cook book.

14820 [Lexington trots] Lexington, Ky., 1974.
          12 p.   illus.   40 cm.

14821 The Liberty Hall cook book. Receipts and recipes,
          collected by the National society of the Colonial
          Dames of America in the Commonwealth of Kentucky.
          [Frankfort?] 1963.
          184 p.   illus.   22 cm.

14822 Liberty saved, or the warnings of an old Kentuckian
          to his fellow-citizens on the danger of electing
          partisans of the old Court of appeals. Louisville,
          W. Tanner, printer, 1825.
          v, [6]-28 p.   19 cm.

14823 Life of Daniel Boone. Dayton O., Ells, Marquis &
          company, 1856.
            vi, 7-288 p.   incl. front., illus. (incl. ports.)
          pl.   18 cm.
          Illustrated t.-p.

14824 The life of John James Audubon, the naturalist.
          Ed. by his widow. With an introduction by Jas.

Grant Wilson. New York, G. P. Putnam & son, 1869.
x, [11]-443 p.   front. [port.]   19½ cm.

14825 Life of Rev. Elisha W. Green, one of the founders of
the Kentucky Normal and Theological Institute...
and over thirty years pastor of the colored Baptist
churches of Maysville and Paris. Written by himself.
Maysville, Ky., The Republican printing office, 1888.
3 p.l., 60 p.   front. [port.]   22 cm.

14826 The life of the pilgrim Joseph Thomas containing
an accurate account of his trials, travels, and
gospel labors, up to the present date. Winchester,
Va., J. Foster, printer... 1817.
372 p.   18 cm.

14827 Lincoln, Abraham, pres. U.S., 1811-1865.
Oration of Abraham Lincoln at the dedication of
the Gettysburg national military cemetery,
November 19, 1863. [Lexington, The Margaret I.
King Library press, 1959]
4 p.   29 cm.
"The text used in this broadside is that of an
apparently unique sheet in the Alfred Whital
Stern Collection in the Library of Congress...
The wooden screw press on which this broadside has
been printed is a copy of the late sixteenth
century Raimondi Press in the Biblioteca Mediceo-
Laurenziana, Florence; it was built during the
years 1926-1930 by Florentine craftsmen working
under the direction of Victor Hammer who had
made the drawings for its construction. The
Margaret I. King Library obtained the press in
1954. The present printing is its first use here.
Gerald M. Stevenson, Jr., set the type and
printed these pages in the summer of 1969."

14828 Lines on the death of the Confederate Gen. Albert
Sidney Johnston, of Ky., who fell at the battle
of "Shiloh," Miss., Sunday, April 6, 1862.
broadside.   25 x 11 cm.

14829 List of Revolutionary war pensioners of Clark
County, Kentucky. Transcribed by Mrs. W. K. McAdams.
[Winchester, Ky., Clark County Historical Society,
n.d.]
1 ℓ., 4, 2 p.   28 cm.

14830 Literary landmarks of Kentucky. Lexington, Research
       and Publication Committee, Kentucky Council of
       Teachers of English, 1961.
           48 p.   illus., map.   21½ cm.   (Kentucky
       English bulletin, v. 11, no. 1, Fall 1961)

14831 Litsey, Edwin Carlile, 1874-
           The eternal flame, a novelette, by Edwin Carlile
       Litsey. Based on the life of Jesus of Nazareth.
       Louisville, Standard printing company, 1937.
           3 p.l., 98 p.   22 cm.
           Author's presentation copy.

14832 Litsey, Edwin Carlile, 1874-
           The race of the swift, by Edwin Carlile Litsey...
       Illustrated with drawings by Charles Livingston Bull.
       Boston, Little, Brown and company, 1905.
           7 p.l., 3-151 p.   front., 3 p.l.   19½ cm.
           Contents. - The race of the swift. - The robber
       baron. - The ghost coon. - The spoiler of the
       folds. - The fight in the tree-bridge. - The
       guardian of the flock. - The king of the northern
       slope.

14833 Littell, William, 1768-1824.
           An epistle from William, surnamed Littell, to the
       people of the realm of Kentucky... Frankfort,
       Printed by William Hunter, 1806.
           40 p.   19 cm.

14834 Littell, William, 1768-1824.
           Festoons of fancy, consisting of compositions
       amatory, sentimental, and humorous in verse and
       prose... Lexington, Ky., University of Kentucky
       publications committee, Margaret Voohies Haggin
       trust, 1940.
           xv, 115 p.   illus., facsim.   22 cm.
       (Kentucky reprints, no. 1)
           Introduction by Thomas D. Clark.

14835 Littell, William, 1768-1824.
           Political transactions in and concerning
       Kentucky, from the first settlement thereof,
       until it became an independent state, in June,
       1792... Frankfort, Ky., From the press of
       William Hunter, 1806.
           81, 66 p.   18 cm.

14836 Littell, Willaim, 1768-1824.
　　　　Reprints of Littell's political transactions
　　　in and concerning Kentucky and letter of George
　　　Nicholas to his friend in Virginia also General
　　　Wilkinson's Memorial. With an introduction by
　　　Temple Bodley. Louisville, John P. Morton &
　　　company, 1926.
　　　　cxxxix, 172 p.　　facsims.　　23½ cm.
　　　(Filson Club publications, no. 31)

14837 Livermore, Mrs. Mary Ashton [Rice] 1820-1905.
　　　　The story of my life: or, The sunshine and
　　　shadow of seventy years... Hartford, Conn.,
　　　A. D. Worthington, & co., 1899.
　　　　730 p.　　23 cm.

14838 Lives of James Buchanan and John C. Breckenridge,
　　　Democratic candidates for the presidency and
　　　vice-presidency of the United States, with the
　　　platforms of the political parties in the presidential
　　　canvass of 1856. Cincinnati, H. W. Derby & co.,
　　　1856.
　　　　2 p.l., 1-88 p.　　front. [port.]　　20 cm.

14839 Livesay, Ann.
　　　　Geology of the Mammoth Cave National Park area.
　　　By Ann Livesay, 1953. Revised by Paul McGrain,
　　　1962. [Lexington, Ky.] 1962.
　　　　40 p.　　illus., map. diags.　　24 cm.
　　　(Kentucky Geological Survey, Series X, 1962;
　　　Special publication, 7)

14840 Lloyd, James T
　　　　Lloyd's steamboat directory, and disasters on
　　　the western waters, containing the history of
　　　the first application of steam, as a motive power;
　　　the lives of John Fitch and Robert Fulton...
　　　History of the early steamboat navigation on
　　　western waters... Full accounts of all the
　　　steamboat disasters... A complete list of
　　　steamboats and all other vessels now afloat on
　　　the western rivers and lakes... maps of the
　　　Ohio and Mississippi river... One hundred...
　　　engravings, and forty-six maps... By James T.
　　　Lloyd. Cincinnati, O., J. T. Lloyd & co., 1856.
　　　　vi, 7-326 p.　　illus. (incl. ports., maps,
　　　facsim.)　　23½ cm.

14841   Lloyd, John Uri, 1849-1936.
            Warwick of the Knobs, a story of Stringtown
        County, Kentucky... with photographic illustrations
        of Knob County. New York, Dodd, Mead & Company,
        1901.
            305 p.   illus.   20 cm.

14842   Logan County, Ky., Homemakers.
            Favorite recipes of Logan County Homemakers.
        [Russellville, Ky.?] 1947.
            60 p.   map.   24 cm.

14843   Logan, John A
            The great conspiracy, its origin and history...
        New York, A. R. Hart & co., 1886.
            810 p.   illus.   23 cm.

14844   Loh, Jules.
            Biggest feud of all. Lexington, Ky., 1975.
            2 p.   illus.   60 x 38 cm.
            Reprinted from Lexington Herald-Leader,
        9 November 1975.

14845   Long, Calista Rosser (Cralle)
            Journal of Calista Cralle Long. A diary
        record of a forty-two day journey; Campbell
        Co., Va., to Union Co., Ky., Dec. 1836 - Jan.,
        1837. Fayetteville, W. Va., Privately printed
        by Armistead Rosser Long, 1940.
            14 p.   25 cm.

14846   Long, Carl Littleton.
            History of the Indian Creek Christian Church,
        Harrison County, Kentucky. Also some fundamental
        articles contributed by authors who labored
        within the church. Cynthiana, Ky., Cynthiana
        Publishing co., 1948.
            61 p.   ports.   21 cm.

14847   Look before you leap; or, A few hints to such
        artizans, mechanics, labourers, farmers and
        husbandmen, as are desirous of emigrating to
        America, being a genuine collection of letters,
        from persons who have emigrated; containing
        remarks, notes and anecdotes, political,
        philosophical, biographical and literary, of the
        present state, situation, population, prospects

and advantages, of America, together with the
reception, success, mode of life, opinions
and situation, of many characters who have
emigrated, particularly to the federal city of
Washington... [London] Printed for W. Row
[etc.] 1796.
1 p.l., xxxvii, [39]-144 p.   22 cm.

14848   Loomis, Henry H
        Lexington legacies, compiled by Henry H.
        Loomis. Lexington, Ky., Robert E. Milward,
        1975.
        68 p.   illus., maps. (1 fold.), facsims.
        19½ cm.

14849   Loughborough, Preston S
        A digest of the statute laws of Kentucky, of
        a public and permanent nature, passed since
        1834, with references to judicial decisions...
        Frankfort, Printed by Albert G. Hodges, 1842.
        viii, 10-693 p.   24½ cm.

14850   Louisville, Ky. Beechmont Younger Woman's Club.
        [Cook book] Club project, United Cerebral
        Palsy of Greater Louisville. Louisville [195-]
        29 p.   illus.   23 cm.

14851   Louisville, Ky. Calvary Episcopal Church.
        A book of favorite recipes compiled by the
        Women's auxiliary of the Calvary Episcopal
        Church, Louisville, Kentucky. [Louisville]
        1923.
        55 p.   22 cm.

14852   Louisville, Ky. Second Presbyterian Church.
        History of the Second Presbyterian Church of
        Louisville, Kentucky. Published in connection
        with its centennial. April 17, 1830 - April 17,
        1930. [Louisville, 1930]
        59 p.   illus.   20 cm.

14853   Louisville, Ky. Twenty-third and Broadway Baptist
        Church.
        Golden Jubilee manual of the Twenty-third and
        Broadway Baptist Church; the old Twenty-second
        and Walnut Baptist Church, Louisville, Ky.,
        organized October 16, 1887. [Louisville, 1937]

4 l., 59 p.   illus.   22 cm.
On cover: 1887-1937.

14854   Louisville, Ky. University. Library.
        Ainslie Hewett bookplate collection. U. of L.
        Library exhibit, Feb, 1-29, 1972.
        3 ℓ.   21½ cm.

14855   Louisville, Ky. Walnut Street Baptist Church.
        History of the Walnut Street Baptist Church
        of Louisville, Kentucky. [Louisville, Ky.] Western
        Recorder [1937]
        91 p.   ports., plates.   23 cm.
        Contents. - 1815-1900, prepared by Dr. T. T.
        Eaton. - 1900-1937, prepared by a committee of
        the Deacons: S. B. Tinsley, R. C. Bowden, Dr.
        W. M. Randall and assisted by Wm. O. Carver, Jr.

14856   Louisville, Ky. Woman's club.
        Favorite recipes. [Louisville] 1938.
        172 p.   24 cm.

14857   Louisville and Cincinnati Packet Company.
        Describing the daily steamer service between
        Louisville, Kentucky, Cincinnati, Ohio, way ports
        and the famous "meet the boat trip." Louisville
        [n.d.]
        cover-title, 17 p.   illus., time table.
        21 cm.

14858   Louisville and Nashville Railroad Company.
        Charter of the Louisville & Nashville R. R.
        Co. with amendments to 1869. Together with the
        general railroad laws of Kentucky and Tennessee.
        And the charter of the Memphis & Ohio R. R. Co.
        Louisville, Ky., Printed by John P. Morton &
        Company, 1869.
        vii, [1], [5]-115 p.   23½ cm.

14859   Louisville and Nashville Railroad Company.
        Parade of progress. [Louisville, Ky.? 1956]
        unpaged.   illus., maps.   28 cm.

14860   Louisville and Nashville Railroad Company.
        Subterranean wonders. Mammoth Cave and
        Colossal Cavern, Kentucky. [Louisville] Louisville

& Nashville Railroad, Passenger Department [n.d.]
48 p.   illus., map.   19½ cm.

14861 Louisville and Nashville Railroad Company.
A tribute to Edward Stockton Jouett, by the
members of the Law Department in the thirteen
states served by the Louisville and Nashville
Railroad Co. Louisville, Ky., 1944.
[4], 15 p.   port.   23 x 28 cm.

14862 The Louisville directory, for the year 1832: to
which is annexed, lists of the municipal, county and
state officers; with a list of various societies,
and their officers. Also, an advertiser. Louisville,
Published by Richard W. Otis, James Virden, printer,
1832.
198 p.   14½ cm.

14863 Louisville flood map showing flooded area of
Louisville, Kentucky, January 1937. Louisville,
Standard printing company, 1937.
map.   71 x 100 cm.

14864 Louisville history "on the air." Being a collection
of historical sketches that were broadcast during
1947 & 1948 over Radio station WHAS. Sponsored
by Louisville Taxicab & transfer co., operators
of yellow cabs. [Louisville, 1949]
92 p.   illus.   19 cm.
"Compiled and edited by Sally V. Woleben"
(verso of t.-p.)

14865 Louisville Hotel, Louisville, Ky.
Table d'hote. Louisville, Morton and Griswold,
printers [1857]
broadside.   30 x 22¼ cm.
Mounted on same page in scrapbook is card
soliciting support for Fayette Hewitt, Democratic
candidate for auditor of public accounts, 1875,
and the card of G. M. Talbott & Bro, proprietors
of Hynes House Livery Stable, Bardstown, Ky.

14866 Luhr, Gary W   ed.
Duties of elected county officials (revised
1976) Revised by Daryl Abner. Edited by Gary W.
Luhr... Frankfort, Ky., Legislative Research
Commission, 1976.

viii, 187 p.   28 cm.   (Informational
bulletin, no. 114)

14867 Luhr, Gary W
        Issues confronting the 1976 General Assembly.
        Prepared by members of the Legislative Research
        Commission staff. Edited by Gary W. Luhr.
        Frankfort, Ky., Legislative Research Commission,
        1975.
        iii, 105 p.   29 cm.   (Kentucky. Legislative
        Research Commission. Informational bulletin, no. 110)

14868 Luhr, Gary.
        Kentucky local planning laws: review and
        analysis, prepared by Gary Luhr. Frankfort, Ky.
        Legislative Research Commission, 1977.
        v, 117 p.   27½ cm.   (Research report, No.
        134)

14869 Lutes, Ann.
        A brief history of Boone County, Kentucky. This
        paper was written January, 1954 and read before
        the Boone County Historical Society on February 18,
        1955. Florence, Ky. [n.d.]
        [16] p.   23 cm.

14870 Luttrell, Juanita Skaggs.
        Kentucky and Tennessee Skaggs, compiled by
        Mrs. Juanita Luttrell and Mrs. Mollie Vicich.
        [n.p., 197-]
        unpaged.   29½ cm.

14871 Lynch, Laurence K
        The structure and long-term growth of Kentucky
        economy, by Lawrence K. Lynch. Lexington,
        Prepared by the Center for Public Affairs, College
        of Business and Economics, University of Kentucky
        [for The Kentucky Council of Economic Advisors]
        1977.
        x, 46 p.   28 cm.   (Kentucky Council of
        Economic Advisors, Policy papers series, no. 2)

14872 Lynd, Samuel W
        Memoir of the Rev. William Staughton, D. D. By
        Rev. S. W. Lynd... Boston, Lincoln, Edmands, &
        co.; Cincinnati, Hubbard and Edmands, 1834.
        vi, [7]-311, [1] p.   front. (port.)   19 cm.

212

14873　Lyons, John A
　　　　　The sesquicentennial of St. Clare's Church
　　　　　on Clear Creek in Hardin County, Kentucky, 1808-
　　　　　1958, by John A. Lyons. [n.p., 1958]
　　　　　13 p.　　cover illus.　　26¼ cm.

14874　Lyons, T　　　　L
　　　　　The English grammar, newly arranged and
　　　　　adapted to the use of schools and private learners.
　　　　　By T. L. Lyons. Lexington, Ky., Noble & Dunlop,
　　　　　printers, 1839.
　　　　　vi, 72 p.　　17½ x 11 cm.

14875　Lyra germanica. Journal for German lyric poetry.
　　　　　v. 1-10. Lexington, Ky., 1966-1975.
　　　　　10 v.　　24 cm.
　　　　　v. 1, no. 1, May 1966, published by Department
　　　　of Languages, Western Michigan University,
　　　　Kalamazoo; v. 1, no. 2, September 1966, published
　　　　by Department of Germanic and Classical Languages,
　　　　University of Kentucky, Lexington; v. 2-10, 1967-
　　　　1975, published by editor, Lexington, Ky.

M

14876　Mabry, John H
　　　　　Census tract street and road index of Lexington
　　　　and Fayette County, Kentucky (December 1, 1962)
　　　　with an appendix on socio-economic areas [by]
　　　　John H. Mabry, Martha C. Ritchie, Joseph M.
　　　　Heidenreich, with cartography by Thomas P. Field,
　　　　Lexington, Ky., Office of the City Manager, 1963.
　　　　　xv, 37 p.　　maps.　　29 cm.

14877　McAdams, Mrs. W　　　　K　　　　comp.
　　　　　List of Revolutionary War pensioners of Clark
　　　　County, Kentucky, transcribed by Mrs. W. K. McAdams
　　　　[n.p., n.d.]
　　　　　1 p.l., 7 typewritten l.　　31 cm.

14878　McAfee, Ky. New Providence Presbyterian Church.
　　　　　Sesqui-centennial celebration. New Providence
　　　　Presbyterian Church, Founded June 6, 1978. Saturday
　　　　and Sunday, June 9 and 10, 1934. McAfee, Ky., 1934.

[8] p.   cover illus.   23 cm.
"Historic New Providence," prepared by Rev. George
B. Thompson: p. [1-3]

14879 McAfee, Nelly (Nichol) Marshall, 1845-1895.
       As by fire... third ed. Harrodsburg, Ky.,
       Published by the author, 1872.
       323 p.   20 cm.

14880 McAfee, Robert Breckenridge.
       Speech of Robert B. M'Afee on education.
       Delivered in the Senate, on the bill providing a
       literary fund for the establishment and support
       of free schools, as amended by attaching thereto
       appropriations for the University, Centre and
       Southern Colleges. [Frankfort? 1819?]
       broadside.   29½ x 47 cm.

14881 Macaulay, Thomas, 1800-1859.
       Specimen pages of a Latin version of Macaulay's
       Life of Johnson, by John H. Neville, of Lexington,
       Ky. Cincinnati, Press of Robert Clarke & co.,
       1886.
       30 p.   18 cm.

14882 McBee, May Wilson.
       The life and times of David Smith, patriot,
       pioneer and Indian fighter. [Kansas City, Mo.,
       E. L. Mendenhall, Inc., printers, 1959]
       [3] l., 84 p.   29 cm.

14883 McBride, James, 1788-1959.
       Pioneer biography. Sketches of the lives of
       some of the early settlers of Butler county, Ohio.
       By James McBride... Cincinnati, R. Clarke & co.,
       1869-71.
       2 v.   front. (port.)   24 cm.   (Half-title:
       Ohio valley historical series. No. 4)
       Biographical sketch of the author, by Laura
       McBride Stembal: v. 1, p. vii-xi.

14884 MacBryde, Nancy.
       The green funeral. [Lexington, Ky., 1959]
       15-18, 23-26 p.   23 cm.
       Reprinted from Stylus, v. 7, no. 2, Spring 1959.

14885 [McCandless, Helen]
The house at Second and Broadway; yesterday and
today. [Louisville, 1936]
17 p.   illus.   23 cm.
Illustrations by Catherine B. Meyer.

14886 McCann, William Ray.
Some descendants of John Keand (McCann) of
Whithorn, Scotland, many of whom lived and died in
Paris, Bourbon County, Kentucky, and were known
as McCanns. [Paris, Ky.? 1953]
31, [52] p.   illus., maps, facsims. $28\frac{1}{2}$ cm.

14887 [McCaslin, Mrs. Elbert]
Historical sketch of the First Baptist Church,
Princeton, Kentucky, 1850-1940. [Princeton, Ky.?
1940?]
cover title, 24p.   illus.   23 cm.

14888 McChord, John H
The McChords of Kentucky and some related families.
The Hynes, Caldwell, Wickliffe, Hardin, McElroy,
Shuck and Irvine families. Louisville, 1941.
56 p.   24 cm.

14889 McClellan, Ely.
An account of the epidemic of cholera, during the
summer of 1873, in eighteen counties of the state
of Kentucky... Cambridge, Printed at the Riverside
Press, 1874.
cover-title, 24 p.   24 cm.
Inscribed by author.

14890 McClung, John Alexander, 1804-1859.
Sketches of western adventure: containing an
account of the most interesting incidents connected
with the settlement of the West, from 1755 to 1794;
with appendix. Also additional sketches of
adventure, compiled by the publishers, and a
biography of John A M'Clung, by Henry Waller.
Covington, Ky., R. H. Collins & Co., 1872.
xxix, 13-398 p.   port., plates.   20 cm.

14891 McClure, Dianna.
The cost of poverty: information for action.
Frankfort, Ky., Legislative Research Commission,
1974.

108 p.   maps, tables.   29 cm.   (Research
report no. 111, new series)

14892 McCord, John A   , 1875-
       Life and labors of Rev. John A. McCord.
       Pineville, Ky., 1961.
           29 p.   illus., front. (port.)   23 cm.

14893 McCormack, Mrs. Arthur Thomas.
           Our pioneer heroine of surgery. [n.p., 1932?]
           109-124 p.   illus.   23 cm.

14894 McCready, John Dudley.
           The collected works of James Lane Allen.
       By John Dudley McCready. Submitted in partial
       fulfillment of the requirements for the degree of
       Master of Arts in the Faculty of Philosophy,
       Columbia University. September, 1922. [New York,
       1922]
           50 p.   29 cm.
       On p. 50 are excerpts from Clark County Deed
       Books showing ancestral properties apparently owned
       by Allen's ancestors. Apparently added to
       original thesis by the transcriber, George Ferdinand
       Doyle of Winchester.

14895 McCready, Richard Lightburne.
           History of St. Luke's Church, Anchorage,
       Kentucky, by Richard Lightburne McCready. [n.p.,
       1940]
           44 p.   illus.   22 cm.

14896 McCreary, James Bennett, 1838-1918.
           Speech in favor of a United States land court
       for the investigation and settlement of private
       land claims in the territories of Arizona and
       New Mexico and the state of Colorado delivered
       in the United States House of Representatives,
       March 31, 1888. Washington, 1888.
           16 p.   23 cm.
       Tipped in at end in article by Paul R. Jordan,
       Tribute paid to McCreary at memorial dedication,
       Louisville Courier-Journal, 17 Nov. 1959.

14897 McDaniel, Ernest, ed.
           Kentucky readings, compiled by Ernest McDaniel.
       With introductions by Thomas D. Clark. Lexington,

Kentucky Cooperative Counseling and Testing
Service, University of Kentucky, 1964.
    [6], 375 p.   illus., maps, facsims.   21 cm.
(Kentucky Cooperative Counseling and Testing
Service, vol. 3)
    Literary map of Kentucky, by Lawrence S. Thompson,
drawn by Charles T. Wade: p. 374-5.
    Illustrations by Robert Herndon.

14898 McDowell, Ephraim, 1771-1830.
    Three cases of extirpation of diseased ovaria,
by Ephraim McDowell of Danville, Kentucky.
Reprinted from the Eclectic repertory, and
analytical review, medical and philosophical
(Philadelphia), VII (April, 1817), 242-244.
With an introduction by Emmet Field Horine, M. D.,
of Brooks, Kentucky. Lexington, University of
Kentucky Library Associates, 1960.
    [8] p.   23 cm.   (Keepsake, no. 7)

14899 [McDowell, Mrs. Katherine Sherwood Bonner]
    Dialect tales, by Sherwood Bonner. New York,
Harper & brothers, 1883.
    187 p.   incl. front., illus., plates.   24 cm.

14900 McElroy, Mrs. Lucy Cleaver, 1860-1901.
    Juletty, a story of old Kentucky, by Lucy Cleaver
McElroy. New York, Thomas Y. Crowell & co. [1901]
    280 p.   front., 15 p.l.   19½ cm.
    Title vignette.
    "Drawings by W. E. Mears": p. 9.

14901 McElroy, Robert McNutt.
    Kentucky in the nation's history... New York,
Moffat, Yard and company, 1909.
    590 p.   illus., maps.   22 cm.

14902 McFarlan, Arthur Crane, 1897-
    Geology of Kentucky... Lexington, University
of Kentucky, 1934.
    531 p.   illus., maps.   23 cm.

14903 McFarlan, Arthur Crane, 1897-
    Geology of the Natural Bridge State park area.
Lexington, 1954.
    31 p.   illus.   (Kentucky Geological Survey.
Series IX. Special Publication. no. 4)

14904 McFarlan, Arthur Crane, 1897-
        Memorial of Arthur McQuiston Miller. [n.p.]
        Geological Society of America, 1936.
            cover-title, 283-287 p.   port.   25 cm.
        "Proceedings of the Geological Society of America,
        1935."
        "Bibliography of Arthur McQuiston Miller":
        p. 284-287.

14905 [McFarlan, Arthur Crane] 1897-
        A report on natural resources. [n.p.]
        Committee for Kentucky [194-]
            39 p.   illus., map, diags.   24 cm.

14906 McFarlan, Arthur Crane, 1897-
        Some old Chester problems - correlations
        along the eastern belt of outcrop, by Arthur C.
        McFarlan and Frank H. Walker. Lexington, Ky.,
        1956.
            37 p.   illus., map., diags. (2 fold.)   24 cm.
        (Kentucky Geological Survey, Series IV, Bulletin,
        no. 20)

14907 Macfarland, William H
        Discourse on the life of Honorable Henry Clay.
        Richmond, H. K. Ellysen, printer, 1852.
            15 p.   21½ cm.

14908 McGann, Agnes Geraldine.
        Nativism in Kentucky to 1860... Washington,
        D. C., Catholic University of America, 1944.
            x, 172 p.   24 cm.
        Ph.D. dissertation, Catholic University of
        America.

14909 McGarvey, John William, 1829-1911.
        Autobiography. Lexington, Ky., College of the
        Bible, 1960.
            93 p.   23 cm.

14910 McGee, L   N
        Burkesville and Cumberland County [Kentucky]
        [Frankfort, 1929]
            broadside.   illus.   28½ cm.
        Reprinted from Kentucky progress magazine, v.1,
        no. 12, p. 21, Aug. 1929.

14911 McGee, L   R
        Kentucky consumer price index, 1969 to first
        quarter 1972. Prepared by Dr. L. R. McGee and
        Dr. C. M. Vaughan... Frankfort, Legislative
        Research Commission, 1972.
        35, 7 p.   tables. $29\frac{1}{2}$ cm.   (Research
        report, no. 70)

14912 McGee, Nora L
        Tales of old Bardstown, compiled by Nora L.
        McGee... [Bardstown, Ky.] Bardstown Woman's
        Club [n.d.]
        [27] p.   illus.   26 cm.

14913 McGill, Josephine, comp.
        Folk songs of the Kentucky mountains. Twenty
        traditional ballads and other English folksongs,
        notated from the singing of the Kentucky mountain
        people and arranged with piano accompaniment by
        Josephine McGill. Introductory note by H. E.
        Krehbiel... New York, Toronto [etc.] Boosey &
        co., 1917.
        3 p.l., 5-106 p.   illus.   (music) $27\frac{1}{2}$ cm.

14914 McGrain, Preston.
        Geology of the Carter and Cascade caves area.
        Lexington, Ky., 1954.
        32 p.   illus.   21 cm.   (Kentucky Geological
        Survey: Ser. IX. Special publication, no. 5)

14915 McGrain, Preston.
        Geology of the Cumberland Falls State park area.
        Lexington, Ky., 1955.
        33 p.   illus., maps, diags.   24 cm.
        (Kentucky Geological Survey, Series IX, Special
        publication, no. 7)

14916 McGrain, Preston.
        Recent investigations of silica sands of
        Kentucky no. 2. Lexington, Ky., 1956.
        32 p.   map, tables, diags.   24 cm.
        (Kentucky Geological Survey, Series IV, Report of
        investigations, no. 11)

14917 Mackaye, Percy Wallace, 1875-1956.
        This fine-pretty world; a comedy of the

Kentucky mountains. New York, Macmillan, 1924.
197 p.   20 cm.

14918   M'Kinley, the poltroon & assassin, in his true colors.
[Frankfort?] October 8, 1811.
broadside.   22 x 27 cm.

14919   McKnight, Martin Marshall.
The Marshalls of Kentucky, their homes and
principal burial ground. [Frankfort, 1931]
28-30 p.   illus.   28½ cm.
Reprinted from Kentucky progress magazine,
v. 3, no. 7, p. 28-30, Mar. 1931.

14920   Mackoy, Harry Brent.
Simon Kenton as soldier, scout, and citizen...
An address delivered Wednesday, August 19, 1936,
at the Blue Licks Battlefield State Park,
Robertson County, Kentucky, on the occasion of the
celebration of the 154th anniversary of the
Battle of the Blue Licks and Commemoration of
the centenary of the death of General Simon Kenton.
Lexington, 1936.
30 p.   front. (port.)   24½ cm.

14921   McLaughlin, James Fairfax, 1839-1903.
Matthew Lyon, the Hampden of Congress, a
biography... New York, Wynkoop Hallenbeck
Crawford company, 1900.
xi, 531 p.   pl., 8 port. [incl. front.]
22½ cm.

14922   McLeod, Don.
Daniel Boone, thirty men cut through Cumberland
Gap. Lexington, Ky., 1976.
broadside.   illus.   28 x 18 cm.
Reprinted from Lexington Herald-Leader,
13 June 1976.

14923   McMechen, James H
Legends of the Ohio Valley; or Thrilling
incidents of Indian warfare. Truth stranger than
fiction. 6th ed. ... Wheeling, West Virginia
printing co., prs., 1893.
112 p.   15 cm.

14924 McMeekin, Isabella (McLennan), 1895-
       Melodies and mountaineers, by Isabella McLennan
McMeekin. Boston, Mass., The Stratford co., 1921.
    5 p.l., 58 p.   front., pl.   18½ cm.

14925 McMurtrie, Douglas Crawford, 1888-1944.
       Check list of Kentucky imprints, 1787-1810,
by Douglas C. McMurtrie and Albert H. Allen.
Louisville, Historical Records Survey, 1939.
       xxvii, 205 p.   28 cm.   (American Imprints
Inventory, 5)

14926 McMurtrie, Douglas Crawford, 1888-1944.
       Checklist of Kentucky imprints, 1811-1820,
with notes in supplement to the check list of
1787-1810 imprints, by Douglas C. McMurtrie and
Albert H. Allen. Louisville, Historical Records
Survey, 1939.
       xiii, 235 p.   28 cm.   (American Imprints
Inventory, 6)

14927 McMurtrie, Henry, 1793-1865.
       The falls of the Ohio, and the adjoining
countries. Engraved for McMurtrie's Sketches.
[Louisville, Ky.? 18 ?]
       38 x 24 cm.   (Kentucky University Library.
Kentucky map facsimile, no. 6)

14928 McMurtrie, Henry, 1793-1865.
       The falls of the Ohio and the adjoining
countries. Engraved from McMurtrie's sketches.
[Louisville, Ky.? 1819?]
       map.   25 x 39 cm.
       Identical with folding map before p. 1 of H.
McMurtrie, Sketches of Louisville and its
environs (Louisville, Printed by S. Penn, June, 1819)

14929 McNamara, Mary C
       "Glory" of the hills. Covington, Ky., 1930.
       232 p.   20½ cm.

14930 McNemar, Richard, 1770-
       The Kentucky revival, or, A short history of
the late extraordinary outpouring of the spirit
of God in the western states of America... with
a brief account of the entrance and progress of
what the world call Shakerism, among the subjects

221

of the late revival in Ohio and Kentucky...
Pittsfield, Reprinted by Phineas Allen, 1808.
148, 28 p.   18½ cm.

14931 McVey, Frank LeRond, 1869-1953.
The gates open slowly, a history of education
in Kentucky. Lexington, University of Kentucky
press, 1949.
321 p.   24 cm.

14932 Madden, John E
Notes on French and German wine [by] John E.
Madden. Lexington, Ky., The author [1961]
20 p.   illus.   17½ cm.

14933 Madden, John E
Notes on French and German wines. Lexington,
Ky., The Thoroughbred press [n.d.]
1 ℓ., 22 p.   illus.   19 cm.

14934 Madigan, Mary Lou S
Your Kentucky Historical Society. [Frankfort,
The Society, 1973?]
unpaged.   illus., diags.   27 cm.

14935 Madison County, Ky. Historical Society.
Madison County sesqui-centennial celebration.
Sponsored by the Madison County Historical Society.
Commemorating the one hundred and fiftieth
anniversary of the formation of Madison County,
Kentucky... Official Souvenir program. Richmond,
Ky., 1937.
cover-title, [16] p.   29½ cm.

14936 Magill, John, 1759-1842.
The pioneer to the Kentucky emigrant;
a brief topographical & historical description
of the state of Kentucky, to which are added some
original verses... Edited, with an introduction
by Thomas D. Clark. Lexington, University of
Kentucky publications committee, Margaret
Voorhies Haggin trust, 1942.
83 p.   22 cm.   (Kentucky reprints, no. 2)

14937 Magnificent scheme! Splendid lottery to be
drawn on the Royal Havana plan! By authority of the
governor and legislature of Kentucky. Kentucky

state lotteries... to be drawn at Covington,
Kentucky, on Monday, December the 31st, 1866...
[Covington? 1866]
broadside. 57 x 43 cm.

14938   Magnum Opus. The great book of the University of
Comus. The paneduct of our national hilaritas,
comprising essays upon the thirteen divisions
of the rituals; sketches of the tredecim doges,
authors of the plan, and a monitorial guide to
the workings of the fellowship... Louisville, Ky.,
Pub. under the direction of the thirteen doges,
1886.
160 p.   illus.   23 cm.

14939   Mahan, Alfred Thayer, 1840-1914.
...The Gulf and inland waters... New York,
Charles Scribner's sons, 1883.
267 p.   fold. maps.   20 cm.
At head of title: The Navy in the Civil War -
III.
Chapter II, "From Cairo to Vicksburg," deals
with naval action on the Ohio, Mississippi,
Cumberland, and Tennessee Rivers in Kentucky.

14940   Mahoney, Ann.
The Cane Ridge Meeting House - a shrine to
church union. Frankfort, Kentucky Historical
Society, 1967.
2 p.   illus.   28 cm.
Reprinted from Kentucky heritage, v. 8, no. 1,
Fall 1967.

14941   Mahr, August C
Shawnee names and migrations in Kentucky and
West Virginia. [Columbus, Ohio] 1960.
155-164 p.   maps.   27 cm.
From the Ohio journal of science, LX (no. 3,
May, 1960), 155-164.

14942   Maierhouser, Fran.
Fort Boonesborough. Louisville, 1977.
14-15 p.   illus.   28 cm.
Reprinted from Rural Kentuckian, v. 31, no. 3,
March 1977.

14943 Maierhouser, Fran.
A man with his head in the clouds. Louisville,
1976.
8-9, 16 p. illus. 28 cm.
Reprinted from Rural Kentuckian, v. 30, no. 8,
August 1976.

14944 Mains, George Preston, 1844-1930.
Francis Asbury, by George P. Mains; with an
introduction by Bishop Daniel A. Goodsell. New
York, Eaton & Mains; Cincinnati, Jennings &
Graham [c1909]
128 p. front. (port.) pl. $16\frac{1}{2}$ x $9\frac{1}{2}$ cm.

14945 Mammoth Cave National Park Association.
A national park in Kentukcy. [n.p., n.d.]
16 p. map. 23 cm.

14946 Mammoth Cave National Park Association.
A national park in Kentucky. [Louisville, Ky.?
n.d.]
30 p. 23 cm.
Cover-title: Now how.

14947 Mammoth Cave National Park Association.
A privilege -- a duty -- an opportunity for
Kentucky. [Louisville, The Association, n.d.]
cover-title, 16 p. illus. $26\frac{1}{2}$ cm.

14948 Manning, John M
Government in Kentucky cities. Lexington,
Bureau of Government Research, University of
Kentucky, 1937.
24 p. fold. diagrs. $29\frac{1}{2}$ cm. (Local
government study, no. 3)

14949 Mansfield, Edward Deering, 1801-1880.
Memoirs of the life and services of Daniel
Drake, M.D., physician, professor, and author;
with notices of the early settlement of Cincinnati.
And some of its pioneer citizens. Cincinnati,
Applegate & co., 1855.
x, 11-408 p. front. [port.] 19 cm.

14950 Mantle and Cowan, firm, Louisville, Ky.
[List of hardware for sale. Louisville, 187-]

broadside. $22\frac{1}{2}$ x $14\frac{1}{2}$ cm.
Printed on both sides.

14951 Manuel, Cathy.
The West's first brick house. Frankfort,
Kentucky Historical Society, 1967.
1 p.   illus.   28 cm.
Reprinted from Kentucky heritage, v. 8, no. 1,
Fall 1967.

14952 Map and directory of information. Lexington
vicinity, Kentucky. Including University of
Kentucky and Fayette county. With indexed
streets. [n.p., 195-]
map.   86 x 55 cm.
"Revised edition."
In folder.

14953 Map of Lexington and Fayette County, Kentucky...
Lexington [1971?]
map.   22 x $25\frac{1}{2}$ cm.

14954 Map of Lexington and suburbs. Fayette county,
Kentucky. Street guide and bus lines. Lexington,
Hurst printing [n.d.]
64 x 46 cm.

14955 Map of Lexington [Kentucky] and suburbs. Fayette
County, Kentucky. [Revised September 1957]
Lexington, Lexington Chamber of Commerce, 1957.
map.   55 x 43 cm.
Street index on verso.

14956 Map of Lexington urban area. Compliments of First
Security National Bank & Trust Company. [Lexington,
1974]
map.   64 x 54 cm.
Index of streets on verso of map.

14957 Marion National Bank, Lebanon, Ky.
100th [one hundredth] anniversary, 1856-1956.
[Lebanon, 1956]
[16] p.   illus., facsims.   23 cm.

14958 Marsh, Ramona.
Shakertown offers special retreat to another
way of life. Lexington, 1975.

broadside.   illus., map.   57 x 27 cm.
Reprinted from Lexington Herald-Leader,
12 April 1975.

14959 Marshall, Walter, 1628-1680.
The gospel-mystery of sanctification, opened,
in sundry practical directions; suited especially
to the case of those who labor under the guilt and
power of indwelling sin. To which is added a
sermon on justification... Lexington, Ky., Printed
by Joseph Charless, and sold at his bookstore,
1804.
xvi, [17]-287 p.   16 cm.

14960 Martin, Asa Earl.
...The anti-slavery movement in Kentucky prior
to 1850... Louisville, The Standard Printing
Company of Louisville, 1918.
165 p.   24 cm.
At head of title: Filson Club publication no. 29.

14961 Martin, Mrs. George Madden, 1866-
The blue handkerchief, by George Madden Martin.
[n.p.] 1911.
290-300 p.   illus.   22 cm.
Reprinted from The Century, v. 83, Dec. 1911.
Illustrated by F. R. Gruger.

14962 Martin, James Walter, 1893-
Comparative state and local government general
expenditure for state institutions of higher
education, by James W. Martin and Dolores S.
Cheek. Lexington, University of Kentucky, 1960.
50 p.   map, tables, diagrs.   28½ cm.

14963 [Martin, James Walter] 1893-
A report on taxation. [n.p.] Committee for
Kentucky [194-]
31 p.   illus., graphs.   24 cm.

14964 Mason, Richard Lee, d. 1824.
Narrative of Richard Lee Mason in the pioneer
west, 1819. New York, Charles F. Heartman [1915]
74 p. incl. front. (port.)   24 cm.   (On
verso of half-title: Heartman's historical
series, no. 6)

14965   Massie, I   N
        Early history of the city of Winchester, by
        I. N. Massie [n.p., n.d.]
        4 p.   23 cm.

14966   Mastin, Bettye Lee.
        Famed homes since destroyed still existed in
        1888. Lexington, Ky., 1963.
        9 p.   illus.   47 x 39 cm.
        Reprinted from Lexington Herald-Leader, 19 May
        1963, p. A-49 - A-57.

14967   Mastin, Bettye Lee.
            Liberty Hall. [Lexington, Ky., 1962]
            broadside.   illus.   56 cm.
        Reprinted from Lexington Herald-Leader, 17 June
        1962.

14968   Mastin, Bettye Lee.
            ...Stone houses [in Kentucky] Lexington, 1972.
            2 p.   illus.   23 x 40 cm.   (Sunday Herald-
        Leader, 6 August 1972, p. 84, 86)

14969   Mastin, Bettye Lee.
            To Millersburg and back. Lexington, Ky., 1975.
            broadside.   illus., map.   44 cm.
        Reprinted from Sunday Herald-Leader, Lexington,
        Ky., 6 April 1975.

14970   Mastin, Bettye Lee.
            What it was like on Poosey and in Garrard.
            broadside.   illus.   60 x 40 cm.
        Reprinted from Herald-Leader, 13 August 1972.

14971   Mastin, Bettye Lee.
            Wildcat stalked Lexington teacher. Lexington,
        Ky., 1976.
            broadside.   illus.   30 x 36 cm.
        Reprinted from Lexington Herald-Leader,
        15 February 1976.

14972   Mather, Cotton.
            Essays to do good, addressed to all Christians,
        whether in public or private capacities. By the
        late Cotton Mather, D.D.F.R.S. To do good, and
        to communicate, forget not. Heb. xiii. 16.
        Improved by the Rev. George Burder. Skillman's

second edition. Lexington, Ky., Printed published
and sold by T. T. Skillman, 1823.
238 p.   18 x 10 cm.

14973 Mathews, Janice.
Veteran remembered. [Louisville, Ky., 1977]
1 p.   port.   30 cm.
Biography of Charles Young of Mays Lick, third
black graduate of U. S. Military Academy.
Reprinted form Rural Kentuckian, v. 31, no. 10,
October 1977.

14974 Matthews, Sue Froman.
A beggar's story, by Sue Froman Matthews...
New York, Chicago [etc.] Fleming H. Revell
company [n.d.]
114 p.   18½ cm.
Inscribed by author.

14975 [Mattingly, L   F   ]
Kentucky: Vol. I. [Lexington, 192-]
unpaged.   illus., facsims., music.   22 x 27½ cm.

14976 Maury, Sarah Webb.
Native trees of Kentucky. A handbook. [n.p.
Kentucky Federation of Women's Clubs, 1910]
140 p.   illus.   22 cm.

14977 Mayer, Joan P
Roger Williams began Iroquois hunt in 1880.
Lexington, Kentucky, 1969.
[2] p.   illus.   32 x 42 cm.
Reprinted from Sunday Herald-Leader, 2 February
1969)

14978 Mayes, Daniel.
An address delivered before the trustees and
faculty of Transylvania University. At the opening
of the session of the law department, on the
7th Nov. 1831. By Daniel Mayes, professor of law.
Lexington, Ky., Printed by N. L. Finnell & J. F.
Herndon, 1831.
17 p.   21½ cm.

14979 Mayes, Daniel.
An address of the students of law, in Transylvania
University, delivered at the beginning of the session

for 1833: by Daniel Mayes, professor of law.
Lexington, Ky., Printed by Tho. J. Pew, Mill
Street, 1833.
27 p.   21½ cm.

14980 Mayes, Daniel.
An introductory lecture delivered to the law
class of Transylvania University, on the 5th
November, 1832. By Daniel Mayes, professor
of law. Lexington, Ky., Printed by H. Savary &
co., book and job printers, 1832.
32, [4] p.   22 cm.

14981 Mayfield, Ky. First Baptist Church.
First Baptist Church, Mayfield, Kentucky,
1844-1944. [Mayfield, Ky.? 1944?]
cover title, [10] p.   plates.   31 cm.

14982 Means, Sterling M
The black devils and other poems, by Sterling
M. Means... Louisville, Ky., Pentecostal
publishing company [1919]
56 p.   20 cm.

14983 [Medina, Louise H   ]
Nick of the woods; or, Telie, the renegade's
daughter. An old melograma in three acts with
music. Adapted by Tom Taggart, New York [etc.]
Samuel French [n.d.]
98 p.   19 cm.
Based on Robert Montgomery Bird, 1806-1854,
Nick of the woods; or, The Jibbenainosay (1837)

14984 Meigs, Charles Delucena, 1792-1869.
A biographical notice of Daniel Drake, M. D.,
of Cincinnati. Prepared by appointment of the
College of physicians of Philadelphia... Read
at the meeting, July, 1853. Philadelphia,
Lippincott, Grambo and co., 1853.
38 p.   33 cm.

14985 Memoir of William Kendrick. [Louisville, Printed by
E. H. Welburn, 1881]
126 p.   18½ cm.

14986 Memoirs of the Lower Ohio valley, personal and
genealogical, with portraits. Madison, Wis.,

229

Federal publishing company, 1905.
2 v.   illus.   26½ cm.

14987   Memorial addresses delivered at Winchester [Ky.]
October 15, 1882, before the Grand Lodge of Ky.,
I.O.O.F. upon the deaths of James L. Ridgely,
Wm. T. Curry [and] Taliaferro P. Shaffner,
together with the resolutions adopted by the
Grand Lodge and the reports of the Committee on
Demises. Louisville, Rogers & Tuley, 1882.
51 p.   24 cm.

14988   Memorial exercises and addresses in honor of James
Kennedy Patterson, president of the University of
Kentucky, 1869-1910. At the Patterson home on
the campus of the University of Kentucky, Sunday,
June 1, 1924. Lexington, 1924.
30 p.   24 cm.

14989   Memorial record of western Kentucky... Chicago and
New York, The Lewis publishing company, 1904.
2 v.   front., ports.   28 cm.
Paged continuously; v. 1: x, [11]-402 p.;
v. 2: 1 p.l., 403-805 p.

14990   Merrill, C   E
"Ole Mose," a Gettysburg incident. [n.p., n.d.]
4 p.   23 cm.

14991   Merton, Thomas, 1915-1968.
Early poems, 1940-42. Lexington, Ky., The Peter
Paul House [1971]
30 p.   24 cm.
This book is bound an unidentified article by
Sarah Lansdell, "In Search of Thomas Merton,"
dated 7 December 1969.

14992   Merton, Thomas, 1915-1968.
Prometheus a meditation. Lexington, 1958.
6 ℓ.   23 cm.

14993   Metcalf, Samuel Lytler.
A collection of some of the most interesting
narratives of Indian warfare in the west, containing
an account of the adventures of Colonel Daniel Boone,
one of the first settlers of Kentucky, comprehending
the most important occurrences relative to its

230

early history- also, an account of the manners,
and customs of the Indians, their traditions and
religious sentiments, their police or civil
government, their discipline and method of war.
To which is added, and account of the expeditions of
Genl's. Harmer, Scott, Wilkinson, St. Clair, &
Wayne. The whole compiled from the best authorities.
By Samuel L. Metcalf. [three lines quotations]
Lexington, Ky., Printed by William G. Hunt, 1821.
   270 p.   21 x 13 cm.

14994 Methodist Church (United States) Conferences.
    Louisville.
      Century of progress, 1846-1946. Hopkinsville,
Ky., Published by the Historical Society for the
centennial session of the Louisville Annual
Conference of the Methodist Church, 1946.
    262 p.   illus., ports. $19\frac{1}{2}$ cm.

14995 Methodist Episcopal Church.
      Delegates of the South and Southwest annual
conference of the convention assembled in the
city of Louisville, May 1st, 1845. New York,
Lith. of G. & W. Endicott [1845?]
    broadside.   80 x 53 cm.
    Contains portraits of William Capers, H. B.
Bascom, William Winans, James O. Andrew, Joshua
Soule, Lovick Pierce, William A. Smith, and
Robert Paine.

14996 Methodist pie (as sung by Bradley Kincaid)
    Lancaster, Ky., Printed by Ky. Valley Press
    [1975]
    broadside.   Music.   29 x 22 cm.
    "This song, collected by Bradley Kincaid, is
believed to have been written here at Camp Nelson.
It was first sung by Bradley Kincaid at the
National Barn Dance at WLS in Chicago about 1926."

14997 Metzenbaum, Howard Morton, 1917-
      A beautiful story about a neighborhood drugstore
in Louisville. [Washington, D. C., 1974]
    S20171-S20172 p.   29 cm.
    Includes article by Ellen Schuhmann, "Drugstore
closing quietly, ending a small bit of history,"

in Louisville Times, 15 November 1974.
Reprinted from Congressional Record, 26 November 1974.

14998   Meyer, Leland Winfield.
Georgetown College, its background and a chapter
in its early history; a contribution to the
centennial anniversary of Georgetown College,
Kentucky... [Georgetown, Ky., 1929]
77 p.   illus.   20 cm.

14999   Meyer, Leland Winfield.
Georgetown College, its early history.
Georgetown, Ky., Frye Printing Company, 1962.
83 p.   illus., ports.   18 cm.
"First published in 1929 under the title
'Georgetown College -- its background and a chapter
in its early history'."
Bibliography: p. 79-81.

15000   Michigan. University. William L. Clements Library.
Fifty Ohio rarities, 1653-1802. Ann Arbor,
1953.
40 p.   port., facsims. (incl. maps)   21 cm.
(Its Bulletin 62)
"The selections were made and the descriptions
written by Mr. Calvin W. Lane of the Clements
Library staff."

15001   Miers, Earl Schenck.
Horse sense, an essay by Earl Schenck Miers.
With woodcuts by Stefan Martin taken from
contemporary sources. Printed at the Spiral Press,
New York, 1970. [Newark, Del.] Curtis Paper
company, 1970.
31 p.   illus.   23½ cm.

15002   Milburn, William Henry.
The lance, cross and canoe; the flatboat,
rifle and plough in the valley of the Mississippi...
New York and St. Louis, N. D. Thompson publishing
co. [1892]
696 p.   illus.   25½ cm.

15003   Miles, Mrs. Emma (Bell) 1879-1919.
The spirit of the mountains, by Emma B. Miles.
New York, J. Pott & company, 1905.

ix, 201 p.   front., plates.   19½ cm.
The chapter entitled "Some real American music"
appeared in Harper's magazine for June 1904.
Contents. - The log church school. - Cabin homes.
- Grandmothers and sons. - Neighbors. The savage
strain. - Supernatural. - The old-time religion. -
Some real American music. - The literature of a
wolf-race. - Conclusion.

15004 Miller, Arthur McQuiston.
...Coals of the lower measures along the
western border of the eastern coalfield...
Louisville, Printed by the Continental printing
company, 1910.
viii, 83 p.   tables (1 fold.), 3 fold.
maps in pocket at end.   26½ cm.
At head of title: Kentucky Geological Survey,
Charles J. Norwood, director. Bulletin no. 12.

15005 Miller, Arthur McQuiston.
The lead and zinc bearing rocks of central
Kentucky, with notes on the mineral veins. By
Arthur M. Miller... Lexington, Kentucky
Geological Survey, 1905.
35 p.   illus.   26 cm.   (Bulletin, 2)

15006 Miller, J   David.
Surface water pollution of the inner Bluegrass
region and its perception by the inhabitants.
Research proposal. [Lexington, Ky., 1971?]
12 p.   29 cm.

15007 Miller, William Harris.
History and genealogies of the families of Miller,
Woods, Harris, Wallace, Maupin, Oldham, Kavanaugh,
and (illustrated), with interspersions of notes
of the families of Dabney, Reid, Martin, Broadus,
Gentry, Jarman, Jameson, Ballard, Mullins, Michie,
Moberley, Covington, Growning, Duncan, Yancey and
others... Richmond, Kentucky, 1907.
728, 127 p.   illus.   24 cm.

15008 Mills, Melbourne.
Uniform laws in Kentucky. Frankfort, Legislative
Research Commission, 1972.
66 p.   29 cm.   (Informational bulletin, no. 37)

15009 Milward, Burton.
       The Confederate soldier monument. [Lexington,
       Ky. 1972]
         2 p.   illus.   29 cm.
       "The following article, the second on the
       Confederate memorials in the Lexington Cemetery,
       is based on accounts published in the Kentucky
       Leader on May 3, May 9 and June 11, 1893."

15010 Milward, Burton.
       Fifteenth anniversary of the Kentucky Civil
       War Round Table, 1953-1968. Compiled by Burton
       Milward, Editor of the News Letter of the Kentucky
       Civil war Round Table. Lexington, Kentucky,
       1968.
         29 p.   illus.   24 cm.

15011 Milward, Burton.
       The first one hundred years of the Transylvania
       Printing Company. [Lexington, Ky., 1972]
         74 p.   illus., facsims.   24 cm.

15012 Milward, Burton.
       Twentieth anniversary of the Kentucky Civil War
       Round Table, 1953-1973. Compiled by Burton
       Milward and Ed Houlihan. Lexington, 1973.
         [32] p.   illus.   24 cm.

15013 Miner, Jessie S
       Trailings, a rhymed sketch-book, by Jessie S.
       Miner. New York, The Lantern press [1930]
         62 p.   20 cm.

15014 Mississippi. Mississippi Library Commission.
       Mississippiana... Jackson, Mississippi
       Library Commission, 1970.
         2 v.   29 cm.
       Contents. v.1. Mississippiana: union catalog.
       v. 2. Mississippiana: union list of newspapers.
       Contains many Kentucky imprints and books relative
       to Kentucky, reflecting the large-scale movement of
       Kentuckians to Mississippi in the first half of
       the nineteenth century.

15015 Mitchell, S   Mitchell.
       A new map of Kentucky with its roads and
       distances from place to place along the stage &

steam boat routes. Philadelphia, S. Augustus
Mitchell, 1846.
    map.   32 x 26 cm.   (Kentucky. University.
Library. Kentucky map facsimile, no. 7)

15016 Mitchell, William M
        The under-ground railroad from slavery to
        freedom. London, 1860.
        xv, 172, xi p.   port.   19 cm.

15017 Moloney, Martha.
        The Kentucky ballot, prepared by Martha Moloney.
        Frankfort, Ky., Legislative Research Commission, 1977.
        v, 103 p.   maps, tables.   27½ cm.   (Research
        report, no. 140)

15018 Moloney, Martha A
        Social security and the teacher. Frankfort, Ky.,
        Legislative Research Commission, 1973.
        57 p.   29 cm.   (Research report, no. 104)

15019 Monson, Thomas.
        Map of Lexington, Kentucky, the blue grass
        capital, with supplemental maps of Fayette county
        and some of the well known stock farms of the
        county... [Lexington? 1948?]
        map.   60 x 60 cm.
        Street index on verso.

15020 Montulé, Édouard de.
        A voyage to North America, and the West Indies in
        1817... London, Printed for Sir R. Phillips and
        co., 1821.
        1 p.l., 102 p.   illus.   21½ cm.
        Tr. from the author's Voyage en Amérique.
        Kentucky, p. 78-83.

15021 Moody, Sid.
        Mountain evangelist no longer on horseback but
        in station wagon. [Lexington, Ky., 1966]
        1 p.   38 cm.
        Reprinted from Sunday Herald-Leader, Lexington,
        Ky., 4 September 1966.

15022 Moody, William Robert, bp., 1900-
        The bishop speaks his mind; convention addresses,

1946-1959. [Lexington, Ky., Keystone Printery, 1959]
150 p.   23 cm.

15023 Moore, Elizabeth Fox.
John Fox, Jr., personal and family letters and
papers. Lexington, University of Kentucky Library
Associates, 1955.
92 p.   29 cm.

15024 Moore, Mike, 1840-
The jolly Irishman. Calhoun, Ky., 1951.
59 p.   port.   17 cm.
Autobiographical.
"A reprint by McLean County News."

15025 [Moore, Thomas Patrick] 1797-1853.
To the citizens of the seventh congressional
district. [Lexington, Ky? 1825?]
14 p.   21½ cm.

15026 Moore, William Cabell.
John Fox, Jr., 1862-1919. [Lexington, University
of Kentucky Library, 1957]
6 l.   28 cm.

15027 Moorman, John Jennings, 1802-1885.
Mineral springs of North America; how to reach,
and how to use them... Philadelphia, J. B.
Lippincott & co., 1873.
294 p.   18½ cm.

15028 Morgan, John Hunt, 1825-1864.
[Autograph letter, 1 p., dated 8 October 1862-
to Gen. Edmund Kirby Smith]
There are six pieces in this group: (1) and
(2), recto and verso of the letter; (3) bookseller's
description of the letters; (4) portrait of Morgan;
(5) description of another Morgan letter of 12
November 1862 from Carnegie Bookshop, Cat. 335, item
313; (6) letter from Warren A. Reeder, Jr., dated
17 October 1973 describing briefly his Morgan
Collection, including this letter.

15029 Morgan, John Hunt, 1825-1864.
Proclamation! To the people of Estill and
adjoining counties... By order of Gen. J. H. Morgan.
R. A. Alston. A. A. Genr'l. Irvine, Ky.,

236

Sept. 22, 1862.
broadside.   27 x 17½ cm.
There is no positive evidence of a press in Irvine
at this time, and the broadside may have been
printed most anywhere, possibly Knoxville, Tenn.,
Lebanon, Ky., Lexington, or even Richmond, Va.

15030 Morgan, Kelly.
Pioneer families of Clay County, Kentucky.
Edited and published by Kelly Morgan and Hazel
Smith Morgan. Manchester, Ky., 1970.
736 p.   illus.   29 cm.

15031 Morgan, Margaret.
The community colleges, University of Kentucky.
Lexington, University of Kentucky Centennial
committee, 1965.
24 p.   illus.   23 cm.

15032 Mori, Samuel.
Zwei briefe aus Amerika. Bern, Buchdruckerei
des "Berner Boten," 1886.
64 p.   20 cm.

15033 Morris, E   Hugh, ed.
Issues confronting the 1978 General Assembly.
Prepared by members of the Legislative Research
Commission staff. Edited by E. Hugh Morris.
Frankfort, Ky., Legislative Research Commission,
1977.
iii, 115 p.   27½ cm.   (Informational
bulletin, no. 126)

15034 Morris, John, ed.
Wanderings of a vagabond. An autobiography.
Edited by John Morris... New York, Published by
the author [1873]
492 p.   20 cm.

15035 Morro, W   C
"Brother McGarvey". The life of President J. W.
McGarvey of the College of the Bible, Lexington,
Kentucky. A publication of the seventy-fifty
anniversary celebration of the College of the
Bible, June, 1940... St. Louis, The Bethany
press [1940]
266 p.   21 cm.

15036   Morse, Jedidiah, 1761-1826, comp.
        The traveller's guide; or Pocket gazetteer of
        the United States; extracted from the latest
        edition of Morse's Universal gazetteer. With
        an appendix... By Jedidiah Morse, D. C., and
        Richard C. Morse, A. M. New-Haven, N. Whiting, 1823.
        2 p.l., 323, [1] p.   front.   [fold. map]
        15½ cm.

15037   Morse, William Clifford.
        ...The Waverlian formations of east central
        Kentucky and their economic values, by William
        Clifford Morse and August F. Foerste. [n.p.]
        Interstate publishing co., 1912.
        16 p.   illus.   27 cm.   (Kentucky geological
        survey, Bulletin no. 16, Serial no. 19)

15038   Morton, J   R
        ...Caleb Powers, appellant, vs. The Commonwealth
        of Kentucky, appellee. Brief for appellant. J. R.
        Morton and J. C. Sims, counsel for appellant.
        Lexington, The Transylvania co. [n.d.]
        183 p.   23½ cm.
        At head of title: Court of Appeals of Kentucky.

15039   Morton, M   B
        Kentuckians are different, by M. B. Morton,
        50 years reporter and editor. Louisville,
        Standard Press, 1938.
        337 p.   front.   (port.)   24 cm.

15040   Morton's manual. The principles of civil government
        in the United States and state of Kentucky. By
        a member of the bar. Louisville, John P. Morton
        and company [1889]
        117 p.   19½ cm.

15041   Mosby, Charles Virgil, 1876-1942.
        A little journey to the home of Ephraim
        McDowell, by C. V. Mosby... St. Louis [Press of
        the C. V. Mosby company] 1939.
        43 p.   front., plates.   18 cm.

15042   Mosgrove, Dallas.
        Kentucky cavaliers in Dixie, or, The reminiscences
        of a Confederate cavalryman... Louisville, Courier-

Journal job printing co., 1895.
265 p.   illus.

15043   Moss, Frank Edward, 1911-
        Senate resolution 205 - Submission of resolution
        designating in the Capitol the Alben W. Barkley
        Room. [Washington, D. C., 1973]
        S20780-S20782 p.   28 cm.
        Reprinted from the Congressional record - Senate,
        19 November 1973, p. S20780-S20782.

15044   Muhlenberg, Henry Augustus, 1823-1844.
        The life of Major-General Peter Muhlenberg,
        of the revolutionary army... Philadelphia,
        Carey and Hart, 1849.
        xii, 13-456 p.   front. [port.]   18½ cm.

15045   Muir, John Wakefield, 1909-
        Bardstown in retrospect. Bardstown, Ky.,
        Wilson & Muir, 1965.
        31 p.   illus.   19 x 25 cm.
        Includes folder at beginning, "Pocket facts,
        historic, beautiful Bardstown," and one at end,
        "Wilson & Muir, bankers."

15046   Munoff, Gerald J
        19th Century photographs from the collections
        of the Photographic Archives, Special Collections,
        University of Kentucky Libraries. Catalog compiled
        by Gerald J. Munoff. January 16 - February 15, 1978,
        Gallery, King Library North, Lexington, 1978.
        [80] p.   cover illus.   22 cm.

15047   Munsell, Joel, Publisher, Albany, N. Y.
        The American genealogist, being a catalogue of
        family histories. A bibliography of American
        genealogy of a list of the title pages of books
        and pamphlets of family history, published in
        America, from 1771 to date. Fifth ed. ... Albany,
        N. Y., Joel Munsell's sons, 1900.
        406 p.   27 cm.

15048   Munsell, Luke, 1790-1854.
        A map of the state of Kentucky, from actual
        survey. Also part of Indiana and Illinois. Frankfort,
        published by the author, 1818.
        Reproduced in three sheets, each 62 x 46 cm.

Accompanying pamphlet, Frances L. S. Dugan,
Footnote to a map (Lexington, Ky., University of
Kentucky Library Associates, Keepsake number 9)

15049 Murray, Ky. Woman's Club.
       Favorite recipes. Murray [n.d.]
       157 p.   23 cm.

15050 Murray State University, Murray, Kentucky.
       The Jesse Stuart creative writing workshop,
       June 26 - July 14, 1972. "Fourth Summer."
       Murray, Kentucky, Murray State University, 1972.
       [12] p.   illus.   24 cm.

15051 Musgrove, Charles Hamilton.
       Club men of Louisville in caricature and verse,
       nineteen hundred twelve. Drawings by P. A.
       Plaschke and associate artists. Verse by Charles
       Hamilton Musgrove... East Aurora, N. Y., The
       Roycrofters, 1912.
       245 p.   ports.   28 cm.

15052 Musical prodigies. Kock's celebrated juvenile
       opera troupe, will give a grand vocal &
       instrumental concert, including the choicest
       gems from the best operas... Louisville,
       Louisville Courier "Lightning Press," Print,
       1857.
       broadside.   41½ x 16 cm.

                            N

15053 Napier, John, 1915-1965.
       The ballad singer, by John Napier. Charcoal
       by Walt Prichard. [n.p., 1973]
       13 p.   illus.   23 cm.

15054 Napier, Sue.
       After half-century, Big Red still races in
       realm of legend. [Lexington, Kentucky, 5 November
       1972]
       2 p.   illus.   58 x 40 cm.
       Reprinted from Sunday Herald-Leader, Lexington,
       Ky., 5 November 1972.

15055 Narrative of the capture and providential escape
of Misses Frances and Almira Hall... Likewise is
added, the interesting narrative of the captivity
and sufferings of Philip Brigdon, a Kentuckian,
who fell into the hands of the merciless savages...
[New York?] 1833.
24 p.   24½ cm.

15056 Nelson, John P
The impact of litter, prepared by John P. Nelson,
John N. Williams, Thurston Howard Reynolds III.
Frankfort, Ky., Legislative Research Commission, 1975.
iii, 203 p.   27 cm.   (Research report, no. 127)

15057 Nelson, John P
Public school finance in Jefferson County.
Prepared by John P. Nelson, John Vaughan Curtis,
Brad Cowgill. Frankfort, Ky., Legislative
Research Commission, 1975.
vii, 119 p.   tables.   28½ cm.   (Research
report, no. 117)

15058 Nelson, John P
Sanitary sewer needs for Jefferson County,
prepared by John P. Nelson [and] Linda B. Wood.
Frankfort, Ky., Legislative Research Commission,
1977.
2 l., 129 p.   27 cm.   (Informational bulletin,
121)

15059 Nettleroth, Henry.
...Kentucky fossil shells. A monograph of
the fossil shells of the silurian and devonian
rocks of Kentucky... Frankfort, Ky., Electrotyped
and printed by E. Polk Johnson, Public printer and
binder, 1889.
245 p., xxxvi pl.   35 cm.
At head of title: Kentucky Geological Survey,
J. R. Procter, director.

15060 Neuman, Fred Gus, 1893-1953.
Irvin S. Cobb, by Fred B. Neuman... Paducah,
Ky., Young printing co., 1924.
4 p.l., 11-37 p. incl. front. (port.)   23 cm.

15061 Neuman, Fred Gus, 1893-1953.
Youth and other things, by Fred G. Neuman...

Paducah, Ky., Young printing company, 1923.
76 p.   23 cm.

15062   Nevin, Alfred, 1816-1890, ed.
Encyclopaedia fo the Presbyterian church in the
United States of America: including the northern
and southern assemblies. Alfred Nevin... editor,
assisted by B. M. Smith... W. E. Schenck...
and other eminent ministers of the church. D. R. B.
Nevin... managing editor... Philadelphia,
Presbyterian encyclopaedia publishing co., 1884.
vii, 9-1248 p.   illus. (incl. facsim.)
ports.   28 cm.

15063   Newman, James A
Yellow popular - Kentucky's state tree. Lexington,
Kentucky, Cooperative Extension Service, Agriculture
and Home Economics [1965?]
3 p.   illus.   29 cm.

15064   Nicholas, George, 1755?-1799.
To the freemen of Kentucky. Considering
myself as accountable to my fellow citizens for my
political conduct, I shall, for your satisfaction,
answer the charges which have been brought against
me, by several anonymous writers. Lexington, March
30th, 1799.
broadside.   24 x 42½ cm.

15065   Nicholasville, Ky. Methodist Church. Annie Bryant
Bible Class.
The home economist. [Nicholasville? n.d.]
52 p.   24½ cm.

15066   Nicholasville. Lexington, Ky. 1974.
12 p.   illus.   40 cm.
Reprinted from Lexington Herald-Leader, 10 November
1974.

15067   Nickles, John M
...The upper Ordovician rocks of Kentucky and
their bryozoa... Louisville, Printed by the Geo.
B. Fetter company, 1905.
64 p.   3 plates.   26½ cm.
At head of title: Kentucky Geological Survey,
Charles J. Norwood, director, Bulletin no. 5.

15068   Noe, James Thomas Cotton, 1864-1953.
        The blood of Rachel. A dramatization of Esther,
    and other poems. By Cotton Noe... Louisville,
    Ky., John P. Morton & company, 1916.
      [6], 150 p.   front.   20½ cm.

15069   Noe, James Thomas Cotton, 1864-1953.
        In Kentucky, by J. T. Cotton Noe, poet laureate
    of Kentucky. Lexington, The Kentucky Kernel press,
    1940.
      3 p.l., 9-86 p.   14½ cm.
    Poems.

15070   Noe, James Thomas Cotton, 1864-1953.
        Leaves of holly (1911-1923) by Cotton Noe.
    [Lexington, Ky.? 1923?]
      [14] l.   18 cm.
    Poems.

15071   Noe, James Thomas Cotton, 1864-1953.
        The legend of the silver band, a tale of
    Kentucky in the eighties. A novelette in verse.
    Louisville, John P. Morton & company, 1932.
      134 p.   21 cm.

15072   Noe, James Thomas Cotton, 1864-1953.
        Lincoln and the mother of Lincoln, by Cotton
    Noe, poet laureate of Kentucky. [Lexington, Ky.,
    1932]
      cover-title, [6] p.   facsim.   28 cm.

15073   Noe, James Thomas Cotton, 1864-1953.
        Southern poets. [Lexington, Ky.? 19--?]
      34 p.   20 cm.

15074   Noe, James Thomas Cotton, 1864-1953.
        Tip Sams of Kentucky and other poems and
    dramas [by] Cotton Noe... Lexington, Ky., The
    Canterbury Club [1926]
      ix p., 1 l., 13-270 p., 1 l.   17½ cm.
    Inscribed by the author.

15075   Noe, James Thomas Cotton, 1864-1953.
        Tip Sams again. A selection of poems by Cotton
    Noe. Lexington, Kentucky, University of Kentucky
    press, 1947.
      225 p.   front. (port.)   24 cm.

15076　Noe, James Thomas Cotton, 1864-1953.
　　　　　The valleys of Parnassus, a selection from the
　　　　poetry of J. T. Cotton Noe. Louisville,
　　　　John P. Morton & company [n.d.]
　　　　　141 p.　　21 cm.

15077　Noll, Arthur Howard, 1855-
　　　　　General Kirby-Smith... Sewanee, Tenn., The
　　　　University press at the University of the South
　　　　[c1907]
　　　　　293 p.　　21 cm.

15078　Noon, and pain, and April. Creative writing class,
　　　　Berea College, 1943-44. Berea, Kentucky,
　　　　Berea College Press, 1944.
　　　　　56 p.　　24 cm.

15079　Norris, Pauline.
　　　　　Collected writings of Willard Rouse Jillson.
　　　　Frankfort, Ky., State Journal company, 1933.
　　　　　15 p.　　front. (port.)
　　　　　"Separate revised issue from the April 1933
　　　　number of the Register of the Kentucky Historical
　　　　Society."

15080　North Middletown [Kentucky] Christian church.
　　　　Christian women's fellowship.
　　　　　[Directory and history of North Middletown,
　　　　Bourbon county, Kentucky. North Middletown,
　　　　1968?]
　　　　　65 l.　　illus.　　15 x 23 cm.

15081　Northern Bank of Kentucky, Lexington.
　　　　　Northern Bank of Kentucky. The following is
　　　　an exhibit of the condition of the Northern
　　　　Bank of Kentucky, made to the Legislature, on
　　　　the 1st day of January, 1838... [Lexington, 1838]
　　　　　broadside.　　55 x 41 cm.

15082　Norton, John Nicholas, 1820-1881.
　　　　　Life of Bishop Ravenscroft... New York,
　　　　General Protestant Episcopal Sunday school
　　　　union, and church book society, 1858.
　　　　　xii, [13]-152 p.　　incl.　　front. [port.]
　　　　15½ cm.

15083　Norwood, Charles Joseph, 1853-1927.
　　　　　The mining laws of the state of Kentucky in
　　　　effect June 17, 1918 compiled by C. J. Norwood,
　　　　chief inspector, Lexington [1918?]
　　　　　xiii, 64 p.　　17 cm.

15084　Norwood, Charles Joseph, 1853-1927.
　　　　　...A general account of the geology of a part
　　　　of Ohio County, by Charles J. Norwood. Frankfort,
　　　　Ky., Major, Johnston & Barret [n.d.]
　　　　　47p.　　28 cm.　　(Kentucky. Geological survey.
　　　　Part V, vol. V, second series)

15085　Norwood, Charles Joseph, 1853-1927.
　　　　　...Report of a reconnaisance in the lead region
　　　　of Livingston, Crittenden, and Caldwell counties,
　　　　including a sketch of their general wealth...
　　　　[Frankfort, Ky., n.d.]
　　　　　45 p.　　illus., maps, part. fold.　　28 cm.
　　　　(Kentucky. Geological survey. Part VII, vol.
　　　　I, second series)
　　　　　At head of title: Geological survey of
　　　　Kentucky, N. S. Shaler director.

15086　Norwood, Charles Joseph, 1853-1927.
　　　　　...Report on the progress of the Survey,
　　　　from the years 1904-1905... Lexington, Ky.
　　　　Louisville, Printed by the Geo. G. Fetter
　　　　company, 1905.
　　　　　56 p.　　24 cm.
　　　　　At head of title: Kentucky geological survey,
　　　　Charles J. Norwood, director.

15087　Norwood, Charles Joseph, 1853-1927.
　　　　　...Report on the progress of the Survey for the
　　　　years 1908 and 1909. [Louisville] The Continental
　　　　printing company, 1910.
　　　　　[4], 127 p.　　tables.　　24 cm.
　　　　　At head of title: Kentucky Geological Survey,
　　　　Charles J. Norwood, director.
　　　　　A stencilled sheet complaining about the policies
　　　　of the public printer is on the verso of the
　　　　front cover.

15088　Notes from the diary of a field and hospital
　　　　surgeon, C.S.A. Reprinted (?) from The American
　　　　medical weekly, Louisville, Kentucky, November 7,

1874. [n.p., n.d.]
   4 p.   23 cm.
A fictitious account of scrotal penetration by
a yankee minie ball, lodgement of same missile
in uterine cavity of a lady attending Confederate
wounded at Vicksburg, her subsequent pregnancy,
and the ultimate union of representatives of two
distinguished Southern families.

15089   Nunley, Scott.
        "Manin." A one-act play. [Lexington, Ky., 1965]
        2 p.   illus.   45 cm.
        Reprinted from Literary Supplement, The Kentucky
   Kernel (University of Kentucky) p. 5-6, 15 April
   1965.

15090   Nunn, Douglas.
        The beef session. [Louisville, Ky., 1950]
        3 p.   illus.   42 cm.
        Reprinted from the Louisville Courier-Journal
   Magazine.

                             O

15090A Obenchain, Mrs. Eliza Caroline (Calvert) Hall, 1856-
        Aunt Jane of Kentucky... With frontispiece
   and page decorations by Beulah Strong. Boston,
   Little, Brown, and company, 1910.
        283 p.   illus.   20 cm.

15091   Obenchain, Mrs. Eliza Caroline (Calvert) Hall, 1856-
        Clover and blue grass, by Eliza Calvert Hall
   [pseud.] With a frontispiece by H. R. Ballinger.
   Boston, Little, Brown & company, 1916.
        5 p.l., 3-229 p.   19½ cm.
        Title within colored ornamental border.
        Contents. - How Parson Page went to the circus.
   - Mary Crawford's chart. - Old mahogany. - Millstones
   and stumbling blocks. - "One taste of the old time."
   - One day in spring.

15092   Obenchain, Mrs. Eliza Caroline (Calvert) Hall, 1856-
        Sally Ann's experience, by Eliza Calvert Hall
   [pseud.]... With a frontispiece by G. Patrick

Nelson and decorations by Theodore B. Hapgood.
Boston, Little, Brown, and company, 1910.
 xii p., 1 ℓ., 45 p.   col. front.   19½ cm.
Green ornamental border.

15093 Obenchain, Mrs. Eliza Caroline (Calvert) Hall, 1856-
 To love and to cherish, by Eliza Calvert Hall
[pseud.]... Illustrated by J. V. McFall. Boston,
Little, Brown, and company, 1911.
 6 p.l., 3-205 p.   front., plates.   17½ cm.

15094 O'Brien, Michael J
 Irish pioneers in Kentucky; a series of articles
published in The Gaelic American, New York, by
Michael J. O'Brien. [n.p., n.d.]
 60 p.   25 cm.

15095 O'Bryan, Paula.
 A student's eye view of Meade County. Frankfort,
Kentucky Historical Society, 1967.
 2 p.   28 cm.
 Reprinted from Kentucky heritage, v. 8, no. 1,
Fall 1967.

15096 Old Bardstown Bourbon recipes. [Bardstown, Ky.]
 The Willett distilling company [c1967]
 38 p.   illus.   23 cm.

15097 Old homes of the Bluegrass. Published to foster
an appreciation of the history of central Kentucky.
[Lexington, n.d.]
 48 p.   illus.   23 cm.

15098 Old Talbott Tavern. [Gettysburg, Pa. 1974]
 broadside.   30 x 23 cm.
 Reprinted from Kentucky edition of The American
Motorist, v. 42, no. 3, July 1974.

15099 [O'Malley, Charles J   ]
 History of Union County, Kentucky... Evansville,
Indiana, Courier co., 1886.
 896 p.   illus.   23 cm.

15100 Omicron, pseud.
 The plan of reform in Transylvania University.
Two letters, one addressed to the academical
faculty and board of trustees; the other to

247

Horace Holley, L.L.D. president. Occasioned by the preamble and resolutions of the faculty and board lately published. By Omicron. From the country-- a friend to reform, Lexington, Ky., 1824.
16 p.   17 cm.

15101 Ord, George, 1781-1886.
Sketch of the life of Alexander Wilson, author of the American ornithology... Philadelphia, H. Hall, 1823.
iv, [ix]-cxcix p.   23½ cm.

15102 O'Rear, Edward Clay, 1863-1961.
A history of the Montgomery County (Ky.) bar. [Frankfort, Ky., 1945]
121 p.   front. (plate) ports.   23½ cm.
Title from binding.

15103 Osborn, Samuel D
The dark and bloody ground. A history of Kentucky. Bristol, Tenn.-Va., Press of the King printing co., 1907.
14 p.   24 cm.

15104 Osborn, Scott Compton, 1913-
A study and contrast of the Kentucky mountaineer and the Bluegrass aristocracy in the works of John Fox, Jr. Lexington, Ky., 1939.
157 p.   26 cm.
M.A. thesis, University of Kentucky.
Vita: p. 157.

15105 Oswald, John W
Beginning a second century. The University of Kentucky academic programs, analysis and prospects. Presented to the Board of Trustees by President John W. Oswald, June 1964. [Lexington, 1964]
45 p.   maps, graphs, tables.   29 cm.

15106 Overstreet, Anne E
The miscellaneous writings (history, biography, bibliography, articles, narratives and poems) of Willard Rouse Jillson, a bibliography, 1907-1965, by Anne E. Overstreet. Vol. II. Frankfort, Ky., The Roberts printing company, 1965.
62 p.   front. (port.)   23 cm.

248

15107   Owen, David Dale, 1807-1860.
         Second report of the Geological Survey in
    Kentucky, made during the years 1856 and 1857
    by David Dale Owen, principal geologist, assisted
    by Robert Peter, chemical assistant; Sidney S.
    Lyon, topographical assistant. Frankfort, Ky.,
    A. G. Hodges, public printer, 1857.
       391 p.   tables.   28 cm.

15108   Owen, David Dale, 1807-1860.
         Third report of the Geological Survey in
    Kentucky, made during the years 1856 and 1857,
    by David Dale Owen, principal geologist, principal
    geologist, assisted by Robert Peter, chemical
    assistant; Sidney S. Lyon, Topographical assistant;
    Leo Lesquereux, paleontological assistant; Edward
    T. Cox, paleontological assistant. Frankfort, Ky.,
    A. G. Hodges, public printer, 1857.
       589 p.   tables.   28 cm.

15109   Owen, David Dale, 1807-1860.
         Fourth report of the Geological Survey in
    Kentucky, made during the years 1858 and 1859,
    by David Dale Owen, principal geologist; assisted
    by Robert Peter, chemical assistant; Sidney S. Lyon,
    Joseph Lesley, topographical assistants; Leo
    Lesquereux, palaeontological assistant; Edward T.
    Cox, geological assistant. Frankfort, Ky.,
    Printed at the Yeoman office, J. B. Major, state
    printer, 1861.
       617 p.   tables (1 fold.)   28 cm.

15110 Owenton, Ky. Beech Grove Baptist Church.
        History of the Beech Grove Baptist Church,
    Owenton, Kentucky, 1852-1952. [n.p., 1952?]
       cover title, [24] p.   ports.   23 cm.
    Preface signed by O. V. Jones.

P

15111   Packard, Alpheus Spring, 1839-1905.
       The Mammoth Cave and its inhabitants, or
    descriptions of the fishes, insects and crustaceans
    found in the cave; with figures of the various

species, and an account of allied forms, comprising
notes upon their structure, development and habits
with remarks upon subterranean life in general. By A. S.
Packard, Jr., and F. W. Putnam, editors of the
American naturalist. Salem, Naturalists' agency,
1872.
 61 p. 2 pl. 29 cm.
 "The following pages were first published in
'The American Naturalist' for December, 1871 and
January 1872, with the exception of the Synopsis
of the family including the Blind fishes of the
cave, which was first published in the 'Annual
Report of the Peabody Academy of Science for
1871.'" - Preface, p. 3.
 Contents. I. The formation of the cave, by
F. W. Putnam. II. The crustaceans and insects, by
A. S. Packard, Jr. III. The blind fishes of the
Mammoth Cave and their allies, by F. W. Putnam.
IV. Synopsis of the family Heteropygii.

15112 ...Paducah lottery of Kentucky for the benefit
of the University of Paducah... to be drawn
at Covington, Saturday, January 25, 1873...
Address: Smith, Simmons & co., Box 91,
Cincinnati, 0. [Cincinnati, 1873?]
 broadside. 25 x 20 cm.

15113 Page, Lawrence M
 The life history of the spot tail darter,
Etheostoma squamiceps, in Big Creek, Illinois,
and Ferguson Creek, Kentucky... Urbana, Illinois
Natural History Survey, 1974.
 20 p. illus., maps, tables, diagrs. 29 cm.
(Biological notes, no. 89)

15114 [Palmer, Elva]
 The romance of Uncle Bill and Aunt Sis. A
story of Kentucky hill folk. Waverly, Ohio,
Rainbow Mountain press, 1954.
 10 p. 15 cm.

15115 Palmer, John McAuley, 1817-
 Personal recollections of John M. Palmer;
the story of an earnest life. Cincinnati, The
R. Clarke company, 1901.
 xvii p., 1 l., 631 p. front., ports., facsims.
24 cm.

15116   Palmer, Vivien M
          Annotated socio-economic bibliography of
        Lexington and Fayette County [Ky.] By Vivien
        M. Palmer and Theressa Ross Garr. Lexington,
        1940?
          125 p.   29 cm.   (Kentucky. University.
        Department of Social Work. Research publication
        no. 1)
          "Prepared with the assistance of Work Projects
        Administration, under official Project No. 664-43-
        3-126."

15117   Panton, J   Hoyes.
          The Mammoth Cave of Kentucky. Louisville, C. G.
        Darnell, 1890.
          [69] p.   14 x 19 cm.

15118   Paris, Ky. Christian Church. Ladies Bible Class.
          Sweets and meats and other good things to
        eat. [Paris?] 1917.
          52 p.   24½ cm.
        Title typed on p. 1.

15119   Park, Clyde William, 1880-
          Steamboat days. [Cincinnati, C. J. Krehbiehl,
        1955]
          30 p.   illus.   16 cm.

15120   Passing of the Rees House; brief history of famous
        old hostelry now being razen to make way for a
        modern building. Transcribed by George F. Doyle,
        M.D., F.A.C.S. [Winchester, Ky., Clark County
        Historical Society, n.d.]
          4 p.   28 cm.

15121   Patterson, James Kennedy, 1833-1922.
          President James K. Patterson on Woodrow Wilson.
        Comments on his attainments and availability for
        the presidency. Personal estimate. [Lexington,
        Ky., 1912]
          4 p.   23 cm.
        Caption title.
        Written in response to a request by Judge
        Samuel M. Wilson.

15122   Payne, Ruth.
          ...Famous historical Kentucky recipes.

Harrodsburg, Mercer County Humane Society, 1976.
3 p.l., ix, 166 p.   illus.
At head of title: Mercer County Humane Society.
Bicentennial Commemorative cookbook.

15123   Pearce, Betsy.
[Kentucky Rivers Coalition] Lexington, Ky.
1976.
3 l.   varying sizes.
Reprinted from The Kentucky Kernel, 21, 22, 25
Oct. 1976.

15124   Pearce, John Ed.
Mr. Cooper says farewell. Louisville, Kentucky,
1972.
[19] p.   illus.   35 cm.
From the Courier-Journal & Time magazine,
Sunday, 5 March 1972, by permission.
Includes letter from author and reprint of
original in Congressional Record, 21 March 1972.

15125   Pearce, John Ed.
Nothing better in the market... Louisville,
Brown-Forman distillers, 1970.
96 p.   illus.   28 cm.

15126   Pearce, John Ed.
What ever happened to Charlie Farnsley?
Louisville, 1972.
6-11 p.   illus.   33 cm.
From the Courier-Journal and Times Magazine,
Sunday, December 31, 1972.
Also includes letters of comment by readers
in issue of 28 January 1973, p. 8-9.

15127   Peavyhouse, William W
Striking facts about Kentucky, historically,
financially, educationally, commercially,
agriculturally, economically, generally...
Frankfort, Ky. [1924]
2 p.l., 35 p.   17 cm.

15128   Peers, Benjamin Orrs, 1800-1842.
An introductory lecture, delivered before
the Lexington mechanic's institute June 20, 1829...
[Lexington, Ky.] Transylvania Press, Printed by

Jos. G. Norwood, Printer to the University, 1829.
32 p.   22 cm.

15129 Peirce, Bradford Kinney, 1819-1889.
Life in the woods; or, The adventures of Audubon...
Eight illustrations. New York, Carleton & Porter
[c1863]
252 p.   incl. front., plates.   15 cm.

15130 [Pelton, Louise]
A brief history of Berea College, Berea, Kentucky,
1963.
12 p.   illus., facsims.   29 cm.
"Prepared by Louise Pelton from: Berea's First
Century, 1855-1955, by Elisabeth S. Peck. Designed
by Jane Harris.

15131 [Pelton, Louise]
A brief history of Berea College. [Berea, Ky., 1972?]
28 p.   illus., map, facsim.   23 cm.
"Text prepared by Louise Pelton and Emily Ann Smith.
Based in part on Berea's First Century 1855-1955
by Elisbeth S. Peck. Designed by Mildred Strikler."
- p. 28.

15132 Perdue, Frances D
Folksong repertoire of Beulah C. Moody.
Bowling Green, Ky., 1976.
15-24 p.   22 cm.
Reprinted from Kentucky folklore record,
v. 22, no. 1, Jan.-Mar. 1976.

15133 Perley, Mae Clement.
The quilt, a pageant of Kentucky's Jewry.
Louisville, Issued by the Jewish Tercentenary
Committee of the Conference of Jewish Organizations.
December, 1954.
56 p.   29 cm.

15134 Perrin, Alfred H
From Bishop Percy (1765) to John Jacob Niles
(1974); 340 books of ballads and songs in the
Berea College collection. [Berea, Ky., 1974]
20 p.   28 cm.

15135 [Perrin, Alfred H   ]
Mountain fiction from Abernethy to Zugsmith,

from 1832 to 1975. 1,132 works of fiction by
Southern Appalachian authors, or with Southern
Appalachian settings. A part of the 9,000
volume Weatherford-Hammond Mountain Collection of
Berea College. Berea, Ky., Hutchins Library, 1976.
34 p.   29½ cm.
"A revised and extended version of mountain
fiction lists published in 1970 and 1972."

15136   Perrin, Alfred H
         Poets of Appalachia, 1813-1975. [Berea, Ky.,
         1975]
         8 p.   29 cm.

15137   Perrin, Alfred H
         Rare books and very special collections at
         Berea College. [Berea, 1977]
         12 p.   illus.   21 cm.

15138   Perrin, Alfred H
         Southern Appalachian mountain lore: Berea
         College's Weatherford-Hammond mountain collection.
         Washington, D. C., 1973.
         36-39 p.   illus.   29½ cm.
         Reprinted from Appalachia, vol. 6, no. 5,
         April-May 1973.

15139   Perrin, Alfred H
         The Weatherford-Hammond Collection of Berea
         College. [Berea, Ky.? 1975?]
         [4] p.   23 cm.
         Folder.

15140   [Perrin, Stephanie D   L   ]
         A fifty-year gathering of county histories...
         Adair to Yancey. 423 mountain county and local
         histories form eight states, "home counties to
         Berea's students... Berea, Ky., Hutchins Library,
         Berea College, 1977.
         2 p.l., 41p.   28 cm.

15141   Perrin, William Henry, d. 1892.
         County of Christian, Kentucky. Historical
         and biographical. Edited by William Henry
         Perrin. Illustrated. Chicago and Louisville,
         F. A. Battey Publishing Co., 1884. Reprinted:

Evansville, Ind., Unigraphic, Inc., 1973.
vi, [3], [19]-656p.   illus.   25 cm.

15142 [Perrin, William Henry] d. 1892?
History of Bourbon, Scott, Harrison and Nicholas
counties, preceded by a brief synopsis of the
Blue Grass region. [Chicago, 1882]
814, 20 p.   illus.   29 cm.
Appended is a typed index to personal names,
compiled by Mrs. William B. Ardery in 1933;
original typescript in this copy is quite dim.

15143 Perrin, William Henry, d. 1892?
Kentucky. A history of the state, embracing a
concise account of the origin and development
of the Virginia colony; its expansion westward,
and the settlement of the frontier beyond the
Alleghanies; the erection of Kentucky as an
independent state, and its subsequent development.
By W. H. Perrin, J. H. Battle, G. C. Kniffin.
Illustrated with numerous engravings. Louisville,
Ky., Chicago, Ill., F.A. Battey & company, 1886.
x, 17-636 p. incl. front., illus., pl.
plates, ports., map.   27½ cm.

15144 Perrin, William Henry, d. 1892?
The pioneer press of Kentucky, from the
printing of the first paper west of the
Alleghanies, August 11, 1787, to the establishment
of the daily press in 1830... Louisville, Ky.,
John P. Morton and company, 1888.
93 p.   illus., facsims.   28 cm.
In subsequent lists of Filson Club publication
recorded as no. 3.

15145 Peter, Robert, 1805-1894.
... Chemical analyses. A. First, second, and
third chemical reports, and chemical analyses of the
hemp and buck-wheat plants, by Robert Peter, M.D.,
etc., chemist to the Survey, and John H. Talbott
and A. M. Peter, assistants. [n.p.] Stereotyped
for the Survey by E. Polk Johnson, public printer,
1890.
180, 165, 92, 39 p.   tables.   26 cm.
At head of title: Geological Survey of Kentucky
[N. S. Shaler, director]

255

15146   Peter, Robert, 1805-1894.
        Chemical examination of the urinary calculi,
in the museum of the medical department of
Transylvania University; with remarks on the
relative frequency of calculus in Lexington,
Ky., and the probable causes. By Robert Peter,
M. D. Professor of chemistry and pharmacy, in
Transylvania University. From the Western
lancet, vol. V, no. 4. Lexington, Ky.,
Scrugham & Dunlop, printers, 1864.
        35 p.   21 x 14 cm.
        Cover title within ornate border.

15147   Peter, Robert, 1805-1894.
        ...Chemical report of the coals, clays,
mineral water, etc. of Kentucky... being the
ninth chemical report in the second series and the
thirteenth since the beginning of the Survey.
Compiled from the laboratory note books by
Alfred M. Peter... Louisville, Printed by the
Geo. G. Fetter co., 1905.
        77 p.   tables. $26\frac{1}{2}$ cm.
        At head of title: Kentucky Geological
Survey, Charles J. Norwood, director, Bulletin
no. 3.

15148   Peter, Robert, 1805-1894.
        The history of the Medical Department of
Transylvania University... Louisville, Ky.,
John P. Morton & company, 1905.
        193 p.   illus.   32 cm.   (Filson Club
publication, 20)

15149   Peter, Robert, 1805-1894.
        Thoughts on medical education in America,
and introductory lecture, delivered in the
chapel of Morrison college, to the medical
students of Transylvania university, on the 11th
November, 1838. By Robert Peter, M.D., professor
of chemistry and pharmacy, in the medical
department of Transylvania university. Published
at the request of the Medical Class. Lexington,
Ky., Printed at the Observer & reporter office,
1838.
        22 p. $17\frac{1}{2}$ x $10\frac{1}{2}$ cm.

15150 Peter, Robert, 1805-1894.
       ...Transylvania University, its origin, rise,
       decline, and fall. Prepared for the Filson Club
       by Robert Peter, M.D., and his daughter, Miss
       Johanna Peter... read at the Club meetings in
       October and November, 1895. Louisville, Ky.,
       John P. Morton and company, 1896.
          202 p.   front. (port.)   32 cm.
       At head of title: Filson Club publications, no. 11.

15151 Peyton, Jim.
          Equal education opportunity in Kentucky.
       Frankfort, Ky., Legislative Research Commission,
       1973.
          77 p.   tables.   29 cm.   (Research report no.
       105, new series)

15152 Phalen, W   C
          The central Kentucky phosphate field. Frankfort,
       Kentucky Geological Survey, 1915.
          [8], 80 p., xix pl. on 11 ℓ. map.   25½ cm.

15153 Phelps, Frank T
          One-time tavern: Carlisle's old Forest Retreat
       finds its place in history. Lexington, Ky., 1976.
          broadside.   illus.   20 x 35 cm.
       Reprinted from Lexington Herald-Leader,
       3 October 1976.

15154 Phillips, Mount Vernon, 1902-
          History of the independent toll bridge in
       Kentucky, 1792-1850. Lexington, Ky., 1930.
          68 p.   fold. map.   29 cm.

15155 Pickard, Madge E
          The midwest pioneer, his ills, cures, &
       doctors, by Madge E. Pickard and R. Carlyle Buley.
       Crawfordsville, Indiana, R. E. Banta, 1945.
          339 p.   illus.   27 cm.

15156 Pickett, John T
          To the army and people of Kentucky...
       My friends have induced me to become a candidate to
       represent the eighth congressional district
       composed of the counties of Henry, Trimble,
       Carroll, Gallatin, Boone, Grant, Kenton and
       Campbell, in the Congress of the Confederate

States... Richmond [Va.] January 8th, 1864.
broadside. $26\frac{1}{2}$ x $17\frac{1}{2}$ cm.

15157 Pickett, Thomas E
The quest for a lost race, presenting the
theory of Paul B. DuChaillu, an eminent
ethnologist and explorer, that the English-
speaking people of today are descended from the
Scandinavians rather than the Teutons-from the
Normans rather than the Germans... Louisville,
Ky., John P. Morton & company, 1907.
229 p.   illus., map.   32 cm.   (Filson
Club publications, 22)

15158 Pierson, Roscoe Mitchell.
The Disciples of Christ in Kentucky, a finding
list of the histories of local congregations
of Christian churches. Lexington, College of
Bible Library, 1962.
63 p.   29 cm.

15159 Pierson, Roscoe Mitchell.
A preliminary checklist of Lexington, Ky.,
imprints 1821-1850... Charlottesville, Va.,
Bibliographical Society of the University of
Virginia, 1953.
155 p. $28\frac{1}{2}$ cm.

15160 Piett, Sam.
The wise man of W-Hollow. [Cincinnati, 1972]
cover, 16-19 p.   illus.   34 cm.
Reprinted with permission from the Enquirer
magazine, Sunday, 2 January 1972.

15161 Pikeville, Ky. First Christian Church.
Gleaners' Class.
Our choicest recipes. Pikeville [n.d.]
109 p. $23\frac{1}{2}$ cm.

15162 Pilcher, Louis.
The story of Hazard, Ky. The pearl of the
mountains... Lexington, Citizens printing co.
[1913]
82 p.   illus.   23 cm.

15163 Pilcher, Louis.
The story of Hazard, Ky. The pearl of the

mountains. Hazard, The Hazard herald and People's
bank [n.d.]
  82 p.   illus.   24 cm.

15164 Pinkerton, Elizabeth W
         The administration of Governor Magoffin with
         relation to the Civil War. Lexington, Ky., 1930.
         59 l.   29 cm.
         M.A. thesis, University of Kentucky.

15165 Pioneer Memorial State Park, Harrodsburg, Ky.
         Visit Old Fort Harrod: a museum of pioneer
         life. Harrodsburg, Ky., Pioneer memorial state
         park [n.d.]
         16 p., illus., map.   25½ cm.

15166 The Pioneers of Kentucky [New York] 1862.
         577-592 p.   illus.   23 cm.
         Reprinted from Harper's new monthly magazine,
         v. 25, no. 149, Oct. 1862.

15167 Pirtle, Alfred.
         ...The Battle of Tippecanoe... Louisville,
         John P. Morton and company, 1900.
         158 p.   illus.   map.   27¼ cm.
         At head of title: Filson Club publication no.
         15.

15168 Pittman, Mrs. Hannah (Daviess) 1840-
         The belle of the Bluegrass county. Studies
         in black and white, by H. D. Pittman. Boston,
         The C. M. Clark Publishing co., 1906.
         5 p.l., v-vii, 424 p.   col. front, 15 pl.
         19½ cm.
         Author's presentation copy.

15169 Pitts, F   E
         Zion's harp: being a choice selection of the
         richest sacred songs not found in the Methodist
         hymn book, and many never before published, with
         several original pieces. Stereotype edition,
         much enlarged. Louisville, Ky., John P. Morton
         & co. [c1852]
         384 p.   12½ cm.

15170 Plan of the Danville theological seminary, under
         the care of the General assembly of the

259

Presbyterian church in the United States of America.
Louisville, Morton & Griswold, printers, 1854.
30 p., 1 ℓ.   18 cm.

15171   [Pohlkamp, Diomede]
St. Martins' Brotherhood, 1872-1947.
Diamond jubilee souvenir book, November, 1947.
[Louisville, 1947]
[36] p.   illus.   30 cm.

15172   A political creed. [Lexington? 1798?]
broadside.   21 x 28 cm.

15173   Pomfrey, J   W
A true disclosure and exposition of the Knights of
the golden circle, including the secret signs,
grips, and charges, of the three degrees, as
practised by the order... Cincinnati, Printed
for the author [1861]
v, [6]-47 p.   15½ cm.

15174   Poor, Peabody, comp.
Haldeman's Picture of Louisville, directory
and business advertiser, for 1844-1845; containing
the historical sketch of the town from 1778 to the
present time, and the trade and statistics of the
city; city and county officers; river distances
and general directory... Louisville, W. N.
Haldeman, 1844.
348 p.   22 cm.

15175   [Pope, John]
To the voters of Fayette, Woodford and Jessamine.
Who is Henry Clay?... [at end] A reply from Mr.
Pope to the handbills issued by Robert Wickliffe,
Esq. will appear in the course of this day. Monday,
Aug. 5, 1816. [n.p., n.d.]
50½ cm.

15176   Pope, Richard M
The College of the Bible, a brief narrative.
Lexington, Ky., 1961.
28 p.   23 cm.

15177   Potts, Eugenia Dunlap.
Idle hour stories. Lexington, Ky., Published

by the author [1909]
   244 p.   19 cm.

15178   Powell, Anna D
        Edward Lindsay Powell, preacher, citizen, friend.
        Louisville, The Herald press [1949?]
        235 p.   illus.   20 cm.

15179   Power, Frederick Dunglison, 1851-1911.
        ...Sketches of our pioneers, by F. D. Power...
        Cleveland, O., The Bethany C. E. company [c1898]
        148 p.   14½ cm.   (Half-title: The Bethany
        C. E. handbook series. [2d series, vol. II])
        At head of title: Hand-book series for the
        Bethany C. E. reading courses.

15180   Powers, Caleb, defendant.
        ...Caleb Powers, appellant advs. the Commonwealth
        of Kentucky, appellee. Brief for appellee. T. C.
        Campbell. [n.p., 190-?]
        At head of title: Commonwealth of Kentucky.

15181   Powers, Caleb, defendant.
        Caleb Powers, appellant, vs. Commonwealth of
        Kentucky, appellee. Brief for appellant. J. R.
        Morton, J. C. Sims, counsel for appellant.
        Lexington, The Transylvania co. [1901]
        183 p.   22½ cm.

15182   Powers, Frederick William.
        In the shadow of the Cumberlands; a story of
        Kentucky mountian life, by Frederick William
        Powers... Columbus, O., The Champlin printing
        company, 1904.
        5 p.l., 192p., 1 ℓ.   front., 11 pl.   20 cm.

15183   Prentice, George Dennison, 1802-1870.
        ...Biography of Henry Clay. New York, Published by
        John Jay Phelps, 1831.
        312 p.   front.   19 cm.
        At head of title: Second edition, revised.

15184   Presbyterian Church (First) Lexington, Ky.
        [History and family directory. Lexington, n.d.]
        unpaged.   illus.   29 cm.
        Historical account based on study by Robert
        Stuart Sanders.

Appended at end is church directory, August
1973, 19 p.

15185 Presbyterian Church (First), Lexington, Ky.
A Presbyterian celebration: the 175th anniversary,
First Presbyterian church, Lexington, Kentucky,
1784-1959. [Lexington, 1959]
64 p.   illus.   21 cm.
"The following history of First Church was
written by Sue McClelland Thierman, a member
of the congregation. The account, devoted
primarily to the early days, is based largely on
a history of the church written and published
this year by Dr. Robert S. Sanders." - p. 21.

15186 Presbyterian Church in the U.S.A. Presbytery
of Cincinnati.
One hundred years of Presbyterianism in the
Ohio valley. Cincinnati, O., 1980.
238 p.   illus., incl. ports.   22 cm.

15187 Presbyterian church in the U.S.A. Synod of
Kentucky.
Address on slavery. [Newburyport? 1836?]
24 p.   18½ cm.
Caption title.
Signed: John Brown, esq., chairman; John C.
Young, secretary.

15188 Presbyterian church in the U.S.A. Synod of
Kentucky.
An address to the Presbyterians of Kentucky,
proposing a plan for the instruction and emancipation
of their slaves, by a committee of the Synod
of Kentucky. Cincinnati, Taylor & Tracy, 1835.
64 p.   23 cm.

15189 Presbyterian Church in the U.S.A. Synod of
Kentucky.
An address to the Presbyterians of Kentucky,
proposing a plan for the instruction of their
slaves. By a committee of the synod of Kentucky.
Newburyport, Charles Whipple, 1836.
36 p.   20 cm.

15190 [Presbyterian church in the U.S.A. Synod of
Kentucky]

Statement and appeal in behalf of Centre college, Danville, Ky. Cincinnati, Elm street printing company, 1873.
19, [1] p.   23½ cm.

15191 Presbyterian church (U.S.), Bowling Green, Ky.
Sesquicentennial celebration of the Presbyterian church of Bowling Green, Kentucky. [Bowling Green, 1968?]
35 p.   illus.   22 cm.

15192 Preston, William, 1816-1887.
Journal in Mexico, by Lieutenant Colonel William Preston of the Fourth Kentucky Regiment of Volunteers, dating from November 1, 1847 to May 25, 1848. [n.p., 192-?]
45 p.   col. map, port.   29 cm.
Designed by Jack Kahane and printed on Arches mould-made vellum. Bound in tooled black leather, inlaid with green and tan leather, forming geometric designs, stamped: Jeanne Huck.

15193 Prewitt [family genealogy] [n.p., n.d.]
22 p., [6] ℓ.   fold. table.   29 cm.

15194 Price, James Franklin.
The Travis family. A remarkable genealogy full of thrilling interest and striking incidents. Marion, Ky., 1926.
89 p.   front.   (port.)   22 cm.

15195 Price, Paul P
Earlington and Hopkins County [Kentucky] [Frankfort, 1929]
broadside.   illus.   28½ cm.
Reprinted from Kentucky progress magazine, v. 1, no. 12, p. 20, Aug. 1929.

15196 Price, Samuel Woodson.
...Biographical sketch of Colonel Joseph Crockett. [Louisville, Ky., 1909]
85, xv p.   illus.   32 cm.
At head of title: Part second [of Filson Club publication no. 24]

15197 Price, Samuel Woodson.
...The old masters of the Bluegrass: Jouett,

263

Bush, Grimes, Frazer, Morgan, Hart... Louisville, Ky., John P. Morton & company, 1902.
181 p.   illus.   27½ cm.
At head of title: Filson Club publications no. 17.

15198 Princeton, Ky. First Baptist Church.
Centennial history of the First Baptist Church, Princeton, Kentucky, March 30, 1850 - March 30, 1950. [Princeton, Ky.? 1950?]

15199 Pritts, Joseph.
Mirror of olden time border life... [2nd ed.] Abingdon, Va., S. S. Miles, 1849.
p., 1 ℓ. [13]-700 p.   23 cm.

15200 A privilege, a duty, an opportunity for Kentucky.
Mammoth Cave National Park Association. Louisville, Ky., The Association [n.d.]
cover-title, [16] p.   illus.   26½ cm.

15201 Professor Rafinesque. Philadelphia, 1831.
328-329 p.   23 cm.
Reprinted from The Monthly American journal of geology and natural science, Vol. I.

15202 Program of exercises in commemoration of the centennial anniversary of the visit to Lexington of the Marquis de Lafayette. Held in connection with the Lexington Sesqui-Centennial celebration. Transylvania College compus, eight o'clock P. M. Wednesday, June 3, 1925. Lexington, Ky., 1925.
[8] p.   illus., ports.   21½ cm.
Contains portraits of Lafayette, Henry Clay, and the reprint of the program of exercises at the reception of General Lafayette by Transylvania University, on 16 May 1825, with introductory ode on Lafayette by Gustavus Adolphus Henry of Christian County, Ky.

15203 Protestant Episcopal Church in the U.S.A.
Lexington (Diocese)
Canons of the Diocese of Lexington adopted by the twenty-sixth annual council, January 31, 1921. Lexington, Ky., Press of J. R. Richardson & co., 1921.
cover-title, 24 p.   23 cm.

15204 Pruett, Rebecca K
The Browns of Liberty Hall... Masonic Home, Ky.,
Masonic home printing offiec, 1966.
35 p.   20½ cm.

15205 The Public library paper. A literary and critical
journal; pub. by the Public library of Kentucky.
v, 1, no. 1-26; May 17 - Nov. 8, 1873. Louisville,
1873.
1 v.   34½ cm.

15206 Public utility. Instructions for the information
and benefit of domestic manufactures in woolen
cloths... South Union, Logan county, Sept. 12,
1815. Russellville, Ky., Printed at the office
of the Weekly messenger [1815]
broadside.   23½ x 25½ cm.

15207 Puckett, Garrett E
History of Jeffersontown Baptist Church.
Centennial celebration, 1845-1945. [n.p.]
1945.
cover-title, 31 p.   illus.   23 cm.

15208 Purdom, Billy Joe.
Kentucky coon hunt. [Columbus, Ohio, 1969]
12-13, 20-22 p.   illus.   29 cm.
Reprinted by permission from Fur-fish-game,
v. 65, no. 12, December 1969.

15209 Pusey, William Allen, 1865-1940.
Giants of medicine in pioneer Kentucky, a
study of influences for greatness, by William
Allen Pusey, A.M., M.D., LL.D. New York, The
Froben Press [1938]
1 p.l., [35]-64 p.   25½ cm.
"Read before the Chicago Society of Medical
History, November 30, 1937; and before the
Filson Club, Louisville, Kentucky, February 7, 1938."
Reprinted from Medical Life, February 1938.
Bibliography: p. 64.

15210 Putnam, Frederic Ward, 1839-1915.
Archaeological researches in Kentucky and
Indiana, 1874... [Boston, 1875]
315-332 p.   24½ cm.

Q

15211 Quisenberry, Anderson Chenault, 1850-1921.
         A brief historical sketch of the newspapers of
       Winchester, by A. C. Quisenberry. Transcribed by
       George F. Doyle. [Winchester, Ky., n.d.]
         1 p.l., 22 typewritten l.   31 cm.

15212 Quisenberry, Anderson Chenault, 1850-1921.
         Clark County and the battle of the Thames.
       [Winchester, Ky., n.d.]
         5 p.   28 cm.
       "From the Winchester Democrat, Oct. 15, 1915."

15213 Quisenberry, Anderson Chenault, 1850-1921.
         Kentucky in the War of 1812... Frankfort,
       Kentucky State Historical Society, 1915.
         222 p.   illus.   24 cm.

15214 Quisenberry, Anderson Chenault, 1850-1921.
         Lopez's expeditions to Cuba, 1850 and 1851...
       Louisville, John P. Morton & company, 1906.
         172 p.   illus.   32 cm.   (Filson Club
       publication, 21)

15215 Quisenberry, Anderson Chenault, 1850-1921.
         Revolutionary soldiers in Clark County, by A. C.
       Quisenberry. Transcribed by George F. Doyle.
       [Winchester, Ky., n.d.]
         1 p.l., 9 typewritten l.   31 cm.

R

15216 Rafinesque, Constantine Samuel, 1783-1840.
         Alsographia americana, or An American grove of
       new or revised trees and shrubs of the genera
       myrica, calycanthus, salix, quercus, fraxinus,
       populus, tilia, sambucus, viburnum, cornus,
       juglans, aesculus &c, with some new genera,
       monographs, and many new sp. in 330 articles,
       completing 1405 g. and sp. as a continuation of
       the Sylva telluriana and North American trees &

shrubs... Philadelphia, 1838.
    76 p.   22½ cm.

15217 Rafinesque, Constantine Samuel, 1783-1840.
        American manuel of the grape vines and the
    art of making wine: including an account of
    69 species of vines, with nearly 300 varieties.
    An account of the principal wines, American and
    foreign. Properties and uses of wines and
    grapes. Cultivation of vines in America; and the
    art to make good wines. With 8 figures...
    Philadelphia, Printed for the author, 1830.
        1 p.l., [5]-64 p., 1 ℓ. 2 pl.   19 cm.

15218 Rafinesque, Constantine Samuel, 1783-1840.
        American manuel of the mulberry trees. Their
    history, cultivation, properties, diseases,
    species and varieties, &c. with hints on the
    production of silk from their barks &c...
    Philadelphia [Pub. by the author for the Eleutherium
    of knowledge] 1839.
        96 p.   21½ cm.

15219 Rafinesque, Constantine Samuel, 1783-1840.
        The American nations; or, Outlines of their
    general history, ancient and modern: including
    the whole history of the earth and mankind in the
    western hemisphere; the philosophy of American
    history; the annals, traditions, civilizations,
    language, &c. of all the American nations,
    tribes, empires, and states. Philadelphia, C. S.
    Rafinesque, 1836.
        2 v. in 1.   19½ cm.

15220 Rafinesque, Constantine Samuel, 1783-1840.
        Analyse de la nature; ou, Tableau de l'univers
    et des corps organisés... Palerme, Aux dépens
    de l'auteur, 1815.
        224 p.   18½ cm.

15221 Rafinesque, Constantine Samuel, 1783-1840.
        The ancient monuments of North and South America.
    2d ed., cor., enl. and with some additions...
    Philadelphia, Printed for the author, 1838.
        28 p.   24½ cm.

15222 Rafinesque, Constantine Samuel, 1783-1840.
       Annals of nature; or, Annual synopsis of
new genera and species of animals, plants, &c.
discovered in North America... First annual
number, for 1820. [Lexington, Ky., Printed by
T. Smith, 1820]
       16 p.   23 cm.

15223 Rafinesque, Constantine Samuel, 1783-1840.
       Caratteri di alcuni nuovi generi e nuove
specie di animali e piante della Sicilia, con
varie osservazioni sopra i medesimi... Palermo,
Per le stampe di Sanfilippo, 1810.
       3 p.l., 105, [2] p.   20 fold. pl.   20½ cm.

15224 Rafinesque, Constantine Samuel, 1783-1840.
       Celestial wonders and philosophy, or The
structure of the visible heavens with hints of
their celestial religion, and theory of futurity...
Philadelphia, Printed for the Central university
of Illinois, 1838.
       135, [1] p.   18½ x 11 cm.

15225 Rafinesque, Constantine Samuel, 1783-1840.
       Circular address on botany and zoology;
followed by the prospectus of two periodical
works; Annals of nature and Somiology of North
America... Philadelphia, Printed for the author
by S. Merritt, 1816.
       36 p.   14 cm.

15226 Rafinesque, Constantine Samuel, 1783-1840.
       Genius and spirit of the Hebrew Bible...
Philadelphia, Printed for the Eleutherium of
knowledge [etc.] 1838.
       264 p.   19 cm.

15227 Rafinesque, Constantine Samuel, 1783-1840.
       The good book, and amenities of nature, or
Annals of historical and natural science...
Philadelphia, Printed for the Eleutherium of
Knowledge, 1840.
       84 p.   24½ cm.

15228 Rafinesque, Constantine Samuel, 1783-1840.
       Improvements of universities, college, and
other seats of learning or education in North

America... Philadelphia, Printed for the
Eleutherium of knowledge, 1839.
1 p.l., 18 p.   24 cm.

15229 Rafinesque, Constantine Samuel, 1783-1840.
Indice d'ittiologia siciliana ossia catalogo
metodico dei nomi latini, italiani, e siciliani
dei pesci, chi si renvengono in Sicilia disposti
secondo un metodo naturale eseguito da un appendice
che contiene la descrizione di alcuni nuovi
pesci siciliani. Illustrato da due piane...
Messina, Presso Giovanni del Nobolo, con
approvazzione, 1810.
70 p.   2 fold. pl.   19 cm.

15230 Rafinesque, Constantine Samuel, 1783-1840.
A monograph of the fluviatile bivalve shells
of the river Ohio, containing twelve genera &
sixty-eight species. Tr. from the French of
C. S. Rafinesque... Philadelphia, J. Dobson,
1832.
vi p., 1 ℓ., [9]-72 p.   front. $19\frac{1}{2}$ cm.

15231 Rafinesque, Constantine Samuel, 1783-1840.
Neogenyton, or Indication of sixty-six new
genera of plants of North America... [Lexington?
Ky.] 1825.
4 p.   24 cm.

15232 Rafinesque, Constantine Samuel, 1783-1840.
Outlines of a general history of America.
Second chronological part: colonial annals of the
Antillian or West Indies islands also Guyana and
Brazil, besides the Boreal and Austral islands,
or the whole of America except Spanish
America and North America. From 1492 to 1775.
Begun in Philadelphia in Octr. 1827. [Philadelphia,
1827]
146 1.

15233 Rafinesque, Constantine Samuel, 1783-1840.
Rafinesque's Atlantic journal. Philadelphia,
1832.
508-515 p.   23 cm.
Reprinted from The Monthly American journal of
geology and natural science, Vol. I.

15234 Rafinesque, Constatine Samuel, 1783-1840.
          Sylva telluriana. Mantis. synopt. New
       genera of trees and shrubs of North America...
       Being a supplement to Flora telluriana...
       Philadelphia, Printed for the author and publisher,
       1838.
          184 p.   23 cm.

15235 Railey, William Edward.
          History of Woodford County... Reprinted from
       the Register of the Kentucky historical society,
       1920-1921. Frankfort, Ky., Roberts printing co.,
       1938.
          449 p.   illus., fold. map.   28 cm.

15236 Railey, William Edward.
          A history of interesting things found in
       the rooms of the Kentucky Historical Society.
       [Louisville, Masonic Home Journal, 19--]
          23 p.   illus.   24½ cm.
          A photograph of the author with biographical
       sketch is mounted in this copy on the verso of
       the title-page.

15237 Railey, William Edward.
          A history of interesting things found in the
       rooms of the Kentucky Historical Society, by
       Wm. E. Railey [Frankfort, Ky., n.d.]
          cover-title.   22 p.   front. (port.)
       23½ cm.

15238 Ramage, James A
          Holman Hamilton, a biographical sketch [by]
       James A. Ramage. Published on the occasion of
       his retirement dinner, April 29, 1975, Lexington,
       Kentucky. [Lexington, 1975]
          26 p.   24 cm.

15239 Ranck, George Washington, 1841-1900.
          The bivouac of the dead and its author... New
       York, Grafton press [c1898]
          73 p.   plates, port.   18 cm.
          Contains the text of the poem.

15240 Ranck, George Washington, 1841-1900.
          Boonesborough, its founding, pioneer struggles,
       Indian experiences, Transylvania days, and

revolutionary annals... Louisville, John P.
Morton & company, 1901.
285 p.   illus.   32 cm.
At head of title: Filson Club publication no.
16.

15241   Ranck, George Washington, 1841-1900.
History of Lexington, Kentucky; its early
annals and recent progress including biographical
sketches and personal reminiscences of the pioneer
settlers, notices of prominent citizens, etc.,
Cincinnati, R. Clarke, 1872.
428 p.   plate.   24 cm.

15242   Ranck, George Washington, 1841-1900.
"The travelling church" an account of the
Baptist exodus from Virginia to Kentucky in
1781 under the leadership of Rev. Lewis
Craig and Capt. William Ellis. With historical
notes. Louisville, Ky., Press of the Baptist book
concern, 1891.
38 p.   22½ cm.

15243   Randolph, Helen Fitz.
Mammoth Cave and the cave region of Kentucky,
by Helen F. Randolph... with bibliography of
Mammoth Cave by Willard Rouse Jillson... first
accurate underground survey by H. Bruce Huffman...
introduction by Dr. H. C. Nelson... Louisville,
The Standard printing company, incorporated, 1924.
153, [3] p.   front., illus., fold. maps.
19 cm.

15244   Rankin, Frank.
Kentucky in the Revolution. Washington, D.C.,
1976.
E2258-E2259 p.   28 cm.
Reprinted from Congressional record, Extensions
of remarks, 30 April 1976.

15245   Ranschoff, Joseph.
Under the northern lights and other stories.
Cincinnati, The Ebbert & Richardson co., 1921.
166 p.   front. (port.)   24 cm.
Contains addresses on "Holmes and Drake" and
"Address on Daniel Drake."

271

15245 Ravens creek. Lexington, Ky., 1960.
          15 ℓ.   illus.   17 cm.

15247 Read, Opie Percival, 1852-1939.
          I remember. New York, Richard R. Smith, inc.,
          1930.
          335 p.   21 cm.

15248 Read, Opie Percival, 1852-1939.
          A Kentucky colonel. Chicago, F. J. Schulte &
          company, 1890.
          342 p.   20 cm.

15249 Read, Opie Percival, 1852-1939.
          Some characters of the old South.
          Illustrations by George Wright. [n.p.] 1919.
          391-400 p.   illus.   24 cm.
          Reprinted from The Century, v. 98, July 1919.
          With this are reprints of articles in the
          Dictionary of American biography, suppl. 2,
          v. 11; Overland monthly, 2d ser., v. 17, 1891,
          on A Kentucky colonel; Oxford companion to American
          literature; Burton Rascoe (of Kentucky), Opie
          Read and Zane Grey, Saturday review of literature,
          v. 21, no. 8, 21 Nov. 1939; and of the section
          of Read entries in the Library of Congress
          catalog.

15250 The Red Mile, 1875-1977. Lexington, Ky., 1977.
          12 p.   illus., map.   28½ cm.
          Reprinted from Lexington Herald, 27 Sept. 1977.

15251 Red River Gorge Legal Defense Fund, Lexington, Ky.
          Help save Red river. [Lexington, Ky., 1974]
          [6] p.   illus., map.   29 cm.

15252 Reed-Hudson, Deborah.
          Alone as a milkmaid. [Lexington, Ky., 1959]
          37-39 p.   23 cm.
          Reprinted from Stylus, v. 7, no. 2, Spring 1959.

15253 Reeves, John Estill.
          Kentucky government. Lexington, 1960.
          113 p.   23 cm.

15254 Republican Party. Kentucky. Executive Committee.
          Beckham vs. Taylor; a pamphlet, series I.

Issued by Republican Executive Committee.
Louisville, Ky., W. P. Jobson printing co.
[190-?]
[9] p.   23 cm.
"The points decided by the courts in this famous
case. Some testimony taken before the Legislative
Board, upon which 200,000 voters were disfranchised."

15255   Retail Merchants Association, Louisville, Ky.
Souvenir booklet. [Louisville? 19--?]
[16] p.   illus.   15 x 23 cm.

15256   Reuthebuck, George.
Society's stepchildren: the mentally retarded.
Frankfort, Ky., Legislative Research Commission,
1974.
34 p.   tables, diagrs.   29 cm.   (Research
report no. 112, new series)

15257   The review of contemporary poetry. v. 1, no. 1-3.
Lexington, Ky., 1949.
3 nos.   23 cm.
No more published.
Editors: James O. Jordan, Myron Bates,
Clement Cockrel, Keller Dunn, Murray Cohen.

15258   Review of government. Lexington, Bureau of
government research, University of Kentucky,
1960-1965.
5 v.   tables.   29½ cm.
Sequence of dates of issues does not
correspond to sequence of issue numbers.
V. 5, no. 8, May 1965, last issued.
V. 3, no. 2, never issued.

15259   Reviews of Jefferson Davis, constitutionalist.
His letters, papers and speeches. Jackson,
Mississippi, printed for the Mississippi department
of archives and history, 1924.
88 p.   illus.   24½ cm.

15260   Reynolds, J   Owen.
History of Epworth Methodist Church, Lexington,
Kentucky, by J. Owen Reynolds. Lexington, A. Z.
Looney & company, 1960.
6 p.l., 37 p.   illus.   21½ cm.

15261 Reynolds, Noah M
          History of the feuds of the mountain parts of
       Eastern Kentucky. Lives of Noah and John Reynolds.
       [n.p., n.d.]
          45 p.   20½ cm.

15262 Rice, Alice Caldwell Hegan, 1870-1942.
          Hoodooed, by Alice Hegan Rice, [n.p.] 1914.
          581-589 p.   illus.   22 cm.
          Reprinted from The Century, v. 88, Sept. 1914.
          Illustrated by F. R. Gruger.

15263 Rice, Alice Caldwell Hegan, 1870-1942.
          Lovey Mary. New York, The Century company, 1903.
          197 p.   illus.   20 cm.

15264 Rice, Alice Caldwell Hegan, 1870-1942.
          A matter of friendship, by Alice Hegan Rice.
       [n.p.] 1910.
          36-41 p.   22 cm.
          Reprinted from The Century, v. 80, May 1910.

15265 Rice, Alice Caldwell Hegan, 1870-1942.
          The nut. Illustrations by W. M. Barger.
       [n.p.] 1919.
          7 p.   illus.   25 cm.
          Reprinted from The Century, v. 99, Nov. 1919.
          With this is the article on Mrs. Rice from the
       Dictionary of American biography, Suppl. 3, 1941-
       1945 (1975); her obituaries in the Louisville Times
       and Lexington Leader, 11 Feb. 1942; articles on her
       and Cale Young Rice in Kunitz and Haycraft, Twentieth
       century authors (1942); the section of entries on her
       and Cale Young Rice in the Louisville Courier-Journal,
       25 Jan. 1943; Library of Congress Catalog; the
       obituary of Cale Young Rice in the Louisville Courier-
       Journal, 25 Jan. 1943; a criticism of Mr. Rice's
       Yolanda in the Literary digest, v. 104, p. 24-25,
       1 Feb. 1890; and a note on Mr. Rice in The Critic,
       v. 45, p. 204-205, 1904.

15266 Rice, Alice Caldwell Hegan, 1870-1942.
          Mr. Opp, by Alice Hegan Rice... With
       illustrations by Leon Guipon. New York, The
       Century co., 1909.
          4 p.l., 326 p.   illus.   18¼ cm.

15267   Rice, Alice Caldwell Hegan, 1870-1942.
        Sandy. New York, The Century company, 1905.
        312 p.   illus.   19 cm.

15268   Rice, David, 1733-1816.
        An essay on Baptism. Baltimore, Printed by
        William Goddard, 1789.
        82 p. $19\frac{1}{2}$ cm.

15269   Rice, David, 1733-1816.
        Slavery inconsistent with justice and good
        policy, by Philanthropos (David Rice) Together
        with a twentieth century afterword [by Jacqueline
        P. Bull and Frances L. S. Dugan] Keepsake number
        3. [Lexington] University of Kentucky Library
        associates, 1956.
        1 ℓ., 42 p. of facsim., [3] p. $15\frac{1}{2}$ cm.

15270   Rice, Laban Lacy, 1870-
        A mountain idyll, by Laban Lacy Rice.
        Nashville, The Baird-Ward press, 1921.
        83 p.   16 cm.

15271   Richardson, Amanda Cranwill.
        Scattered leaves. Poems from a collection of
        poems lost during the war. By Amanda Cranwill
        Richardson. Louisville, John P. Morton &
        company, 1895.
        viii, 96 p.   15 cm.

15272   Richardson, Charles Henry.
        The molding sands of Kentucky, a detailed
        report covering the field examination,
        mechanical analysis, and industrial evaluation of
        the principal molding sand deposits of the state...
        Frankfort, Kentucky Geological Survey, 1927.
        [12], 240 p.   illus., maps. $24\frac{1}{2}$ cm.
        (Kentucky Geological Survey, ser. VI, v. 29)

15273   Richardson, Paul D
        Participation in organized activities in a
        Kentucky rural community. By Paul D. Richardson
        and Ward W. Bauder. Lexington, Kentucky
        Agricultural Experiment Station, University of
        Kentucky, 1953.
        28 p.   map, tables.   (Kentucky Agricultural
        Experiment Station, Bulletin, 598)

15274 Richardson, R
Kentucky agricultural school. No. II.
Frankfort, Ky., 1858.
82-83 p.   24 cm.
Letter addressed to J. B. Bowman as general
agent of Kentucky University, Harrodsburg.
Reprinted from Kentucky Farmer (Frankfort),
v. 1, no. 6, December 1858.

15275 Ridenour, George L
Early times in Meade County, Kentucky...
Louisville, Ky., Western recorder, 1929.
107, [1] p. incl. plates. front.   20 cm.

15276 Ridgeway, Florence Holmes.
Developments in library service Kentucky.
A review by Florence H. Ridgeway... [Berea]
Berea College Press, 1940.
20 p.   23 cm.
Bibliography: p. 19-20.

15277 Riley, Herbert Parks.
The College of Arts and Sciences, University
of Kentucky. Lexington, University of Kentucky
Centennial Committee, 1965.
40 p.   24 cm.

15478 River drift. An accumulation of pictures, data and
stories of the inland waterways and the men and
that carried the nation's commerce in days gone
by. St. Louis, The Waterways journal [1969]
[32] p.   illus.   24 cm.

15279 Rives, Hallie Erminie, 1876-1956.
Hearts courageous. Illustrated by A. B. Wenzell.
New York, Grosset and Dunlap [1902]
407 p.   illus.   20 cm.

15280 Robbins, A
Nature's wonderland. Hickman, on the bluffs
of the Mississippi is the gateway to the
famous Reelfoot Lake. [Frankfort, Ky., 1932]
6-12, 45-46 p.   illus.   28½ cm.
Reprinted from Kentucky progress magazine,
v. 4, no. 11, p. 6-12, 45-46, July 1932.

15281   Roberts, James R
        Financing of mass transportation operations,
        prepared for the Interim Joint Committee on
        Public Utilities and Transportation by James R.
        Roberts. Frankfort, Ky., Legislative Research
        Commission, 1977.
            viii, 39 p.   tables.   27½ cm.   (Research
        report, no. 135)

15282   Roberts, Joseph K
            ... Geology and mineral resources of the
        Jackson Purchase region, Kentucky, by Joseph
        K. Roberts and Benjamin Gildersleeve. Paleozoic
        geology, by Louise Barton Freeman. Published in
        cooperation with the Tennessee Valley Authority.
        Printed by authority of the state of Kentucky.
        Lexington, 1950.
            114 p.   illus., graphs, tables, 3 fold.   maps
        in pocket at end.   24 cm.
            At head of title: University of Kentucky.
        College of Arts and Sciences. Kentucky Geological
        Survey. Arthur C. McFarlan, director. D. J.
        Jones, state geologist. Series IX. Bulletin - no. 4.

15283   Robertson, George, 1790-1874.
            An address delivered at Camp Madison, on the
        Fourth of July 1843. Frankfort, Ky., Hodges, Todd
        & Pruett, printers, 1843.
            32 p.   21½ cm.

15284   Robertson, George, 1790-1874.
            Introductory address on the history and
        nature of equity; by the Hon. George Robertson,
        L.L.D., professor of natural and constitutional
        law, and equitable jurisprudence, in Transylvania
        university. Delivered November, 1837. Lexington,
        Ky., Printed by Edwin Bryant, 1838.
            22 p.   21 x 13 cm.

15285   Robertson, Harrison, 1856-1939.
            The opponents, by Harrison Robertson...
        new York, Charles Scribner's sons, 1902.
            vi, 1 ℓ., 355 p.   19½ cm.

15286   Robertson, Harrison, 1856-1939.
            The pink typhoon, by Harrison Robertson.

New York, C. Scribner's sons, 1908.
2 p.l., 196 p.   front.   18 cm.

15287   Robertson, Harrison, 1856-1939.
Red Wood and blue, by Harrison Robertson...
New York, C. Scribner's sons, 1900.
2 p.l., 324 p.   19½ cm.

15288   Robertson, James Rood.
... Petitions of the early inhabitants of
Kentucky to the General Assembly of Virginia,
1769-1792. Louisville, John P. Morton &
company, 1914.
246 p.   front. (port.)   27 cm.
At head of title: Filson Club publication
no. 27.

15289   Robertson, Mabel D
Kentucky administrative regulations, prepared
by Mabel D. Robertson... Frankfort,
Legislative Research Commission, 1976.
[6], 26 p.   21½ cm.   (Informational
bulletin, no. 118)

15290   Robinson, Lee Lamar.
Kentucky in Washington. History in brief of
participation of Kentucky, through Kentuckians,
in affairs at Washington, 1792-1928... Louisville,
The Standard printing company, inc., 1928.
143 p.   illus.   27½ cm.

15291   Rodman, Hugh.
Yarns of a Kentucky admiral... Indianapolis,
The Bobbs-Merrill company [1928]
320 p.   illus.   23 cm.

15292   Rogers, James Richard, 1840-
The Cane Ridge meeting-house, by James
R. Rogers; to which is appended the autobiography
of B. W. Stone, and a sketch of David Purviance
by William Rogers. Cincinnati, The Standard
publishing company [1910]
237 p.   incl. front., plates, ports.   20 cm.

15293   Rogers, John C
The story of Louisville neighborhoods.
Portland, Clifton, Highlands, The Point,

Germantown, Butchertown, Beechmont, West End,
Limerick, Parkland, Crescent Hill, Downtown.
Louisville, The Courier-Journal and The
Louisville Times, 1955.
  36 p.   illus., map.   27 cm.
A series of articles in the Louisville Times,
May, 1955. Reprinted by permission.

15294 Rogers, Robert M
       The 125th regiment, Illinois volunteer infantry...
       Champaign, Ill., Gazette steam print, 1882.
         226 p.   front. (port.)   22 cm.
       Campaign in Kentucky, p. 21-53.

15295 [Roland, Clayton]
       New Liberty. A brief history of Owen county's
       oldest town. Reprint of a feature article appearing
       in the News-Herald, Owenton, Kentukcy, on Oct. 18,
       1956.
         [8] p.   illus.   23 cm.

15296 A roll of the officers in the Virginia line,
       of the Revolutionary army, who have received
       land bounty, in the states of Ohio and Kentucky...
       Chillicothe, Latham & Leonard, 1822.
         20 p.   16 cm.

15297 Roll, William H
       A short description of Kentucky coals.
       Lexington, Engineering Experiment Station,
       College of Engineering, University of Kentucky,
       1962.
         36 p.   maps, tables.   24 cm.   (Engineering
       Experiment Station, Bulletin, v. 17, no. 1)

15298 Rose, David B   G
       The Louisville Foundation...   Louisville, The
       Franklin Printing Co. [1949]
         23 p.   illus.   23 cm.

15299 Rothert, Otto Arthur, 1871-1956.
       The Filson Club and its activities, 1884-1922.
       A history of the Filson Club, including lists of
       Filson Club publications and papers on Kentucky
       history prepared for the club, also names of
       members. Louisville, John P. Morton & co., 1922.

64 p.   24½ cm.   (Filson Club publications,
no. 32)

15300   Rothert, Otto Arthur, 1871-1956.
        A history of Muhlenberg County... Louisville,
        John P. Morton & co., 1913.
        496 p.   illus.   25 cm.

15301   Rothert, Otto Arthur, 1871-1956.
        A history of the Filson Club, 1884-May 15, 1934.
        Louisville, 1934.
        139-147 p.   24 cm.
        In The Filson Club history quarterly, vol. 8,
        no. 3, July 1934. The entire issue is reprinted
        here, with permission of the Director of the
        Filson Club, since it contains supporting
        information of Mr. Rothert's article.

15302   Rothert, Otto Arthur, 1871-1955.
        A history of the Unity Baptist Church,
        Muhlenberg County, Kentucky, by Otto A. Rothert.
        Louisville, Ky., Press of J. P. Morton & co.,
        incorporated, 1974.
        2 p.l., 59 p.   illus.   (incl. facsim.)
        20½ cm.

15303   Rothert, Otto Arthur, 1871-1956.
        ... The story of a poet: Madison Cawein.
        His intimate life as revealed by his letters and
        other hitherto unpublished material, including
        reminiscences by his closest associates; also
        articles from newspapers and magazines and a
        list of his poems... Louisville, John P. Morton
        & company, 1921.
        xi, 545 p.   illus.   24 cm.
        At head of title: Filson Club publication
        no. 30.

15304   Rothert, Otto Arthur, 1871-1956, comp.
        Young E. Allison memorial meeting, Henderson,
        Kentucky, June 24, 1933; proceedings compiled
        for publication by Otto A. Rothert... [Louisville,
        1933]
        1 p.l., p. [181]-208.   25 cm.
        "Reprinted from the Filson club history
        quarterly... October, 1933."

280

Includes contributions by Otto A. Rothert,
William Fortune and J. Christian Bay.

15305 Rowan, John, 1773-1843.
Report of John Rowan, esq., in relations to the
late decision of the Court of Appeals, on the
replevin and endorsement laws, and of Supreme
court of the United States on the occupying
claimant laws of Kentucky. Frankfort, Ky.,
Printed by J. H. Holeman, 1823.
31 p.   23 cm.

15306 Royce, Jack F
The preservation of Land Office records...
Frankfort, Kentucky, Legislative Research
Commission, 1971.
27 p.   illus., facsims.   27½ cm.
(Informational bulletin, no. 89)

15307 Rudd, Robert W
Trends in Kentucky agriculture. By Robert W.
Rudd and D. Milton Shuffett. Lexington, Kentucky
Agricultural Experiment Station, University of
Kentucky, 1956.
74 p.   tables, diags.   24 cm.   (Kentucky
Agricultural Experiment Station, Bulletin, 653)

15308 The run for the roses; a history of the Kentucky
derby. [New York, W. A. Taylor & Company, n.d.]
[16] p.   illus., fold. table.   17½ cm.

15309 Runyon, Keith.
Fox hunting in Kentucky. Louisville, Ky.,
1972.
3 p.   illus.   58 x 40 cm.
Reprinted from Louisville Courier-Journal and
Times, Section G, 12 November, 1972.

15310 The Rupp legacy. Lexington, Ky., 1977.
12 p.   illus.   37 cm.
Reprinted from Lexington Herald, 13 Dec. 1977.
Appended are twenty-two items from Lexington
Herald and Kentucky Kernel, 11-28 Dec. 1977 and
one from the Kentucky Alumnus, winter 1977-1978.

15311 Russell, J
Maps of the state of Kentucky, with the

adjoining territories. London, H. D. Symonds, 1794.
map.   37½ x 44 cm.

15312 Rutherford, Susan B
       The Derby dictionary. Lawrenceburg, Ky., 1941.
       [12] ℓ.   illus.   24 cm.

                            S

15313 Sacajawea fesitval, August 6-7-8-9-10, 1970,
       Cloverport, Ky. [Cloverport, 1970]
           cover-title., 48 p.   illus.   22 cm.
       Includes five pages of ms. history of Cloverport
       by Mrs. Frank A. Smith, "Cloverport historian."

15314 Safford, William Harrison, 1821-1903.
           The life of Harman Blennerhassett. Comprising
       an authentic narrative of the Burr expedition:
       and containing many additional facts not
       heretofore published. Chillicothe, O., Ely,
       Allen & Looker, 1850.
           239 p.   incl. front.   20 cm.

15315 St. Aloysius College, Louisville, Ky.
           The catalogue of St. Aloysius College, Louisiville
       Ky., for the academical year 1851-'52. Louisville,
       Printed at the office of the Journal, 1852.
           16 p.   22 cm.

15316 St. John, Percy Bolingbroke, 1821-1889.
           Queen of the woods; or, the Shawnee captives.
       A romance of the Ohio. New York, Beadle and
       company [1868]
           129 p.   16½ cm.   (Beadle's dime novels,
       no. 174)

15317 ... St. Joseph's Parish, Bowling Green, Ky.
       1859-1959. [Bowling Green? 1959?]
           cover-title, [12] p.   illus.   18½ cm.
       At head of title: Centennial souvenir.

15318 ... St. Peter Claver Church, Louisville, Kentucky.
       [Louisville? 1932?]

cover-title, [28] p.   illus.   28 cm.
At head of title: 50th anniversary.

15319   Sanders, Harlan, 1890-
        [Statement to Special studies subcommittee of
        House committee on government operations in
        August 1971] [Washington, D.C., 1971]
        p. H 10338-H 10340.   29 cm.   (Congressional
        record, v. 117, no. 165, 3 November 1971)
        Introduced by Mr. Randall of Missouri. Contains
        biographical statement about Col. Sanders.

15320   Sanders, Robert Stuart.
        Annals of the First Presbyterian Church,
        Lexington, Kentucky, 1784-1959... Louisville,
        The Dunne press, 1959.
        192 p.   illus.   24 cm.

15321   Sanders, Robert Stuart.
        Gleanings from West Lexington Presbytery, 1799-
        1935; Ebenezer Presbytery, 1820-1935; Lexington-
        Ebenezer Presbytery, 1930-1950. Lexington, Ky.,
        Lexington-Ebenezer Presbytery, 1952.
        66 p.   23 cm.

15322   Sanders, Robert Stuart.
        An historical sketch of Springfield Presbyterian
        Church, Bath County, Kentucky. Frankfort, Ky.,
        Roberts Printing Company, 1954.
        115 p.   plates, ports.   23 cm.

15323   Sanders, Robert Stuart.
        An historic sketch of the Ebenezer Reformed
        Presbyterian Church, Jessamine County, Kentucky.
        [1st ed.] Frankfort, Ky., Roberts Print. Co., 1954.
        71 p.   illus.   23 cm.
        Author's presentation copy.

15324   Sanders, Robert Stuart.
        History of the Louisville Presbyterian
        Theological Seminary, 1853-1953. [Louisville]
        Louisville Presbyterian Theological Seminary,
        1953.
        100 p.   illus.   24 cm.

15325   Sanders, Robert Stuart.
        History of Walnut Hill Presbyterian Church

(Fayette County, Kentucky)... Introduction by
J. Winston Coleman, Jr. Frankfort, Ky., Kentucky
Historical Society, 1956.
    88 p.   illus.   24 cm.
    Appended in front is article from Lexington
Herald, 5 June 1973, describing the church as an
entry in the National Register of Historic Places.

15326 Sanford, Washington L   1825-   comp.
    History of Fourteenth Illinois cavalry and
the brigades to which it belonged; compiled
from manuscript history by Sanford, West, and
Featherston, and from notes of comrades...
Chicago, R. R. Donnelley & sons company, 1899.
    347 p.   19 cm.

15327 Sauer, Carl Ortwin, 1889-
    Geography of the Pennyroyal; a study of the
influence of geology and physiography upon the
industry, commerce and life of the people, by
Carl Ortwin Sauer... assisted by John B.
Leighly, Kenneth McMurry, Clarence W. Newman...
Frankfort, Ky., The Kentucky geological survey,
1927.
    303 p.   front., illus., maps, diags.   24 cm.
(Kentucky geological survey, ser. VI, Geologic
reports, v. 25)
    Bibliography: p. 293-298.

15328 Scenic and historic Garrard. Garrard and the
    Lake Herrington. Lancaster, Ky., published by
Garrard County Board of Commerce [n.d.]
    12 p.   illus., map.   23 cm.

15329 [Schoolcraft, Henry Rowe] 1793-1864.
    Western scenes and reminiscences: together with
thrilling legends and traditions of the red men
of the forest. To which is added several
narratives of adventures among the Indians.
Auburn [N.Y.] Derby & Miller; Buffalo,, Derby,
Orton & Mulligan, 1853.
    v, [5]-495 p.   col. front., illus., pl.   23 cm.

15330 Schrader, Floyd F
    Water. Lexington, Ky., 1946.
    123 p.   illus., map, tables (1 fold.), diags.
    24 cm.   (Kentucky Geological Survey, Series

VIII, Reprint, 10)
Reprinted from Bulletin of the Bureau of School
Service, College of Education, University of
Kentucky, vol. 18, no. 2, December, 1945, pp.
44-123, for the Department of Mines and Minerals.

15331   Schten, Edward V
Educational television for Kentucky. Frankfort,
Ky., Legislative Research Commission, 1961.
55 p.   29 cm.   (Research report no. 3)

15332   Schten, Edward V
Insurance on state property in Kentucky.
Lexington, Ky., Bureau of Government Research,
University of Kentucky, 1960.
30 p.   29 cm.

15333 Schten, Edward V
Professional licensing in Kentucky. Lexington,
Bureau of Government Research, College of Arts
and Sciences, University of Kentucky, 1960.
40 p.   22 cm.

15334   Schwab, Edith C
Condemnation: 1970-1972 supplement. Frankfort,
Legislative Research Commission, 1972.
iii, 17 p.   28 cm.   (Informational
bulletin, no. 101)

15335   Schwab, Edith C
Eminent domain in Kentucky. Frankfort, Ky.,
Legislative Research Commission, 1973.
116 p.   tables.   29 cm.   (Research report
no. 101, new series)

15336   Schwab, Edith M
Motor vehicles: certificates of title and
taxation. Prepared by Edith M. Schwab [and]
Donald F. Roney. Frankfort, Ky., Legislative
Research Commission, 1975.
144 p.   29 cm.   (Research report, no. 119)

15337   Schwarzweller, Harry K
Sociocultural origins and migration patterns of
young men from eastern Kentucky. Lexington,
Kentucky Agricultural Experiment Station, 1963.

285

29 p.   maps, diags., tables.   24 cm.
(Bulletin 685)

15338 Schwendeman, Gerald.
         Lexington, Kentucky. Urban land use. [Lexington,
       1965]
         27 p.   maps, tables.   29 cm.   (Kentucky
       study series, 1)

15339 Scott, Charles.
         Frankfort, [Ky.] January 13th, 1812. Being
       delegated by the officers who served during
       our Revolutionary war... [Frankfort, 1812]
         19 x 32 cm.

15340 Scott, R   H
         Speech in House of Representatives of Kentucky,
       Monday, March 11, 1912. [n.p., 1912?]
         12 p.   23 cm.

15341 Scribblings by the Scribblers' club. Lexington,
       Kentucky, 1926.
         52 p.   17½ cm.

15342 Scrugham, Mary, 1885-
         ... The peaceable Americans of 1860-1861;
       a study in public opinion... New York, Columbia
       University [etc., etc.] 1921.
         125 p.   21½ cm.   (Studies in history,
       economics and public law, ed. by the Faculty of
       political science of Columbia University, vol.
       xcvi, no. 3; whole no. 219)
         Published also as thesis (Ph. D.) Columbia
       University, 1921.

14343 Sea, Sophie Fox.
         "That old-time child, Roberta," her homelife
       on the farm, by Sophie Fox Sea. Louisville,
       Printed by John P. Morton and company, 1892.
         84 p.   illus.   22 cm.

15344 [Sealsfield, Charles] 1793-1864.
         The Americas as they are; described in a tour
       through the valley of the Mississippi. By the
       author of "Austria as it is." London, Hurst,
       Chance, and co., 1828.
         [x, 221] p.   20 cm.

15345 Seems Southern to we. [Lexington, Ky., Office of
       Minority Student Affairs, University of Kentucky,
       1977]
          64 p.   illus.

15346 The sesquicentennial addresses given at Christ
       Church, Lexington, Kentucky, as part of the
       150th anniversary celebration. By Dr. Raymond
       F. McLain and the Rt. Rev. William R. Moody,
       on May 19 and 26, 1946. [Lexington? 1946]
          cover-title, 11 p.   23 cm.

15347 75 years in the Bluegrass, 1865-1949. [Lexington,
       Ky., Transylvania Printing Co., 1940]
          [11] p.   23 x 10 cm.
          A historical sketch of the First National
       Bank and Trust Company, Lexington, Ky.

15348 Shackelford, Nevyle.
          Wildflowers of Kentucky. Lexington, Cooperative
       Extension Service, College of Agriculture,
       University of Kentucky [195-?]
          63 p.   illus.   23 cm.
          Cover-title.

15349 Shakers.
          A memorial, remonstrating against a certain act of
       legislature of Kentucky, entitled "An act to
       regulate civil proceedings against certain
       communities having property in common" — and
       declaring, —"That it shall and may be lawful to
       commence and prosecute suits, obtain decrees and
       have execution against any of the communities
       of people called Shakers, —without naming or
       designating the individuals, or serving process
       on them, otherwise than by fixing a subpoena
       on the door of their meeting-house, &c.
       Approved Feb. 11, 1828. [Harrodsburg, Ky.,
       Printed at the Union office, 1828]
          8 p.   22 cm. (in binding 35 cm)
          Caption title.
          Signed by the communities of Pleasant Hill and
       South Union, "Officially represented by their
       responsible agents, John R. Bryand, Eli McLean."

15350 Shakertown at Pleasant Hill, Ky., Inc.
          Paul Sawyier (1865-1917) An exhibition of

287

the artist's work held at Pleasant Hill, Kentucky,
June 1- June 14, 1964. [n.p., 1964?]
  cover-title., 28 p.   illus.   21 cm.

15351 Shaler, Nathaniel Southgate, 1841-1906.
    The autobiography of Nathaniel Southgate Shaler.
    With a supplementary memoir by his wife. Boston
    and New York, Houghton Mifflin company, 1909.
    481 p.   illus.   25 cm.

15352 Shaler, Nathaniel Southgate, 1841-1906.
    ... Kentucky, a pioneer commonwealth...
    Third ed. Boston, Houghton, Mifflin, 1886.
    433 p.   fold. map.   19 cm.

15353 Shall the free men of Kentucky secure their
    rights? [Lexington? 1798?]
    broadside.   26 x 23½ cm.

15354 Shannon, Jasper B
    A survey of the natural resources and population
    trends of Kentucky River valleys, by J. S. Shannon...
    [Lexington] Bureau of Government Research,
    University of Kentucky, 1937.
    [6], 28 p.   28 cm.   (Studies in regionalism
    in Kentucky, 1)

15355 Sheffey, Daniel, 1770-1830.
    The Honorable D. Sheffey, [member of Congress
    from Virginia] to his constituents. [Circular]
    [Lexington, Ky., From the press of Thomas T.
    Skillman, 1813]
    16 p.   21 cm.

15356 ... Shelby College lottery of the state of
    Kentucky... to be drawn in Covington,
    Kentucky, on Saturday, February 27th, 1864...
    [n.p., 1865?]
    broadside.   51 x 13½ cm.

15357 [Shelby, Isaac] 1750-1826.
    Battle of King's Mountain... [Lexington, Ky.,
    Thomas Smith, 1823]
    24 p.   20 cm.

15358 Shelby, Isaac, 1750-1826.
    [Call for volunteers in the War of 1812]

[Frankfort, Kentucky Historical Society, n.d.]
manuscript.   1 ℓ.   29 x 22½ cm.

15359   Shelby, Lucy Goodlow, 1862-1957.
Grassland days and grassland ways. Lexington,
Ky., 1957.
30 p.   ports.   24 cm.

15360   Shely, Forest Wyatt.
This is Friendship. Sinai, Ky., Friendship
Baptist Church, 1959.
47 p.   illus., ports.   23 cm.

15361   Sherley, Douglass, 1857-
Love perpetuated: the story of a dagger.
Christmas 1884. [Louisville, Ky.? 1884]
[2, 20] p.   French fold.   20 cm.
Appended at end is Sharon M. Reynolds,
"Kentucky House Has Maine Roots," Lexington
Herald-Leader, 17 April 1977, Section E,
p. 1-2, concerning Sherley home on Wolf Run
Creek, Fayette County, known as Birch Nest Farm.

15362   Shewmaker, William Orpheus, 1869-
The Pisgah book, 1784-1909: a memorial,
a lesson, an inspiration. [n.p.] 1909.
72 p.   plates.   25 cm.

15363   Shine, Frances Smith Dugan.
The rare book room of the Margaret I. King Library.
Lexington, University of Kentucky Library Associates,
1968.
8 p.   illus.   29 cm.

15364   Shine, Lee.
... A comparison of five mortals' trip to
Hades. Lexington, 1953.
16 p.   20 cm.
At head of title: Phi Beta Kappa, University
of Kentucky. Award for outstanding undergraduate
writing, number III.

15365   Short, Charles Wilkins.
Biographical memoir of doctor Frederick Ridgely;
late of Lexington, Kentucky. (From the
Transylvania journal of medicine, &c. No. III,
August, 1828) Lexington, Ky. Printed by

Joseph G. Norwood, 1828.
8 p.   21 cm.

15366   Shuck, Richard H   1851-1877.
Confessions of Richard H. Shuck, a member of the
Owen and Henry county marauders, of the state of
Kentucky. Written by Jesse Fears. Frankfort, Ky.,
Printed at the Kentucky yeoman office, Major,
Johnston & Barrett, 1877.
35 p.   22½ cm.

15367   Siebert, Wilbur Henry, 1866-
The Tory proprietors of Kentucky lands, by
Professor Wilbur H. Siebert... Columbus, O., The
F. J. Heer Printing Co., 1919.
26 p.   23 cm.
"Reprinted from Ohio Archaeological and Historical
Quarterly, vol. XXVIII, no. 1, January, 1919."

15368   Siebert, William Henry, 1866-
Kentucky's struggle with its loyalist
proprietors. [n.p., 1920?]
113-126 p.   22 cm.
Running caption: M.V.H.R., vol. VII, no. 2.

15369   Simms, William Gilmore, 1806-1970, ed.
War poetry of the south... New York, Richardson
& company, 1866.
482 p.   20 cm.
Includes poems of Mrs. Annie Chambers Ketchum
(1824-1904) of Georgetown, Ky.

15370   Simpson, Louisiana (Wood)
The cat who lives at Ashland. Illustrated by
Harriett McDonald Holladay. Lexington, Ky.,
Garden Club of Lexington, 1963.
18 p.   illus. (1 col.)   22 cm.

15371   Sims, Richard.
Evaluation of Jefferson County private sewage
disposal rates. Prepared by Richard Sims.
Frankfort, Ky., Legislative Research Commission,
1977.
vi, 59 p.   29 cm.   (Research report, no. 144)

15372   Sinclair, Ward.
Senator Huddleston - Man from the Blue Grass

State. [Washington, D.C., 1973]
S6410-S6412 p.   30 cm.
Reprinted from Congressional Record, 3 April
1973. Includes speech by Huddleston, "The
National Democratic Party and Kentucky's role
in it."

15373 Singer, James W
A history of the Baptist Church at Stamping
Ground, Kentucky, by J. W. Singer. Frankfort,
Ky., Roberts Printing Co. [1951?]
67 p.   illus.   23 cm.

15374 Sipes, Georgia.
The man who made Boone immortal. Frankfort,
Kentucky Historical Society, 1967.
2 p.   28 cm.
Reprinted from Kentucky heritage, v. 8, no. 1,
Fall 1967.

15375 Sisk, Morgan E
The fishes of west Kentucky, by Morgan E. Sisk
and Paul L. Smith. [Lexington, Ky.] 1969.
54-68 p.   23 cm.
Reprinted from Transactions of the Kentucky
Academy of Science, v. 30, nos. 3-4, 1969.

15376 Skaggs quarterly. [Leland, Ill.?, 197]
2 nos.   19½ cm.
V. 1, no. 1 and 2, probably the only ones
published.

15377 Skean, Marion Holcomb, comp.
Circle left! Folk-play of the Kentucky
mountains. Collected by Marrion Holcomb Skean.
Homeplace, Ary, Ky., Sponsored by the E. O.
Robinson Mountain Federation, 1939.
2 p.l., 3- 48 p.   incl. illus. (music)
diagrs.   23 cm.

15378 ... Sketch of the life and some of the principal
speeches of Henry Clay. Compiled from the
latest and best authorities. Cincinnati,
Published by U. P. James [1854]
111 p.   front. (port.)   22½ cm.

15379   A sketch of the life of General Thomas Metcalf.
        [Lexington, Ky.? 1828?]
        27 p.   23 cm.

15380   The Sky Land Company, Middlesboro, Ky.
        The story of the Pinnacle. Middlesboro
        [Three States Print. co., 1929?]
        16 p.   illus.   18 x 10 cm.

15381   Slocum, Charles Elihu.
        The Ohio country between the years 1783 and
        1815, including military operations that twice
        saved to the United States the country west of
        the Alleghany mountains after the Revolutionary
        war... New York, G. P. Putman's sons, 1910.
        321 p.   23 cm.

15382   Smallwood, Robert.
        Beattyville and Lee County [Kentucky]
        [Frankfort, 1929]
        broadside.   illus.   28½ cm.
        Reprinted from Kentucky progress magazine,
        v. 1, no. 12, p. 19, Aug. 1929.

15383   Smith, Earl Hobson.
        The favored of the gods... A drama in five
        acts introducing to the public one of the
        loveliest of Greek myths. Lexington, The
        Kentucky Playmakers [n.d.]
        61 p.   18½ cm.

15384   Smith, Earl Hobson.
        President Lincoln. A two hour play in three
        acts with three scenes each... Harrogate, Tenn.,
        The Lincoln book company, 1940.
        97 p.   front. (port.)   20 cm.

15385   Smith, Earl Hobson.
        Stephen Foster, or, Weep no more my lady...
        a biographical play... Knoxville, Tenn., The
        Foster Players [1940]
        136 p.   illus., music.   23 cm.
        "Third edition."

15386   Smith, Earl Hobson.
        ... Tainted souls, a play that is different...
        Lexington, Ky., Press of James M. Byrnes co.

[n.d.]
    64 p.   17 cm.
    Inscribed by author.
    At head of title: The Kentucky Playmakers
present to the public.

15387 Smith, Eli, 1787-1839.
    A funeral sermon on the death of Governor
Madison, delivered before the legislature of
Kentucky and the citizens of Frankfort,
December 8th, 1818. Frankfort, Ky., Gerald
& Kendall -- Printers, 1817.
    26 p.   20 cm.

15388 Smith, George Gilman, 1836-1913.
    Life and labors of Francis Asbury, bishop of the
Methodist Episcopal church in America...
Nashville, Tenn., Publishing house M. E. church,
South, Barbee & Smith, agents, 1896.
    xv, 311 p.   front. [port.]   19 cm.

15389 Smith, Hal.
    Berea's Bess Gilbert retires. [Berea, 1973]
    4p.   29 cm.
    cover illus.
    In pocket at end: Article by Alfred H. Perrin,
"130 Friends gather for tribute to Miss Bess
Gilbert," The Berea Citizen, 26 April 1973 and
"BC Names Marsh as Librarian," Lexington Herald,
22 June 1973.

15390 Smith, Henry Clay.
    Outline history of the wilderness of Kentucky
and the religious movements of the early
settlers of our country and the church history
of the North Middletown community. Paris, Ky.,
Frank Remington, printer [1923]
    91 p.   front. [port.]   illus.   18 cm.

15391 Smith, Hubbard Madison, 1820-1907.
    Historical sketches of old Vincennes,
founded in 1732; its institutions and churches,
embracing collateral incidents and biographical
sketches of many persons and events connected
therewith, by Hubbard Madison Smith, M.D. Vincennes,
Ind. [Indianapolis, Press of W. D. Burford] 1902.
    288 p.   incl. front., illus., ports., map.   20 cm.

15392 Smith, J   Allan.
       The College of Agriculture and Home Economics,
       University of Kentucky. Lexington, University
       of Kentucky Centennial Committee, 1965.
       62 p.   illus.   23 cm.

15393 Smith, J   Soule.
       Kentucky River scenery. [Louisville? 1890?]
       broadside.   illus. on verso.   29 x 23 cm.
       Originally published in the Louisville
       Times, 12 July 1890.

15394 Smith, J   Soule.
       Kentucky river scenery. [n.p., n.d.]
       [6 l.]   illus.   26, 19 cm.
       This text consists of a typed title-page,
       a typescript of the original text, and a dim
       silver print of the original pamphlet, probably
       unique, in the private library of Lawrence S.
       Thompson.
       The article was published originally in the
       Louisville Times of 12 July 1890 on the occasion
       of the editorial excursion to the Kentucky river.
       It was written by J. Soule Smith ("Falcon").

15395 Smith, J   Soule.
       The mint julep, the very dream of drinks.
       From the old receipt of Soule Smith, down in
       Lexington, Ky. [Lexington, Ky.] The Gravesend
       press, 1949.
       [8], 9 p.   18½ cm.

15396 Smith, James, 1737-1812.
       An account of the remarkable occurrences in
       the life and travels of Colonel James Smith...
       during his captivity with the Indians in the years
       1755, '56, '58 & '59... Written by himself.
       Philadelphia, J. Grigg, 1831.
       xi, [13]- 162 p.   15 cm.

15397 Smith, Mrs. Lilla May (Hall) 1860-
       Down our way, by Lilla Hall Smith... New
       York, Dodd, Mead and company, 1911.
       4 p.l., 3-341 p.   front.   19½ cm.
       Cover illustration by John Rae.

15398   Smith, Margarete C
            Cloverport. Looking back... by Margarete C.
        Smith. Cloverport, Ky. [197-?]
            15 p.   illus.   28 cm.

15399   Smith, Mattie S
            Miss Claire's pupils, by Mattie S. Smith...
        Fulton, Kentucky, The National Baptist
        Publishing House, 1905.
            311 p.   20 cm.

15400   Smith, Phillip S
            The past twenty-five years of Epsilon Chapter
        of Beta Theta Pi, 1948-1973 [by Phillip S.
        Smith and Robert T. Carter. Danville, Ky., 1973]
            5 p.   27½ cm.
            Appended at end of program for 125th anniversary
        banquet of Epsilon Chapter of Beta Theta Pi at
        Centre College on 14 April 1973, invitation to the
        celebration, ticket for functions, a sheet with
        words to four Beta Theta Pi songs, and "Oldest
        Fraternity in State Plans Anniversary Celebration
        at Centre" (Lexington Herald, 10 April 1973,
        p. 17), "Former Senator [John Sherman Cooper]
        Speaks: Betas Called Bulwark of Centre at Banquet"
        (Kentucky Advocate [Danville], 15 April 1973,
        p.1, 17), "At Beta Anniversary Fete" (Lexington
        Herald, 17 April 1973, p. 15)

15401   Smith, William Townsend.
            A complete index to the names of persons,
        places and subjects mentioned in Littell's
        Laws of Kentucky. A genealogical and
        historical guide... Lexington, The Bradford
        Club press, 1931.
            313 p.   22½ cm.

15402   Smith, Zachary Frederick, 1827-1911.
            ... The Battle of New Orleans, including
        previous engagements between the Americans and
        the British, the Indians, and the Spanish
        which led to final conflict on the 8th of
        January, 1815... Louisville, John P. Morton &
        company, 1904.
            209 p.   front. (port.), illus., maps.   32 cm.
            At head of title: Filson Club publications, no. 19.

15403 Smith, Zachary Frederick, 1827-1911.
        ... The Clay family. Part first. The mother
    of Henry Clay, by Hon. Zachary F. Smith... Part
    second: The genealogy of the Clays, by Mrs.
    Mary Rogers Clay... Louisville, John P. Morton
    & co., 1899.
       252 p.   illus.   32 cm.
       At head of title: Filson Club publications no.
    14.

15404 Smith, Zachary Frederick, 1827-1911.
        School history of Kentucky from the earliest
    discoveries and settlements to the year 1891...
    sixth ed. Louisville, The Courier-Journal
    job printing company, 1891.
       288 p.   illus., fold. map.   20 cm.

15405 Smyth, Samuel Gordon, 1859-
        Rafinesque, the errant naturalist. Read
    before the Montgomery County Historical Society,
    Norristown, Pa., April 26th, 1919. [Norristown?
    1919?]
       22 p.   23 cm.

15406 Sneed, W   H
        Capital [!] removal. Public aspects of the
    question. By a committee of citizens of
    Frankfort. History of location. By Judge W. H.
    Sneed. Legal aspects of the case. By Judge
    William Lindsay. Frankfort, Ky., Geo. A. Lewis
    book and job printer, 1891.
       51 p.   plates (1 fold.)   24 cm.

15407 Society of Colonial Wars in the Commonwealth of
    Kentucky.
        Yearbook... 1917. To which is added a calendar
    of warrants for land in Kentucky, granted for
    services in the French and Indian War. [n.p.,
    1917?]
       154 p.   facsims.   24 cm.

15408 Somerset, Ky. Presbyterian Church.
        The Somerset cook book. Somerset, Ky., 1907.
       116 p.   23 cm.

15409 Somerset, Lake Cumberland, Daniel Boone National
       Forest, Burnside [Kentucky] [n.p., n.d.]
          32 p.   illus., map.   22½ cm.

15410 Sons of the American Revolution, Kentucky Society.
          A three-fold anniversary celebration. I. 150th
       anniversary of the first settlement of Kentucky,
       June 16, 1774. II. 149th anniversary of Battle of
       Lexington, April 19, 1775. III. 30th anniversary
       of founding of the Kentucky Society, Sons of the
       Revolution, June 24, 1894... [Lexington, Ky., 1924]
          [4] l.   facsim.   16 x 21 cm.
          On last leaf is facsimile of a military warrant
       granted by Lord Dunmore, to Sergeant James
       Buford, on 19 April 1774, upon which was located,
       on 5 August 1775, the first survey within the
       corporate limits of the city of Lexington.

15411 Sons of the Revolution in the State of Kentucky.
          Constitution and by-laws. [Lexington, Ky., n.d.]
          14 p.   17 cm.

15412 Sophonisba Preston Breckinridge, 1866-1948.
       [Chicago, 1948]
          417-450 p.   port.   24 cm.
          "Reprinted from the Social service review, vol.
       24, no. 4, December 1948."

15413 The South in the building of the nation; a
       history of the southern states designed to record
       South's part in the making of the American nation;
       to portray the character and genius, to chronicle
       the achievements and progress and to illustrate the
       life and traditions of the southern people...
       Richmond, Va., The Southern historical publication
       society [c1909-12]
          12 v.   col. fronts., plates (part col.) ports.
       (part col.) map, facsims.   24 cm.
          Vol. 1-4, 7-12, 1909; v. 5-6, 1910.
          Contains bibliographies.
          Contents. - v. 1-3. History of the states, ed.
       by J.A.C. Chandler. - v. 4. Political history,
       ed. by F. L. Riley. - v. 5. Economic history,
       1607-1865, ed. by J. C. Ballagh. - v. 6. Economic
       history, 1865-1909, ed. by J. C. Ballagh. - v. 7.
       History of the intellectual life, ed. by J. B.
       Henneman. - v. 8. History of southern fiction,

ed. by E. Mims. - v. 9. History of southern
oratory, ed. by T. E. Watson. - v. 10. History
of the social life, ed. by S. C. Mitchell. -
v. 11-12 Southern biography, ed. by W. L.
Fleming.

15414 Southard, Mary Young, ed.
        Who's who in Kentucky; a biographical assembly
    of notable Kentuckians, ed. by Mary Young Southard,
    Ernest C. Miller, co-editor. Louisville, Standard
    printing co., 1936.
        582 p.   illus.   25½ cm.

15415 Southeastern Kentucky Regional Library Cooperative.
        Appalachian/Kentuckiana bibliography. [Jackson,
    Ky? 1972?]
        29, 17, 11, 7, 5, 4 p.   28 cm.

15416 Southeastern Kentucky Regional Library Cooperative.
        Appalachia/Kentuckiana. Second edition.
    [Jackson, Ky.] 1974.
        80 p.   27 cm.

15417 Southern Baptist Convention.
        Proceedings of the twenty-fifth session of the
    Southern Baptist Convention held with the First
    Baptist Church, Lexington, Ky., May 6-10, 1880.
    Louisville, Ky., A.C. Caperton & co., 1880.
        79 p.   22 cm.

15418 Southern Baptist Theological Seminary. The first
    Thirty years. 1859-1889. [Edited by] John R.
    Sampey... Baltimore, Wharton, Barron & co., 1890.
        217 p.   18½ cm.

15419 Southern Railway System.
        [Portfolio of six color photographs of scenes
    along the Southern tracks in Kentucky and
    Tennessee mountains. Washington, D. C., 1975]
        6 sheets.   29 x 45 cm.

15420 A souvenir of Wilmore. The home town, the progressive
    town, the town of opportunity. [n.p.] 1914.
        [12] p.   illus.   23 cm.
        Cover-title.

15421   Spanning the centuries. Centennial supplement of
         the Kentucky Kernel. February 5, 1965. Lexington,
         Ky., 1965.
            34 p.   illus.   29 cm.

15422   [Spears, James E   ]
            The Wooldridge monuments: "Strange procession
         which never moves." Bowling Green, Ky., 1976.
            10 p.   illus. 22 cm.
            Reprinted from Kentucky folklore record, v. 22,
         no. 1, Jan.-Mar. 1976.

15423   Spears, Woodridge.
            Feudalist. New York, The Fine editions press,
         1946.
            40 p.   19½ cm.
            At end is article on Mr. and Mrs. Spears, Ann
         Bevins, "Remote Greenup Community Basis for
         'Stuart Country'". Lexington Herald-Leader,
         4 February 1973.

15424   Special souvenir programme of the presentation of a
         portrait bust of Governor Isaac Shelby as Kentucky's
         gift to Memorial Continental Hall at the Twentieth
         Continental Congress of the National Society of the
         Daughters of the American Revolution, April 17 to
         22, 1911, Washington, D.C. [n.p. 1911?]
            [8] p.   illus.   23 cm.
            Includes biographical sketch of Isaac Shelby and
         notes on Shelby at Point Pleasant (10 October 1774),
         King's Mountain (7 October 1813), and Governor
         James T. Morehead's tribute to Shelby at
         Boonesborough, Ky., 25 May 1840.
            With this is included Presentation and dedication
         by Kentucky Society, Sons of the Revolution, of
         monument and tablet commemorating sesquicentennial
         anniversary of inauguration of Isaac Shelby as
         first governor and first session of the General
         Assembly of Kentucky in Lexington June 4, 1792.
         Ceremonies on Fayette County Court House Square,
         Lexington, Kentucky, June 4, 1942. 4 p.
         24 cm.

15425   The speeches of Henry Clay, delivered in the
         Congress of the United States; to which is
         prefixed a biographical memoir, with an appendix,
         containing his speeches at Lexington and

Lewisburg, and before the Colonization Society at
Washington; together with his address to his
constituents on the subject of the late presidential
election. Philadelphia, 8 vo. pp. 381. [Boston,
1827]
    425-451 p.   20½ cm.
Reprinted from North American Review, v. 25 (1827)
A review.

15426   Speed, Thomas, 1841-1906.
    ... The Political Club, Danville, Kentucky,
1786-1790. Being an account of an early Kentucky
society from the original papers recently found...
Louisville, John P. Morton and company, 1894.
    166 p.   32 cm.
At head of title: Filson Club publication no. 9.

15427   Speed, Thomas, 1841-1906.
    Who fought the battle. Strength of the Union
and Confederate forces compared. An address by
Capt. Thos. Speed before the Army corps society
of Louisville, Ky., January 26, 1904. [Louisville,
Ky., Press of F. G. Nunemacher, 1904]
    cover-title, 31 p.   25½ cm.

15428   Speed, Thomas, 1841-1906.
    The Wilderness Road, a description of the routes
of travel by which the pioneers and early
settlers first came to Kentucky... Louisville,
Ky., John P. Morton & co., 1886.
    75 p.   fold. map.   26 cm.
In subsequent lists of Filson Club publication
recorded as no. 3.

15429   Spelman, John A
    At home in the hills. Glimpses of Harlan,
Kentucky, through the linoleum block and
the woodcut. Pine Mountain, Ky., Pine Mountain
print shop [1939]
    87 p.   illus.   28 cm.
Inscribed by author.

15430   Spencer, John H
    A history of Kentucky Baptists. From 1769 to
1885. Including more than 800 biographical
sketches... the manuscript revised and corrected

by Mrs. Burrilla B. Spencer... Cincinnati,
J. R. Baumes 1885.
2 v.   illus., fold. map.   24 cm.

15431   Spencer, John H
The life of Thomas Jefferson Fisher, the
celebrated pulpit orator and evangelist; with
a masonic address and a fragment of a sermon.
Louisville, J. P. Morton & co., 1866.
208 p.   front. [port.]   20 cm.

15432   Stacy, Helen Price.
Historians voice objections to proposed
Paint Lick Dam. Lexington, 1972.
broadside.   illus.   30 x 38 cm.
Reprinted brom Sunday Herald-Leader, Lexington,
16 July 1972, p. 61.

15433   Stacy, Helen Price.
Old Cooper house at West Liberty believed to
have been built in 1870. Lexington, Ky. 1973.
1 ℓ.   illus.
Reprinted from Lexington Herald, 11 April 1973,
p. 8.

15434   Stallons, Malcolm.
Unchanging Amish stick to old ways. Lexington,
Ky., 1975.
broadside.   illus.   59 x 36 cm.
Reprinted from the Sunday Herald-Leader,
12 October 1975, p. A-5.

15435   Staples, Charles Richard, 1875-1954.
The history of pioneer Lexington (Ky.)
1779-1806... Lexington, Ky., Transylvania press,
1939.
[10], 361 p.   map.   23½ cm.

15436   Starling, Edmund L
History of Henderson county, Kentucky... Henderson,
Ky., 1887.
844 p.   illus.   23 cm.

15437   Starling, Edmund L
History of Henderson County, Kentucky, by Edmund
L. Starling. Comprising history of county and city,
precincts, education, churches, secret societies,

leading enterprises, sketches and recollections, and
biographies of the living and dead. Illustrated.
Henderson, Ky. 1887. Reprinted, Evansville, Ind.,
Unigraphic, Inc., 1972.
[844] p.   illus.

15438 Stevens, Harry R
         Six twenty; Margaretta Hunt and the Baker-
       Hunt foundation. Covington, Ky., 1942.
         131 p.   illus.   21½ cm.

15439 Stevenson, Dwight E
         The Bacon College story: 1836-1865...
       Lexington, Ky., The College of the Bible,
       1962.
         56 p.   illus., chart.   24 cm.

15440 Stevenson, Dwight E
         Lexington Theological Seminary, 1865-1965.
       The College of the Bible century. St. Louis, The
       Bethany press [1964]
         495 p.   23 cm.
         Includes special section of Lexington Herald-
       Leader for 7 March 1965 dedicated to the centennial
       (12 p.), by various authors, and an article by
       Jim Morrissey, "Solid at 100 - The College of the
       Bible," Louisville Courier-Journal Magazine,
       14 February 1965, p. 24-28. Both are extensively
       illustrated.

15441 Stierlin, L
         Der Staat Kentucky und die Stadt Louisville,
       mit besonderer Berücksichtigung des deutschen
       Elements. Louisville [Ky.] Gedruckt in der
       Offizin des Louisville Anzeigers, 1873.
         2 p.l., [3]-234, 51, xxiiii p. pl.   22 cm.

15442 Stiles, Joseph Clay, 1795-1875.
         A letter of Alexander Campbell, in reply
       to an article in the Millennial harbinger.
       Lexington, Ky., Lexington intelligencer print,
       1838.
         57 p.   20½ cm.

15443 Stillwell, Lucille.
         Born to be a statesman: John Cabell
       Breckinridge. Caldwell, Idaho, The Caxton

printers, 1936.
196 p.   illus., map inside front cover.
20 cm.

15444   Stitzel-Weller co., Louisville, Ky.
Spoon bread and other deep south delights.
Louisville, Ky. [1972]
20 p.   illus.   23 cm.

15445   Stokes, Bess D
Methodism in Wayne County, Kentucky, 1802-1974.
[By] Bess D. Stokes and Elizabeth F. Duncan.
Somerset, Ky., The Commonwealth Journal Printing
Co. [1974?]
106, A-R p.   illus., map.   23 cm.

15446   Stoltz, Charles, 1864-1931.
The tragic career of Mary Todd Lincoln, by Dr.
Charles Stoltz.   South Bend, Ind., Priv. print.,
The Round Table, 1931.
5 p.l., [15]-62p., 1 ℓ.   port.   23 cm.

15447   Stone, Barton Warren, 1772-1844.
History of the Christian church in the West.
With illus. by Riley B. Montgomery and William
Clayton Bower, and a foreword by Roscoe M. Pierson.
Lexington, Ky., The College of the Bible, 1956.
53p.   illus.   23 cm.
Reprinted from several issues of the Christian
Messenger.

15448   Stone, Barton Warren, 1772-1844.
Letters to James Blythe, D. D.   Designed as a
reply to the arguments of Thomas Cleland, D. D.
against my address, 2d edition, on the doctrines
on trinity, the Son of God, atonement, &c...
Lexington, Ly., Printed by William Tanner,
Monitor office, 1824.
163, [1] p.   17½ cm.

15449   Stone, William Leete, 1792-1844.
Border wars of the American revolution.   By
William L. Stone...   New-York, Harper & brothers,
1845.
2 v.   15½ cm.   (On cover: The Family library.
no. 167-168)

15450 The story of 75 years. St. Frances of Rome [Church,
Louisville, Ky. Louisville, 1962?]
64 p.   illus.   24 cm.

15451 Straten-Ponthoz, [Gabriel] A[uguste] van der, comte.
Onderzoek naar den toestand der land-verhuizers
in de Vereeingde Staten van Noord-America...
Utrecht, W. H. Van Heijningen, 1847.
2 p.l., 124 p.   fold. map.   23½ cm.

15452 Strickland, William Peter, 1809-1884.
The pioneers of the West; or, Life in the woods.
By W. P. Strickland. New-York, Carlton & Phillips
[c1856]
403 p.   incl. front., 8 pl.   18 cm.

15453 Strong, T
Episcopal tract--no. 1 Candid examination of
the Episcopal church, in two letters to a friend...
Lexington, Ky., Printed by William G. Hunt, 1821.
23 p.   17 cm.

15454 Strosberg, Don.
Publications and theses on Appalachian resource-use
topics by University of Kentucky personnel. A
preliminary working bibliography. Prepared for
participants in the University's Program for
improving the quality of life in Appalachia. By
Don Strosberg, Jackie Bondurant, Sue Johnson,
Connee Davis. Development paper no. 2, Center
for Developmental Change, University of Kentucky.
April 29, 1972. Lexington, 1972.
29 p.   30 cm.

15455 Strosberg, Don.
Regulation of the building industry in Kentucky.
Prepared by Don Strosberg. Frankfort, Ky.,
Legislative Research Commission, 1977.
v, 87 p.   27½ cm.   (Research report,
no. 147)

15456 Stuart, Jane.
A man of her own faith. Lexington, Ky.,
Bluegrass Publishing Co., 1974.
20-21, 26-28 p.   29½ cm.
Reprinted by permission from The Bluegrass woman
(Lexington, Ky.) v. 1, no. 1, Spring 1974.

Correspondence between author and Lawrence S. Thompson at end.

15457 Stuart, Jesse Hilton, 1905-
          Animal personalities. Huntington, W. Va.,
       Tri-State Audubon Society and Department of
       Biological Sciences, Marshall University, 1971.
          3-4 p.   illus.   29 cm.
          Reprinted from Call Notes, v. XXVIII, March
       and May, 1971.

15458 Stuart, Jesse Hilton, 1905-
          Autobiographical reminiscence. [Kansas City,
       Mo., 1960]
          58-64 p.   21½ cm.
          Reprinted from University of Kansas City
       review, v. 27, 1960.

15459 Stuart, Jesse Hilton, 1905-
          Characters versus farmers. [Richmond, Va., 1972]
          26-29 p.   port.   24 cm.
          Letter from author precedes article.
          Reprinted from the Phi journal, v. 52, no. 1,
       Winter, 1972.

15460 Stuart, Jesse Hilton, 1905-
          The Cistern. Muncie, Indiana, Ball State
       University, 1972.
          13-30p.   26 cm.
          Reprinted from Forum, v. 13, no. 3, 1972.

15461 Stuart, Jesse Hilton, 1905-
          E.P. [n.p., 1972?]
          [2] p.   illus.   29 cm.
          Reprinted from Today's Education - NEA   Journal.

15462 Stuart, Jesse Hilton, 1905-
          Famous Kentucky author rediscovers his homeland.
       Lexington, Ky., 1974.
          broadside.   port., map.   45 x 30 cm.
          Reprinted from Lexington Herald and Leader,
       7 December 1974.

15463 Stuart, Jesse Hilton, 1905-
          [Four poems] [Huntsville, Ala., Huntsville
       literary association, 1967]
          62-65 p.   19½ cm.
          Reprinted from Poem, No. 1, November 1967.

Contents: By the bend in the road. - Too
soon too early. - Two cypresses. - At fifty-eight.

15464 Stuart, Jesse Hilton, 1906-
Going to the Fourth. [Frankfort, Ky., 1968]
211-221 p.   22 cm.
Reprinted from the Register of the Kentucky
Historical Society, v. 66, no. 3, July 1968.

15465 Stuart, Jesse Hilton, 1905-
The Good Samaritan. Greenup, Ky., 1973.
1 p.   port.   60 x 45 cm.
From the Greenup News, vol. 116, no. 6,
8 February 1973.
Inscribed.

15466 Stuart, Jesse Hilton, 1905-
He saw the sun this time. Tucson, Ariz., 1972.
196-208 p.   24 cm.
Reprinted from Arizona quarterly, v. 28, no. 3,
1972.
Includes poem, "To Jesse Stuart, " by Read
Bain.

15467 Stuart, Jesse Hilton, 1905-
How not to write a novel. [Fern Creek,
Kentucky, Kentucky State Poetry Society, 1972]
12-17 p.   23 cm.
Reprinted from Pegasus, v. 2, no. 2, Summer 1972.

15468 Stuart, Jesse Hilton, 1907-
If I were seventeen again. [n.p.] 1954.
38, 121-125 p.   illus.   29 cm.
Reprinted from Country gentleman, November
1954.

15469 Stuart, Jesse Hilton, 1905-
Islands in the sun; a Kentucky author discovers
a natural wonder close to home. Louisville,
1975.
72-75 p.   illus.   35 cm.
Reprinted from The Courier-Journal and
Times Magazine, 4 May 1975.

15470 Stuart, Jesse Hilton, 1907-
Kentucky is my land. [n.p., 1947?]

5 p.   28 cm.
Reprinted from Country gentleman, 1947.

15471   Stuart, Jesse Hilton, 1905-
        A land and its people. [Frankfort, Ky., 1970]
        221-230 p.   23 cm.

15472   Stuart, Jesse Hilton, 1905-
        Letter to August Derleth. Madison, Wis.,
        Wisconsin Academy of Science, Arts and Letters,
        1973.
        5-7 p.   port.   29 cm.
        Reprinted from Wisconsin Academy review, v. 19,
        no. 2, March 1973.

15473   Stuart, Jesse Hilton, 1905-
        Lost sandstones and lonely skies. [n.p., 1956]
        386-388 p.   26½ cm.
        Reprinted from Southwest review, XLI (1956)
        386-388.

15474   Stuart, Jesse Hilton, 1905-
        Muleback. From "The thread that runs so true."
        [Cincinnati, Glenmary home missioners, 1971]
        14-15 p.   illus.   28½ cm.
        Reprinted from Glenmary's challenge, v. xxxiv,
        no. 2, summer 1971.

15475   Stuart, Jesse Hilton, 1905-
        My Appalachia. [Charleston, W. Va., Morris
        Harvey College, 1972]
        8 p.   24 cm.
        Reprinted from From the hills, 1972.

15476   Stuart, Jesse Hilton, 1907-
        My father's fifty acres. Illustrations by
        W. Kirtman Plummer. [n.p., 1955]
        37, 84-85 p.   illus.   27½ cm.
        Reprinted from Better farming, January 1955.

15477   Stuart, Jesse Hilton, 1905-
        My seven year plans. [Richmond, Va., 1970]
        44-45 p.   24 cm.
        Reprinted from Phi Kappa Journal, v. 50, no. 4,
        Fall, 1970.
        Letter from author precedes article.

15478   Stuart Jesse Hilton, 1905-
            Naomi. [Nashville, Tenn., 1972]
            28-31 p.   port.   29 cm.
            Reprinted from the Peabody reflector, v. 45,
        no. 2, Spring, 1972.
            Letter from author and correspondence with
        editor follows article.

15479   Stuart, Jesse Hilton, 1905-
            No street address. [Madison, Wis., 1972]
            15-16 p.   22 cm.
            Reprinted from Wind, v. 2, no. 5, Summer 1972.

15480   Stuart, Jesse Hilton, 1905-
            Our summer symphony. Huntington, W. Va.
        Tri-State Audubon Society and the Department of
        Biological Sciences, Marshall University, 1971.
            7-8 p.   29 cm.
            Reprinted from Call notes, v. XXVIII, Sept. 1971.

15481   Stuart, Jesse Hilton, 1905-
            Revolution in Greenup County. [New York, 1957]
            20-25 p.   illus.   29 cm.
            Reprinted from American Petroleum Institute
        Quarterly, Autumn 1957.

15482   Stuart, Jesse Hilton, 1905-
            Stabilizing a generation. [Edgewater, Md., 1973]
            4-5 p.   illus.   25½ cm.
            Reprinted from Scimitar and song, vol. XXXV,
        Dec. 1972 - Jan./Feb. 1973, no. 1.
            Includes poems by Jane Stuart on p. 3.

15483   Stuart, Jesse Hilton, 1905-
            "There shall not be left here one stone upon
        another." Louisville, Ky., 1977.
            221-233 p.   22 cm.

15484   Stuart, Jesse Hilton, 1905-
            Uncle Sam married an angel. Muncie, Indiana,
        Ball State University, 1972.
            11 p.   port.   26 cm.
            Reprinted from Forum, v. 13, no. 3, 1972.

15485   Stuart, Jesse Hilton, 1905-
            Washington is a swell place! [n.p., 1945]
            243-246 p.   26½ cm.
            Reprinted from Southwest review, XXX (1945), 243-246.

15486 Stuart, Jesse Hilton, 1905-
       Why I think Album is my best. [Lincoln, Neb.,
       1956]
       32-37 p.   22 cm.
       Reprinted from Prairie Schooner, v. 30, 1956.

15487 Stuart, T   G
       Notes on Henry Clay, by Colonel T. G. Stuart.
       Transcribed by George F. Doyle, M. D., F.A.C.S.
       [Winchester, Ky., 194-]
       2 p.   22 cm.

15488 Stuart, T   G
       The origin and derivation of the names of towns
       and places in Clark County by Colonel T. G.
       Stuart. Transcribed by George F. Doyle
       [Winchester, Ky., n.d.]
       1 p.l., 9 typewritten l.   23 cm.

15489 Stuart, T   G
       Preemption rights to Kentucky not possessed
       by the Indians, by Colonel T. G. Stuart.
       Transcribed by George F. Doyle. [Winchester, Ky.,
       n.d.]
       3 typewritten l.   23 cm.

15490 Subterranean Wonders. Mammoth Cave - Colossal
       Cavern, Kentucky. For distribution through the
       newspapers represented by Frederic J. Haskin.
       Louisville, Louisville and Nashville Railroad
       [191-?]
       cover-title, 46 p.   illus.   20 cm.

15491 Sulzer, Elmer Griffith.
       Twenty-five Kentucky folk ballads. Volume
       I. Collected arranged, and edited by Elmer
       Griffith Sulzer... Lexington, Transylvania
       Printing Company [1938]
       28 p.   music.   27 cm.
       No more published.

15492 Sutton, Carol.
       A visit in New York with Mrs. Irvin Cobb.
       Louisville, Ky., 1964.
       broadside.   illus.   57 x 38 cm.
       Reprinted from the Courier-Journal, 26 April
       1964, Section 3, p.1.

With this is a reprint of the article in the
Dictionary of American biography, Suppl. 3, 1941-
1945 (1975); obituaries from Newsweek, 20 Mar. 1944,
p. 98-99, and Time, 20 Mar. 1944; and of the
section of Cobb entries in the Library of Congress
catalog.

15493 Sutton, William Loftus, 1797-1862.
       A history of the disease usually called typhoid
       fever, as it has appeared in Georgetown and its
       vicinity, with some reflections as to its causes
       and nature. Louisville, Maxwell, 1850.
           iv, 127 p.   22 cm.

15494 Sweeney, Mary E
       War cook book, by Mary E. Sweeney, head of Home
       Economics Department, University of Kentucky...
       [and] Linda B. Purnell, assistant in foods and
       nutrition, University of Kentucky. [Louisville,
       Mayes printing company, 1918]
           108 p.   20 cm.

                            T

15495 Talley, Brooks H
       Falmouth reservoir. Frankfort, Ky., Legislative
       Research Commission, 1972.
           50 p.   maps (four fold. in pocket at end),
       tables.   29 cm.

15496 Taney, Mary Florence.
        Kentucky pioneer women, Columbian poems and
       prose sketches. Cincinnati, Press of R. Clarke
       and company, 1893.
           3 p.l., 5-99 p.   20½ cm.

15497 Tanner, Henry, comp.
       The Louisville directory and business advertiser
       for 1859-60... Louisville, Maxwell & co., 1859.
           xvi, [17]-330 p.   23½ cm.

15498 Tapp, Hambleton.
       The Confederate invasion of Kentucky, 1862, and

the Battle of Perryville, October 8, 1862.
47 p. map. 29 cm.
Inscribed by author.

15499 Tapp, Hambleton.
The road back. The Confederate armies again
move into Kentucky. [n.p., 1960]
[4] p. illus. 28 cm.
Also includes essay by Tapp on the Battle of
Perryville, 8 October 1862.

15500 Tarascon, Berthoud and co., firm, merchants,
Philadelphia.
An address on trade with the western country,
1806. Together with a twentieth century afterword
[by Frances L. S. Dugan and Jacqueline P. Bull.
n.p., 1957]
cover-title, facsim (13 p.), [3] p. 21 cm.
(University of Kentucky Library Associates.
Keepsake. no. 4)
At head of title: Lewis Tarascon.
Original title page reads: An address to the
citizens of Philadelphia, on the great advantages
which arise from the trade of the western country...
By Messrs. Tarascon jun., James Berthoud and
co. Philadelphia: Printed for the addressers, 1806.

15501 Tarascon, Louis Anastasius, 1759-
L.A. Tarascon, to his friends &c. ...
Louisville, 1836.
14 p. 14½ cm.

15502 Taylor and his campaigns. A biography of Major-
General Zachary Taylor, with a full account of
his military services. With 27 portraits and
engravings. Philadelphia, E. H. Butler & co.,
1848.
3 p.l., [9]-128 p. front. port. illus.
17½ cm.

15503 Taylor, John, 1752-
A history of ten Baptist churches, of which
the author has been alternately a member: in
which will be seen something of journal of the
author's life, for more than fifty years. Also
a comment on some parts of Scripture; in which
the author takes the liberty to differ from

other expositors. Frankfort, [Ky.] Printed by
J. H. Holeman, 1823.
300 p.   18 cm.

15504   Taylor, M   Lee
Trends in the size and distribution of the
southern population. By M. Lee Taylor and
Robert Roberts. Lexington, Kentucky Agricultural
Experiment Station, University of Kentucky, 1963.
32 p.   maps, tables.   24 cm.   (Kentucky
Agricultural Experiment Station, Bulletin, 684)

15505   Taylor, Reuben Thornton.
A pageant to celebrate the founding of
LaGrange, Oldham County, Kentucky, 1827-1927...
[LaGrange, Ky., The Oldham Era, 1927]
[28] p.   23 cm.

15506   Temple, Wayne Calhoun, 1924-   ed.
Lincoln's marriage ceremony. Harrogate,
Tenn., Lincoln Memorial University Press, 1960.
7 p.   23 cm.
Cover-title: "Limited edition published for
the members of the National Lincoln-Civil War
Council."
Bibliography: p. 7.

15507   Temple, Wayne Calhoun, 1924-
Mary Todd Lincoln as a "sailor". [Harrogate,
Tenn., 1959]
101-110 p.   illus.   27 cm.
Reprinted from the Fall 1959 Lincoln Herald.

15508   Temple, Wayne Calhoun, 1924-
Mrs. Mary Edwards Brown tells story of
Lincoln's wedding. Edited by Wayne C. Temple...
Harrogate, Tenn., Lincoln Memorial University
press, 1960.
8 p.   23½ cm.
"Limited edition published for the members of
the National Lincoln-Civil War Council."

15509   Terry, Jimmy.
Fairs - Kentucky style! Frankfort, Kentucky
Historical Society, 1967.
2 p.   28 cm.

Reprinted from Kentucky heritage, v. 8, no. 1, Fall 1967.

15510   Thatcher, Benjamin Bussey, 1809-1840.
Indian traits, being sketches of the manners, customs, and character of the North American natives... New York, Harper & brothers, 1854.
2 v.   front. illus., port.   15 cm.

15511   Thatcher, Benjamin Bussey, 1809-1840.
Tales of the Indians; being prominent passages of the history of the North American natives. Taken from authentic sources... Boston, Waitt & Dow, 1831.
253 p.   front.   17 cm.

15512   Thiessen, Reinhardt.
Oil shales of Kentucky, a series of four economic and morphological discussions of the Devonian shales of this Commonwealth, by Reinhardt Thiessen, David White, and Charles Stevens Crouse, presented with three separate geological papers by Author McQuiston Miller, Walter H. Bucher, and Charles Stevens Crouse... Frankfort, Kentucky, Kentucky Geological Survey, 1925.
[8], 242 p.   illus., fold. maps, tables.
24½ cm.   (Kentucky Geological Survey, ser. VI, v. 21)

15513   Thomas, Daniel Lindsey.
Kentucky superstitions, by Daniel Lindsey Thomas... and Lucy Blayney Thomas... Princeton, N. J., Princeton University press, 1920.
334 p.   23½ cm.

15514   Thomas, David, 1732-ca. 1815.
The observer trying the great reformation in this state, and proving it to have been originally a work of divine power. With a survey of several objections to the contrary, as being chiefly comprised in Mr. Rankin's review of the noted revival, lately published. Sent with an address to a friend in the country... Lexington, Printed by John Bradford [1802]
v, [7]-42 p.   19 cm.

313

15515   Thomas, Mrs. Jeannette (Bell) 1881-
         Devil's ditties, being stories of the Kentucky
         mountain people told by Jean Thomas, with the songs
         they sing; Cryil Mullen drew the illustrations.
         Chicago, W. Wilbur Ratfield, 1961.
             vii, [1], 180 p.   illus.   26½ cm.
         "The ballads [words and music]": p. 69-178.
         "Foreword" by Lucy Furman: p. iv.

15516   [Thompson, Algernon Smith Dickson] 1922-1962.
         The enchanted village, a story for Sarah Beth
         and Mary Lawrence. Christmas, 1957. [Lexington,
         Kentucky, 1957]
             14 ℓ.   illus.   18½ cm.
         Manuscript.
         A "roman à clef" in the form of a children's
         book, with references to persons and places in
         Lexington and Bourbon County, Kentucky.

15517   Thompson, Algernon Smith Dickson, 1922-1962.
         The Western review and miscellaneous magazine.
         New York, 1946.
             119 p.   23 cm.
         Reproduced electrostatically from only available
         copy in Columbia University, by permission of
         the executor of Mrs. Thompson's estate.

15518   Thompson, Charles Lemuel, 1839-1924.
         Times of refreshing. A history of American
         revivals from 1740 to 1877, with their philosophy
         and methods. Chicago, L. T. Palmer & co.;
         Philadelphia, W. R. Thomas; [etc., etc.] 1877.
             xvi, 13-483 p.   19½ cm.

15519   Thompson, Ed Porter.
         History of the First Kentucky Brigade...
         Cincinnati, Caxton publishing house, 1868.
             931 p.   illus.   25 cm.

15520   Thompson, Ed Porter.
         History of the Orphan Brigade... Louisville,
         Lewis N. Thompson, 1898.
             1104 p.   illus.   25 cm.

15521   Thompson, Frank B
         The spirit of old Kentucky. [Louisville and
         Owensboro, Ky.] Glenmore distilleries [n.d.]

314

cover-title, [28] p.   illus., diags.
14 cm.

15522 Thompson, J   J   of Brookville, Miss.
A history of the feud between the Hill and
Evans parties of Garrard County, Ky. The most
exciting tragedy ever enacted on the bloody
grounds of Kentucky. By Lieut. J. J. Thompson.
Cincinnati, U. P. James [1854?]
xiii, [15]-112 p.   24 cm.
Cover title: Kentucky tragedy! A history of the
bloody renconters, street fights, battles, &c.

15523 Thompson, Lawrence Sidney, 1916-
The Anvil Press of Lexington, Kentucky.
[Nashville, Tenn., 1960]
10-12 p.   30 cm.
Reprinted from Southern observer, 1960.

15524 Thompson, Lawrence Sidney, 1916-
Books at the University of Kentucky.
[Louisville, Ky., 1950]
58-65 p.   table.   25 cm.
Reprinted from Filson Club History Quarterly,
v. 24, 1950.

15525 Thompson, Lawrence Sidney, 1916-
Essays on the folklore of Kentucky and the
Ohio Valley... Lexington, Kentucky, Erasmus
Press, 1971.
various pagination.   24 x 29 cm.
A collection of fifteen reprints from various
journals.
Contents. 1. Folklore in the Kentucky novel.
2. The negro in Kentucky fiction. 3. Bluegrass
and bourbon: the colonel of Kentucky fiction.
4. More buzzard lore. 5. A vanishing science
[folk medicine] 6. Hogs in Ohio Valley
superstition. 7. Sparrows in Bluegrass
superstition. 8. Rites of sepulcher in the
Bluegrass. 9. Marriage and courtship customs
in the Ohio Valley. 10. The broom in the Ohio
Valley. 11. Some notes on the folklore of
tobacco and smoking. 12. Kentucky snake
superstitions. 13. Hoppy-toads in the Ohio
Valley. 14. The water of life in the Ohio Valley
[Bourbon whiskey] 15. The owl in the Ohio Valley.

15526   Thompson, Lawrence Sidney, 1916-
         The Filson Club. [New York, 1972]
         457-459 p.   27 cm.
         Reprinted from Encyclopedia of library and
         information science, v. 8.

15527   Thompson, Lawrence Sidney, 1916-
         Foreign travellers in the south 1900-1950.
         Lexington, Kentucky, 1954.
         187 p.   25½ cm.
         Reprints of articles from various southern
         historical periodicals.
         Partially in manuscript.

15528   Thompson, Lawrence Sidney, 1916-
         German travellers in the South from the
         colonial period through 1865. [Chapel Hill,
         N. C., 1972]
         62-74 p.   24 cm.
         Reprinted from the South Atlantic Bulletin,
         v. 37, no. 2, May 1972.
         Includes Kentucky.

15529   Thompson, Lawrence Sidney, 1916-
         Hogs in Ohio Valley superstition, by Lawrence
         S. Thompson. [Bowling Green, Ky., 1965]
         59-61 p.   21½ cm.
         Reprinted from the Kentucky Folklore Record,
         vol. X, no. 4, Oct.-Dec. 1964.

15530   Thompson, Lawrence Sidney, 1916-
         The Kentucky novel, by Lawrence S. Thompson
         and Algernon D. Thompson. [Lexington] University
         of Kentucky Press [1953]
         172 p.   21 cm.

15531   Thompson, Lawrence Sidney, 1916-
         Kentucky tradition... Hamden, Conn., The
         Shoe string press [1956]
         225 p.   25 cm.
         Map on end papers.

15532   Thompson, Lawrence Sidney, 1916-   ed.
         The lewd versus the prude. Lexington's great
         pornography controversy, 1977-1978. Documents
         on provincial attitudes on sexuality. Compiled
         by Lawrence S. Thompson from The Lexington Herald,

316

The Kentucky Kernel, and posted broadsides,
arranged in 116 items. Lexington, 1978.
116 1.   illus.   varying size.

15533 [Thompson, Lawrence Sidney] 1916-
Literary map of Kentucky. Art work by Charles
T. Wade, Jr. [Lexington, Ky.] Kentucky library
association, 1959.
map.   32 x 67 cm.   illus.

15534 Thompson, Lawrence Sidney, 1916-
Mr. Beadle and the folklorists, by Lawrence S.
Thompson. Chillicothe, Ohio, Ohio Valley Folk
Research Project, Ross County Historical Society,
1961.
2 p.l., 6 numb. l.   28 cm.   (Ohio Valley
folk publications, n.s., no. 72)

15535 Thompson, Lawrence Sideny, 1916-
The moon in Kentucky and elsewhere.
[Lexington, Ky., 1973]
[4] p.

15536 Thompson, Lawrence Sidney, 1916-   ed.
Newspaper clippings and broadsides relating
to the Red River Dam controversy, 1969-1976.
Compiled by Lawrence S. Thompson. Lexington,
Ky., 1976.
166 newspaper articles, 8 broadsides.   illus.,
maps.   varying sizes.

15537 Thompson, Lawrence Sidney, 1916-
Printing and collections of printing in
Kentucky. [New York, Asia Publishing Houes,
1965]
508-514 p.   24 cm.
Reprinted from Library science today (New York,
Asia Publishing House, 1965; homage volume for
S. R. Ranganathan)

15538 Thompson, Lawrence Sidney, 1916-
The rediscovery of Kentucky. Chicago, 1957.
19-24 p.   29 cm.
Reprinted from The American book collector, VIII,
no. 4, December 1957)

15539   Thompson, Lawrence Sidney, 1916-
        Scandinavian travellers in the South.   [Lexington,
        Kentucky, 1971]
        6 p.   37 cm.
        A paper presented to the Scandinavian Section of
        the South Atlantic Modern Language Association,
        Atlanta, Georgia, 6 November 1971.

15540   Thompson, Lawrence Sidney, 1916-
        Some Kentucky snake superstitions, by Lawrence
        S. Thompson.   Chillicothe, Ohio, Ohio Valley
        Folk Research Project, Ross County Historical
        Society, 1959.
        2 p.l., 6 numb. l.   28 cm.   (Ohio Valley
        Folk publications, n.s., no. 16)

15541   Thompson, Lawrence Sidney, 1916-
        Sparrows in Bluegrass tradition, by L. S.
        Thompson.   [Lexington, Ky., 1963]
        3 p.   22 cm.

15542   Thompson, Lawrence Sidney, 1916-
        Victor Hammer in Kentucky, von Dr. Lawrence
        S. Thompson.   Wien, 1954.
        cover-title, 7 p.   21 cm.
        "Sonderabdruck aus Biblos. Österreichische
        Zeitschrift für Buch- und Bibliothekswesen,
        Dokumentation, Bibliographie und Bibliophilie.
        Vienna.   Jg. 3 (1954), Heft 1, Seite 87-91."

15543   Thompson, Lawrence Sidney, 1916-
        Whiskey in Kentucky folk belief.   [Bowling
        Green, Ky., 1974]
        35-38 p.   23 cm.
        Reprinted from Kentucky folklore record, v. 20,
        no. 2, 1974.

15544   Thompson, Stith, 1885-
        Shipley, Mitchell, and Thompson families.
        Notes based in part on researches of Kate A.
        Thompson.   Bloomington, Indiana, 1964.
        various pagination.   charts, maps.
        29½ cm.

15545   Thomson, C   T   , ed.
        Lindsay Hughes Blanton, an appreciation of
        his life and work.   Edited by C. T. Thomson,

Ph.D.   Lexington, Ky., Transylvania press, 1980.
44 p.   illus.   25½ cm.

15546   Thomson, John Lewis.
History of the Indian wars and wars of the
revolution of the United States... With
additions and corrections. Illustrated with
numerous engravings, from designs by W. Croome
and other artists. Philadelphia, J. B.
Lippincott & co., 1873.
iv, vii-xii, 13-402 p.   incl. illus., plates,
ports.   24½ cm.

15547   Thornton, Kitty ("Mrs. James W. Thornton")
Women in Fayette County history, by Kitty
Thornton (Mrs. James W.)... Prepared by
Fayette County homemakers, September, 1974.
[Lexington, University of Kentucky, College
of Agriculture, Cooperative Extension Service,
1974]
[30] p.   29 cm.

15548   Thoroughbred Record marks its 100th anniversary.
[Lexington, Ky., 1974]
1 p.   port., illus.   27 cm.
Reprinted from Sunday Herald-Leader, 3 February
1974, p. D-10.

15549   Thrilling stories of the forest and frontier.
By an old hunter. Philadelphia, H. C. Peck
& Theo. Bliss, 1858.
295 p.   illus.   20 cm.
Contains account of Indian attack of Mrs.
Scragg's house in Bourbon County, Kentucky, 11
April 1787 (p. 216-260, and fight of Robert and
Samuel M'Afee with Indians in Mercer County,
Kentucky, in May 1781 (p. 248-252)

15550   Through the years. [Lexington, Ky.? 194-?]
347 p.   illus.   24 cm.

15551   Thruston, Rogers Clark Ballard.
Some recent finds regarding the ancestry of
General George Rogers Clark... Louisville, 1935.
34 p.   illus., chart, facsims.   26 cm.

319

15552 Tilton, James.
          General orders. Adjutant general's office,
       Olympia, W. T., Nov. 2d, 1855. General Orders no.
       1. [Olympia? 1855?]
          broadside.   32 x 24½ cm.
          Incipit: 1st. The company D, Capt. Wallace
       raised and organized in Steilacoom, is accepted
       and mustered into service... Explicit: By order
       of the acting governor. James Tilton, adjutant
       general of the volunteer forces of Washington
       Territory.

15553 Timbered tunnel talk. News of Kentucky Covered
       Bridge Association. Newport, Ky., 1965-
          v.   illus.   29 cm.
          Library has v. 1, no. 2, Summer 1965, and
       Supplement, 1965.

15554 Tipton, Ida.
          Descendants of Ephraim McDowell to gather
       for celebration. Lexington, Ky., 1971.
          broadside. illus.   19½ x 40 cm.
          Reprinted from Lexington (Ky.) Sunday
       Herald-Leader, 3 October 1971.

15555 Tipton, L   H
          History of Greenup Association, 1841-1941,
       by L. H. Tipton. [n.p., 1941?]
          39 p.   ports.   23 cm.

15556 To do and to teach, essays in honor of Charles
       Lynn Pyatt, presented by his friends upon his
       retirement from The College of the Bible, June
       1953. Lexington, The College of the Bible,
       1953.
          186 p.   21 cm.

15557 To the citizens of Kentucky... The period is
       rapidly approaching when we shall be called
       upon by our country to exercise one of the
       most important privileges that belongs to a
       free people... [n.p., 1845?]
          broadside.   61 x 29 cm.
          Hummel, 714.
          Signed by "C." (Clay?) of Bourbon County.
          Original in Duke University Library.

15558 Tobacco and the Civil war. Being a true account
       of certain events in the terrible struggle...
       [Washington, Tobacco institute] 1961.
          [3] p.   illus.   31 cm.
       "Reprinted from Tobacco news, June 1961."

15559 Todd, John, 1750-1782.
          Memorandum book of John Todd written during
       September 1774 on a march against the Indians
       from Camp Union, Virginia, to the Ohio river.
       A facsimile of the original in the Margaret I.
       King Library, University of Kentucky, with a
       foreword and transcription by Jacqueline Bull...
       [Lexington, Ky.] University of Kentucky Library
       associates, 1964.
          [24] p.   incl. facsims.   21½ cm.
       (Keepsake no. 13)

15560 Todd, Lyman Beecher, 1832-
          An historical address delivered before the
       Lexington and Vicinity Bible Society, at the
       celebration of its semi-centennial anniversary,
       October 30, 1887, in the First Presbyterian
       Church, Lexington, Kentucky, by Lyman Beecher
       Todd, and published by the Society. Lexington,
       Transylvania Printing Company, 1887.
          cover-title, 17 p.   21 cm.
       Author's presentation copy.

15561 Todd, Lyman Beecher, 1832-
          Kentucky medical necrology, by L. Beecher
       Todd... Louisville, John P. Morton & co.,
       1877.
          44 p.   23 cm.
       Reprinted from the Transactions of the Kentucky
       State Medical Society, April, 1887.
       Author's presentation copy.

15562 Todd, Robert S
          [Manuscript drafts of wills of 14 July 1849]
          2 l.   24½ cm.
       The wills of Robert S. Todd, drawn up two
       days before his death, were declared invalid for
       the lack of two witnesses. Thus his estate,
       including his slaves passed to his children,
       Mary Todd Lincoln being one. This circumstance
       caused Abraham Lincoln to be a slaveowner.

321

These manuscripts were originally in the collection
of the late William H. Townsend of Lexington and
were photographed in 1953. Location of originals
is unknown at present (1971).

15563   Tom Marshall of Kentucky. [New York, 1867]
354-359 p.   23½ cm.
Reprinted from Harper's new monthly magazine,
v. 35, 1867.

15564   Tompkins, Hamilton Bullock.
Burr bibliography. A list of books relating
to Aaron Burr... Brooklyn, N. Y., Historical
printing club, 1892.
89 p.   21 cm.

15565   Tornado!!! The results of the April 3, 1975,
tornado in Breckinridge and Meade Counties,
Hardinsburg, Ky., The Breckinridge County Herald-
News [1974]
cover-title, 100 p.   map, illus.   28 cm.
Mainly photographs.
Appended at end are clippings from Lexington
Herald Leader and Louisville Courier-Journal and
Times for 30 March 1975, the anniversary of the
great tornado of 1974.

15566   [Toulmin, Harry] 1767-1824.
A description of Kentucky, in North America:
to which are prefixed miscellaneous observations
respecting the United States. [London] Printed
in November, 1792.
iv, [5]-121, [3] p.   map.   21½ cm.
Map accompanied by explanatory leaf.
Pages 117-119 contain a letter received
"since the preceding account was printed"
dated: Feb. 2, 1793.
Published anonymously.

15567   Toulmin, Harry, 1767-1824.
Review of the criminal law of the Commonwealth
of Kentucky. Published under the authority of
the legislature. By Harry Toulmin & James Blair.
Frankfort, Ky., from the press of W. Hunter,
printer to the state, 1804.
468 p.   24 cm.

15568 [Toulmin, Harry] 1767-1824.
Thoughts on emigration. To which are added, miscellaneous observations relating to the United States of America: and a short account of Kentucky... [London] Printed in October 1792.
vi, [7]-24, iv, [5]-121, [3] p. map. 22 cm.
Map accompanied by leaf with descriptive letterpress.
The second part has special t.-p.: A description of Kentucky, in North America to which are prefixed miscellaneous observations respecting the United States, Printed in November, 1792.
Pages 117-119 contain a letter from Mr. Imlay received "since the preceding account was printed", dated: London, Feb. 2, 1793.

15569 A tour of historic Louisville and surrounding areas. Louisville, Brown and Williamson tobacco corporation, 1965.
47 p. illus. 17½ cm.

15570 A tour of historic Louisville and surrounding areas. [Louisville] Brown & Williamson Tobacco Company, 1968.
46 p. illus., maps. 19 cm.
Revised edition.

15571 Town House, Danville, Ky.
Danville, Ky. Cradle of the Commonwealth. [Danville, 1970?]
map. illus. 26 x 35 cm.

15572 Townsend, Charles, 1857-
Uncle Tom's cabin; a melodrama in five acts, arranged by Charles Townsend... New York, H. Roorbach, c1889.
44 p. 19 cm. (On cover: Roorbach's American edition of acting plays, no. 18)
On cover: New version.

15573 Townsend, Dorothy Edwards ("Mrs. John Wilson Townsend) 1915-
The life and works of John Wilson Townsend, Kentucky author and historian, 1885-1968...

Lexington, Ky., Printed by the Keystone Printery,
1972.
90 p.   front. (port.)   24 cm.
Four letters from author to Lawrence S.
Thompson in pocket at end (27 April, 4 May, 13 May,
and 15 May [two pages])

15574 Townsend, John Wilson, 1885-1968.
American imprints inventory. No. 25. Supplemental
check list of Kentucky imprints 1788-1820.
Including the initial printing of the original
Kentucky copyright ledger, 1800-1854, and the
first account of the run of Baptist Minutes in
the collection of Mr. Henry S. Robinson. Louisville,
Historical records survey, Service Division, Work
projects administration, 1942.
241 p.   28½ cm.

15575 Townsend, John Wilson, 1885-1968.
James Lane Allen. The address at the unveiling
of the Allen Fountain of Youth in Gratz Park,
opposite Transylvania University, Lexington,
Kentucky, Sunday afternoon, 15 October, 1933...
[Lexington] Transylvania University Press, 1933.
unpaged.   29 cm.
Reproduced from typewritten copy.

15576 Townsend, John Wilson, 1885-1968.
James Lane Allen... Louisville, Ky.,
Courier-Journal job printing company, 1927.
120 p.   front. (port.), illus.   24 cm.

15577 Townsend, John Wilson, 1885-1968.
Kentuckians in history and literature... New
York and Washington, The Neale publishing
company, 1907.
189 p.   21 cm.

15578 Townsend, John Wilson, 1885-1968.
Kentucky: mother of governors, by John Wilson
Townsend... Frankfort, Kentucky State Historical
Society, 1910.
50 p., 1 ℓ., incl. front. (port.)   23 cm.
"The first volume of the Kentucky Historical
Series." - Editor's introduction, by Mrs.
Jennie C. Morton, p. [9]

15579   Townsend, John Wilson, 1885-1968.
        ... The life of James Francis Leonard; the
        first practical sound-reader of the Morse
        alphabet... Louisville, John P. Morton & company,
        1909.
            85 p.   illus.   32 cm.
            At head of title: Filson Club publication no.
        24, Part first.

15580   Townsend, John Wilson, 1885-1968.
            Lore of the meadowland... Lexington, Ky.,
        Press of J. L. Richardson & co., 1911.
            34 p.   24 cm.
            Contains three biographies.

15581   Townsend, John Wilson, 1885-1968.
            Richard Hickman Menefee. New York and
        Washington, The Neale publishing company, 1907.
            320, iii p.   illus.   24 cm.

15582   Townsend, John Wilson, 1885-1968.
            The story of the Phoenix Hotel. Lexington,
        Ky., Kentucky University [i.e, Transylvania
        University] 1908.
            302-311 p.   illus.   27 cm.
            Reprinted from the Transylvanian, v. 16, no. 8,
        May 1908.

15583   Townsend, John Wilson, 1885-1968.
            Supplemental list of Kentucky imprints, 1788-
        1820, including the initial printing of the
        Kentucky copyright ledger, 1800-1854, and the
        first account of the run of Baptist Minutes in
        the collection of Mr. Henry S. Robinson. Edited
        by John Wilson Townsend. Louisville, Ky.,
        Historical Records Survey, Service Division,
        Work Projects Administration, 1942.
            xii p., 1 ℓ., 241 p.   28 cm.   (American
        imprints inventory, 25)

15584   Townsend, John Wilson, 1885-1968.
            Three Kentucky gentlemen of the old order.
        Frankfort, Ky., The Roberts Printing Company,
        1946.
            51 p.   25 cm.
            Inscribed by author.

15585 Townsend, William Henry, 1890-1964.
          The most orderly of disorderly houses...
       Lexington, Kentucky, Privately printed, 1966.
          [9] p.   illus., port.   19½ cm.
          Mounted at end is article from Lexington Herald,
       18. XII. 70, p. 45, "Bricks from Pauline's 'House'
       to be sold as 'collector's [!] items," dealing
       with the career of Pauline - - - -, 627 Clay
       Street, Bowling Green, Kentucky.

15586 Townsend, William Henry, 1890-1964.
          The boarding school of Mary Todd Lincoln.
       A discussion as to its identification between
       C. Frank Dunn and William H. Townsend, originally
       published in the Sunday Herald-Leader of
       Lexington, Kentucky... Lexington, Privately
       printed, 1941.
          41 p.   front., port.   23 cm.

15587 Tracie, Theodore C   1836-
          Annals of the Nineteenth Ohio battery, volunteer
       artillery; including an outline of the operations
       of the Second division, Twenty-third army corps;
       lights and shadows of army life, as seen in the
       march, bivouac and battlefield... Cleveland,
       O., Pub. for the Battery committee by J. B.
       Savage, 1878.
          xvi, 17-470 p.   19 cm.

15588 Tracy, Susan.
          Before the present "Old State House".
       Frankfort, Kentucky Historical Society, 1967.
          1 p.   illus.   28 cm.
          Reprinted from Kentucky heritage, v. 8, no. 1,
       Fall 1967.

15589 Transylvania College.
          ... Rafinesque memorial papers, October 31,
       1940. Lexington, Ky., Transylvania College,
       1942.
          108 p.   facsim.   23 cm.   (Transylvania
       College bulletin, v. 15, no. 7)
          Portrait of Rafinesque on cover.
          In pocket at end are three clippings on
       Rafinesque's "ghost", from Lexington Herald,
       28 Oct. 1976, and Kentucky Kernel, 29 Oct. 1976.

15590 Transylvania College.
The Transylvania library, founded in 1784.
Lexington, Ky., 1919.
51 p.   illus., facsims.   24 cm.
(Transylvania College bulletin, vol. II, no. 3,
November, 1919)

15591 Transylvania University.
Addresses delivered at the inauguration of
Rev. Lewis W. Green, D.D., as president of
Transylvania University and state normal school,
November 18, 1856. Frankfort, Ky., A. G.
Hodges, printer, 1856.
40 p.   21 cm.
Address of Dr. Lewis W. Green": p. 4-35.

15592 Transylvania University.
A catalogue of the officers and students of
Transylvania university. Lexington, Kentucky,
January, 1825.
15 p.   21½ cm.

15593 Transylvania University.
Catalogus senatus academici, eorum qui munera
at officia gesserunt quique alicujus gradus laurea
donati sunt in Transylvaniensi, Lexingtoniae in
Republica Kentuckiensi.   Lexingtoniae, Gulielmo
Tanner, typographo, 1824.
20 p.   23 cm.

15594 Transylvania University.
Clarissimo Johanni Adair, Armigero Gubernatori
Honoratissimo Gulielmo Taylor Barry, LLD, Armigero,
Vice-gubernatori; senatoribus et delegatis
Reipublicae Kentuckiensis; curatoribus colendis
et aestimandis Universitatis Transylvaniensis;
Reverendo Horatio Holley, A.M. AAS, Praesidi, Toti
senatu academico; venerandisque ecclesiarum passim
pastoribus; universis denique ubicunque terrarum.
Humanitatis cultoribus, reique publicae nostrae
literatae autoribus; these hasque, juvenes in
artibus initiati, [twenty-seven names in two columns]
humillime dedicant. Aulae academicae Lexingtoniae,
in Republicae Kentuckiensi, sexto idus sulii,
anno salutis MDCCCXXII, rerumque publicarum
foederatarum Americae summae postestatis XVLII.

327

[Lexingtoniae] e typis Gulielmi Gibbes Hunt [1822]
20 p.   22½ cm.

15595 Transylvania University.
The order of exercises in the chapel of
Transylvania university. A collection of original
pieces in honour of the arrival of General
Lafayette, the hero, patriot, and philanthropist,
a defender of American independence, a companion
of Washington, and a devoted friend of liberty
and equal laws in Europe and America. Lexington,
Fayette county, Kentucky, May, 1825.
16 p.   20 cm.

15596 Transylvania University.
Transylvania journal of medicine... Extra.
A catalogue of the officers and students of
Transylvania University. Lexington, Kentucky.
January, 1830. Lexington, Kentucky, Printed by
J. G. Norwood, Short street, 1830.
16 p.   23½ cm.

15597 Trent, Paul.
Citizens opposed razing of Belle Breazing [!]
house. Lexington, Ky., 1962.
broadside.   illus., facsim.   46 x 30 cm.
Reprinted from The Kentucky kernel, v. 53, no. 62,
9 February 1962.

15598 [Trimble, Ernest Greene]
A report on labor. [n.p.] Committee for
Kentucky [1947]
31 p.   illus.   24 cm.

15599 Triplett, Frank.
History, romance and philosophy of great
American crimes and criminals... with personal
portraits, biographical sketches, legal notes
of celebrated trials, and philosophical disquisition
concerning the causes, prevalence and prevention
of crime... New York and St. Louis, N. D. Thompson
& company, 1884.
xxiv, 33-659 p.   incl. front., illus.
[incl. ports.]   23 cm.

15600 [Triplett, Robert]
An account of Bon Harbor, in the state of

Kentucky, on the Ohio River one hundred and
sixty miles below the falls. London, E. Palmer
and son, 1849.
39 p.   22 cm.

15601   [Triplett, Thomas]
To the public.   [n.p., n.d.]
31 p.   22 cm.

15602   Triplette, Ralph R
Land use at selected interchanges on interstate
Highway 75 in north-central Kentucky, Ralph R.
Triplette, Jr. Lexington, Department of
Geography, University of Kentucky [1966]
viii, 37 p.   illus., maps.   28 cm.
(Kentucky study series, 3)

15603   ... Trustees' House: Shakertown at Pleasant Hill.
1975 [n.p., 1975]
broadside.   illus.   30 x 23 cm.
At head of title: Famous inns of Kentucky.

15604   Tuckerman, Henry Theodore, 1813-1871.
Biographical essays. Essays, biographical
and critical; or, Studies of character. By
Henry T. Tuckerman... Boston, Phillips,
Sampson and company, 1857.
iv, [5]-475 p.   21 cm.

15605   Turner, Justin G
The thirteenth amendment and the Emancipation
proclamation. Los Angeles, The Plantin press,
1971.
17 p.   facsims.   21½ cm.

15606   Tuttle, Charles Richard, 1848-
History of the border wars of two centuries,
embracing a narrative of the wars with the
Indians from 1750 to 1874... Chicago, C.A. Wall
& company, 1874.
608 p.   front., port.   23 cm.

15607   200 [Two hundred] years: Kentucky impact on the
nation. Lexington, 1976.
22, [4] p.   illus.   58 cm.
Reprinted from Sunday Herald-Leader, 4 July
1976, and Herald and Leader, 5 July 1976.

329

Partial contents. - Thomas S. Watson, Early
Kentucky rated name of Dark and Bloody Ground. -
Betty Ellison, Mrs. Lincoln, genteel, refined,
gaining new historical image. - Marilu Dauer,
Kentuckians by thousands flocked to take part in
America's war with Mexico. - Linda Carnes,
War of 1812 was popular in state. - Lu Williams,
Civil War was struggle for neutrality. - Tom
Carter, Pioneers' determination helped win
American Revolution. - Sue Alexander, Coal has
been Kentucky's major industry. - Jack Lewyn,
Tobacco production began when earliest settlers
moved into state. - Betty Cox, Kentucky River,
early highway for settlers, still has traffic. -
Ron Cordell, TVA's Kentucky Dam brought flood
control to wide area. - Don Walker, Paducah
became early atomic city. - George C. Wright and
Harold Greene, Lexington black achievements
cited. - John Alexander, Great Revival shook
Kentucky, saw creation of two denominations. -
Marti Martin, Hatfield-McCoy feud most famous. -
Frank T. Phelps, Man o' War captured hearts of
old-time race followers.

U

15608   Uncle Johnny Furlong, café owner. [Lexington, Ky.,
        1965]
            broadside.   port.   38 x 23 cm.
            Reprinted from Lexington Herald, 8 July 1965.
            Includes photographic portrait by John Mitchell,
        42 x 34 cm.

15609   The ungrateful god.   1956 prose writing publication.
        [Berea, Kentucky, Berea College Press, 1956?]
            55 p.   24 cm.

15610   United Daughters of the Confederacy.   Kentucky
        Division. Lexington Chapter.
            Book of choice recipes. Lexington, Ky.,
        1908?
            48 p.   illus.   23 cm.

15611 U. S. Bureau of Agricultural Economics.
       Economic and social problems and conditions of
       the southern Appalachians. Washington, D. C.,
       Government printing office, 1935.
         184 p.   maps (incl. one fold. map in pocket
       at end), graphs, tables.   30 cm.

15612 U. S. Bureau of Refugees, Freedmen and Abandoned
       Lands.
       Freedmen's affairs in Kentucky and Tennessee.
       [Washington, D.C., 1868?]
         51 p.   24 cm.

15613 U. S. Congress.
         ... An Act for the government of the territory
       of the United States south of the river Ohio.
       [n.p., n.d.]
         broadside.   29 x 22½ cm.
         At head of title: Congress of the United
       States: at the second session, begun and held
       at the City of New-York, on Monday, the fourth
       of January, one thousand seven hundred and ninety.
         Signed by Thomas Jefferson, Secretary of
       State over titles of Frederick Augustus Muhlenberg,
       speaker of the House of representatives, John
       Adams, vice-president of the United States, and
       president of the Senate, and George Washington,
       president of the United States. Washington's
       approval is dated 25 May 1790.
         Accompanied by brief explanatory note signed
       by Lawrence S. Thompson.

15614 U. S. Congress.
         [Eulogies of John Sherman Cooper]
       [Washington, D.C., 1972-73]
         S17401-S17415 p, E280 p.   29 cm.
         Reprinted from the Congressional Record, 11
       October 1972.
         Contains speeches by Senators Young, Mansfield
       Mathias, Stennis, Harry F. Byrd, Jr., Allen,
       Hansen, Robert C. Byrd, Goldwater, Beall, Cotton,
       Jordan, Allott, Brooke, Boggs, Schweiker,
       Sparkman, Kennedy, Hruska, Saxbe, Roth, Dale,
       Weicker, Griffin, Fannin, and Rep. Tim Lee
       Carter.
         Clippings with photograph on the proceedings
       from New York Times and Washington Star mounted

at end.
At end is an article by Bill Straub, "Cooper
reminisces," Kentucky Kernel (Lexington), 1
February, 1973.

15615 U. S. 42d Cong., 3d sess., 1872-1973.
Memorial addresses on the life and character of
Garrett Davis (a senator form Kentucky)
delivered in the Senate and House of Representatives...
Dec. 18, 1872. Published by order of Congress.
Washington, Govt. print. off., 1873.
47 p.   27 cm.

15616 U. S. 51st Cong., 2d sess., 1890-1891.
Memorial addresses on the life and character
of James B. Beck (a senator from Kentucky)
delivered in the Senate and House Representatives,
August 23 and September 13, 1890. Prepared in
accordance with joint resolution of Congress,
and under the direction of the Joint Committee
on Printing, by W. H. Michael... Washington,
Government Printing Office, 1891.
146 p.   20½ cm.

15617 U. S. 53d Cong., 3d sess., 1894-1895.
Memorial addresses on the life and services
of Marcus Claiborne Lisle (late a representative
from Kentucky) delivered in the House of
Representatives and Senate, fifty-third Congress,
Third session... Washington, Government Printing
Office, 1895.
55 p.   front. (port.)   28½ cm.   (53d
Cong., 3d sess., House misc. doc. no. 83)
Published by order of Congress.

15618 U. S. 56th Congress, 1st sess., 1899-1900.
Memorial addresses on the life and character
of Evan E. Settle (late a representative from
Kentucky) delivered in the House of Representatives
and Senate, 50th Congress, 1st session.
Washington, Government Printing Office, 1900.
73 p.   front. (port.)   27 cm.

15619 U. S. 68th Cong., 2d sess., 1924-1925. House.
James C. Cantrill. Memorial addresses
delivered in the House of Representatives of the
United States in memory of James C. Cantrill,

332

late a representative from Kentucky. Sixty-eighth
Congress. March 1, 1925. Washington, U. S.
Govt. Print. Off., 1925.
　　3 p.l., 63, [1] p.　　front. (port.)　　23 cm.
(68th Cong., 2d Sess. House. Doc. 666)

15620　U. S. 82d Cong., 1st sess., 1951.
　　Memorial addresses held in the House of
Representatives and Senate of the United States,
together with remarks presented in eulogy of
Virgil Munday Chapman, late a senator from
Kentucky. Washington, U. S. Govt. Print. Off.,
1951.
　　115 p.　　front. (port.)　　23 cm.

15621　U. S.　　84th Cong., 2d sess., 1956.
　　Memorial addresses held in the Senate and
House of Representatives of the United States,
together with remarks presented in eulogy
of Alben William Barkley, late a senator from
Kentucky. Washington, Government Printing
Office, 1956.
　　161 p.　　front. (port.)　　24 cm.

15622　U. S.　Congress.　House.
　　[Remarks on death of Maurice Hudson Thatcher
in Washington, D.C., on 6 January 1973.
Washington, 1973]
　　5 ℓ.　　29 cm.
　　From Congressional Record, 9 January 1973,
H 150, E73; 11 January 1973, H 205, H 206,
E 168; 18 January 1973, H 298, H 299; 24 January,
1973, H 298, H 299; 24 January, 1973, H 478 -
H 480, H 1050 - H 1051.

15623　U. S.　Congress.　House.
　　Robert C. Wickliffe (late a representative
from Louisiana) Memorial addresses delivered
in the House of representatives of the United
States, sixty-second congress, proceedings in
the House, February 23, 1913, proceedings in
the Senate, June 11, 1912... Washington, 1913.
　　69 p.　　front. (port.)　　27 cm.

15624　U. S.　Congress.　Senate.
　　Tributes to Marlow Cook upon retirement from the
U. S. Senate. [Washington, D. C., 1974]

S22629-S22634.   29 cm.
Reprinted from Congressional Record, 20 December
1974.
Portrait of Sen. Cook from Lexington Herald-Leader,
28 December 1974, at end.

15625 U. S. Defense Department.
United States Army Training Center, Armor,
Fort Knox, Kentucky. [Fort Knox? 197-?]
unpaged.   illus.   29 cm.
Includes parts of 11th Battalion, Company E,
Training period 13 Oct. 1969 - 5 Dec. 1969.

15626 U. S. Engineer Dept.
Index map of Big Sandy, Levisa & Tug Rivers.
Ky. and W. Va. Cincinnati [n.d.]
map.   84 x 55 cm.
Scale: 4 miles x 1 5/8 in.
"U. S. Engineer Office, Cincinnati, O. To
accompany report of Survey of Big Sandy River.
H.F. Hodges. Capt. Corps of Engrs. U.S.A. H. Doc.
235 56 2."

15627 U. S. Forest Service.
... Kentucky's forest resources and industries.
O. Keith Hutchinson and Robert K. Winters, forest
economists, Central states forest experiment
station, Forest service. Washington, D.C., U. S.
Government printing office, 1953.
56 p.   illus., maps, diags. $26\frac{1}{2}$ cm.

15628 U. S. Forest Service.
Red River Gorge, land of arches. Daniel Boone
national forest in Kentucky. [Washington,
D. C., n.d.]
10 l.   illus., map.   22 x 28 cm.

15629 U. S. Forest Service.
Red River gorge, land of arches. Daniel Boone
National Forest in Kentucky. [n.p., 197-]
[20] p.   illus., maps. $21\frac{1}{2}$ x 28 cm.

15630 U. S. Forest Service.
Scenic Red River gorge, land of natural bridges.
Daniel Boone National Forest, Kentucky. [n.p., 197-]
folder, 3 p.   illus., map on verso of folder.
24 cm.

15631 U. S. Laws, statutes, etc.
Extracts from the revenue laws of the United
States: comprehending such parts of the excise
laws, - laws laying duties on licenses for
selling wines, &c. - on riding carriages, - on
property sold at auction, - and on stamps; as
appears best calculated for the information of
such as have not an opportunity of perusing the
laws of the general government. Lexington,
Printed by J. Bradford, 1798.
26 p.   20 cm.

15632 U. S. Laws, statutes, etc., 1797-1799 (5th Cong.,
1st-3d sess.)
The several acts relative to the stamp duties,
passed at the late and present sessions of
Congress, and which will become payable from
and after the first day of July, 1798. To which
is added, a table of the several duties, by
which they may be seen at one view. Washington,
Ky., From the press of Hunter & Beaumont, 1798.
23 p.   15½ cm.
An act laying duties on stamped vellum,
parchment and paper, with amendment.

15633 U. S. Office of Education. Division of Higher
Education.
Public higher education in Kentucky. Report to
the committee on functions and resources of state
government... [Frankfort, Ky., 1951]
185 p.   tables.   29 cm.   (Kentucky.
Legislative Research Commission. Research
publication, 25)

V

15634 Vague. Lexington, Xi Chapter of Chi Delta Phi,
University of Kentucky, 1946-1951.
6 v.
One volume a year, each as no. 1.
Library has v. 1, 3, 5, 6.

15635 Van Cleve, Benjamin, 1773-1821.
Harrod's Old fort, 1791, as described and

platted in Benjamin Van Cleve's manuscript
biographical memorandum dating from the year
1773, by Willard Rouse Jillson... Van Cleve's
original map reproduced. Frankfort, Ky., The
Kentucky State historical society, 1929.
[14]p.   illus.   20 cm.
Facsimile of original manuscript and the
transcript of it, on opposite pages.

15636 Van Fleet, Donald.
Alternative programs for suspended and
expelled children. Part I: An evaluation of
alternative programs for suspended and expelled
children, prepared by Donald Van Fleet. Part II:
Educational program for suspended or expelled
children, presented by Department of Education,
Department of Human Resources. Frankfort, Ky.,
Legislative Research Commission, 1975.
iii, A-10, B-34 p.   28 cm.   (Research
report, no. 126)

15637 Van Fleet, Donald.
Veterinary needs in Kentucky, including an
exploration of possible new professional programs
at Murray State Universtiy. Study supervised and
compiled by Donald Van Fleet, LRC Staff. Report
prepared by Booz, Allen and Hamilton; advisory
Committee for a Veterinary School Study,, Clarence
R. Cole, Donald Van Fleet. Frankfort, Ky.,
Legislative Research Commission, 1975.
various pagings.   maps, tables.   27 cm.
(Kentucky. Legislative Research Commission.
Research report no. 123)

15638 Vanlandingham, Kenneth E
The fee system in Kentucky counties...
Lexington, Kentucky, Bureau of Government Research,
College of Arts and Sciences, University of Kentucky,
1951.
38 p.   24 cm.

15639 Vanlandingham, Kenneth E
Financial management in Kentucky counties...
Lexington, Kentucky, Bureau of Government Research,
College of Arts and Sciences, University of Kentucky,
1951.
98 p.   24 cm.

15640   Van Meter, Benjamin F
        Genealogies and sketches of some old families
        who have taken a prominent part in the development
        of Virginia and Kentucky especially, and later of
        many other states of this union... Louisville,
        John P. Morton & company, 1901.
        182 p.   illus.   25½ cm.

15641   Vanover, Frederic D
        James Taylor Adams, a brief biography, by
        Frederic D. Vanover. Louisville, Dixieana
        Press, 1937.
        15, [1] p.   23 cm.
        Title on cover: James Taylor Adams, mountain
        poet, historian, with photograph of Adams at his
        typewriter.

15642   Vaughn, Laurence Meredith.
        Just the little story of Cumberland Gap. By
        Laurence Meredith Vaughn. Middlesboro, Ky.,
        Middlesboro Chamber of Commerce, 1927.
        16 p.   illus.   24 cm.

15643   Vaughn, Neil.
        Gratz Park: where history was made. Lexington,
        Ky., 1963.
        2 p.   illus.   47 x 39 cm.
        Reprinted from Lexington Herald-Leader, 19 May
        1963, p. A-72, A-74.

15644   Venable, Emerson, 1875-   ed.
        Poets of Ohio; selection representing the
        poetical work of Ohio authors from the pioneer
        period to the present day, with biographical
        sketches and notes. Edited by Emerson Venable.
        Cincinnati, The Robert Clarke company, 1909.
        356 p.   21 cm.
        Includes selections from Sarah Morgan Bryan
        Piatt, 1836-1919, of Lexington, Ky.

15645   Verhoeff, Mary.
        ... The Kentucky mountains. Transportation and
        commerce, 1750 to 1911. A study in the economic
        history of a coal field... Volume I. Louisville,
        John P. Morton & company, 1911.
        208 p.   illus.   32 cm.

At head of title: Filson Club publication
no. 26
V. II never published.

15646   Verhoeff, Mary.
        ... The Kentucky River navigation... Louisville,
        John P. Morton & company, 1917.
            257 p.   illus., fold. map.   24 cm.
        At head of title: Filson Club publication no. 28.

15647   Vicich, Mollie.
            Kentucky Skaggs, compiled by Mrs. Millie Vicich
        and Mrs. Juanita Luttrell. [n.p., 197]
            unpaged.   29½ cm.

15648   Vickery, Oliver, ed.
            The Kentucky colonels handbook. [Ed. by Oliver
        Vickery and John E. Goddard] Louisville,
        Kentucky Colonels Directory, Brown Hotel [1930]
            64 p.   19 cm.
        Contains text of "In Old Kentucky" by Judge
        J. B. Wyatt and "Sentiment" by James Ball Naylor.
        Inscribed by Col. Vickery.

15649   Victor, William B
            Life and events... Cincinnati, Applegate &
        co., 1859.
            vii, [9]-232 p.   22 cm.

15650   Virginia. General Assembly, 1798-1799.
            Resolutions of Virginia and Kentucky, penned
        by Madison and Jefferson, in relation to the
        Alien and sedition laws; and debates, in the
        House of Delegates of Virginia, in December, 1798,
        on the same. Richmond, R.I. Smith, 1832.
            72, 183 p.   21 cm.

15651   Virginia. State Library. Dept. of Archives
        and History.
            ... List of the colonial soldiers of Virginia.
        Special report of the Department of Archives and
        History for 1913. H. J. Eckenrode, archivist.
        Richmond, D. Bottom, superintendent of public
        printing, 1917.
            91 p.   23½ cm.
        Published also in Virginia. State Library,

Richmond. 13th annual report, 1915/16. Richmond, 1917.
List of references: p. 15-16.

15652   Visscher, William Lightfoot, b. 1842.
Blue grass ballads and other verse, by William Lightfoot Visscher. New York and Boston. H. M. Caldwell company [1900]
221 p.   front.   21 cm.
Includes some poems in Negro dialect.

W

15653   Wahlgren, Sue F
Orphan society has served community since 1833. Lexington, Ky., 1973.
2 p.   illus.   30 cm.
Reprinted from Lexington Herald-Leader, 4 February 1973.

15654   Walk in the still nights. Creative writing class, 1948-49. Berea, Kentucky, Berea College Press [1949?]
64 p.   24 cm.

15655   Walker, C   B
The Mississippi valley, and prehistoric events: giving an account of the original formation and early condition of the great valley; of its vegetable and animal life; of its first inhabitants, the mound builders, its mineral treasures and agricultural developments. All from authentic sources. Burlington, Ia., R. T. Root, 1879.
1 p.l., 5-539 p.   23$\frac{1}{2}$ cm.

15656   Walker, Courtenay J
Circuit court case activity in Kentucky 1950-1960. Frankfort, Ky., Legislative Research Commission, 1961.
unpaged.   map, tables, diagrs.   28$\frac{1}{2}$ cm.
(Information bulletin, no. 30)

15657   The Walker Foxhound. [Washington, D. C., 1973]
E4089-E4091 p.   27$\frac{1}{2}$ cm.

Reprinted in the Congressional record (extension
of remarks), 14 June 1973. Original article in
Garrard County News, Lancaster, Ky.

15658 Walker, Tom L
        History of the Lexington post office from
        1794 to 1901. With additional important
        postal information. Comp. by Tom L. Walker,
        assistant postmaster. Lexington, Ky. [E. P.
        Veach (?)] 1901.
        199 p.   illus.   19 cm.

15659 Walker, Wilma J
        Residential location selectivity of
        Appalachian return migrants: an eastern Kentucky
        case study. [Lexington, Ky., 1972]
        18 p.   28 cm.

15660 Wall, Bennett H
        The struggle to make a great university.
        [Lexington, 1978]
        8-11 p.   ports.   28½ cm.
        Reprinted from The Kentucky Alumnus, v. 48,
        no. 1, winter 1977-78.

15661 Wall, Maryjean.
        Reflections on Man o'War. [Lexington, Ky.,
        1973]
        1 p.   18 cm.
        Reprinted form the Sunday Herald-Leader,
        Lexington, Ky., 16 December 1973.

15662 Wallace, Frances Jane (Todd), 1817-1899.
        Mrs. Frances Jane (Todd) Wallace describes
        Lincoln's wedding. Edited by Wayne C. Temple...
        Limited edition published for Members of the
        National Lincoln-Civil War Council. Harrogate,
        Tenn., Lincoln Memorial University Press, 1960.
        12 p.   22½ cm.

15663 Wallace, Jack C
        Map, City of Danville, Kentucky, showing
        streets, parks, schools and places of principal
        interest. Danville, Published by Danville-Boyle
        County Chamber of Commerce [n.d.]
        56 x 45 cm.   Scale: ½ in. = 500 feet.

Appended to map is undated illustrated folder
captioned Danville, Kentucky, birthplace of the
Commonwealth.

15664 [Walls, David]
Appalachia. [Lexington, University of Kentucky
Library, 1976]
6 p. 29 cm. (Kentucky. University.
Libraries. Subject guide to research, 12)

15665 Walton, Blaine C
Memories... today and the tomorrows. [n.p.]
1959.
29 p. 23 cm.
Poems.

15666 Waltz, Mrs. Elizabeth (Cherry) 1866-1903.
The ancient landmark; a Kentucky romance, by
Elizabeth Cherry Waltz... New York, McClure,
Phillips & co., 1905.
5 p.l., ix-xviii, 3-269 p. 20 cm.

15667 Waltz, Mrs. Elizabeth (Cherry) 1866-1903.
Pa Gladden; the story of a common man, by
Elizabeth Cherry Waltz. New York, The Century
co., 1903.
ix, 338 p. incl. 7 pl. front. 20 cm.

15668 Warland, J   B
The prize song. The Whig chief. Written by
J. B. Warland, Esq./Hon. Henry Clay/ of the
Boston Clay CLub, no. 1. [Boston? n.d.]
1 ℓ., 3-5 p. cover illus., music. 36 cm.
Includes words.
The original of this text was in the possession
of Elliott Shapiro, 118 West 79th Street, New
York, in February 1943. The original cannot
now be located. The present "photostatic" copy,
possibly now unique, is in the library of
Lawrence S. Thompson, Lexington, Kentucky.

15669 Warren, Edward L
The First Presbyterian Church in Louisville
from its organization in 1816 to the year 1896.
By Rev. Edward L. Warren, D. D. Reprinted from
Memorial history of Louisville. Chicago, 1890.
36 p. front. (port.) 29 cm.

15670   Warren, Jack R
        A study of magnetic anomalies associated
        with ultrabasic dikes in the western Kentucky
        fluorspar district. Lexington, Ky., 1956.
        38 p.   illus., graphs, tables.   24 cm.
        (Kentucky Geological Survey, Series IX, Bulletin,
        19)

15671   Warren, Louis Austin, 1885-
        Souvenir of Abraham Lincoln's birthplace,
        Hodgenville, Kentucky. Morganfield, Ky.,
        Munford Publishing Company [1927]
        [28] p.   illus.   28½ cm.

15672   Watson, Henry Clay, 1831-1869.
        Nights in a block-house; or, Sketches of
        border life: embracing adventures among the
        Indians, feats of the wild hunters, and exploits
        of Boone, Brady, Kenton, Wetzel, Fleshart, and
        other border heroes of the West.
        448 p.   incl. front., illus., plates, ports.
        23 cm.

15673   Watson, Thomas S
        Diarist recounts Perryville battlefield
        "slippery with blood". Lexington, Ky., 1976.
        broadside.   ports.   16 x 37 cm.
        Reprinted from Lexington Herald-Leader,
        9 October 1976.
        Excerpts from and commentary on diary of
        Robert Belt Taylor.

15674   Watson, Thomas S
        Early settlements terrorized: Indians
        destroyed Kentucky settlement of Kincheloe-
        Polk Station. Lexington, 1976.
        broadside.   illus.   42 x 36 cm.
        Reprinted from Lexington Herald-Leader, 27
        June 1976.

15675   Watson, Thomas S
        First wireless. Lexington, Ky., 1976.
        broadside.   port.   34 x 14 cm.
        Reprinted from Lexington Herald-Leader, 11 July
        1976, p. C-4.
        Nathan B. Stubblefield's invention of radio.

15676 Watterson, Henry, 1840-1921.
        George Dennison [!] Prentice. A memorial
        address delivered before the legislature of
        Kentucky in the hall of the House of representatives
        on the evening of Wednesday, February 2nd, 1870...
        Cincinnati, R. Clarke & co., 1870.
        1 p.l., [5]-27 p.   24 cm.

15677 Watts, E   C
        History of Methodism in Clark County [Ky.]
        by Rev. E. C. Watts. Winchester, Ky. [n.d.]
        1 p.l., 40 numb. 1.   30 cm.

15678 Wayland, John W
        The Bowmans, a pioneering family in Virginia,
        Kentucky and the Northwest Territory... Staunton,
        Va., The McClure company, 1943.
        185 p.   illus., maps.   24 cm.

15679 [Weaver, Rufus]
        Man in our image: the same man the eugenist
        would make, by S. Auk [pseud.] Lexington, Ky.
        Commercial printing co., 1940.
        333 p.   21½ cm.

15680 Webb, Ben J
        The centenary of Catholicity in Kentucky...
        Louisville, Charles A. Rogers, 1884.
        594 p.   illus.   24 cm.

15681 Webb, William S
        An archaeological survey of Guntersville
        basin on the Tennessee river in northern Alabama,
        by William S. Webb... and Charles G. Wilder...
        Lexington, University of Kentucky press 1951.
        278 p.   78 pl.   tables (part. fold),
        maps (part fold.)   24 cm.
        Professor Webb related his studies at
        Guntersville with his extensive investigations of
        Indian cultures in Kentucky and elsewhere in the
        valleys of the Tennessee and Ohio rivers.

15682 [Webber, Charles Wilkins] 1819-1856.
        The romance of forest and prairie life:
        narratives of perilous adventures & wild hunting
        scenes... London, H. Vizetelly [1853]
        239 p.   incl. front.   17½ cm.

343

15683 Webster, Noah, 1758-1843.
         The American spelling book; containing the
      rudiments of the English language, for the use
      of schools in the United States; by Noah Webster,
      Esq. The revised impression, with the latest
      corrections. Stereotyped by C. N. Baldwin,
      New York. Lexington, Ky., Published by W. W.
      Worsley, 1823.
         163 p.   16½ cm.
      Cover-title, in double ruled border.

15684 Webster, Pauline Tabor.
         Important auction. The private collection of
      Pauline Tabor (Webster), author of "Pauline's"
      memoirs of the madam of Clay Street, May 24,
      25, & 27, 1973. 10:00 A. M. daily. Larmon
      Mill Road, Bowling Green, Kentucky. [Murfreesboro,
      Tenn., Jones Realty and Auction Company, 1973]
         [44] p.   illus.   23 cm.
      At end is a smaller brochure announcing the sale
      with a picture of Mrs. Webster on cover. 8 p.
      23½ cm.

15685 Weik, Jesse W
         Letter to Jesse W. Weik by William H.
      Herndon, 5 January 1889.
         ℓ., 4 p. of facsimile.   28 cm.
      Preceded by anonymous introductory essay,
      "Abraham Lincoln, a Man of Total Integrity."
      Weik relates a story about Lincoln told to
      him by Joshua F. Speed.

15686 Weller, Stuart.
         Geology of the Cave-In Rock quadrangle,
      detailed report on the stratigraphic structure
      and areal distribution of the rocks south of
      the Ohio River and in the vicinity of Marion,
      Kentucky... Presented with five separate
      miscellaneous papers by James H. Gardner, Wilbur
      Greeley Burroughs, James S. Hudnall, Lewis Cass
      Robinson, and Lucien Beckner... Frankfort,
      Kentucky, Kentucky Geological Survey, 1927.
         [10], 282 p.   illus., maps, diags., tables.
      24½ cm.   (Kentucky Geological Survey, ser. VI,
      v. 26)

15687 Wells, J   K
       A short history of Paintsville and Johnson
       county. [Paintsville, Ky.] Published by the
       Paintsville Herald for the benefit of the Johnson
       County Historical Society [1962]
       39 p.   illus., fold. map., port.   23 cm.

15688 Welsh, Joseph S
       Harp of the West: a volume of poems. Cincinnati,
       Printed by Dawson and Fisher, 1839.
       1 p.l., [9]-204 p.   front.   18 cm.

15689 The Western farmer's almanac, for the year 1826...
       Calculated for the meridian of Lexington, Ky.
       And will serve, without any sensible variation,
       for the states of Tennessee, Ohio, Indiana,
       Illinois, and Missouri. By James W. Palmer.
       Lexington, Printed by W. W. Worsley, for self
       and James W. Palmer, Lexington, and John P.
       Morton, Louisville [1825]
       36 p.   19½ cm.

15690 The western farmer's almanac, for the year 1827...
       Calculated for the meridian of Lexington, Ky.
       And will serve, without any sensible variation,
       for the states of Tennessee, Ohio, Indiana,
       Illinois, and Missouri. Lexington, Printed by
       W. W. Worsley, for self and J. W. Palmer,
       and John P. Morton; Louisville [1826]
       24 p.   19½ cm.

15691 Western farmer's almanac, 1895-1897. Louisville,
       Ky., John P. Morton & company, 1895-97.
       3 v.   illus.   24 cm.
       No more published?

15692 Western Kentucky University.
       The Kentucky building. [Bowling Green, Ky.,
       1975]
       13 p.   illus.   29 cm.
       "The articles are reprinted from vol. 45, no. 2,
       fall 1975 edition of Western Alumnus."

15693 Wetmore, Alexander, 1793-1849.
       The pedlar. Lexington, University of Kentucky
       library associates, 1955.
       [3] l., 35 p.   facsim.   (University of

Kentucky library associates, Keepsake no. 2)
Introductory matter by Scott C. Osborn,
ℓ. 2-3.

15694 Wheatley, Ky. Dallasburg Baptist Church.
The challenge of Christ on the one hundredth
anniversary, Dallasburg Baptist Church, Wheatley,
Kentucky, 1851-1951. [Wheatley, Ky.? 1951?]
[16]p.   incl. illus.   23 cm.
"The History of the Dallasburg Baptist Church,
1851-1951": p. [6-11]

15695 Wheeler, Patton Galloway.
First report of the Constitution Revision
Committee to the Legislative Research Commission.
Frankfort, Ky., Legislative Research Commission,
1960.
51 p.   29 cm.   (Research report, no. 2)

15696 Whitaker, Fess, 1880-
History of Corporal Fess Whitaker. [Louisville,
Standard Printing co., 1918]
152 p.   illus.   24 cm.

15697 White, E   P
Clay's quick step, from a favorite French
air, arranged by E. P. White. Boston, Oliver
Ditson [n.d.]
3 ℓ., port., music.   36 cm.
The original of this text was in the possession
of Elliott Shapiro, 118 West 79th Street, New York,
in February 1943. The original connot now be
located. The present "photostatic" copy, possibly
now unique, is in the library of Lawrence S.
Thompson, Lexington, Kentucky.

15698 White, George W
Early geology in the Mississippi Valley, an
exhibition of selected works held in the University
of Illinois Library at Urbana, November, 1962.
By George W. White and Barbara O. Slanker. Urbana,
University of Illinois, 1962.
26 p.   23 cm.

15699 White, Martin Marshall, 1904-
The University of Kentucky project at Bandung in
its fifth year 1961. Lexington, 1961.

33 p.   cover illus.   29½ cm.
"Contract between the University of Kentucky
and the International Cooperation Administration.
Contract ICA/W 688."

15700   White, Mrs. Peter A
The Kentucky housewife, a collection of recipes
for cooking, by Mrs. Peter A. White.   Chicago and
New York, Belford, Clarke & co., 1886.
316 p.   20 cm.

15701   Whitley, Mrs. Wade Hampton.
Comprehensive index to W. E. Arnold, A history
of Methodism in Kentucky, vol. 1 (Louisville,
Herald press, 1935) Lexington, University of
Kentucky Libraries, 1960.
14 p.   23 cm.   (Kentucky. University.
Libraries. Occasional contribution, no. 110)

15702   Whitman, Walt, 1819-1892.
"Kentucky" - Walt Whitman's uncompleted poem.
Fragments edited with a commentary by Harry R.
Warfel. Lexington, University of Kentucky
Library Associates, 1960.
16 p.   facsim.   29 cm.   (Keepsake, no. 8)

15703   Whitsitt, William H
Life and times of Judge Caleb Wallace, some
time a justice of the Court of Appeals of the
State of Kentucky... Louisville, John P. Morton
& company, 1888.
151 p.   32 cm.
In subsequent lists of Filson Club publications
recorded as no. 4.

15704   Whittaker, Frederick.
The brave boy hunters of Kentucky, by Capt.
Frederick Whittaker... Cleveland, The Arthur
Westbrook company, 1908.
99 p.   cover illus.   19 cm.

15705   Whittlesey, Walter R
... Catalogue of first editions of Stephen C.
Foster (1826-1864) by Walter R. Whittlesey and
O. G. Sonneck... Washington, Government printing
office, 1915.

347

79 p.   24 cm.
At head of title: Library of Congress.

15706 Who's who in Kentucky; a biographical dictionary of
       leading men and women of the Commonwealth...
       Volume one. Chicago, Larkin, Roosevelt & Larkin,
       1947.
          1084 p.   24½ cm.
          No more published?
          Not arranged alphabetically; no index; includes
       many individuals with only tenuous associations
       with Kentucky.

15707 Wickliffe, Robert, 1775-1859.
          An address to the people to the people of
       Kentucky, on the subject of the Charleston &
       Ohio rail-road. Lexington, Ky., N. L. Finnell,
       Pr., Observer & reporter office, 1838.
          40 p.   23 cm.

15708 Wickliffe, Robert, 1775-1859.
          A further reply of Robert Wickliffe, to the
       billingsgate abuse of Robert Judas Breckinridge,
       otherwise called Robert Jefferson Breckinridge.
       Lexington, Ky., Kentucky gazette, Print., 1843.
          69 p.   22 x 14 cm.

15709 Wickliffe, Robert, 1775-1859.
          The Shakers, speech of Robert Wickliffe. In
       the Senate of Kentucky, January, 1831. Frankfort,
       A. G. Hodges, 1832.
          32 p.   17½ cm.

15710 [Wickliffe, Robert] 1775-1859.
          To the freemen of the county of Fayette.
       Lexington, Kentucky Gazette, print, 1845.
          22 p.   21 cm.

15711 Wickliffe, Robert, 1815?-1850.
          An address delivered on the occasion of
       laying the corner stone of the new medical
       hall, of Transylvania University, July, 1839.
       Lexington, Ky., Noble & Dunlop, printers, 1839.
          29 p.   21 cm.

15712 Wickliffe, Robert, 1815?-1850.
          An oration delivered before the Transylvania

Whig society, February 22d, 1835... Lexington, Ky.,
N. L. Finell, Observer and reporter office, 1835.
28 p.   20 cm.

15713 Wickliffe, Robert, 1815?-1850.
Speech of R. Wickliffe, Jr. ... delivered in
the National convention of the Whig young men of
the United States, assembled at Baltimore, May
4th & 5th, 1840. Lexington, Ky., Observer and
reporter print, 1841.
28 p.   22 cm.

15714 Wigham, Eliza.
The anti-slavery cause in America and its
martyrs. London, A. W. Bennett, 1863.
vii, 168 p.   18½ cm.

15715 Wildwood, Warren, pseud.
Thrilling adventures among the early settlers,
embracing desperate encounters with Indians,
Tories, and refugees: daring exploits of Texan
rangers and others... Philadelphia, J. E.
Potter, 1862.
384 p.   illus.   19½ cm.

15716 Wiley, William.
Locally administered city pension systems.
Prepared by William Wiley. Frankfort, Ky.,
Legislative Research Commission, 1977.
iv, 125 p.   tables.   29 cm.   (Research
report, no. 143)

15717 Wilkinson, Ann Biddle.
Letters of Mrs. Ann Biddle Wilkinson from
Kentucky, 1788-1789, with an introduction and
note by Thomas Robson Hay. [Philadelphia]
The Historical society of Pennsylvania [1932]
33-55 p.   port.   26½ cm.
Reprinted from the Pennsylvania magazine of
history and biography, volume LVI, number 1,
January, 1932.

15718 Williams, John Augustus, 1824-1903.
In memoriam: remarks on the life and character
of General Samuel L. Williams. By his nephew,
John Augustus Williams... Delivered before
the Church of Christ, at Somerset, Montgomery

Co., Ky., on the 20th of October, 1872, and
published by the request of many brethren.
Cincinnati, R. Clarke & co., 1872.
23 p.   24½ cm.

15719 Williams, John Augustus, 1824-1903.
Thornton, a Kentucky story, by John Augustus
Williams... Cincinnati, F. L. Rowe, publisher,
1900.
viii, 304 p.   14 cm.

15720 Williams, Mary Ida.
Living in Kentucky; the story of old Kentucky
homes from log cabin to Greek revival. [n.p., n.d.]
xii, 95 p.   illus.   24 cm.

15721 Williams, U   V
History of Franklin Baptist Association from
1815 to 1912 by Dr. U. V. Williams and Rev. F. W.
Eberhart. [Frankfort, Ky.? 1912?]
26 p.   illus.   21 cm.

15722 Williamson, Judith.
Older Kentuckians: their needs. Prepared by
Judith Williamson and Jeffrey Raines. Frankfort,
Ky., Legislative Research Commission, 1971.
30, 29 p.   tables.   29½ cm.   (Research
report, no. 62)

15723 Willis, George Lee, 1862-
History of Shelby County, Kentucky, written,
compiled and edited by Geo. L. Willis, sr.,
under the auspices of the Shelby County
Genealogical-Historical Society's Committee on
printing... [Louisville, Ky., C. T. Dearing
printing company, inc.] 1929.
268 p.   plates, facsim.   23½ cm.
"Official statistics and records including
Shelby County marriages, 1792-1800, and a list
of Revolutionary soldiers from Shelby County,
p. [207]-268."

15724 Willis, George Lee, 1862-
Kentucky constitutions and constitutional
conventions. A hundred and fifty years of state
politics and organic-law making. [Frankfort, Ky., 1930]
77 p.   illus.   27 cm.

15725 Willis, Nathaniel Parker, 1806-1867.
           Health trip to the tropics. By N. Parker Willis,
       New-York, C. Scribner, 1853.
           xiii, [11]-421, xxiii p.   18 cm.

15726 Willson, Augustus Everett, 1846-1931.
           Message of Augustus E. Willson, governor of
       Kentucky, to the General assembly of the
       Commonwealth of Kentucky, January 4, 1910.
       [Frankfort? 1910?]
           52 p.   24 cm.

15727 Wilmot, Franklin A
           Disclosures and confessions of Frank A. Wilmot,
       the slave thief and negro runner. With an
       account of the under-ground railroad. Philadelphia,
       Barclay & co. [1860]
           1 p.l., 13-38 p.   incl. 3 pl. [incl. front.]
       25½ cm.

15728 Wilson, Gordon.
           Folklore of the Mammoth Cave region, by Gordon
       Wilson, Sr. ... Ed. by Lawrence S. Thompson...
       Bowling Green, Ky., Kentucky folklore society,
       1968.
           112 p.   22½ cm.   (Kentucky folklore series,
       no. 4)

15729 Wilson, Gordon.
           Folkways of the Mammoth Cave region.
       [Bowling Green, Ky.?] 1962.
           64 p.   illus., map.   24 cm.
           Inscribed by author.

15730 Wilson, Joyce.
           New Hope Church [Owsley County, Ky.]
       Lexington, Ky., 1976.
           broadside.   illus.   21½ x 21½ cm.

15731 Wilson, Leonard Seltzer, 1909-
           Settlement forms in the northwest Cumberland
       plateau of Kentucky. [Minneapolis, 1938]
           [8] p.   maps.   23 cm.
           "Reprint from Proceedings of the Minnesota
       Academy of Science, v. 6, 1938."

15732   Wilson, Mary Helen.
            A citizens' guide to the Kentucky constitution,
        compiled by Mary Helen Wilson. Frankfort, Ky.,
        Legislative Research Commission, 1977.
            iii, 118, 38 p.   28 cm.   (Research report,
        no. 137)

15733   Wilson, Mary Helen.
            A look at the Kentucky General Assembly, by
        Mary Helen Wilson. Frankfort, Legislative Research
        Commission, 1976.
            24 p.   21½ cm.
        Second (revised) edition.

15734   Wilson, Mary Helen.
            A perspective of constitutional revision in
        Kentucky. Prepared by Mary Helen Wilson.
        Frankfort, Legislative Research Commission, 1976.
            iii, 64 p.   27 cm.   (Informational bulletin,
        no. 119)

15735   Wilson, Robert Burns, 1850-1916.
            Life and love: poems, by Robert Burns Wilson.
        New York, Cassell & company, limited [1887]
            viii p., 1 ℓ., 268 p.   18½ cm.

15736   Wilson, Robert Burns, 1850-1916.
            Until the day break; a novel, by Robert
        Burns Wilson... New York, C. Scribner's sons,
        1900.
            3 p.l., 330 p.   20 cm.

15737   Wilson, Samuel Mackay, 1871-1946.
            Additional notes on Matthew Harris Jouett,
        Kentucky portrait painter. [Louisville, 1940]
            102 p.   26½ cm.
            A supplement to article in Filson Club History
        Quarterly, April, 1939, and to John Hill Morgan,
        Gilbert Stuart and his pupils, 1939.

15738   Wilson, Samuel Mackay, 1871-1946.
            Andrew Jackson; an address delivered on the
        Plains of Chalmette, New Orleans, La., on January
        8, 1915, at the centennial celebration of the
        battle of New Orleans, held under the auspices
        of the Louisiana historical society, by Samuel
        M. Wilson... [Louisville, Ky., Press of the

Westerfield-Bonte co., 1915]
cover-title, 43 p. pl., 2 port. (incl. front.)
map, plan.   23 cm.
"Appendix. Birthplace of Andrew Jackson": p.
[37]-43.

15739 Wilson, Samuel Mackay, 1871-1946.
Battle of the Blue Licks, August 19, 1782,
by Samuel M. Wilson... Lexington, Ky., 1927.
143 p.   front. (facsim.)   illus. (map)
25½ cm.
"Authorities": p. 118-122.

15740 Wilson, Samuel Mackay, 1871-1946.
Book collecting. Lexington, Ky., Privately
printed, 1937.
15 p.   19 cm.

15741 Wilson, Samuel Mackay, 1871-1946.
The first land court of Kentucky, 1779-1780.
An address... before the Kentucky State Bar
Association at Covington, Kentucky, July 6, 1923
(reprinted, with the addition of notes, appendices,
and illustrations from the Proceedings of the
twenty-second annual meeting of the Association,
1923) Lexington, Ky., 1923.
164 p.   facsims.   26½ cm.

15742 Wilson, Samuel Mackay, 1871-1946.
Henry Clay; an address by Hon. Samuel M.
Wilson... Lexington, Ky., 1931.
24 p.   23 cm.   (Reprint from the Proceedings
of the Thirtieth annual meeting of the Kentucky
State bar association, 1931)

15743 Wilson, Samuel Mackay, 1871-1946.
History of the United States Court for the
Eastern District of Kentucky... Lexington, Ky.,
1935.
39 p.   ports.   27 cm.

15744 Wilson, Samuel Mackay, 1871-1946.
Jeffersonian democracy; an address delivered
before the Young Men's and Young Women's Democratic
Clubs, of Franklin County, at their Jefferson
Day dinner, Frankfort, Kentucky, April 13, 1933.
Lexington, Ky., 1933.

26 p.   23 cm.
Cover title.

15745 Wilson, Samuel Mackay, 1871-1946.
        John Filson in Pennsylvania. Louisville, Ky.,
        1939.
            179-201 p.   facsim.   26 cm.
        On cover: Reprinted from The Filson Club
        History quarterly, Louisville, Kentucky, October,
        1939.

15746 Wilson, Samuel Mackay, 1871-1946.
        The "Kentucky Gazette" and John Bradford,
        its founder. [New York] 1937.
            102-132 p.   25½ cm.
        "Reprinted from Papers of the Bibliographical
        Society of America, volume XXXI, part 2, 1937."

15747 Wilson, Samuel Mackay, 1871-1946.
        Matthew Harris Jouett, Kentucky portrait
        painter. A review. Louisville, 1939.
            75-96 p.   facsims.   26 cm.
        Reprinted from The Filson Club History
        Quarterly, Louisville, Kentucky, April, 1939.
            A review of E. A. Jonas, Matthew Harris Jouett,
        Kentucky portrait painter (1787-1827), 1938.

15748 Wilson, Samuel Mackay, 1871-1946.
        A new constitutional convention, both
        necessary and expedient, by Samuel M. Wilson...
        Lexington, Ky., [n.p.] 1931.
            39 p.   23 cm.

15749 Wilson, Samuel Mackay, 1871-1946.
        The relation of the Ohio river and its valleys
        to the discovery of the Mississippi by De Soto.
        Louisville, 1942.
            55-66 p.   27 cm.
        "Reprinted from The Filson club history quarterly,
        Louisville, Kentucky, January, 1942, volume 16,
        no. 1."

15750 Wilson, Samuel Mackay, 1871-1946.
        A review by Samuel M. Wilson of "Isaac
        Shelby and the Genêt mission," by Dr. Archibald
        Henderson... Lexington, Ky., 1920.
            52 p.   23 cm.

15751 Wilson, Samuel Mackay, 1871-1946, comp.
          Souvenir of the commemoration of the bicentennial
       anniversary of the birth of George Washington, by
       the Kentucky society of the Sons of the Revolution,
       the John Bradford historical Society and
       Daughters of the American revolution in Kentucky,
       prepared and presented by Samuel M. Wilson.
       Lexington, Ky., 1932.
          19 p.   23 cm.
       "The oration of the Honorable James Brown
       [Eulogy on the late illustrious citizen George
       Washington] here reprinted, was published in full
       in the Kentucky Gazette for February 6, 1800."

15752 Wilson, Samuel Mackay, 1871-1946.
          Sovereignty: a commencement address before the
       faculty, graduates and students of the Jefferson
       School of law at Louisville, Ky., May 31, 1922...
       Louisville [1922?]
          38 p.   29 cm.

15753 [Wilson, Samuel Mackay] 1871-1946.
          Susan Hart Shelby. A memoir by S. M. W. ...
       Lexington, Ky., 1923.
          66 p.   front., pl., ports.   28 cm.

15754 Wilson, Samuel Mackay, 1871-1946, ed.
          A symposium of tributes to Lexington on the
       occasion of the Sesqui-centennial of its
       birth; Lexington named, June 4, 1775, 150th
       birthday commemorated June 4, 1925. Edited by
       Samuel M. Wilson, published under the auspices
       of the General committee. Lexington, Ky.
       [Transylvania printing co.] 1925.
          79, [1] p.   23½ cm.

15755 Wilson, Samuel Mackay, 1871-1946.
          Tercentenary of the Westminster Assembly;
       an address delivered in the First Presbyterian
       Church, Lexington, Kentucky, Sunday, November 14,
       1943. Lexington, Ky., 1944.
          [8] p.   23 cm.

15756 Wilson, Samuel Mackay, 1871-1946.
          Washington's relations to Tennessee and
       Kentucky. [n.p., n.d.]
          21 cm.   26 cm.

15757 Wilson, Samuel Mackay, 1871-1946.
West Fincastle - now Kentucky. Louisville,
Kentucky, The Filson club, 1935.
65-94 p.   illus.   28 cm.
Reprinted from the Filson club history quarterly,
IX, no. 2, 1935.

15758 Wilson, Samuel Mackay, 1871-1946.
William H. Mackoy; first president of Kentucky
State Bar Association. An address by Samuel M.
Wilson; delivered Thursday, June 3, 1937, in
Louisville, Kentucky at the annual meeting of the
Kentucky State Bar Association. Louisville, Ky.,
1937.
26 p.   port.   19 cm.
Bibliography: p. 26.

15759 Winchester, Ky.
Reasons why all progressive citizens of Winchester
should vote against the proposed "electric light"
franchise. [Winchester, n.d.]
broadside.   28 x 21 cm.

15760 Winchester, Kentucky. Commissioner.
Commissioner's sale of land! by virtue of a
decree of the Clark Circuit Court, in the suit of
Harrison Thomson, &c., vs. Jane Chenault, &c., I
will on the 9th day of June, 1857, sell to the
highest bidder on the premises, about 750
acres of land! in Clark County... Winchester,
May 25th, 1857.
broadside.   24½ x 31½ cm.

15761 Witherspoon, Pattie French.
Through two administrations, character
sketches of Kentucky. Chicago, T. B. Arnold, 1897.
110 p.   19½ cm.

15762 Woman's Club, Louisville, Ky.
Legal opinions supporting Woman's Club of
Louisville. [Louisville, Ky.? 1926?]
16 p.   24 cm.
Opinions by Samuel M. Wilson et al.

15763 Wood, Edith.
To the westward (an historical play in five
scenes) [n.p., n.d.]

iii, 13 p.   27 cm.
On cover: "To the westward": historical play
commemorating the first exploration of Kentucky
by Dr. Thomas Walker.

15764 Woodbridge, Hensley Charles, 1923-
          Articles by Jesse Stuart: a bibliography.
       [Murray, Ky., Kentucky Library Association, 1959]
          89-91 p.   24½ cm.
       Reprinted from Bulletin of the Kentucky Library
       Association, XXIII, no. 3 (July, 1959), 89-91.

15765 Woodbridge, Hensley Charles, 1923-
          Jesse and Jane Stuart: a bibliography. Murray,
       Ky., Murray State University, 1969.
          144 p.   illus.   24 cm.

15766 Woodbridge, Hensley Charles, 1923-
          Jesse Stuart: a bibliography... With essays by
       Roland Carter, Lawrence Edwards, H. H. Kroll,
       E. H. Smith, and Jesse Stuart. Harrogate,
       Tenn., Lincoln Memorial University Press, 1960.
          74 p.   23 cm.

15767 Woodbridge, Hensley Charles, 1923-
          Jesse Stuart: a bibliography for May, 1960-
       May, 1965, by Hensley C. Woodbridge. [Frankfort,
       Ky., 1965]
          349-370 p.   23 cm.
       "Reprinted from the Register of the Kentucky
       Historical Society, v. 63, no. 4, October, 1965."

15768 Woodford Bank and Trust Company, Versailles, Ky.
          The Woodford Bank and Trust Company, Versailles,
       Kentucky. Into the second quarter of the second
       century. [Versailles, 1977]
          [24] p.   illus.   23 cm.

15769 Woodford County. Lexington, Ky., 1976.
          12 p.   illus.   37 cm.
       Reprinted from Sunday Herald-Leader, 12
       September 1976.
          Partial contents. - Dottie Bean, Much of Blue
       Grass tradition evident in Woodford. - Jackie
       Nelson, Clifton: river town has seen many wondrous
       times. - David Fried, County formed from Fayette
       in 1788. - Mike Smith, County has produced some

357

great athletes. - Jackie Nelson, Margaret Hall
has simple elegance. - Mary Buckner, Gov. A. B.
Chandler loves Versailles. - Jackie Nelson,
Midway shops liven street. - Midway College -
Jackie Nelson, Aura of history marks Pisgah Church.

15770 Woodworth, Samuel, 1784-1842.
        The hunters of Kentucky; or, The Battle of New
     Orleans. [n.p., n.d.]
        broadside.   33 x 21½ cm.

15771 Woolsey, F   W
        New Parisian wine in old bottles...
     Photographed by Richard Nugent. [Louisville, Ky.,
     1977]
        [4] p.   illus.   28 cm.
        Appended at end: Estate bottled Cane Ridge
     chelois dry red wine. Produced and bottled at the
     Colcord Winery, Paris, Bourbon County, Kentucky
     Paris, Ky., The Colcord Winery [1977?]
     4 p.   14 cm.

15772 Work Projects Administration, Kentucky.
        Medicine and its development in Kentucky.
     Compiled and written by the Medical historical
     research project of the Work Projects
     Administration for the Commonwealth of Kentucky.
     Sponsored by the State Department of Health of
     Kentucky and the Kentucky State Medical
     Association. Louisville, Ky., Standard
     printing company, 1940.
        373 p.   illus.   24 cm.

15773 The World almanac, 1868. [New York, The World,
     1868]
        108 p.   20 cm.
        Kentucky, p. 90-92.

15774 The world, or Instability. A poem. In twenty
     parts, with notes and illustrations...
     Philadelphia, J. Dobson; London, O. Rich,
     1836.
        248 p.   21½ cm.

15775 Worsley and Smith, Lexington, Ky.
        Lexington's second city directory, published
     by William Worsley and Thomas Smith for the

year 1818, by J. Winston Coleman, Jr. ... Lexington,
Winburn Press, 1953.
19 p.   facsim.   24 cm.

15776 Worsley's & Smith's Kentucky almanac, and farmer's
calendar, for the year 1819; being the third
after leap year. The 43d of American independence,
after the 4th of July; the 31st of the Federal
government, and the 28th of this commonwealth,
after the 1st day of June... Calculated for the
meridian of Lexington, Kentucky and will serve
without any sensible alteration, the states of
Ohio, Indiana, Illinois, Tennessee and Virginia.
Lexington, Printed at the office of the Kentucky
Reporter, by Worsley & Smith [1818]
47, [1] p.   19 cm.

15777 Wraxall, Sir Frederick Charles Lascelles,
3d bart., 1828-1865.
The backwoodsman; or, Life on the Indian
frontier. Edited by Sir S. F. Lascelles
Wraxall, bart. With illustrations by Louis
Guard, engraved by John Andrew. Boston,
T.O.H.P. Burnham; New York, O. S. Felt,
1866.
302 p.   front., 7 pl.   19 cm.

15778 Wright, Charles L
The family doctor; a new specialty. Prepared
by Charles L. Wright and George L. Riegling.
Frankfort, Ky., Legislative Research Commission,
1971.
120 p.   maps, tables.   29½ cm.   (Research
report, no. 61)

15779 Wright, Charles W
A guide manual to the Mammoth Cave of Kentucky.
Louisville, Bradley & Gilbert, 1860.
61 p.   15½ cm.

15780 Wright, Ray Herbert.
History of Cox's Creek Baptist Church.
Written on the occasion of the one hundred and
fiftieth anniversary of its constitution by
Ray H. Wright and Elsie Southwood Wright. Cox's
Creek, Ky., Published by L. S. Chambers, 1935.
28, [8] p.   illus.   21 cm.

Mounted at end is church program for 3 Oct. 1943
(4 p., illus.) for dedicatory exercises for new
building.

15781 Writers' Program, Kentucky.
In the land of Breathitt. Compiled by the
workers of the Writers' Program of the Work
Projects Administration in the State of Kentucky...
Northport, N. Y., Bacon, Percy & Daggett [n.d.]
165 p.   illus.   22½ cm.
"Sponsored by the Breathitt County Board of
Education."

15782 Writers Program, Kentucky.
Union County, past and present; compiled
by workers of the Kentucky Writers' Project
of the Work Projects Administration... American
guide series... Sponsored by the Union County
Fiscal Court. Louisville, Schuhmann printing
company, 1941.

15783 Writers' Project, Kentucky.
Lexington and the Bluegrass country. Written
by workers of the Federal Writers' Project of
the Works Progress Administration for the state
of Kentucky. Sponsored by the city of Lexington.
Lexington, E. M. Glass, publisher, 1938.
8 p.l., 149 p., 1 ℓ., 16 p. of maps and illus.
21 cm.
In pocket at end of this copy is unidentified
clipping of article by Cummings Parker, Horse
bridges in Fayette County.

15784 Wunz, Gerald A
Farm game habitat evaluation in Kentucky.
A final report. [Frankfort, Ky.? 1959?]
[6] l., 133 p.   illus., maps, diagrs.
29 cm.
Covers period 1 April 1951-30 June 1959.

15785 Wurtz, George B
Just in fun. A few poems by George B.
Wurtz for the edification of his friends.
[Lexington, Ky., The Hurst press, 1948]
85 p.   front. (port.)   24 cm.

360

15786 Yandell, David Wendell, 1826-1898.
        Reply to the attack of Dr. E. S. Gaillard.
        By D. W. Yandell... Louisville, J. P. Morton
        and company, 1871.
        cover-title, 20 p.   22 cm.
        "Reprinted from the American practitioner for
        July, 1871."

15787 Yandell, Lunsford Pitts, 1805-1878.
        History of the Medical department of the
        University of Louisville: an introductory lecture,
        delivered on November 1st, 1852... Louisville,
        Printed at the office of the Journal, 1852.
        38 p.   22½ cm.

15788 The year of the Cats. 32 steps to UK's 1978
        NCAA Championship. [Lexington, Ky., 1978]
        36 p.   illus.   37 cm.
        Reprinted from Sunday Herald-Leader, 2 April
        1978.

15789 Youmans, E   Grant.
        Aging patterns in a rural and an urban area
        of Kentucky. Lexington, Kentucky Agricultural
        Experiment Station, University of Kentucky, 1963.
        80 p.   tables, graphs.   24 cm.   (Kentucky
        Agricultural Experiment Station. Bulletin 681)

15790 Young, Bennett Henderson, 1843-1919.
        ... The Battle of the Thames in which Kentuckians
        defeated the British, French, and Indians, October
        5, 1813, with a list of the officers and privates
        who won the victory... Louisville, John P.
        Morton and company, 1903.
        274 p.   illus.   27½ cm.
        At head of title: Filson Club publication
        no. 18.

15791 Young, Bennett Henderson, 1843-1919.
        ... The prehistoric men of Kentucky. A
        history of what is known of their lives and habits,
        together with a description of their implements
        and other relics and of the tumuli which have
        earned for them the designation of mound

builders... Louisville, John P. Morton & co., 1910.
343 p.   illus.   32 cm.
At head of title: Filson Club publication no. 25.

15792   Young, Bennett Henderson, 1843-1919.
Complaint of Bennett H. Young et al. against
the Synod of Kentucky, 1908. Harmony and
adjudication of church courts and memorandum
of points bearing upon complaint. [n.p., 1908?]
23 p.   25 cm.

15793   Young, Bennet Henderson, 1843-1919.
Lay effort among the masses. An address
delivered in Horticultural Hall, Philadelphia,
by Bennett H. Young, of Louisville, Ky., May
24th, 1888, at the celebration of the centennial
of the first General Assembly of the Presbyterian
Church in America. Philadelphia, MacCalla & company,
1888.
14 p.   24½ cm.

15794   Young, Bennett Henderson, 1843-1919.
History of the Battle of Blue Licks. Louisville
[Ky.] John P. Morton and company, 1897.
xi, [1] 101 p.   plates.   25 cm.

15795   Young, David M
... Kentucky's recources. Minerals...
Reprinted from Bulletin of the Bureau of School
Service, College of Education, University of
Kentucky, vol. 18, no. 2, December, 1945, pp.
274-314, for the Department of Mines and Minerals.
Lexington, Ky., 1948.
275-312 p.   illus., graphs.   24 cm.
At head of title: Commonwealth of Kentucky.
Department of Mines and Minerals. Harry Thomas,
chief. Division of Geology. D. J. Jones,
State geologist, Lexington. Series VIII, reprint 9.

15796   Young, John Clarke, 1803-1857.
An address on temperance; delivered at the
court house in Lexington, Ky. Lexington, Ky.,
Printed for the Society by T. T. & W. D. Skillman,
1834.
28 p.   22 cm.

15797 Young, John Clarke, 1803-1857.
           Address of Rev. John C. Young, delivered at
       his inauguration as president of Centre College.
       Danville, Nov. 18, 1830. Lexington, Ky., Printed
       by T. T. Skillman--Luminary office, 1830.
           11,[1] p.   21 cm.

15798 Young, John Clarke, 1803-1857.
           Redemption by the blood of Christ. A sermon
       preached in the Presbyterian church, in
       Harrodsburg, Ky., on Sunday, March 13, 1831. By
       Rev. John C. Young. President of Centre college.
       Lexington, Ky., Printed by Thomas T. Skillman, 1831.
           16 p.   20 x 12 cm.

15799 Young, Lot D   , 1842-
           Reminiscences of a soldier of the orphan
       brigade, by Lieut. L. D. Young, Paris, Kentucky.
       Louisville, Ky., Courier-Journal job printing
       co., n.d.
           99 p.   23 cm.

15800 A youth's history of the great Civil War in the
       United States from 1861 to 1865... New York,
       Van Evrie, Horton & co., 1866.
           xiv, [15], 16-384 p.   illus.   18 cm.
           Anti-abolitionist.
           "Campaign in Kentucky": p. 156-165.

                              Z

15801 Zeitlin and Ver Brugge, booksellers, Los Angeles.
           The Anderson papers, Los Angeles [1976?]
           12 p.   28 cm.
           Contains letters from Robert Clough Anderson,
       Jr. (1788-1826), John J. Crittenden, Henry Clay,
       and James Monroe, among others.

15802 Zettlemoyer, Charles L
           Some aspects of higher education in Kentucky.
       Staff data collected for the Advisory Committee
       on Higher Education. Prepared by Charles L.
       Zettlemoyer, Kenneth H. Thompson, Jr., Lance M.
       Liebman, Michael L. Ades. Frankfort, Ky.,

Legislative Research Commission, 1963.
xii, 121 p.   maps, tables.   29 cm.   (Research
report, 14)

15803   Zettlemoyer, Charles L
Timberlands taxation in Kentucky. Prepared by
Charles L. Zettlemoyer [and] Michael Ades.
Frankfort, Ky., Legislative Research Commission,
1963.
ix, 19 p.   29 cm.   (Research report, 15)

WITHDRAWAL